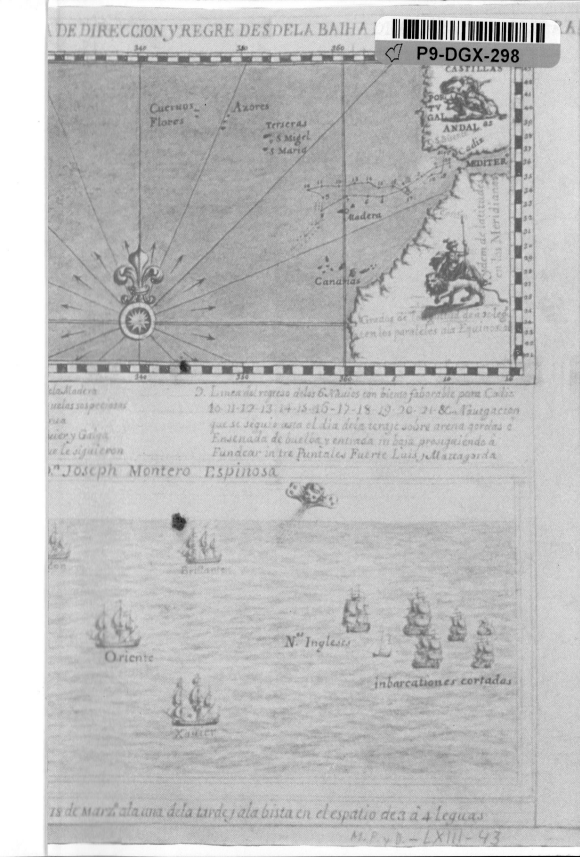

A DE DIRECCION Y REGRE DESDELA BAIHA

Cueruos
Flores
Azores
Tenceras
S Migel
S Maria

CASTILLAS
PORTVGAL
ANDAL.
MEDITER.

Madera

Canarias

ela Madera
uelas sospecosas
ua
uier y Galga
se le siguieron

9. Linea del regreso delos 6 Nauios con biento fauorable para Cadiz
10·11·12·13·14·15·16·17·18·19·20·21·&c. Nauigacion
que se siguio asta el dia dela teraje sobre arena gordas ó
Ensenada de buelos y entrada in baja prosiguiendo a
Fundcar in tre Puntales Fuerte Luis y Mattagorda

n Joseph Montero Espinosa

Brillante

Oriente

N.º Ingleses

inbarcaciones cortadas

Xavier

ns de Marzo ala una dela tarde y ala bista en el espatio de 3 á 4 leguas

M.P. y D. — LXIII — 43

THE HIDDEN GALLEON

THE HIDDEN GALLEON

*The true story of a lost Spanish ship
and the legendary wild horses of Assateague Island*

By John Amrhein, Jr.

To Bill

John L Amrhein

New Maritima Press

ISBN 978-0-9796872-0-4

Library of Congress Control Number: 2007935481

New Maritima Press, LLC
P.O. Box 1918
Kitty Hawk, North Carolina 27949
www.newmaritimapress.com

In Memory of

Mary Ellen Sutliff
1949-2001

The Honorable Albert D. Alberi
1944-2004

WILSON E. "CHIP" BANE
1963-2007

Table of Contents

*SOMEDAY THE HIDDEN GALLEON
WILL BE EXCAVATED, PRESERVED,
AND HOUSED IN ITS OWN MUSEUM.
THIS BOOK IS DEDICATED TO THAT IDEA.*

"Everyone should do all in his power to collect and disseminate the truth in the hope that it may find a place in history and descend to posterity"

General Robert E. Lee, C.S.A.
Grand Nephew of Thomas Lee
Acting Governor of Virginia 1750

Acknowledgments

The beginning of every project, by definition, is always the most important. This adventure started with my grade school friend and diving buddy, Greg Sutliff. Thanks Greg. Later, my best friend and loving wife, Delphine, provided me the opportunity to take on the project of writing this story and her editing skills were invaluable. Without her it would never have happened. Along the way were my new partners Bill Bane, Chip Bane, Ned Middlesworth, Gene Parker, Albert Alberi, and Bill Holloway, who all had faith in me and the project and to each I owe a great deal of thanks.

My researchers were invaluable. Not enough can be said for the contribution of Victoria Stapells-Johnson who began researching the Spanish documents in 1980 and whom I was fortunately able to reunite with in 2001 and who carried the story beyond my greatest expectations. I also appreciate her husband Richard's patience and the photographs. Her assistants were Genoveva Enriquez Macias, Esther González Pérez, and Guadalupe Fernández Morente.

The international team also included: Charles Stuart (1980), Simon Niziol and Tim Hughes and Associates in London; John Flora in California; Norma Cantu, San Antonio, Texas; and the Honorable Father Juan José Hernández O. H. in Spain. George Ryskamp, Associate

Professor of History at Brigham Young University gave us guidance at the archives in Cádiz. To the many unnamed archivists and librarians who assisted me in my own research, thanks. Dave Horner, one of the first to write about *La Galga*, helped ignite the flame. A special thanks to David Wegner of the David Taylor Research Center and Hugh Benet of the Star Spangled Flag House, Baltimore. Mort Wood provided some valuable anecdotes. David Owen and Charles McKinney your involvement was valuable as well as timely. Doug Sachse took my case when others wouldn't. Thanks to Chip Johnson who loaned us his boat. And to Shane Cook for his insight and suggestions.

Attorneys Peter Hess and David Horan your contributions are remembered. Susan Olive gave her legal review. Dr. Eugene Lyons and Duncan Mathewson of Treasure Salvors helped fill in the blanks on the legend. Edwin Bearss and Larry Points of the National Park Service both were of great help. To my employer, Beach Realty and Construction, Kitty Hawk, North Carolina for their patience. I would like to thank from SEA, Ltd: Vincent and Phyliss Bredice, John Mathisen, Charles Gordon, Dr. Richard Passwater, and Donald Parks. I recognize here the valuable contributions made by Alan Riebe, Daniel Koski-Karell, Richard Cook, and Ben Benson in their hunt for *La Galga*. To Guy Banks and Clarence Bowden, thanks for the upfront at the 2004 Pony Swim at Chincoteague. Charlie Mazel shared his knowledge with me at a chance meeting at Jost Van Dyke. Annie Alberi opened the files of her late husband and my former partner, Albert Alberi, whose role was pivotal. Nat Steelman and Ronnie Beebe shared the legend with me.

To the Internet which saved years of work and tens of thousands of dollars. My editors were tremendous. Connie Buchanan set the course. Others that followed were Lori Lisi whose critical eye challenged me. Ann Buskirk literally came aboard to fine tune the manuscript and with Buddy Hullett became cheerleaders from the sidelines. Julie Robert and Molly Lynde read the manuscript and gave me their unique points of view. Robert Pruett and the staff at Brandylane Publishers, Inc., Richmond, Virginia brought it to press. To my artist, Tom Dean, for his rendering of Grandpa Beebe and the legend and for his future efforts. Matt White contributed the musket drawing. St. Rosalia who was always there and to the One who wrote this story, as I am only the narrator.

Additional recognition must be given to Chip Bane for his splendid drawings of the cannon, and the Interior View of *La Galga*. And to his father, Bill Bane, who has spent several thousand hours building a scale model of *La Galga* from scratch which will enable us all to fully appreciate this historic ship.

For the many sources used in this book, please consult the Notes and Bibliography at the end.

INTRODUCTION:
A Legend and a Shipwreck

The brown stallion snorted the salt air, reared, and then careened down the sandy beach. Ten more of these frolicking playful creatures followed his lead as they galloped along the flat wet sand laid bare by the receding tide of the Atlantic Ocean. These horses were wild and free. They owned this island of sand dunes, pine forests, and salt marshes called Assateague Island.

The horses were not alone today as two youngsters named Paul and Maureen Beebe stood and watched them silhouetted by the early morning sun on this crisp early spring day.

Paul and his younger sister had come over the channel from Chincoteague Island with their grandfather, Clarence Beebe. Anxious to see the wild ponies, the adventurous children ran far up the beach as Grandpa moored his skiff.

Later, their attention was interrupted when they heard Grandpa hallooing from down the beach as he rushed to catch up. Young Paul, mesmerized by the ponies as they disappeared in the distance, paid no heed to him. Grandpa, after finally catching up with them, said they needed to get back home.

> Still entranced by his vision of the wild herd, Paul said, "Is it true, Grandpa, about the Spanish galleon being wrecked?"

> "And the ponies swimming ashore?" added Maureen.

Grandpa pretended to ignore them as he reminded his grandchildren that Grandma was waiting for them back home on Chincoteague.

> "Grandpa!" reminded Paul. "Is it true about the Spanish galleon and the ponies? Or is it a just a legend like the folks over on the mainland say?"
> "'Course it's true!" replied Grandpa. "All the wild herds on Assateague be descendants of a bunch of Spanish hosses."
> "Then it's not a legend?" Maureen asked.
> "Who said 'twasn't a legend?" Grandpa exclaimed.
> "'Course it's a legend. But legends be the only stories as is true!"

This scene was depicted in the book *Misty of Chincoteague*, published in 1947 by Marguerite Henry. This same scene was played out again in 1961 in the movie, *Misty*, based on the book. It is a fictional children's story based on real life people like the Beebe family and the wild ponies that have roamed Assateague Island for centuries.

Chincoteague and Assateague are barrier islands located on the Atlantic seaboard of the rural Eastern Shore of Virginia. Chincoteague Island lies across a narrow channel from Assateague Island where the ponies roam free. This wild unspoiled barrier island is located along the coasts of Maryland and Virginia. Today the island stretches from the inlet at Ocean City, Maryland, which opened in 1933, to Chincoteague Inlet to the south, a distance of about twenty-seven miles. Assateague State Park, operated by the State of Maryland, controls the land from the inlet at Ocean City to the Assateague Island National Seashore Park operated by the National Park Service. The National Park ends at the Maryland-Virginia border and the Chincoteague National Wildlife Refuge, managed by the U.S. Fish and Wildlife Service, occupies the remainder of the island ending at Chincoteague Inlet. Assateague and Chincoteague are Indian names, Assateague meaning "a place across" and Chincoteague, "beautiful land across the waters."

In 1945, Marguerite Henry heard of the wild Spanish horses, the legend of their origin, and the pony pennings held at Chincoteague every summer. She traveled the following year from Freeport, Illinois, to Chincoteague Island in search of a story and to see the ponies for herself. When she arrived, she met the family of Clarence and Ida Beebe, local ranch owners who kept horses and participated in the annual roundup. She also met a woman named Victoria Watson Pruitt, considered to be the best authority on the island's history. Mrs. Henry consulted with Mrs. Pruitt and the Beebes about the roundup, the pennings, the auction, and the legend of the Spanish shipwreck. The story captivated her. While she was there, she purchased a colt she named *Misty*. Inspired by her experiences at Chincoteague, she wrote a story about them. In 1947, the book became an immediate success, earned awards, and later became a movie released by Twentieth Century Fox. Her story included the real life characters of Grandpa and Grandma Beebe, and Ralph and Maureen, their grandchildren.

When the first English settlers arrived at the barrier islands in the latter 1600s, they made no mention of wild horses on Assateague or anywhere else. They did, however, begin using Assateague to pasture their own cattle and horses since there was no need for fencing, and the beach and marsh grasses provided ample forage. This former practice is well documented in local records.

The barrier islands proved to be an efficient and profitable way to care for livestock. But then something happened. Probably the greatest storm ever recorded to hit Assateague was on October 7-8, 1749. This storm wracked the coast from South Carolina to New England. A contemporary account from the *Maryland Gazette* of October 18, 1749, gave a harrowing description of the devastation and loss:

In Worcester County, in this province, the tide rose to a prodigious height, and has done considerable damage. Capt. Newbold's sloop is now lying high and dry in an apple orchard: the losses sustained there, in drowning of cattle, horses etc, are very great. The sea broke over an island in the said county called Phoenix Island, on which were between 4 and 500 head of cattle, and 60 horses: whereby all the cattle were drowned but five, and all the horses except one. The damage in Worcester County is computed at about 10,000.

And in the following edition:

Every day brings fresh accounts of the damage done by the late storm, mentioned last week. On the sea side, in Worcester County, we are told that the tide ran up into the woods upwards of two miles higher than it usually rose before.

"Phoenix Island" is Fenwick's Island or the present coast of Ocean City, Maryland.

In Hampton, Virginia, they fared no better: "The like storm has not been known in the memory of our oldest man." The tide had raised fifteen feet perpendicular and "forced ships ashore where the water was never before known to flow." Along Assateague Island, inlets opened up and channels clogged as the ocean met Chincoteague Bay.

This storm not only wiped out most of the livestock, but surely altered the barrier island itself. The people who owned Assateague prior to the storm were documented as having horses and cattle on the island. After 1749, records showed they had few or none.

The year after the Great Storm of 1749, there was a horrendous West Indian hurricane that propelled a fleet of Spanish ships up the east coast of America whereupon a Spanish warship was driven ashore upon the desolate beaches of Assateague Island. Her name was soon forgotten by the early settlers of Chincoteague and the nearby mainland, but the event was not, as the mystery of the origin of the wild ponies became fused with the oldest memories of the Spanish shipwreck.

Years later, it was noted that the wild horses on the island were much smaller than those on the mainland. Henry A. Wise, who was born and raised in Accomack County and later became governor of Virginia (1856-1860), described them as a "race of very small, compact, hardy horses, usually called beach horses," which were believed to have been on Assateague since long before the American Revolution. Wise also said that these horses were so small that a tall man might straddle one and "his toes touch the ground on each side."

Sometime around the end of the eighteenth century, a festival was started where the ponies, or "beach horses" as they were called, were rounded up and the younger ones auctioned off. It was an event marked with a great festival and celebration. In 1835, an observer of the festival noted:

> The rustic splendor, the crowds, and wild festivity of the Assateague horse-pennings, scarcely retain a shadow of their ancient glory. The multitudes of both sexes that formerly attended those occasions of festal mirth, were astonishing. The adjoining islands were literally emptied of their simple and frolic loving inhabitants, and the peninsula itself contributed to swell the crowd, for fifty miles above and below the point of meeting. All the beauty and fashion of a certain order of the female population, who had funds, or favorites to command a passage, were sure to be there.

In 1877, *Scribner's Monthly* published an article on Chincoteague Island, the Assateague ponies, and the annual pony penning. The author, Howard Pyle, was told that there was a "vague tradition" on Chincoteague Island that the horses had escaped from a vessel wrecked on the southern end of Assateague and that the Indians then carried the survivors to the mainland. The horses were left to themselves to roam the island.

Today, the pony penning and festival are still carried on. The tradition was revived in 1925 to benefit the Chincoteague Volunteer Fire Department and is held during the last week of July each year.

CATCHING A PONY.

Scene from a nineteenth century pony penning at Chincoteague Island.
From Scribner's Monthly. Vol. 13, Issue #6, April, 1877.

In good weather, nearly fifty thousand people flock to the little island of Chincoteague to witness the event. The horses are rounded up and swam across the channel, paraded through town, and then corralled for the auction. The horses today are larger than the ones described in previous centuries.

The origin of the horses remains an ongoing debate. In 1968, the National Park Service historian published a report on the historical background of Assateague. His conclusion was that the horses descended from stock abandoned by the seventeenth century colonists. He had no knowledge of the decimation of the horses in 1749. He did mention that there was a Spanish shipwreck in 1750, but he concluded that there was no basis for the legend that the wild ponies originated from a Spanish shipwreck.

Now the oldest inhabitants of Chincoteague, like the Watsons,

CROSSING TO ASSATEAGUE.

Scene from a nineteenth century pony swim. *From Scribner's Monthly. Vol. 13, Issue #6, April, 1977. Courtesy of the Library of Congress.*

Whealtons, and Lewises, will tell you that these horses came from a shipwreck and disagree with the skeptics in the National Park Service. Victoria Watson Pruitt, one of those who originally conveyed the legend of the lost Spanish galleon to Marguerite Henry, was born Victoria Watson on April 20, 1884. Her family reached back to the early eighteenth century in Accomack County, Virginia, and neighboring Worcester County, Maryland. Her grandparents owned land on Assateague beginning in the 1790s.

Before she died, she wrote down for future generations her belief in the tradition passed on to her. It is included in her papers preserved at the Eastern Shore Public Library in Accomack, Virginia. On the page entitled "Doubters of the Shipwreck & Storm," Mrs. Pruitt laments,

> Some people tried to discredit the story of the Spanish shipwreck as a source [from] which the ponies came. Others would like (now that the ponies are famous and have made

Assateague and Chincoteague the talk of the entire country for beautiful ponies) to claim the honor.

But go where you will, up and down the Atlantic Seaboard, from Maine to Florida you will not find the ponies. In fact Assateague is home of their forefathers and its good enough for them.

The opinion of some experts in the big city, those who have come down to Chincoteague to manage the wildlife and tourists, is that the Spanish shipwreck legend is unfounded.

But in direct contradiction to this and because of some remarkable events in the twentieth century, other experts, government officials, and a public fascinated by the shipwreck legend put their faith in an incredible story of shipwreck, treasure, and ponies, related not to a Spanish warship lost in 1750, but to a ship that never sailed. That shipwreck story was the genius of a calculating con man.

The Hidden Galleon at last separates fact from fiction and asks for you to decide if "Legends be the only stories as is true!"

CHAPTER ONE
The King's Ship

A Spanish warship closely resembling *La Galga* built in the English fashion *From the Album of the Marqués de la Victoria, Courtesy of the Museo Naval, Madrid.*

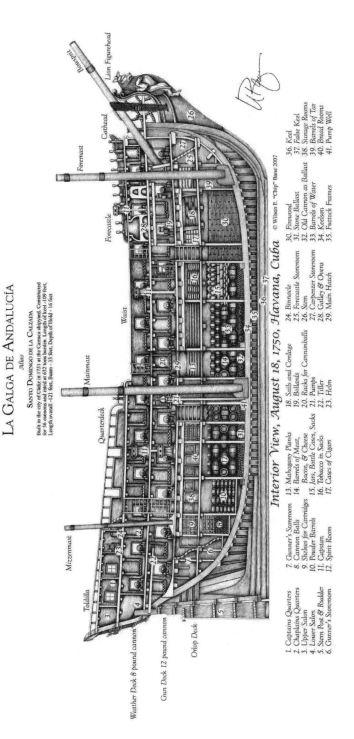

LA GALGA DE ANDALUCÍA

Alias

SANTO DOMINGO DE LA CALZADA

Built in the city of Cádiz in 1731 at the Carraca shipyard. Constructed for 56 cannons and rated at 632 tons burden. Length of keel -109 feet, Length overall -121 feet, Beam - 33 feet, Depth of Hold - 16 feet

© Wilson E. "Chip" Bane 2007

Interior View, August 18, 1750, Havana, Cuba

1. Captains Quarters
2. Chaplains Quarters
3. Upper Salon
4. Lower Salon
5. Stern Post & Rudder
6. Gunner's Storeroom
7. Gunner's Storeroom
8. Cannon Balls
9. Shelves for Cartridges
10. Powder Barrels
11. Capstan
12. Spirit Room
13. Mahogany Planks
14. Barrels of Meat, Bacon, & Cheese
15. Jars, Bottle Cases, Sacks
16. Tobacco in Sacks
17. Cases of Cigars
18. Sails and Cordage
19. Bollards
20. Racks for Cannonballs
21. Pumps
22. Tiller
23. Helm
24. Binnacle
25. Forecastle Storeroom
26. Stem
27. Carpenter Storeroom
28. Galley & Ovens
29. Main Hatch
30. Firewood
31. Stone Ballast
32. Old Cannon as Ballast
33. Barrels of Water
34. Keelson
35. Futtock Frames
36. Keel
37. False Keel
38. Storage Rooms
39. Barrels of Tar
40. Bread Rooms
41. Pump Well

Interior View of *La Galga drawn by Chip Bane.*

August 13, 1750
Havana, Cuba

It was a sunny day like most in this tropical city that was the hub of Spain's colonial empire in the New World. Spain and her colonies were still suffering from the effects of the late conflict, known as King George's War to the English. It had been not quite two years since the English warships under the command of Admiral Charles Knowles had devastated the fleet of Admiral Andrés Reggio just outside the harbor entrance. Havana, with its population of nearly 30,000, was a magnificent city with its ornate stone and stucco buildings and plazas and avenues adorned with palm trees and flowering tropical flora. But the Spanish stronghold had declined during the last nine years of conflict into a hell hole of disease, shortages of every kind, and a malaise, magnified by the late summer heat.

Just outside the fortified city, a Spanish warship named *La Galga* was moored to the pier at the Royal Dockyard loading her cargo and supplies for her long overdue voyage to Spain. Her captain, Don Daniel Huony, was there, just as he had been every day since the first of November, overseeing the process of overhauling the aging ship. Word was now circulating around Havana that final preparations for the fleet's departure were being completed.

In the heart of the city, a weary priest named Father Juan Garay de Concepcíon stood outside the convent hospital of San Felipe y Santiago, run by his order San Juan de Dios. He and his two assistants watched the loading of a cart that was to take them and their baggage to the warship now being loaded at the Royal Dockyard. Father Garay had received permission from Governor Francisco Cagigal de la Vega to return to Spain on the naval vessel. He was an important man, having served as commissary general of the order San Juan de Dios, a religious sect founded in 1550 that maintained a chain of hospitals in Spain and in the New World. The fifty-eight-year-old priest had spent the last nine years in Peru restoring discipline in the convents and hospitals of his order in South America. The viceroy of Lima, in recognition of his service, was funding his trip home. He had recently arrived at Havana after sailing from Callao to Panama, where he crossed the isthmus by wagon to Porto Bello and boarded the *Nuestra Señora de Begoña*, which brought him to this hot and unhealthy city. There were many sick people in the hospital that needed caring for but his orders, thankfully, instructed him to return to Spain.

After the many chests, bags, and hampers were loaded, he and his assistants climbed onto the back of the cart. The driver, with a shout and a snap at the reins, urged the donkey forward and they headed east to the waterfront. They wanted to escape the stench of the streets as soon as possible. Garay's legs dangled from the rear as the creaking cartwheels rumbled down the narrow cobblestone streets. Five blocks away, they pulled into the parade grounds in front of the Governor's Castle, or fort, called the Real Fuerza. They stopped for a moment as they saw a contingent of armed soldiers escorting a group of prisoners coming over the drawbridge that spanned the protective moat around the fort. Garay learned from his driver that they were destined for the same ship he was about to board. The cart fell in before the column of prisoners.

Garay enjoyed the view of the ships and the harbor and the sea breeze that stirred the occasional palm tree. It was fresher than the dank air of the streets, but the waters of the harbor still bore the foul smell of human and animal waste.

The cart turned south and proceeded along the seawall that bordered the harbor, followed by the prisoners, who were urged ahead by their uniformed guards armed with muskets tipped with bayonets. Father Garay tried to avoid eye contact with them, as their physical condition was disturbing. He was a compassionate man, but he was a Spaniard and they were the enemy, or had been anyway. At least they were fit enough to serve, unlike the crippled and disease-ridden he had left at the hospital.

Unlike Garay, the prisoners had no bags or luggage. All they had was the scarce tattered clothing on their backs and the shackles around their wrists. Yet, they were relieved to be out of the prison. It was a sunny day and to them the air was delightful compared to their dank cells inside the Governor's Castle.

Each man had his own story for being there. Most of them were English and had been captured by Spanish privateers who could not accept that the war had ended two years ago.

Among the decrepit imprisoned seamen was a Scotsman named Andrew Connell, who had been master of the schooner *Musquito*, owned by William Pitt, a member of Britain's Parliament, and future prime minister of England. Captain Connell had left the Mosquito Shore at Honduras in February of 1750 on a routine trip to Jamaica but was becalmed off the west end of that island and carried by a strong current to the coast of Cuba off Cape Cruz. He was boarded by the Spanish *Guarda Costas* in a quarter galley under the command of Don Francisco, who tied Connell to the main shrouds and immediately began to plunder the ship. He beat the crew cruelly, and forced them to confess that they were "contraband dealers" by means of thumb screws. The tortured crew told the Spaniards where Captain Connell had hidden 280 dollars in gold and silver. Connell and his crew were then carried to Trinidad, where his vessel was searched again by the lieutenant governor, Don Francisco Guterez. The crew were then forced to carry mortar and stones for the construction of one of the King's new buildings. In Trinidad, there were other prisoners as well. Connell witnessed one man's refusal to work. He had his head placed in the stocks, and when it would not close properly, Guterez jumped up and down on it nearly choking the man to death. Two others were placed in the stocks and beaten with a cane by the brutal governor.

In March, Andrew Connell and two of his crew were taken to Havana and immediately put in prison in the Governor's Castle, nearly naked, and fed very little. Since his two men did not volunteer to serve on board the Spanish men-of-war, they were taken by force and placed aboard one of them in April. Connell pleaded with Mr. Britt, the governor's interpreter, to see his official condemnation so that he might present a defense. He was told those papers were put on board *La Galga*, now loading at the dockyard, to be reviewed back in Spain.

In prison, Captain Connell met other captains and crewmen who had suffered the same misfortunes of weather to come too close to Cuba and were now headed for *La Galga* at the dockyard. Captain

James Maloney, sailing from Jamaica to London in the ketch *Shepardess*, was disabled in a storm and put into Mariel Harbor, west of Havana. He then took his ketch to Havana for repairs, whereupon complete, he was arrested and put in prison. He was accused of carrying Spanish commodities and stealing eight sacks of tobacco. These men did, in fact, volunteer for service. They were told that they could stay in prison and "eat rock stones" or volunteer for service on board *La Galga*. They chose the latter.

There was also Captain Edward Ford, who had been captured while fishing in a small boat off Grand Cayman. And Captain Guillermo Francisco Lossiur, of the French packetboat, the *Fox*, and his second in command, Jean Coquelin, and Mathew Lublan, surgeon from the *Young Theodore*, a Dutch sloop. These men were being taken to Spain on the pretense of legal redress. There were other men of various nationalities who had no privilege or status as the others. They were lowly crewman, like William Edgar of Philadelphia, when they were captured. Edgar had been ordered to serve as a gunner on *La Galga*.

When the caravan arrived at the docks they found more armed soldiers under the command of Lt. Diego Guiral, *capitán* of the marines. He was a veteran soldier and had served aboard *La Galga* since 1740.

Captain Huony was aboard, standing at the quarterdeck rail, observing the tedious process of loading supplies and cargo. Although he was discouraged by his latest command, he enjoyed the smell of fresh paint and tar that had permeated the ship since her recent overhaul.

Ashore, and at the base of the pier, sat Thomas Velando, the master of supplies, sheltered beneath a makeshift awning of sail cloth. He had served aboard *La Galga* since the Battle of Toulon in 1744. Today, with quill in hand, he began to fill out the cargo register as the loading began.

Father Garay approached and disclosed that he had in various hampers and chests 4,800 pesos in gold doubloons and also other valuable items of gold and silver he had collected during his tour of duty. He had been advised that *La Galga* was not serving as a treasure ship on this voyage, and he would have to assume responsibility for his valuables.

The prisoners were safely on board and were under heavy guard since the shackles had been removed so they could perform the labor that was expected of them. Velando nodded to the sergeant, and Garay's luggage was carried aboard. Garay dispatched the cart driver with a nod and a piece of eight and proceeded to his cabin located in the aft section of the gun deck. He passed a Franciscan priest named Juan Martin who had signed on three days before as chaplain who, after a warm introduction, followed him and his assistants to his cabin.

Anchored in the harbor were five merchant ships waiting impatiently for the loading of *La Galga* to be completed. Each had stopped in Havana to take on more cargo and supplies before returning to Spain. The *Nuestra Señora de Guadalupe*, alias *La Nympha* alias *La Augusta Celi*, under Captain Juan Manuel Bonilla, had left Veracruz, Mexico, on May 30. Bonilla was loaded with 350,000 pesos in treasure and that much more in cochineal, animal skins, and logwood. The *Nuestra Señora de Los Godos*, under Don Pedro Pumarejo, had sailed from Veracruz on June 14 with over 600,000 pesos in treasure and other valuable cargo. Captain Huony was very familiar with this ship as he had taken it from the English in 1746. During the end of the late war, Huony had commanded the sixty-gun *El Fuerte* and had captured the *Harrington*, as she was known then, off the coast of Jamaica.

The two treasure ships had sailed from Cádiz, Spain, to Veracruz the year before and were behind schedule returning to Spain. They had hoped to sail with the treasure fleet of General Benito Spinola the previous November but were held up in Mexico. By the time they had arrived, Spinola had left. Bonilla, who had lost his last cargo in 1747 to English privateers, was skittish even though the war had been over for two years. He took advantage of his long friendship with Don Francisco Cagigal de la Vega, the current governor of Havana, and quietly suggested that he have an armed escort back to Spain.

Three more ships had come in and joined the protection of *La Galga*. Two were from Cartagena, Columbia. *El Salvador*, Master Don Juan de

Cruañes and her owner Don Jacinto de Arizon, was loaded with cocoa, and with sixteen chests of silver and four chests of gold coins valued at 140,000 pesos. The *San Pedro*, a Portuguese vessel licensed to sail with the Spanish, under Captain John Kelly, arrived carrying 150,000 pesos in cocoa, logwood, and treasure in silver coins, gold doubloons, silverware, jewelry, two gold bars, and thirteen silver bars. The third ship was the *Nuestra Señora de Soledad y San Francisco Xavier*, master and owner, Don Joseph Respaldiza. He would have been ready sooner but the ship that he sailed from Spain, the *San Antonio de Padua y Nuestra Señora del Rosario*, was lost on January 19 in a hurricane near Veracruz, after he had successfully landed his cargo there. He purchased the *Soledad* and was granted permission at Veracruz to load the *Soledad* with a cargo of cocoa from Maracaibo and 48,000 pesos in silver. These captains wanted to take advantage of *La Galga's* heavy armament and sail with her back to Spain. They made a direct request to Don Lorenzo Montalvo, the port minister, to have *La Galga* escort them. Montalvo agreed since the readiness of *La Galga* coincided with theirs and, of course, Governor Cagigal de la Vega was in agreement thanks to the persuasion of Captain Bonilla.

 La Galga de Andalucía, alias *Santo Domingo de la Calzada*, was built in the city of Cádiz in 1731 and rated at 56 cannons, 632 tons burden, and had an overall length of 120 feet. Called the *Greyhound* in English, as her builder, Juan de Casanova, followed a sleek English design in her construction that predicted a fast sailer. She had seen varied service in the Mediterranean, the Spanish coast, and voyages to Mexico and South America. She had expected to sail earlier that summer after undergoing six months of long overdue maintenance and repairs. She also had been ordered to carry tobacco products from the Royal Tobacco Company in Havana, but the summer rains had delayed the tobacco harvest and its transportation to the waiting ships. When the tobacco was received, it had to be properly packaged for safe passage on board ship. *La Galga's* sailing date had been pushed into late July. Besides carrying tobacco, she was loaded with mahogany for the King's opulent palace being built in Madrid.

Lorenzo Montalvo, the Port Minister of Havana, suggested that the King's zumaca, a vessel similar to a brigantine called the *Nuestra Señora de Mercedes*, be refitted as well and carry some of the mahogany and tobacco back to Spain, otherwise the ship would fall totally into disrepair if she remained in Havana. Captain Huony dutifully accepted this new task. The ships were then loaded with the mahogany planks, or in reality, beams. Some were over two feet wide and almost five inches thick—265 on *La Galga* and 69 on the *Mercedes*. Before departure, Juan García Barrosa was given command of the *Mercedes*.

As the crew loaded aboard chests that had been removed from the wagon on the pier, Thomas Velando dutifully recorded them into the register. One chest had 500 pesos to cover expenses for the petition filed by the French captain, Guillermo Losiur, of the packetboat *Fox*, which had been captured by a Spanish privateer. Another box containing 400 pesos for the appeal of taxes owed by the privateer who had captured the *Fox* was also registered.

On August 14, Joseph de la Cuesta y Velasco, the ship's purser, tallied a total crew of 199 which included the officers, soldiers, sailors. Thirty of these were ship's boys. There were also four cabin boys and four servants for Captain Huony. This was far short of her war time complement, which sometimes exceeded four hundred.

La Galga was nearly ready. Thomas Velando recorded in the register that there were four sealed chests of documents that had been transferred from *Los Godos* to *La Galga* by order of Don Juan Francisco de Güemesy Horcasitas, the Count Revilla Gigedo and Viceroy of Mexico. These were destined for officials in Spain.

The final task was the loading of fresh supplies of meat which consisted of some calves, hogs, and many chickens. Stored in the tightly packed holds were barrels of salted pork, beef, and fish. Sacks of beans and rice, dried fruit, jars of olives, raisins, almonds and figs, casks of biscuit, barrels of aguardiente, and many bottles of red wine, were loaded days before.

On Monday, August 17, the register was closed and certified by Pedro Antonio de Florencia, Chief Notary of the Registers, and *La Galga*, with the six other ships, made final preparations to sail the following morning. *La Galga* was towed out into the harbor to join the others.

The next morning, Captain Huony observed the tide begin to ebb.

"Señor Echaniz, stand by to make sail and signal the fleet," he barked to his second in command, Lt. Manuel Echaniz. A signal flag was hoisted and the capstan began to turn, raising the massive anchor from the bottom of Havana harbor. Barefoot seamen scurried about the deck and into the rigging to prepare the sails. Father Martin, with Father Garay at his side, gave his blessing to the men and the ships and prayed for a safe voyage. The other ships repeated this long-awaited procedure. *La Galga* then led them single file through the narrow harbor mouth that was often barricaded by a massive chain connected to each side of the entrance. To their left was a fortification called the *Castillo de la Punta*, and on their starboard beam was the *Castillo del Morro*, which made Havana nearly impenetrable by its enemies. The nearly sixty soldiers on board stood along the rails on each side of the ship, presenting their muskets while the gunners returned the salute of cannon fire from the forts. Huony smiled. He was finally headed home. The balmy wind filled the billowing sails; the rigging snapped tight. *La Galga* now surged ahead—her lion figurehead fixed its gaze on the horizon.

After *La Galga* cleared the harbor, Joseph de la Cuesta y Velasco, the ship's purser, reported to Captain Huony that instead of the total crew of 199 reported days before departure, by last count they were down to 193. Joseph de los Rios, master of sails, was among the missing.

The ships tracked northeast to the entrance of the Straits of Florida, known as the Bahama Channel to the Spanish. The weather was pleasant and they rejoiced at being at sea. On the fourth day out, Pedro de León Gomez, ship's boy, died and Father Martin presided over the prescribed ceremony of burial at sea.

La Galga and the other ships were experiencing a northerly head wind from the western edges of a storm system. Captain Huony did not realize that as he entered the Straits, a hurricane was about to pass north of the Bahama Islands at a point where he would ordinarily turn eastward toward Spain. The makeshift fleet proceeded along the Florida coast—on course and unaware of their rendezvous with hell.

CHAPTER TWO
Twelve Days

The Hell Storm. *From a NASA Satellite image.*

Day One: Tuesday, August 25, 1750
Off of the North Coast of Florida

At dawn on August 25, the fleet was northeast of Cape Canaveral, Florida; the northerly winds increased in strength intermittently as bands from the hurricane licked the fleet. The animals below deck became restless and so did Captain Huony.

"Señor Izaguirre, reef the main and tighten those shrouds!" And to the helmsman, Huony bellowed, "Steer two points to the east!" Izaguirre repeated the commands to his subordinates and the crew set to the task.

The skies started to darken that afternoon. There was now no doubt in Huony's mind what was facing him on the horizon. There was much work to be done.

"House and the secure the guns! Close all ports and secure the hatches! Señor Izaguirre, get men to the tops, prepare to take in sail and take down the yards of the top gallants!" Huony continued with detailed instructions for everyone above and below decks.

By 4:00 p.m., the wind abruptly changed from north to west, then south, and by nine in the evening, clocked southeast. The crew now realized they were in a full hurricane.

Darkness fell on the fleet as the invisible monster continued its assault—even so, the hapless ships were able to remain together. They prayed for deliverance. If they could hold on until morning, they believed the hurricane would move past them. From the quarterdeck Huony peered out into the darkness. A little to the south he glimpsed several lights from the other ships, but they would quickly disappear behind the mountains of water. Below decks, the common crew swung in their hammocks or prostrated themselves on the deck floor. Even sitting up was difficult.

With the mainsail reefed and topsails still set, Huony and his officers retired to the main salon joined by Fathers Garay and Martin where they ate ham, biscuit, and beans and sipped aguardiente, a Spanish brandy, brought up from the storage room by Henry Dalton, one of Huony's four servants. Dalton had served him previously on the warship *El*

Fuerte the year before.

The fleet remained on the northeastern edge of the storm, driving with the wind and the northbound currents. *La Galga*, however, was being forced off the wind by the punishing waves and began to run downwind, northwest toward the coast. Suddenly, the top foremast snapped and fell into the violent sea. Above and below decks the crew manned three of the four pumps to remove the rain and seawater that was beginning to flood the holds. The fires in the iron ovens were extinguished out of precaution.The ship moaned as the hellish wind strummed the rigging like a bass fiddle.

The officers' conversation was interrupted as the door flew open and Juan Bernardo Mayonade, *La Galga's* pilot, stood dripping in the dim light of the lantern. The ship's officers could see his wild bloodshot eyes smarting from the saltwater that still ran from his face. "Captain, the hurricane has not veered a single point," he blurted as he stood rubbing his eyes to clear his vision. "We are in the Gulf Stream riding the northbound current. It appears that we are locked in place with the winds and being propelled at a frightful rate. I have to remind you, sir, that on our present course, and based on our last position, we are being driven toward the shoals of Cape Hatteras on the coast of Carolina."

No one needed further explanation. Even Captain Huony's servant, Henry Dalton, knew what dangers lay ahead. They could survive the hurricane only to be dashed to pieces on that notorious sandbank.

After inspecting the storm damage, Captain Huony returned to the salon and sat down again with his officers. Sleep was out of the question. In an effort to soothe the fears of the younger officers, he began the tale of a prior storm:

"Gentlemen, I am here today because I have survived this before," he began. "On July 13, 1733, I was in command of the *San Joseph*, alias *El Africa*, a newly built warship of seventy guns. I sailed with General Don Rodrigo de Torres y Morales, commander of the New Spain Fleet that consisted of nineteen ships carrying over twelve million pesos in registered treasure for His Majesty Ferdinand's father, King Philip V. I was waiting for *El Africa* to be completed when the treasure ships arrived at Havana. *El Africa* was loaded with tobacco and I was given the responsibility of guarding the treasure ships. On the second day out, off the Cabeza de los Martires, we encountered a fierce hurricane and were driven toward the offshore reefs. The general signaled us to turn around and return to Havana. I lost sight of the fleet and was forced to continue only with a jury-rigged foremast. The lookout could see the breakers on the reefs so we let go two storm anchors and found bottom at 220 feet, just in time to save the ship from disaster. We found ourselves off Cayo Largo. On the 17th, we discovered the *Populo* sunk to her poop deck and the *Nuestra Señora de los Delores* dismasted off the next island to the north. With much effort, we rescued the survivors, repaired our ship, and after six days departed for Spain, where we arrived on September 25. In January, I returned to Florida to assist in the salvage of treasure that then returned to Spain the following year."

"So it is you that I have heard about, the lucky Irishman," piped Ensign Marcenaro. And the others nodded. "Yes, your reputation is legend," added Diego Guiral, *capitán* of the marines. "But this time there will be no anchoring in the Bahama Canal."

Huony nodded in recognition of this harsh reality. There really was nothing much he could do as the ill-fated fleet labored before the wind.

Day Two: Wednesday, August 26, 1750
Off of the Coast of Georgia

The fickle wind finally made up its mind. First it was west, then north, and now, since 9:00 p.m. the night before, it was blowing out of the southeast a full hurricane. The foremast had been broken in several places and repairs were underway. With great difficulty men ascended the rigging as the ship pitched and rolled, replaced the foretopmast, and bent and reefed new canvas. Huony could see that the main mast was suffering; some of the shrouds and chains were starting to give. This was because the rigging was rotten, and several shrouds and chains that supported the mast were missing when the ship sailed from Havana.

Huony scanned the horizon, occasionally catching glimpses of the other struggling ships as they crested on wave tops.

Immediately after the storm hit, the *Nuestra Señora de los Godos* remained upwind of *La Galga,* and the fleet became separated, so Captain Pumarejo furled his mizzen sail and was able once again to close with the convoy by 8:00 p.m. The wind was so strong now that shouted words were blown overboard before they could be heard. The wind-driven rain bit the skin like a swarm of stinging insects. The ships could only go where the wind and Gulf Stream currents told them to as Mother Nature continued propelling them north toward the Carolina coast.

In *La Galga's* salon, Captain Huony started to relate another adventure to his officers when, suddenly, there was a purple flash of lightning that illuminated the white heaving mountains outside. Everyone gasped. Through the mullioned window, *Los Godos* was seen skidding down a wave like a piece of worthless flotsam.

At 3:00 a.m., Captain Pumarejo on *Los Godos* was in distress. Forced to cut down his mizzenmast, he lost control of his ship, which in turn allowed a hammering sea to take out his rudder. He lay broadside to the waves and out of control as water flooded his first deck and his launch and boat were badly damaged. An anchor was cut loose to lighten his bow, and then he was able to fix his tiller and regain control of the ship.

"I am lucky," continued Huony. "In 1739, I was commander of the sixty-two-gun *LanFranco* and the fifty-eight-gun *Incendio,* which left Veracruz on February 2 carrying millions in treasure. Hours out of port, we were hit by a great storm forcing us back to the harbor. The *Incendio* was able to return and anchor, but the *LanFranco* came in with sails up and out of control, cutting the anchor cable to the *Incendio,* causing her to be driven ashore. We were undermanned and couldn't bring her under control for two days. Later, we finally tied to the huge mooring rings under the lee of the fortress of San Juan de Ulúa. The 734 chests of silver, 8 chests of silverware, and nearly 3,500 slabs of copper on board *LanFranco* narrowly missed going to the bottom."

The most relieved to hear these stories was his servant, Henry, who was wild-eyed with fear. They seemed to calm him a bit as he appreciated hearing the experiences of his captain and master.

"And then there was the war that had commenced that same year and I was put in charge of the defense of Boca Chica during Admiral Vernon's siege. Yes, I am lucky, but I know the sea and promise you if this old ship will hold together, we will be celebrating in Cádiz in a few weeks."

To himself, Huony was not so sure. He had to break free of the storm's tenacious grip if they were going to survive.

Day Three: Thursday, August 27, 1750
Somewhere Off of the Coast of South Carolina
The Wind South Southeast

The pumping continued and Father Martin and Father Garay were busy hearing confessions of the resting crewmen. In the salon, Huony and his officers studied the charts of the American coast. They had not been able to take a position from the sun for several days.

"Gentlemen, we are in an unfortunate situation. We don't know where we are," said Huony as he pointed to the chart and indicated Cape Fear, Cape Lookout, and Cape Hatteras, on the North Carolina coast. Each cape lay north and to the east of the other, jutting out into the Atlantic resembling enormous teeth in the cavernous mouth of some nightmarish sea monster. "But most assuredly we know where we are headed!"

When dawn broke, Pumarejo on *Los Godos* found himself alone; the rest of the fleet was out of sight. The eye of the storm lay well off Charleston, South Carolina, and was nearly stalled. Charleston was only now starting to get some rain.

La Galga and the *Mercedes* were farther north on the east side of the vortex as they had been able to keep more sail up. Captain Huony noted in his log that the wind continued with a vengeance, and the sea was extremely rough and dense. Realizing that getting clear of the Carolina coast was critical, he continued with his mainsail up and his mizzen reefed. By nightfall the wind became "fiercely furious" forcing them to lower the foretopmast.

Bonilla, Pumarejo, and the others were south and out of sight of Huony. None of the ships could see one other, but they all were still being pushed together, north toward the coast. They were all aware of the dangers lying ahead at the shoals of Cape Hatteras, the killer of ships.

Pumarejo on *Los Godos* was nearing the eye of the hurricane and experiencing increasing intensity of the wind and seas. Two of his pumps were out of order and the other two constantly manned. By now, nearly all of the cows and pigs had been killed by being dashed about below decks. Pumarejo ordered them thrown overboard as well as most of her cannon and the iron oven.

Day Four: Friday, August 28, 1750
Southeast of Cape Fear, North Carolina

L a Galga was now east of *Los Godos*. The topmast of the foremast, having been repaired two days before, was in danger of being lost again as the shrouds and chains had finally come loose. The topsail was kept furled. At 3:00 a.m., after the crew secured the foremast, they climbed the mainmast rigging and cut down the main topmast. The crew quickly furled the sails and brought in the yards before the hurricane winds could snatch them away. In an attempt to reinforce the masts, the crew passed two preventer shrouds formerly used in the topmasts to the mainmast pole and two others to the foremast. Wedges were placed in the mainmast channel to stop it from moving. The ship was now totally at the mercy of the waves which were pounding the ship so hard she began to split open from the doorway of the forecastle toward the bow. Water began to pour through the openings flooding the bow. The men pumped faster. The weighted bow would not ride over the waves. In the forecastle and waist, ropes were stretched across the ship, tied to framing members, and bound together. With the aid of a crowbar, they twisted the ropes to draw the sides together. Izaguirre, the boatswain, consulted with the carpenter about the condition of the bow. They decided to cut one of the main anchors loose, which eased some of the strain, leaving only two large anchors remaining.

On board *Los Godos*, Pumarejo sighted the *Guadalupe* to the windward; her mizzenmast was missing. They signaled each other and both turned south hoping to avoid Cape Lookout, but they soon became separated again. At dusk, the wind let up a bit, but Pumarejo was still in a desperate situation. With only two pumps working, the crew could barely keep the ship afloat; he and the chaplain even took turns pumping while swimming in water up to their waists. At 9:00 p.m., the new tiller broke, once again exposing the ship to broadside seas. Iron bolts popped loose as the wooden ship twisted. With the forecastle going under with every sea, the lion figurehead at her bow was ripped off. Now, with eleven-and-a-half feet of water in her hold, their only hope of salvation was in the hands of the Virgin Mary.

On board *La Galga*, Captain Huony was concerned that the safety of his ship was in the hands of an incomplete and undesirable crew. They consisted of ill-trained Mexicans and prisoners who were uncooperative. The treasure fleet of General Spinola had taken the best available men the preceding fall.

While *La Galga* had been in Mexico preparing for her return to Havana, proclamations enlisting crew were posted in Mexico City and Veracruz. There were few takers. After repairs had been completed on *La Galga* in Havana, Lorenzo Montalvo agreed with the Huony's suggestion to offer an advance payment of twenty pesos to entice crew to enlist. Montalvo knew that Huony wanted to leave as soon as possible to avoid the dangers of the hurricane season. Don Francisco Cagigal de la Vega, the governor of Havana, published an edict to that effect. There were still few volunteers.

Montalvo's solution was to use "forced recruits." This included Spaniards as well as any foreigners still remaining in Havana since the end of the war. At the end of 1749, there were only seventeen prisoners remaining who were awaiting sentencing or were carrying out their time. Many had already opted to finish their terms in the mines, on galleys, or in the fortresses around Havana. In May, while *La Galga* was still at La Machina, the careening yard near the Governor's Castle, some had the good fortune to get away. In the early morning hours, they stole a crown boat from the harbor and were seen by sentries at the dock, on board *La Galga*, and across the harbor at the Divine Sheppard's Battery, as they rowed to freedom through the harbor mouth. Captain Huony was forced to make an accounting of his crew to verify that they had not come from his ship. Those prisoners unable to escape took service aboard ship as a better alternative to continued imprisonment.

Day Five: Saturday, August 29, 1750
East of Cape Lookout, North Carolina

At 3:00 a.m., *La Galga* continued to roll and on every recovery the main mast strained the chains and channels that tied the supporting shrouds to the side of the ship. The mast finally became so loose that it snapped, cracking below the weather deck. Huony ordered the men to take axes to the downed mast and rigging to get it overboard before more damage was done. A little before 7:00 a.m., the foretopmast, sail, and mizzen yard gave way going overboard. There were now only two pumps working, continually manned by the soldiers, but water kept coming in through the bow. At noon, after consultation with the other officials, Huony ordered that the cannon forward of the mainmast be thrown overboard—a textbook maneuver to elevate the bow. This was an extremely dangerous and difficult task with the waves crashing across the heaving decks. The ship rode higher, but the nineteen-year-old hull was not holding up to the constant battering; she still wanted to split open. The bruised and battered crew were growing weaker; there had been no hot food for days.

Before dawn, *Los Godos* had lost her foremast, which was critical in controlling the ship. As it went overboard, it carried two small anchors with it. Then, the mainmast came down. The situation was now so bad they were dumping cargo and supplies overboard, along with mattresses of the officers and passengers, everything but the treasure that was now weighting down the ship. At 8:00 a.m. and again at half past nine, they were hit by a great sea, knocking out all of the oakum in the deck seams. This increased the flow of water to the holds. The seawater was now running through, drenching the food, sails, and gunpowder rooms. The men at the pumps were totally dispirited. Captain Pumarejo and his chaplain were even forced to take turns. They had little hope of survival, but still, with that in mind, they continued manning the pumps and trying to repair the ship.

By this time the fate of the *Nuestra Señora de Soledad* and *El Salvador* had been decided. *El Salvador* was dashed onto the sand banks at Cape Lookout, drowning all but three men and a boy. Captain Cruanes was lost. The ship broke up and was buried under seven feet of sand. To the north, at Drum Inlet, the *Soledad* ran ashore in shallow water and rolled over on her side. Miraculously, everyone survived. When the sun came up, Don Joseph Respaldiza began salvaging his ship. He was soon joined by the four survivors from *El Salvador*. Soon they would find the launch, various cargo, and a number of dead seaman along the beaches, all believed to have come from *Los Godos*.

Day Six: Sunday, August 30, 1750
North of Cape Hatteras

On Sunday the 30th, *La Galga's* chaplain, Father Martin, celebrated Mass below deck as the soldiers and sailors, soaking wet, huddled amongst the cannon and prayed. The sounds of the pumps and the creaking and groaning of the ship's wooden frames nearly drowned out their hymns.

The wind had not let up, and in Captain Huony's own words:

> The frigate had become a marble at the mercy of the waves and without direction for lack of sails, coming apart as it rolled. The water aboard increased so that three pumps were at work constantly. Twisted lashings were added to those already in the middle deck and fore castle. The wind eased slightly, the rain stopped and the sun could be seen between the clouds so that at midday we surmised and with inexplicable pleasure that we had come round Cape Hatteras which is the furthest south of Carolina and on whose shoals we had feared wrecking. Thanks be to God for the strength of extra natural force of the currents to the east which freed us of these and that it was thereby possible to reach Virginia.

"Captain Huony, sir! I need to speak with you!" implored Diego Guiral, capitán of the marines. Huony motioned to follow him into the salon. *La Galga* lay southeast of the Virginia Capes.

"Sir, Señor Mayonade, our pilot, says that he is unfamiliar with these waters and the crew has learned of this and are getting very upset. One of our prisoners, the Irish Catholic captain named Maloney, says he can help as he is familiar with this coast."

"Señor Guiral, fetch Maloney and Mayonade and bring them here! Summon the other officers for a full council."

Guiral returned shortly with the two men, and after the council listened to both of them, they recommended relieving Mayonade from navigational responsibilities, and Huony gave pilot duties to

James Maloney. It was decided that they would make for the port of Virginia.

After the two left, Huony nodded to Guiral. "Have a guard keep an eye on him at all times."

Huony ordered that everyone would now take turns at the pumps. Three more cannon were thrown overboard. James Maloney turned *La Galga* northwest, hoping to make Chesapeake Bay with only the spritsail yard and fore-topmast stay sail jury rigged to the foremast pole. The wind, however, would not cooperate and the wind veered southwest, forcing them farther out to sea. They added some sail to the foremast to gain more control and attempted to head for land.

At dawn, Juan Manuel Bonilla aboard the *Guadalupe* had sounded twenty brazas (110 feet) of water and realized that the North Carolina coast was close by. He was unaware of the fate of the *Soledad* and *El Salvador* not far away. That evening, he safely anchored five leagues south of Ocracoke Inlet, North Carolina, and one league from shore. The *Guadalupe* was in a shattered condition; the only timber standing was the base of her fore and main masts. The men were at all four pumps desperately trying to keep her free. With no rudder and no masts, he was forced to wait for the angry sea to subside before rowing ashore in the ship's boat to find out exactly where they were.

Los Godos had not yet met her end. By half past twelve the crew of *Los Godos* had finished reinforcing the body of the ship. The wind suddenly died, but the sky said it was not over. At 2:00 p.m., the wind slammed them from the southeast, and they ran under bare masts north, north-northwest, and north-northeast at almost six miles per hour in a heavy following sea. Pumarejo was convinced, "We are persuaded to die."

Day Seven: Monday, August 31, 1750
Off of the Mouth of Chesapeake Bay, Virginia

Huony was able to take a position from the sun and found himself at latitude 37°. He was well out of sight of land and he estimated he was about 120 miles directly off of Cape Henry, the southern cape of Chesapeake Bay. *La Galga* lay in the eye of the storm. The winds were light from the east. As they lay becalmed, the monster storm continued its northerly path, soon to engage its resting pray once again.

La Galga's crew were now totally exhausted, wet, and too weak to reset a jury mast. Now that the wind had eased, they removed the jib boom from the heaving bow and hoisted it onto the pole of the mizzenmast with a topgallant sail. In the hopes of finding approaching land, soundings were taken regularly, but they found no bottom. The east winds were beginning to veer again.

By 8:00 a.m. on *Los Godos*, Captain Pumarejo's luck was starting to change. The wind started to abate, and the skies cleared. His noon sight placed him at 36° 40 minutes. *Los Godos* was about twenty miles south of Chesapeake Bay, but was much closer to land than *La Galga*. Knowing from this position that land was due west, he sailed in that direction in search of a landing.

Day Eight: Tuesday, September 1, 1750
Off Watchapreague, on the Coast of Virginia

Huony had taken advantage of the break in the weather to make repairs. He found two seams in the bow storeroom open above the lower wale, which he ordered recaulked and pinned with canvas. The crew made wells to collect the sea water, so it could be pumped out along with the putrid human and animal waste that had accumulated in the bilge. They gained on the incoming water and reduced it to six feet. Huony had just purchased some precious time.

South and inshore of him, *Los Godos* continued west toward shore. Pumarejo sighted land at 9:00 a.m. By noon, he was two leagues from shore and at 36° 38 minutes north. He saw a creek that looked like a port entrance and sailed for it. About three miles out, he dropped anchor in six brazas (approximately thirty-two feet) of water. He was a little north of Currituck Inlet, situated at the border between North Carolina and Virginia. Captain Pumarejo raised a Spanish flag and fired his remaining cannon repeatedly. A canoe finally came out to greet them at about five in the afternoon. The men in the canoe told the Spaniards that two English ships had sunk three days before, leaving only one boy as a survivor, and that they were out to salvage what they could. The Spaniards were informed that they were fifteen miles from the Virginia Capes, where they could get a pilot and go into Hampton, Virginia. The men in the canoe offered to guide them, but they would have to wait until dawn. That night, the water remained at seven feet in the hold as *Los Godos* rode at anchor awaiting sunrise.

Day Nine: Wednesday, September 2, 1750
East of Chincoteague Island, Moderate Breezes

The wind was northwest making it difficult for *La Galga* to claw her way toward land. At 5:00 p.m., and with great joy, they sounded a little over two hundred feet of water. But still, the coastline eluded them. The pumping continued, but even though they could not see land, the sounding lead had lifted their spirits. If the weather would continue to improve, salvation was now possible. The south edge of the hurricane's eye wall was moving towards them.

Pumarejo on *Los Godos* was enjoying the same moderate weather and raised anchor at 2:30 in the morning. At 12:30 that afternoon, off Cape

Henry, Virginia, two vessels approached his ship. To his surprise, one was *San Pedro*, Captain Kelly. The other was a Spanish sloop named *La Marianna*, which had left Campeche, Mexico, for Santo Domingo and had been blown out of the Caribbean and found herself in company with *San Pedro*.

The three disabled vessels had to wait for a pilot to come out from Hampton, Virginia, so they anchored off of Cape Henry that night. Luckily the weather had eased. It looked as if the worst were behind them.

Day Ten: Thursday, September 3, 1750
Off of the North Coast of Maryland

Before dawn, *La Galga* was still working north westerly toward shore when the wind picked up again from the southwest and ranged to the north.

"Ship, ho! A brig on the starboard beam!" cried the lookout, as the rising sun outlined the horizon.

"Fire a distress signal—one minute intervals! Come about!" shouted Captain Huony. The brig quickly faded away on the horizon without acknowledging the signal. *La Galga* turned back to the north.

By 10:00 a.m., they sighted land, the first since they left Havana, but at noon they were prevented from taking a sun sight because of the cloudy skies, therefore, they were uncertain of their position. *La Galga* was now some three or four leagues from land when the wind switched to the northeast blowing a gale. Huony decided it was pointless to try to sail north into the wind in such a bad condition. James Maloney, the English prisoner now acting as pilot, recognized the bend in the coast at Fenwick's Island, which is on the border of Maryland and Delaware. He knew they were close to entering Delaware Bay. When the crew heard this, some of the English sailors moved to the forecastle in agitation and shouted that they wanted to go on to Philadelphia. They did not want to remain in the open sea when the hurricane backed around. Huony was now dead set on the Virginia Capes so he ordered some soldiers to arrest six of the "principal troublemakers" and put them in shackles in the *toldilla*, located on the poop deck. *La Galga* turned south with the roaring wind.

At 7:00 p.m., the weather became so severe that they lay to rather than risk running ashore in the dark. A watch was posted with a sounding lead to make sure the ship remained offshore. The same coastline they prayed to see was now something to be avoided.

La Galga's age was starting to become a factor as the seething Atlantic continued to batter her hull. Her nineteen years of age was a factor but her design and intermittent maintenance was taking its toll. The late war had left scarce supplies and men to do the work. Her present voyage was an unexpected one as her retirement from the Spanish Navy had been planned over two years before. Her last intended voyage in the service of King Ferdinand VI was to be from Cádiz to Veracruz, then on to Havana to be sold to the *Real Compañía de la Habana* and serve out her last days as a merchant vessel. Before her arrival in Havana, however, the Real Compañía had rejected the idea of the purchase.

La Galga's reputation as being a bit unseaworthy due to her defective design was known to many, including Captain Huony. He had been told to load bulky packages of *astilla*, or tobacco stems, in Havana. His only heavy cargo was the mahogany planks, and without sufficient ballast or heavy cargo, *La Galga* would be a tender sailer. Huony reminded the governor of this and told him he had the concurrence of the minister of shipbuilding and the director of the Real Compañía in this matter. Huony said he was even considering cutting back her masts to discourage foundering. If he had to carry the astilla, he proposed that if the bundles were small enough, they could be stuffed into spaces amongst the other cargo, but since he had no direct authority from Spain ordering him to ship any of it on board, he was entitled to refuse it.

Ultimately, the astilla was loaded on board the *Nuestra Señora de Guadalupe* commanded by the governor's old friend, Juan Manual Bonilla. The King would have to pay the freight.

In Havana, Captain Huony oversaw the entire careening and repairs for *La Galga*, which began in November of 1749. On her last trip from Veracruz carrying treasure, she was reported to be leaking. This had postponed her trip on to Spain.

The wooden sheathing was removed from the hull, the seams were calked, and new sheathing installed. Hundreds of iron bolts were removed, holes rebored and bolts replaced. Six inches of false keel were added to protect the backbone of the ship. Windows, gunports, and doorways were retrimmed. Some of the gun carriages needed overhauling and iron fastenings replaced.

The rudder was removed, resheathed in lead, and the pintals were relined.

Inside the ship, a new deck was built for the gunpowder room and the bread storage rooms received new bulkheads. In the steerage area, two new storerooms were built, one on each side.

Even the launch and the lifeboat received a thorough refit, and finally the ship was painted inside and out.

Huony worried constantly about the beating his ship was taking. For ten days, the old ship defied his silent expectations. Perhaps they would make it.

At eight in the morning, *Los Godos, San Pedro,* and *La Marianna* weighed anchor and proceeded into the Chesapeake Bay. The ships sailed against a strong ebb tide, and by 3:30 in the afternoon, they were forced to drop anchor, again having proceeded only three leagues up the bay. They would have to wait again for an incoming tide. The winds resumed gale force on September 4, but they were now northeast with driving rain, which helped push them up the Bay, but once the tide began to run they would anchor again. This process would be repeated with each favorable tide until the next day, when they arrived off Hampton, Virginia, and reported to the Naval Officer, Wilson Cary. He warned Captain Pumarejo and the others not to unload any cargo until the president of the council and acting governor of Virginia, Thomas Lee, had given his permission. Otherwise it would be confiscated. The customs officials knew they had seen *Los Godos* before. During the war it had been the English ship *Harrington*, and had been captured by Huony in 1747. But the English officials could take no open retribution since the war was over.

The *Nuestra Señora de los Godos*, as she was now called, was leaking badly. There was not an adequate harbor at Hampton, so the Spanish ships proceeded to Norfolk, where they arrived on September 7 and anchored in the Elizabeth River within cannon shot of town. The bone-weary crews were forced to stay at the pumps to keep the ships afloat; otherwise, they would sink and settle to the river bottom weighted down with gold and silver. Many of the towns' people came out to witness them. The adults told the children about the huge treasures that these ships carried. Old and young alike fantasized about chests stacked upon chests of gold, silver, and jewels in the cargo holds. There was enough treasure on these ships to buy the whole town of Norfolk. The Spaniards on board returned their gazes and wondered what was going to happen next.

Day Eleven: Friday, September 4, 1750
Off of Assateague Island

At 1:00 a.m., soundings showed that *La Galga* had drifted into four brazas (twenty-one feet), dangerously close to shore. They sailed eastward to deeper water, where they lay to until dawn. The sun rose but unseen as *La Galga* sailed along the coast within sight of land toward the Virginia Capes with only a spritsail and the jury rigged foremast. At 8:00 a.m., the ship shuddered to a stop, knocking crewmen to the deck. They had hit a reef or sand bar. A huge wave lifted the ship and dropped it hard again. Soundings were ordered—there was only sixteen feet of water. *La Galga* continued to pound the bottom, and the crew was convinced that their end was near as the ship trembled and shuddered. If the ship broke apart now, there most likely would not be any survivors as they were miles from shore. Captain Huony estimated they struck at least twenty-five times within the next thirty minutes before they cleared the sand bar and sounded twenty-five to thirty-five feet of water. Huony rejoiced, "God was willing however to save us." The English crew were so convinced they were going to die that they wanted to kill James Maloney since he was acting as the pilot. *La Galga* was still in one piece and floating, but she had suffered the loss of her rudder and some exterior sheathing. Without a rudder, they no longer had control of the ship.

The terrified crew shouted, "If the northerly hits, we will all perish! To land! To land, to save our lives!" *La Galga* continued sailing out of control for another half an hour, and then Captain Huony ordered the two remaining great anchors set. There were also two small kedge anchors, but they would be of little use in the storm. With great difficulty, the crew dropped anchor with a cable of twenty-two inches, and a second with a shorter and smaller thirteen-inch hurricane hawser. They were now inshore of the reef. After this last demonstration, Huony thought that the loss of *La Galga* was not yet certain and convinced the crew that they needed time to formulate a plan for going ashore. The winds had subsided and were variable.

"Señor Echaniz, prepare for a landing. Ready the boats and have the men construct a raft from the spare masts and downed spars. Post an armed guard at the bow and let no one near those cables unless I order it!"

By 3:00 in the afternoon the winds increased, the crew let out a cry once more to go ashore before nightfall. Captain Huony said that they would not be ready by then, and it was too dangerous to consider landing in the dark. The beaches of Assateague Island disappeared as the sun descended behind the distant trees.

Huony had hoped that this delay of running his ship ashore would give the weather a chance to improve. Unfortunately, it got worse. It started to rain and the winds set in from the east-northeast blowing a strong gale. Seawater began to rise again in bow of the ship, and the crew made a gallant effort at the pumps to keep her free. On the evening of September 4, the loss of the ship was now assured. The chaplain, Father Juan Martin led the soldiers and sailors in prayer for a safe landing. It was the feast day of St. Rosalia.

Unknown to Huony, the *Mercedes* lay to the southeast of him, helpless in the turbulent sea, with her rudder, bowsprit, and launch gone. There was no control of the vessel and Captain Barrosa would only put up sail when the wind had the notion to blow them toward land.

Day Twelve: Saturday, September 5, 1750
Anchored Ten Miles Off of Assateague Island

Captain, the cable of the best anchor just parted," shrieked Izaguirre. It was now dawn of the 5th. The wallowing ship was barely holding with only one anchor as the gale force winds tested the lone anchor cable.

"Izaguirre, hurry the men with that raft," Huony implored.

By 11:00 a.m.., the raft was completed and lowered over the side. The crew, except for those at the pumps, began assembling on deck. The water continued to rise in the hold. Intermittent squalls obliterated the view of the coastline.

"Señor Echaniz, cut that hawser. We're going in," Huony ordered with relief. It was 2:00 p.m. "Have your men get their arms ready and keep them dry. Señor Izaguirre, get some barrels of biscuit from the storeroom and put them in the upper cabins. Tell the men to retrieve their belongings." Confessions of the crewmen had been heard days before.

They drifted for two hours as the ship proceeded stern first toward the beach, but then the easterly winds grabbed the spritsail and turned her around. Without a rudder, the ship veered back and forth. The crew's attention was now totally focused on the beach as they could see sand dunes and cedar trees coming into view as the beach drew closer. The landfall that they had prayed for was about to become a reality. The crew anxiously looked, first to the approaching shore, and then to the coamings around the hatches, as seawater was now about to engulf the hold and sink the desperate ship. The shoreline rose and fell with the sea.

Thuuump! Her hull brushed the bottom and lifted, but then it hit harder and harder with each sea. At 4:00 p.m., *La Galga* ground to a temporary halt.

"Lower the boats," croaked Huony. The launch and skiff were dropped on the lee side of the ship in the calmer water. The invisible sun started to set, so Huony decided that everyone was to remain aboard. The waves continued to lift and drop the ship as the tide rose. *La Galga* moved closer to shore, and the boats alongside began to fill with water as they slammed against the ship's hull. That night, the officers and crew huddled in the forecastle and quarterdeck cabins and prayed that the ship would hold together.

At dawn, Sunday, the 6th of September, the weather had eased somewhat and, although cloudy, the rain had stopped. They saw their launch and skiff on the beach broken and useless. The raft tied alongside was also coming apart. Also on the beach, they observed another vessel that had run ashore the previous morning. Huony, with difficulty, climbed to the roof of the damaged forecastle and looked down at the surf. He, like the others, had become accustomed to the moving decks and now, even though they were now stationary, the exhausted Spaniards continued to stumble about.

They were very close to the beach as Huony could see the retreating waves creating a dangerous undertow, making the short trip to safety a very precarious one. Some of the crew started to make their own plans. In the commotion, Father Martin and Father Garay passed out communion.

They were now close enough to the beach that some sailors who were considered good swimmers attached a lifeline to *La Galga's* bow and attempted to swim ashore with the line to attach to the wreck on the beach. They were unsuccessful as there were still huge waves, and the undertow pulled them back. The English prisoner named Captain Edward Ford volunteered to swim in with a flask containing a letter from Huony to the governor of Virginia asking for assistance, as they had estimated they were on Virginia's coast. Fortunately, he made it and went in search of help. For awhile the winds had increased again driving huge waves crashing against the windward side of the ship, sending torrents of foam and water across the decks. The soldiers and sailors braced themselves with each breaking wave as the ship was nudged ever closer the beach. Seawater had now totally flooded the holds through the deck openings. Huony ordered three barrels of biscuit thrown overboard to wash ashore in the waves. This would help sustain them after landing. Those who had gotten their chests and baggage topside threw them over as well, hoping to retrieve them once ashore. Hours later the winds diminished and the angry sea began to subside. Night fell and Captain Ford stood by and listened as the sea breeze carried the moans and prayers of those on board over the breaking waves.

At dawn on the 7th, the sun shone bright and the winds relaxed. Some of the crew and prisoners risked going in on a topmast that had been used for the raft. Others found their own pieces of wreckage. Seeing the success of Captain Ford the day before, three of the ship's boys jumped overboard with bags of money tied to their waists. They drowned as the receding waves pulled them under. Andrew Connell and a few other prisoners grabbed some wreckage and floated to shore. Connell's ordeal that started with being captured by the Spanish, then tortured off Cuba, and finally confined to hard labor in Trinidad, was now over.

On the beach, Captain Ford had found help from some Indians. Word was sent to the mainland. Ford sent a message back aboard to Huony informing him, "We're on the island of Azetegue on the border of Maryland and Virginia." He reported that the governor was two hundred miles distant, but some canoes were on the way. One came a little later, having been dragged overland from another part of the island. When the canoe arrived, they were able to carry the lifeline to the wreck on the beach, but the canoe then broke up in the surf and washed ashore.

A second raft was built from the yards of the topsail mast. With the line now secured from the ship to the beach, the crew were able to pull themselves ashore while balancing themselves on the raft as it precariously pitched and rolled atop the cresting waves. The raft was returned to the ship by a second line that had been tied to the raft. During one of these trips, the raft capsized and all the people were trapped underneath. Two chests of silver slipped off as well. By a miracle, everyone escaped but one soldier named Andrés Almoguera. In their haste to reach the shore, the last crewman to leave was confused and cut the return line so the raft broke up on the beach. One of the prisoners acting as gunner, William Edgar of Philadelphia, did not wait to be carried in and drowned as he tried to go it alone in his bid to escape.

That night, the Spaniards on the beach found comfort around a fire and rested. Those on board ship were able to relax a bit as the seas had calmed and were consoled as well by the glow of the fire that reassured them that they too would be ashore by the next day.

By the Tuesday the 8th, there was a crowd of survivors standing on the beach. Most everyone stayed close to the water's edge to assist those coming ashore and to escape the biting flies and mosquitoes. A third raft was put together using the first beam of the forecastle and another yard. Because the sea had calmed a little, a few more trips were made, but then the waves became stronger and the new raft came apart on the beach. There was now no way to get the last thirty souls ashore, which included Captain Huony and his chief officers. Those aboard ship were very anxious to get to the beach, but they would soon trade one misery for another.

Later, another canoe arrived, and in four or five trips, and at great risk of capsizing, Huony and his officers were brought ashore. On the last trip, the exhausted Captain Huony, with his hat under his arm, dropped into the canoe, with his boatswain, Francisco Izaguirre, the purser Joseph de la Cuesta y Velasco, and Diego Guiral, capitán of the marines. Their voyage was over.

When the canoe rode up onto the beach, the crew gave Huony a rousing cheer led by Manuel Echaniz.

As Captain Huony stood on the beach surveying his ship, he contemplated his options. Some Englishmen had also arrived from the mainland, eyeing what they believed to be a treasure ship as they saw some heavy chests coming ashore. He summoned his officers to council. They could see that *La Galga's* hull was covered with sand, and there was two feet of water over her gun deck and up to the windows of the lower saloon. Her heavy stern was sitting farther out in deeper water.

"Gentlemen, what is your opinion on attempting to salvage our ship?" Huony asked.

The other officers stressed the point that the crew were too exhausted to attempt such a feat. Then one of them said, "Let's burn the ship, sir, and keep her out of the hands of the English." Huony was quick to quell the idea and pointed out that they were not at war and that these Englishmen were their ticket home. Since there was no food or water to be found on the island, their time was limited.

The English offered to shuttle the distressed Spaniards to the mainland, thinking that as soon as they were gone, they would plunder the wreck of all the valuables they believed to be on board.

Unknown to Captain Huony, and not quite forgotten by the English, was that his good friend the notorious privateer, Don Pedro Garaicochea, had plundered shipping along this coast several years before during the late war. Garaicochea had been operating in his ship the *Nuestra Señora del Carmen*. But his ship was better known to the English by her alias, *LA GALGA*. This was, perhaps, an unfortunate coincidence for Huony. The locals patiently awaited retribution; *La Galga* was going to be theirs.

"Señor Velasco, assemble everyone for inspection and account for all hands. Have some soldiers surround the effects we have saved," Huony commanded.

Velasco reported 187 hands present. The last accounting at sea was 193. They found that a soldier named Joseph Guzman had remained on board ship, either too frightened to leave, or most likely, in a desperate attempt to save his valuables. As for the others, Huony said, "Praise God only five drowned in this tragedy." No one was lost aboard ship.

This was an amazing feat. For thirteen days, men climbed masts and rigging, and struggled on open decks making repairs. Not a single man had been lost. Only going ashore did people drown and then it was out of haste.

Not only did almost everyone survive, but a number of officials were able to save some of their personal possessions, which included some money, silverware, clothes, and some small chests. Others lost everything they owned. Huony was able to bring ashore nine chests, which included at least one chest of silver and hampers full of clothes and documents.

That night, they all rested on the beach, exhausted from their ordeal at sea. They divided up the biscuit and what little water they had brought with them.

The next morning, the 9th, a number of canoes and small shallow draft sailing vessels called *periaugers* had come over from the mainland, having heard about the Spanish wreck. The English told Huony that the closest town was Snow Hill, Maryland, where he could find sustenance for his crew and then passage to Norfolk. They were willing to help, but they also wanted the wreck. Huony said that he could not surrender the ship to them as the "owner of the land" was the owner of the wreck.

The Spaniards straggled to the west side of the island and began boarding. They looked back to see the English climb onto the wreck.

Twelve miles up the Bay, the Spaniards landed. The prisoners and some of the crew began to desert and headed for Philadelphia. Most of them stuck with Huony and walked the eight miles overland to town.

As the caravan of Spaniards marched toward Snow Hill, they passed little farm houses and the English settlers at work in their fields. Everyone stopped what they were doing, including the slaves, as this colorful band of soldiers and sailors paraded past them. The children waved. They had seen shipwreck survivors before, but nothing like this. It was a crew from one of those legendary Spanish galleons. The whole countryside was soon buzzing with the news. Huony and his crew entered Snow Hill on September 10.

Snow Hill was a small village made up of mostly little wooden houses resting on logs set against the banks of the black waters of the narrow Pocomoke River. There was a tavern and an Anglican church and a Presbyterian church. This was the county seat of Worcester County, which had just been formed in 1742 out of the larger county of Somerset.

After the Spaniards' ordeal at sea and their exhausting experience at Assateague followed by their march overland to town, Snow Hill was a welcome site. Here Huony learned that *Los Godos* and *San Pedro* had made it safely into Norfolk.

The county sheriff, John Scarborough, who was now aware of the Spaniards' arrival, presented himself to Captain Huony. Scarborough, a man of influence, was also a delegate from Worcester County to the Lower House in Annapolis. Huony related to him the purpose of his mission, the hurricane, the condition of his ship on Assateague, and that before he left Assateague, the locals had begun plundering the wreck. Scarborough assured him that he would do all he could to protect the wreck, but his first priority was to find food, water, and shelter for the Spaniards.

Scarborough had observed the number of chests that had been brought into town and some of them were noticeably very heavy; these he believed to be full of silver. The quiet little village was now in an uproar—rumors about a Spanish treasure ship ashore on Assateague spread, arousing the populace. The sight of the Spaniards, basically unarmed but still in their uniforms, conveyed a sense of vulnerability to the English in Snow Hill. Scarborough decided to go over to Assateague and have a look.

On September 12, Sheriff Scarborough arrived at the wreck. He was overwhelmed by what he saw. There lay a crippled Spanish warship with her masts down, many cannon still at the ready, and two kedge anchors held in place at her bow with the golden lion figurehead staring menacingly at the beach; the sea was rolling through her lower decks spewing water out of the open gun ports. Sand had piled up around the hull. On board and on the beach were a number of Virginia plantation owners with their slaves methodically looting the ship. Others from Maryland stood by hoping to get a chance to join in. Some of these men were even magistrates and Accomack County justices. Many small items that could be easily taken were accumulating on the beach and were being readied for transport to the mainland. The stern area, which included the officers' cabins, was ransacked. Furniture, small arms, and other personal items had been taken. Scarborough watched helplessly as a gang of slaves were slinging a cannon to lift it overboard. Others were now cutting the rigging loose and collecting blocks, deadeyes, tools, and fastenings.

He climbed on board and descended to the gun deck, which was covered with several feet of water. Others were wading about inside, searching for items worth taking. Bales of tobacco leaf wrapped in canvas were floating to the top of the hold and recovered. They were then opened, and the sodden tobacco was cast out of the wrappers and examined for hidden treasure. As Scarborough stood in the swirling sea water peering into the flooded hold, he could see the mahogany planks lashed to the bottom of the hold. All of the storage rooms below the gun deck were flooded and inaccessible. There was more tobacco in the hold, and in the forward storage room were sails and rigging yet to be taken. Sheriff Scarborough stared down a wooden gangway that descended into watery darkness. He reflected on the heavy chests the Spaniards had brought to Snow Hill. He was no seaman but Scarborough knew that the heaviest cargo, cargo like chests of silver pieces of eight, was always stored in the lowest part of the ship, down that flooded gangway. Others, who had the same realization, began to dismantle the ship. Burning was out of the question.

One of the looters was William Gore, who had a sizable plantation on the mainland and owned all of Assateague up to the Maryland-Virginia line. Scarborough told him and the others to "go easy" with the looting until he could consult with the Maryland governor. The people about the wreck told Scarborough that the ship was in Virginia and of no concern to the Maryland governor. They were abusive and disrespectful to the sheriff, doing their best to run him off.

Back in Snow Hill, Captain Huony realized that his crew had further diminished in size and ordered his purser, Joseph Velasco, to take roll call again. He was now down to 122 men and ship's boys. Huony found two sloops, which he hired to take him and the remaining crew on to Norfolk, Virginia. They loaded on board their salvaged possessions, which included chests of personal belongings, government documents, and money. After nearly a week in Snow Hill, they departed, floating down the narrow Pocomoke passing swamps and plantations of the English until they reached the broad waters of Pocomoke Sound and the Chesapeake Bay. Here the sloops hoisted sails and proceeded down the Chesapeake to Norfolk, Virginia, where they arrived on September 19.

While Captain Huony was en route to Norfolk, Sheriff John Scarborough wrote his report of the wreck to Maryland's governor, Samuel Ogle. He reported that more than two hundred small arms, swords, and bayonets, as well as rigging, tools, and "coppers of large and small sizes" had been salvaged. He said the mahogany was still on board and should be gotten before the ship "bursts with the sea and sinks into the land."

Scarborough described his harsh treatment at the wreck by the "Virginia Gentlemen" and repeated what they said about the wreck being in Virginia. But he also told the governor that there were people living on the beach who said the ship was two miles inside of Maryland. Scarborough sought to draw the governor into the controversy over the location of the wreck. He prefaced his letter to him saying, "I thought it my duty to write to your Excellency to have your Oppinion whose Property She is as the Spaniards has left her…."

When Scarborough returned to Snow Hill, he sent his report on to Governor Ogle in Annapolis. Before Scarborough's report was received in Annapolis, the *Maryland Gazette* of September 16 reported the exaggerated news of the fleet as told to them by a man who had just come in from Norfolk:

A fleet of Spanish Ships, consisting of three Men of War, one of 20, one of 60, and one of 80 Guns, six Merchantmen, two register ships, a brigantine, and a sloop bound from Havannah for *Old Spain,* were dispers'd at Sea by hard Gales of Wind, and the Brigantine, having on board a good many Chests of Money, was drove ashore on *Machapungo* Shoals, and lost, but the Crew and part of the Money saved; the two Register Ships having the Governor of Havannah and his Family on board, and Twelve Million Pieces of Eight, lost their masts, but fortunately got into *Norfolk* in *Virginia,* where they are now refitting. They know not what became of the Men of War, the Merchantmen and the sloop.

News of the loss of the Spanish fleet was spreading throughout the colonies. More details appeared in the *Pennsylvania Gazette* of September 17. Captain James Maloney, who had escaped his confinement on board *La Galga* and fled with many others to Philadelphia, reported to the *Gazette* and described his ordeal and gave his account of the wreck. He said the storm was the worst he had ever experienced. In his words, the ship had hit "Chincoteague shoals" on September 4 and ran ashore on "Chincoteague Island" on September 6. That same day the *Boston News Letter* featured a story about the Spanish treasure fleet of Admiral Spinola, which had left the previous November and arrived in Cádiz in July. The Men-of-War *Fénix, Dragon,* and *Real Familia* had brought in a huge treasure, which the paper listed in detail:

> A sacramental Chalice with 238 Emeralds
> A small chest full of emeralds, and Jewels in Gold
> Several Jewels of Gold, with 140 Emeralds
> Two Almond Pearls
> A Regal Crown
> A Silver Chalice
> And for the King,
>
> A Silver Trunk containing two Pear Pearls, one of 35 and half carats, the other 34 ¾ Carats

The Gold and Silver coin amounts

On the King's Account	840,297 Dollars
For the Holy Crusado	50,000
For the Holy Places in Jerusalem	13,916
For the Trade	14,237,011
Gold in bars	252,396
Silver work'd up	104,914
Brute Emeralds work'd up	26,515 stones
Pearls	1,924
Bazoard	350 lb. &c."

As this news circulated, everyone's attention was focused on the wrecked Spanish ships.

In Annapolis on September 23, the next issue of the *Maryland Gazette* followed up on the latest about the Spanish fleet:

Since our last, we have collected some further account of the *Spanish* Fleet, which met with bad weather at Sea, and were, some of them, forced into *Norfolk*. We are assured that the whole fleet, which left the *Havannah*, consisted of three Galleons, four Register Ships, one Brigantine, and one Sloop, under convoy of one *Spanish* Man of War of 50 guns: They were parted at Sea by bad weather. One of the Galleons, a Register Ship, and the Sloop are at *Norfolk*, have brought in a vast sum of money; the Galleon had 350 chests of dollars on board, and a great quantity of Cochineal, Sugar, Indigo, Cocoa, and Dying Wood: One passenger on board her had 200,000 Dollars, and a great quantity of Diamonds. They lost all their masts and flung over all of their guns, which were 40, at Sea: and when she came into *Norfolk*, had fourteen feet of water in her hold. The other ship belongs to the *Portuguese*, her cargo consisting of Cocoa, Cochineal, and Money: having 600,000 Dollars register'd, and a great quantity besides. The Brigantine, as we mentioned, was lost; but all, or the greatest Part of her Money saved; The

Man of War, called (in English), the *Greyhound*, commanded by Capt. *Omness*, an *Irish* Gentleman, after losing all her Masts, Rudder, and guns at Sea, drove ashore on *Machapungo* Shoals, off *Worcester* County, in this province, with seven feet of water in her Hold; where she now lies a wreck. After she struck, the People hoisted out her Boats, but they stove along side, being about a quarter Mile from the Shore; after which they made a Raft, on which they brought a good deal of Money ashore; but two men, and two chests of Money, were wash'd off and lost; and two other men, attempting to swim ashore, had so much Money round their waists that they sunk with it, and were drowned. The Captain hired two sloops to carry his Men, and what Money they could save, round to *Elizabeth*, in *Virginia*. She had on board, besides money, *Spanish* Snuff, *Spanish* Tobacco, and a great quantity of Mahogany, the best which could be got, for the King of *Spain's* new Palace at *Madrid*. The people at and about *Worcester* County, are every day, in good weather, fishing what they can out of her, and have found a considerable Booty.

The next day, when Scarborough's report was read to the governor and council, Governor Ogle immediately issued a warrant directed to Sheriff Scarborough to recover the salvaged items from those "Several Evil Minded Persons:"

These are therefore Strictly to Charge & Command you the said Sheriff to Seize and take into your Possession and Safe keep the same untill the Right thereto shall be Lawfully determined all the Guns Tackle Apparel Equipment and other Materialls of the said Ship and all and every Part of the Money Goods Wares and Effects of every kind & quality whatsoever.... Hereof you are not to fail as you shall answer the Contrary at your Peril.

Governor Ogle, who was now in his third term as governor since 1731, appeared to take no position on which jurisdiction the wreck lay in as asked by Scarborough, and his written instructions referred to the wreck only as lying "on or near the Shoar" of Worcester County. Sheriff Scarborough continued his efforts to gain control of the wreck.

Captain Huony arrived in Norfolk, Virginia, on September 19, where he was warmly greeted by Captains Pedro Pumarejo of the *Nuestra Señora de los Godos* and John Kelly of the *San Pedro*. He also was introduced to Captain Don Antonio Tanasio Anaya of the sloop *La Marianna* from Campeche, which had come into Norfolk with the other two. When he met with Pumarejo, he was brought up to date on the fate of the other ships.

Captain Juan Manuel Bonilla had gotten the *Nuestra Señora de Guadalupe* towed into Ocracoke Inlet, which lay a little south of Cape Hatteras on the Outer Banks of North Carolina. The *Nuestra Señora de Soledad* was ashore at Drum Inlet and Don Joseph Respaldiza was hurriedly salvaging his cargo. *El Salvador* was totally lost.

The week before, word had reached Norfolk the the *Nuestra Señora de Mercedes* had run ashore near Machapungo Inlet north of Cape Charles. Captain Barrosa and his crew were safe but nothing was saved. A Virginia merchant and customs agent named Peter Hog wrote from the wreck site to Captain Pumarejo in Norfolk on September 13 to advise them of the loss and offered his services to the King of Spain. By then, the locals led by the Powell brothers who lived on the mainland in Northhampton County set fire to the wreck to get at its contents and were able to get the sails, rigging, and some parcels of money. Captain Barrossa and his crew wouldn't join Huony at Norfolk until September 30.

Huony was totally exhausted from his ordeal. Instead of personally going to Williamsburg to meet President Lee, the acting governor of Virginia, he sent the *Guadalupe's* pilot, Felipe García, who had just come up from Ocracoke, and his own chaplain, Father John Martin, to act as interpreter. They went to discuss the strict customs regulations that were being imposed on the ships in Norfolk. President Lee was informed by the Spaniards that *La Galga* lay in Virginia under his jurisdiction. After the meeting, Huony was able to obtain a license to send the cargoes of the three ships in the harbor back to Spain. As commander of the fleet at sea, responsibility for the ships and their crews still remained with him. Captain Bonilla needed help at Ocracoke to bring his cargo and valuables to Norfolk. Norfolk would become the command center for the Spaniards as they made plans to return to Spain with their treasure.

On October 8, Governor Ogle wrote to President Lee in Virginia to inform him that people from Virginia were looting a wreck that he now claimed was in the province of Maryland. President Lee never responded. On October 17, Governor Ogle wrote to Sheriff Scarborough instructing him to arrest anyone who was known to be looting the wreck and even anyone who would hinder the execution of his orders.

Unknown to Captain Huony, officials at the wreck site of *La Galga* were in disagreement as to which jurisdiction she lay in. Huony knew that he was very close to the border, but had been told before he left Assateague that he was in Virginia. Sheriff Scarborough claimed the wreck had to be in Maryland. The locals from both jurisdictions continued to plunder the wreck.

In Norfolk, Huony was told about the continued looting, the controversy over jurisdiction, and what appeared to be a resolution of that controversy. He learned that a recent storm had broke open the hold of the ship releasing over two hundred mahogany planks into the sea that washed ashore south of the boundary line. The mahogany was bought by a merchant in Snow Hill, Maryland.

The planks were property of King Ferdinand VI, destined for his new palace, so Huony was duty bound to demand restitution. In the first week of November, he wrote to Governor Sam Ogle in Annapolis whereupon his letter was read before the governor and council on November 14:

Honorable Sir:

His Catholick Majesty's Ship the *Greyhound* I commanded, having wrecked upon the Island of Assateague the 6th of the expired N: S:, the Country People, telling me She lay in Virginia, was the Motive that made me write to the President, giving him an Account of My Misfortunes that Occasioned my being castaway in his Government &c. But now understanding, that by a late experiment of an East Line drawn (to know the bounds) its found, She lyes within twice her length of it in Maryland, I see its to you I should give the aforesaid Account as Governor of that Province, wherefore I hope you will excuse my Mistake, as proceeding from a wrong Information, & consequently involuntary in me....

Governor Ogle immediately penned his response to Huony in Norfolk:

Sir:

I have this day received your Letter in Relation to the Loss of his Catholick Majesty's Ship the *Greyhound* under your Command, And you may be Assured of all the Assistance, that lies in my Power, in recovering such of the Effects as have been Plundered out of the said Ship by any of the Inhabitants of this Province and indeed without waiting till I heard from you I thought it my duty, as soon as the News of your Misfortune arrived at this Place, to use my utmost endeavours to Secure as many of them as Possible, in order to their being delivered, to such as might have Authority to demand the same, for the Use of his Catholick Majesty Conformable to the Treaties of Peace and friendship that happily Subsist between the two Crowns. If I might Presume to give you any Advice, it would be to Authorize some Person to Receive the Mahogany and the Other Effects, who, by the Assistance of the Several Governments concerned, might Recover more of them than can well be Contrived by any other means am heartily for the Occasion of this Correspondence and am with very great Regard Sir.

Sam Ogle

Captain Huony departed Norfolk, Virginia, for Spain on January 10, 1751, without receiving any compensation for the mahogany or any other items confiscated by Sheriff Scarborough of Worcester County, Maryland. Later, the Colonial government of Virginia recovered some of the salvaged items in the hands of some citizens of Accomack County, which were then sold at auction and the proceeds turned over to Captain Huony's attorney, Peter Hog. After Huony's letter was read before the governor and council in Annapolis, it was duly filed away, where it lay for centuries in Maryland's archives.

This would become the single most important letter that he ever wrote.

CHAPTER THREE
Hooked

The Bait

"...By a late experiment of an East line drawn (to know the bounds) it's found, she lies within twice her length of it in Maryland." —Don Daniel Huony

As I entered the National Archives Building in Washington, DC, one evening in March of 1978, I once again read the words below the statue flanking the entrance: "What is past is prologue." I was there to review Civil War records related to some naval engagements. Documenting shipwrecks was my goal.

I had asked for some records, and while I was waiting, I noticed several shelves close by stacked with green volumes lettered in gold. It was a series of colonial records for the State of Maryland called *The Archives of Maryland*. There were over fifty volumes. *Were they indexed?*

I pulled a volume off the shelf without regard for the date printed on the book's spine, opened it to the index, and proceeded to the letter "S" for shipwreck. I was immediately rewarded. Turning to the referenced pages, I found a document concerning the Spanish ship the *Greyhound*, or *La Galga* in Spanish, which wrecked in 1750. I recognized this ship as the same one mentioned in Dave Horner's *The Treasure Galleons*. Horner's book had contained details about a number of Spanish galleons, one of which was the *Nuestra Señora de Atocha*, the shipwreck made famous by Mel Fisher and his Florida-based company, Treasure Salvors, and discovered in 1975. Horner had placed *La Galga* at Old Currituck Inlet, North Carolina.

As I read on, this document gave me the exact location of *La Galga's* final resting place, far from North Carolina. The letter was written in November, 1750 by Don Daniel Huony, captain of *La Galga*, to Governor Samuel Ogle of Maryland. In his letter, he said he thought he was cast ashore in Virginia on Assateague Island, but was later informed, while waiting in Norfolk to return to Spain, "that by a late experiment of an East line drawn (to know the bounds) its found, she lies within twice her length of it in Maryland...."

I was stunned. Having read quite a bit about shipwrecks, I had never seen such a precise description for the location of a wreck. I would usually see a reference such as so many "miles" or "leagues" from some known point or inlet. The older the wreck, the more imprecise the description of its location tended to be. Mel Fisher was still looking for the mother lode of the *Atocha* after nine years of searching off of the Marquesas in the Florida Keys. He had located scattered artifacts from the wreck, which narrowed the search area, but he still had many square miles yet to search.

My heart pounding with excitement, I returned to my apartment and called my diving buddy, Greg Sutliff, who was living in Richmond, Virginia, my hometown. I briefed him on my discovery and told him that I thought we could easily locate *La Galga*. But we would need a magnetometer and a boat to get us out to the site.

Greg and I had been diving together since 1972 and had been friends since grade school. Our underwater adventures were mostly in the rivers and quarries around Richmond. My first diving experience was at age fourteen at Nassau, Bahamas, on a family vacation. I never got over that first encounter with the underwater world as I marveled at the angel fish, parrot fish, clown fish, and other neon-colored denizens of the deep that darted about the multicolored corals. In the crevices, I glimpsed beautiful blue and yellow wrasses swimming about and a lazy moray eel that gave me an evil look. It was more spectacular than I could have imagined. The only previous underwater images I had ever seen had come from the family's black and white television. It was 1964. Adding to my excitement, above and not far away, MGM was filming *Thunderball*, the James Bond action/adventure movie. I knew that some day that I would eventually take up diving.

Greg and I had talked about buying a boat together following our days together at Benedictine High School. After graduating from the University of South Carolina, I took a job with Blue Cross in Richmond auditing hospitals. Greg was working for his father's company, Sutliff Tobacco. After a few months, I saved enough money to make the joint purchase. We became the proud owners of a fifteen-foot baby-blue ski boat.

Neither of us could wait until spring to go water skiing. Our solution—go rent some wet suits. We consulted the phone book and found W&W Dive Shop out on West Broad Street and paid them a visit. While we were there, Bob White, the owner, talked of wreck diving and hunting for underwater artifacts. He proudly showed us some photos of Civil War artifacts that he had recovered in nearby rivers. In his display case were Revolutionary War cannonballs and bar shot, which look like dumbbells and are fired into ship's rigging. Greg and I looked at each other and then at the pictures. We got our wet suits and went outside.

Greg burst out "Man, did you see that stuff?!"

"We need to get certified!" I said with equal enthusiasm.

While we were driving, we talked more about scuba diving and artifact finding than water skiing. We decided to enroll in the next YMCA scuba diving course. It was only weeks away, and Bob White would be our instructor.

Right after the diving course started, Greg and I began buying our dive gear. We wanted to be ready as soon as the course was over. For our first "treasure hunt," we decided to go the James River above Bosher's Dam and explore the waters in front of Bellona Arsenal, a foundry that made cannon and shot during the Civil War. In 1864, near the end of the war, Colonel Ulric Dahlgren of the U.S. Cavalry attacked Richmond. The Confederate Rebels in control of the arsenal could see the approaching Union Army from the hilltop. They threw cannon, shot, and various weapons and foundry equipment into the river to prevent their capture by the Northern soldiers. The Rebels also sank a barge, which legend said had carried two twelve-pound caliber brass field cannon on the end. In 1962, some divers, guided by an eyewitness account passed on in 1924, had located the barge and an iron cannon and cannon mold that they lifted out of the water with a crane. They also tried to lift the front of the barge but their attempt failed when it broke. It was said then that whatever was on the stern of the barge, which was jutting out into the river, was driven deeper into the river bottom. This event was memorialized by the placement of the cannon and mold on a permanent foundation between the riverbank and the side of Old Gun Road.

Divers had combed the bottom for years retrieving many artifacts. *Would there be anything left for us?* To improve our odds, we bought an underwater metal detector from J. W. Fishers in Taunton, Massachusetts. From the description, it sounded sensitive enough to locate even small artifacts. Even though our certification course was not yet complete, we were ready.

By June, we had our certification cards, which gave us the ability to buy air, so we set out one Sunday to water ski and to dive. When our boat arrived in front of Bellona Arsenal, we debated where to anchor. Unsure what would be the best location, we set up about twenty-five yards from shore in front of the arsenal hill. We plunged over the side, and I carried the metal detector. The water was only about ten feet deep, but we had visibility of only about a foot. With the earphone tucked inside my diving hood to hold it in place, I began to swim randomly about, moving the detector back and forth in front of me, waiting to hear a high-pitched whine as it passed over some metal object.

Before long, the first sounds came through the earpiece. I centered over the hit and then started digging blindly. Feeling something hard, I pushed my hand deeper alongside of it. When I pulled it free of the mud, I quickly realized it was only a beer can, having held many of these before. I vowed never again to toss my refuse in the river. I moved on and found a pop top and another can. Frustration began to set in over the amount of trash on the bottom.

Then it happened. The next hit was stronger, and I had to dig deeper. I reached into the hole I had dug and pulled out a six-pound cannonball. I felt Greg next to me so I grabbed his arm and put his hand on it. His underwater yell sounded like a squeal. It was our first treasure!

Topside, we took turns holding the cannonball and later showed it to many of our friends who were out skiing that day. I never got over it. I called the office the next morning and said I wasn't coming in. I refilled the air tanks and returned with my brother Mike where we then recovered several more cannonballs, which included a fifty-pounder.

Greg and I would later return and find even more artifacts. We eventually made a few diving trips to the Bahamas and Florida Keys, but our treasure hunting was put on hold when the real world got a grip on us.

In 1976, I had a job offer to go to Washington, DC, to work for Psychiatric Institutes of America as a government reimbursement specialist. The company owned hospitals in Virginia, Washington, and across the U.S. I had sworn that I would never live in a big city. My goal was to find a quiet place near the water, not concrete sidewalks and rush-hour traffic. But I was tired of my job, tired of Richmond, and my social life was stalled (everybody was getting married). So, I took the job. At the same time, Greg, who was married with two kids, had left his father's company and decided to go to commercial diving school. We stayed in touch.

Washington, DC, was rejuvenating, everyone was single, and at twenty-six, I was really having fun. My job took me around the country, and the promotions and pay raises came annually. I was climbing the corporate ladder, and it couldn't have been better.

But I soon became disillusioned with the business world, partly because I was constantly dealing with government rules and regulations that made little sense and seemed to add nothing to real productivity, and also because I was frustrated by the pettiness and incompetence of some of my superiors. My daydreams took me out on the water.

Greg would call me sometimes to help him with his diving business. This gave me the opportunity to go diving again and forget the confines of my Georgetown office. Greg was now a certified commercial diver and trained me to use surface-supplied air and communications gear. As we were doing this, we starting talking about treasure hunting and our past diving experiences.

"You know, Greg, I could start researching dive sites like Bellona Arsenal and shipwrecks and maybe we could make some money at this," I said more than once. I told him that the National Archives and Library of Congress were available in DC and would be a great place to "look stuff up." So in September of 1977, I started researching Civil War era wrecks. It was a little confusing at first because I had not been in a library since my college days and even then not very often. But after learning my way around the various collections, I decided that I would catalog every wreck that could be documented in the State of Virginia.

By March of 1978, my list was growing as well as my obsession. It was then, that fateful evening, that I became ensnared by the story of *La Galga*.

After reading Captain Huony's letter, I was convinced that locating the wreck would be a piece of cake. It also seemed worthwhile as additional research in contemporary newspapers described several chests of money being lost off of a raft as it was being carried ashore. I hoped there would be more.

But I then found that the discovery of Captain Huony's letter in the Maryland Archives was no great discovery at all. Since it was printed in 1913, the location was repeated in local histories and some tourist literature and was known to many. Now the question loomed, if it was so easy to find, why hadn't anyone found it before? Had anybody else tried to find it? I reasoned that if they had, they would have found it and I would've already read about it. It would at least been mentioned in one of the many books on shipwreck discoveries. As this logic played on my mind, I became convinced that I would be the first to go hunt for *La Galga* simply because it hadn't been discovered yet.

I dove into the map collections at the Library of Congress and studied the evolution of cartography for the Eastern Shore of Virginia and Maryland. I found that seventeenth and eighteenth century maps were not drawn to scale and Assateague Island wasn't even shown until late in the eighteenth century. Some maps showed the boundary near latitude 38°, two miles south of the present boundary, and by the end of the eighteenth century maps showed the boundary as exactly latitude 38°. But even if research couldn't establish with absolute certainty where the line actually lay, I figured a couple of days of good weather with a magnetometer in tow would be all that was necessary.

Since we didn't have a magnetometer or a boat that could get us the twelve miles from the safety of Chincoteague Inlet to the wreck site, we weren't in a position to pursue it. Soon after that, I made the decision to buy a magnetometer made by J.W. Fishers, the same company from which I had purchased the metal detector years before. This device could be towed behind a boat, and it would detect anomalies in the earth's magnetic field created by ferrous metals. A magnetometer is as essential to treasure hunting as scuba gear is to diving. It was my prized possession—and it nearly emptied my bank account.

We put *La Galga* on the back burner and continued our occasional weekend forays in rivers, hoping somehow to turn a buck and then graduate to ocean search and salvage. We discovered that rivers, with their relatively easy access, weren't good hunting grounds because items could easily be salvaged contemporary with their loss.

In the summer of 1978, I would go down to Richmond on weekends and rendezvous with Greg and his petite wife, Mary Ellen, whom I had known since first grade. We would go look in rivers for wrecks or places like Bellona where things were reported to have been thrown in the water. What we really wanted was to find a cannon, but mostly we found junk. The wrecks we looked for were not where they were supposed to be. We found that they were often raised shortly after they were sunk or they had been blown up and buried deep in the bottom. We even looked for the cannon jettisoned from the USS *Minnesota* during her engagement with the *Merrimack* in the Civil War after she had run aground in Hampton Roads, but there was nothing to be found. We dove off the beach at Yorktown where we saw the mast of a Revolutionary War-era ship lying across the bottom, but we found no artifacts where others had.

By midsummer of 1979, we hadn't had any success and the subject of *La Galga* came up again. "Look," I said to Greg, "I am going to find a researcher in Spain and find out what I can about this wreck. If you can get the boat, we'll have a real good shot at this." Greg thought it over and agreed. Our only chance of a successful find was to hit the ocean. Our planning began.

That fall, I wrote to the Archivo General de Indias in Seville, Spain, for the purpose of locating a researcher. It is at this archive that most of the documents relating to Spain's operations in the New World are located. Greg and I then took off for some diving in the Florida Keys where we scouted the outer reefs hoping to find something from one of the many ships that had met their end there. We had no luck, but our "treasure fever" intensified when we visited Mel Fisher's Galleon Museum in Key West and saw firsthand the silver bars and gold and silver coins he had recovered from the *Atocha* and *Santa Margarita*. Our thoughts ran wild with the idea of finding our own Spanish galleon.

I did not hear anything from Spain for months. Finally in December, I received a letter from Mrs. Victoria Stapells Johnson, a Canadian who was an expert at reading the old Spanish documents housed at the Archivo General de Indias. I would find out later that she had played an important role in the discovery of the *Nuestra Señora de La Concepción* two years before. She was working for Peter Earle who, while writing a book about the wreck, discovered the lost logbook of William Phipps who had first salvaged the wreck in 1687. Through another researcher, she introduced Peter Earle to Burt Webber who ultimately found the wreck in 1978 with the help of the logbook.

Victoria did not get started until March of 1980, and then the information started to flow. One of the first things she had found was *La Galga's* cargo manifest. Notations on the document showed that it had actually traveled aboard the ship and been rescued by Captain Huony and returned to Spain. I thought to myself how fortunate that at least one artifact from the ship still existed. She found no report from Captain Huony.

La Galga's manifest gave us some disappointing news. It stated clearly that she "was not a treasure ship." It did mention some 900 pieces of eight, a tantalizing chest that contained various pieces of worked silver and gold, and 4,800 pesos in gold doubloons which belonged to a priest named Juan Garay de Concepcíon. Also listed were large amounts of tobacco for the Royal Treasury, and described in the Maryland archives was a shipment of mahogany for the King's Palace. Greg and I rationalized that salvaging the ship could still be worth our while. We had read about the Spaniards' penchant for smuggling money and valuables to avoid the King's tax, and if Father Garay's chest of gold was still there, we would be richly rewarded.

In Captain Huony's letter found in the Maryland Archives, he stated that everything worth taking had been salvaged by the locals. Many of the wrecks in Florida from the 1715 and 1733 Spanish treasure fleets had been heavily salvaged directly after their loss, yet they yielded riches to modern salvors; likewise with *Nuestra Señora de la Atocha* that

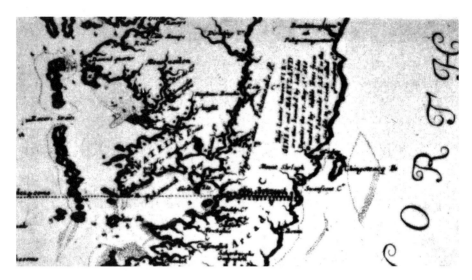

Part of map drawn by Augustine Herman in 1670. This map would be the basis for almost all future maps until 1751. Chincoteague Island is shown but Assateague is omitted. The notation in the upper right describes the Maryland–Virginia boundary as, "marked by DUBBLE Trees from the Pocomoke EAST to the seaside to a crooke called Swansecute Cr." This line is shown as a due east line. *Courtesy of the Library of Congress.*

Part of "A Map of the Most Inhabited Part of Virginia Containing the Whole Province of Maryland with Part of Pennsylvania, New Jersey and North Carolina." Drawn by Joshua Fry & Peter Jefferson in 1751." *Courtesy of the Library of Congress.* Note the Calvert-Scarborough line is still depicted as due east and lies south of latitude 38°, although the map says 1688, it was drawn in 1668.

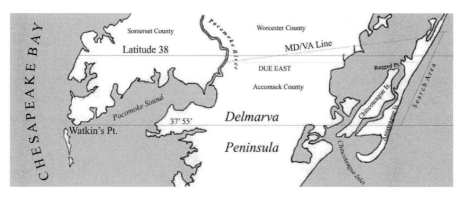

In 1751, Somerset County, Maryland's boundary ended at Watkin's Point at 37' 55"
and the south side of the Pocomoke Sound and east at Pocomoke River. Worcester
County was separated from Accomack, Virginia by the Calvert-Scarborough line.
The starting point of Scarborough in 1668 was the east side of the Pocomoke River.
Scarborough, by intention or mistake, used his compass to run an east line to the
seaside creating the error and controversy over the boundary. Note that the starting
point is below latitude 38° just as it was in 1751 as shown in the illustration at bottom
of page 58. The dotted line is the intended course for Scarborough. The present MD/
VA line is noted. President Thomas Lee of Virginia described the boundary in 1750
as ending about latitude 38°. Later eighteenth century maps showed the boundary
as latitude 38°. With these parameters, the search area was delineated. This is also
shown in chart below. *Illustration by the author.*

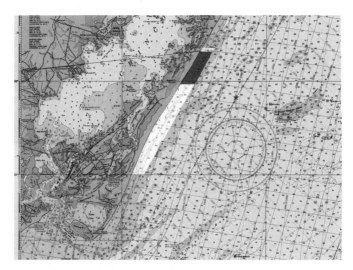

Delineation of search areas for *La Galga*. The dark area was the most probable, lying
between the present boundary and just below latitude 38°, which is the due east
extension from the point of origin on the Pocomoke River. The lightened areas north
and south were deemed possible but unlikely. *Taken from NOAA Chart #12211, Fenwick
Island to Chincoteague Inlet, 1980.*

sank in 1622 at the Marquesas Keys southwest of Key West.

While Victoria was busy in Spain, I focused on locating documents in Maryland, Virginia, and North Carolina relative to the fleet. This included the contemporary newspapers from Philadelphia, New York, Annapolis, Williamsburg, Charleston, and London. I located a letter dated September 29, 1750, from President Thomas Lee, acting governor of Virginia, to the Duke of Bedford that described the boundary between Maryland and Virginia as, "Our Northern Bounds are divided from Maryland by a line drawn East from Watkins Point the South side of Pocomoke on the Eastern Shore to the Atlantick Ocean and ends about latitude 38°." Previous searches of eighteenth century maps showed the same thing. The boundary was a line due east across the Eastern Shore at latitude 38°. I noted that the present line was a tangential line from Pocomoke River on the west side of the Delmarva Peninsula that ended about a mile and a half north of latitude 38°. I found that this line had been drawn in 1668 by Edmund Scarborough, surveyor general of Virginia, but that he made the mistake of following his compass and did not allow for the predicted magnetic variation. After further study of Huony's letter, I deduced that the "experiment" of a new boundary line pushed the boundary south of some preconceived location. The boundary line was certain to be an unsettled issue. I considered President Lee's letter very important because its date was contemporary to the loss of *La Galga*.

Some of the early maps and charts depicted latitude 38° as being nearly five miles south of where it actually is today, or approximately latitude 37° 55'. I figured that this would have to be the extreme southern limit of the search area. The wreck would then lie between this line and the current boundary line, a distance of almost seven miles.

English accounts described the ship as being a quarter of a mile from shore. A Spanish document located by Victoria said a "musket shot from shore." I reasoned that it still would be a relatively easy find because *La Galga* would be within several hundred yards of the beach in a narrow corridor and most likely in the vicinity of latitude 38°, or how that degree of latitude was determined in 1750.

In April, Greg bought a twenty-two-foot Aquasport center console, which we could trailer to Chincoteague Island, Virginia, and easily motor from there through the inlet to the search area. We already had the dive gear, electronics, pumps, and light dredging equipment. Our plan now was to get the boat to a safe place at Chincoteague and leave it. We figured it would take only a few weekends to find the wreck and then we could start bringing up treasure. On April 23, I rendezvoused with Greg at Chincoteague. We drove around and found Tom's Cove Campground, which provided a boat ramp and a place to safely leave our boat during the week. Camping was the only way we could afford to stay and work every weekend since we both had already expended quite a bit of money. The hunt would begin the following weekend, on May 3, 1980.

On Sunday, April 27, I went to my office to check messages since I was to be out of town on Monday. I found one I would never forget, and it would change my life forever.

There was a piece of paper taped to my phone with a newspaper clipping from Friday's *Wall Street Journal*:

And written below was a note from my co-worker Kevin Holecko, "Looks like you're too late!"

SALVAGE VENTURE
After 5 yrs. we have located several wrecks off the Delmarva coast. One has over $100,-000,000 in gold & silver. Require working partners w/capital to form salvage company. Principals have over 30 yrs experience in this business. S.E.A. Ltd., 1 Manklin Ct., Berlin, MD 21811. 301/641-

From the April 25, 1980 *Wall Street Journal*. The Mart section. *Courtesy of the Wall Street Journal.*

CHAPTER FOUR
Storm on the Horizon

August 9, 1955
Baltimore Harbor

Powerful tug boats nudged ARD-16, a U.S. Navy floating dock, toward its rendezvous with another dry dock owned by the Maryland Shipbuilding and Dry Dock Company. Inside the awkward craft rested a centuries-old wooden warship rescued from decay and neglect. She had been docked at Boston, Massachusetts, since the end of World War II before beginning her final voyage to Baltimore. There was a great celebration attended by dignitaries, the media, and a cheering crowd on shore. The USS *Constellation* that had been built in Baltimore in 1797 had finally returned home.

Unknown to many, but not all, the ship now cradled in the dry dock was built in 1854 at Norfolk, Virginia, only two hundred yards from where the original *Constellation* had been dismantled the year before. She was not the original *Constellation* that had been launched in Baltimore on September 7, 1797, as the first frigate to be commissioned in the U.S. Navy.

But today, among the cheering crowd, was a very proud young man named Donald Stewart who had been actively involved for the last two years in the effort to rescue this rotting relic. Stewart had been a volunteer member of the *Constellation* Committee that had been formed to bring the ship to Baltimore and to raise funds for her preservation.

The City of Baltimore had great plans to restore the seedy Inner Harbor from decay and neglect. The homecoming and restoration of the *Constellation* was to be the centerpiece of this revival. The new life planned for the *Constellation* marked the beginning in a new life for Donald Stewart. He had a fascination with old ships and history in general. He had grown up on Warren Avenue, only a few blocks from the South Baltimore docks. To escape the harsh reality of the city streets, he would visualize himself aboard the ships as they came and went from Baltimore to ports all over the world. He would sit and draw crude sketches of them and spend hours fantasizing how they could take him anywhere he wanted to go. Stewart entertained his friends with tall stories and exaggerations and quickly learned a fundamental weakness in human nature—people will readily believe what they want to believe. He had become street smart at an early age.

After high school and some art classes at the University of Baltimore, Donald Stewart went to work at the B&O Railroad as a clerk-typist. He devoted his spare time to reading books about ships and shipwrecks, and he avidly followed the news of treasure discoveries in the Florida Keys.

Closer to home, there were accounts of other wrecks that had captured his imagination. In January 1949, he had read a short article in *The Baltimore Sun* about a Spanish warship named the *La Galga* (*Greyhound*) that had run ashore on Assateague in 1750. Also mentioned was an unidentified Spanish ship wrecking off Ocean City, evidenced by Spanish coins having been found on the beaches there, dating as late as 1820. The article described a third vessel called the *Ocean Bird* lost near Ocean City in 1799.

Galleon Is Wrecked

In 1750, a Spanish galleon, the "Greyhound," Daniel Huony, master, ran aground on Assateague Island. When news of the wreck spread, people from Maryland and Virginia went to the scene and carried away all its cargo and even strippea the decks of their planks

On January 5, 1799 the English sailing vessel, "Ocean Bird," sank near Ocean City during a storm.

Another unidentified Spanish ship is believed to have been wrecked on the Ocean City shoals in 1820 during a storm. Legend has it that this ship was carrying a cargo of "pieces of eight." A number of golden coins have been found there from time to time.

From the Baltimore *Evening Sun*, January 4, 1949. *Courtesy the Baltimore Sun.*

At work, Stewart fantasized about salvaging sunken galleons, while pecking away at his manual typewriter. He vowed then that some day he would go hunt for *La Galga*.

In the spring of 1952, while Stewart was working at the B&O Railroad and lobbying for the return of the *Constellation*, he had heard about a cave-in at Clement Street in Baltimore caused by the collapse of a tunnel from an old mine. Donald Stewart told authorities investigating the collapse that he had a map drawn by General Ben Butler of the Union Army showing a maze of tunnels that had been an underground military fortress. With this map, Stewart said that he could locate a cache of Civil War weapons and powder. *The Baltimore Sun* featured a story about Stewart and these mysterious tunnels. Stewart had claimed he was writing a book about them.

That same night, a group of Maryland arms collectors held a meeting and invited Donald Stewart to speak about his project. He told them about his upcoming book, *Thunder Under the Bolus*, and described his "treasure map" that would lead them to the cache of Civil War weapons. He even showed them a pistol of certain Civil War vintage that he claimed to have discovered in the tunnels. Stewart went on to tell them that he had no personal interest in the weapons and that the collectors could have them. He just wanted to write the story.

The collectors left the meeting agreeing to lend Stewart a hand in a couple of days. Afterwards, they reconvened at a bar in downtown Baltimore and were soon enticed by Stewart to make the assault on the tunnels that night. Dressed in business clothes and armed with flashlights provided by Stewart, they descended through a manhole into the city sewer system. Stewart led them through a dark tunnel that he said had just collapsed that morning. One of the collectors, an engineer, commented that it looked like the cave-in had happened long ago. Nevertheless, Stewart persuaded them to start digging into the rubble. They soon dislodged a brick that fell into a cavity on the other side of the wall. It appeared that they had discovered another tunnel. Suddenly, from the other side, a man's arm reached through the opening, startling everyone. They had broken into the basement of a welding company, and the owner, who was alarmed and in no way amused, called the police. After they arrived, they carried everyone to jail for questioning. The police released everyone once they had heard the story and recognized Stewart. Apparently, they were familiar with his bizarre behavior.

Stewart was asked numerous times by the media and the gun collectors to produce the map, but he never did. Some members of the gun collectors club did some investigating and learned that the pistol he "found" had actually been purchased from an antique dealer. His hoax was written off as the publicity stunt of a man running for office. As for the tunnels, it was proven that they were dug well before the Civil War. After numerous searches, no weapons were found. *Thunder Under the Bolus* was never published.

Donald Stewart was a man surrounded by controversy and mystery. He had a disarming and confident manner and was likable and trustworthy. His lack of physical stature accentuated these personality traits. He had claimed, at the time, that his interest in historic ships came from his experience salvaging Spanish treasure ships in the Florida Keys. The truth was he couldn't even swim.

In May of 1956, he left the B&O Railroad and took the job of night watchman aboard the *Constellation*, apparently without any background checks. Donald Stewart loved his new job at the *Constellation*. He liked being surrounded with the history of the old ship and the atmosphere of the city dock. Before long he was wearing a captain's uniform. He felt important—he had a new identity. He was later given the job of supervisor of the *Constellation* and stepped up to the financial challenges of restoring the deteriorating ship. By early 1958, the committee's first public fund-raising campaign netted a $9,532 loss, which prompted Dr. R. Walter Graham, the comptroller for the City of Baltimore, to call for the sinking of the ship rather than to continue to pay any more grant money to the committee.

Dr. Graham already was quite sure that the ship was not the original *Constellation*. On March 16, 1958, Dr. Graham appeared on television in Baltimore with Stewart and Leonard Cushing, the custodian and the historian for the ship, and Howard Chapelle, a naval historian, to debate that issue. Stewart was wearing a Merchant Marine captain's uniform with gold stripes on the sleeve. Dr. Graham asked him where he had obtained his master's license, but he got no answer. Dr. Graham had heard that shortly after high school, the FBI had picked up Stewart while he was masquerading in a naval officer's uniform. This latest display of fantasy had come as no surprise to him.

With the ship already in a financial crisis, the question as to its 1797 origins surfaced again. Howard Chapelle and John Lyman, another noted maritime historian, came forward to say that their research indicated that Baltimore had the wrong ship.

Now the future of the *Constellation*, the committee, and even Stewart's position remained uncertain, with scarce funds and mounting evidence that this was not the original *Constellation*. If the *Constellation* preservation program were terminated, Stewart would be out of work and that would mean most likely another boring menial job.

On April 27, 1958, Donald Stewart made an extraordinary revelation that would change the course of the controversy. He said he had been collecting documents since 1956 to support the committee's claim of the *Constellation*'s 1797 origin, and by January 1957, he said that he had obtained all of the late President Franklin D. Roosevelt's files and plans for the ship from 1794 to the present time. Roosevelt had been the former Assistant Secretary of the Navy under Woodrow Wilson. In April 1958, Stewart reported that he had located among the records of the Bureau of Ships at the National Archives a letter written by FDR to the Chief of the Bureau of Construction and Repair dated July 13, 1913. The letter carried the identity stamp of the National Archives. Stewart provided what he described as an exact transcription and noted that the original contained the stamp.

He retyped copies and sent them to the Bureau of Ships and to his friend, Admiral Earnest M. Eller, who was also on the committee and was Director of Naval History for the U.S. Navy. Suspicious, the Bureau of Ships anonymously sent a copy to Howard Chapelle, who was now at the Smithsonian Institution. Eller immediately contacted the

Roosevelt Library and requested a thorough search for all of the data that Roosevelt claimed to have had before him in 1913 when he wrote this "letter" to the Bureau of Ships. The library staff found nothing.

At the Smithsonian, Chapelle was quick to analyze the document and immediately doubted its authenticity. The content contradicted other documents, and the document itself could not be located in the National Archives.

But the "original" was indeed found later in the National Archives. This apparent forgery had been inserted into Record Group 19. A later analysis showed the onionskin document to be larger than the other documents in the file. The paper had the letterhead typed on instead of printed or blank as it should have been for a carbon copy. There were fourteen typographical errors, a habit that Donald Stewart found hard to correct. However, it had the rubber stamp used to mark National Archives documents, and it was sitting in the National Archives. This would confuse and convince later researchers who would review the document.

The document convinced Admiral Eller that the ship now floating in Baltimore Harbor was built in 1797. Fund-raising by the committee turned the corner and the money began to come in. In June 1959, Leon Polland joined the committee as a volunteer and acted as chairman of the Construction and Repair Committee and architect. His experience was with steel-hulled ships as a draftsman and engineer. He was not a historical researcher and also found the shift to wooden hull construction confusing. Polland reviewed the *Constellation* files for historical context before formulating a reconstruction plan. There he found the FDR letter and other "research" that had been done by Donald Stewart. These documents contained a convincing blend of actual historical facts and complete fabrication.

After analyzing the ship's construction, Polland formed the hypothesis that the original ship had been lengthened by twelve feet, and this was the reason for the differences of opinion on the *Constellation's* age. Inside the middle of the ship, he thought he saw evidence of sectioning and an addition. He declared, "His theory must now be taken as fact...." Then, only eight days later, a plan was produced (apparently by Stewart), which supposedly came from the Franklin D. Roosevelt Library. This undated drawing with FDR's initials demonstrated almost exactly what Polland had only theorized. It showed a mid-ship lengthening scheme. This lengthening theory was the bridge between the new ship that was built in 1854, and the belief of the *Constellation* Committee that the ship in Baltimore Harbor was built in 1797.

The *Constellation* went into dry dock in May 1960, and further repairs and construction analyses were initiated. On the evening of May 19, a workman was extracting copper bolts and spikes from the ship at the turn of the bilge and produced a spike with the date "1797" stamped on it. He turned it over to the night watchman and signed an affidavit before Donald Stewart. Stewart, who attested the affidavit with his own signature, signed as "Justice of the Peace at Large" for Baltimore City.

Leon Polland was elated. He now proclaimed, "*Constellation* gives every indication of bearing more original structure and form than has ever been hoped for by this committee...." Howard Chapelle, however, was becoming even more skeptical. His comment was, "This is very strange.... It is highly unlikely that a spike or bolt would show a date...."

Chapelle examined a drawing in the *Constellation* files, which he proclaimed to be "doctored." This infuriated members of the Committee, including Donald Stewart.

By 1962, fund-raising was lagging again, and the Committee was looking for ways to invigorate these efforts. They brainstormed the idea of approaching the National Park Service to have the ship declared a national landmark. Charles Scarlett, a committee member and prominent businessman, and Admiral Eller were the driving forces behind this effort. The Park Service wanted documentation. What they got was a copy of an article entitled "Yankee Racehorse: The U.S.F. *Constellation*," which was published in the Maryland Historical Society's magazine in March 1961, and was co-authored by Leon Polland, John Schneid, Charles Scarlett, and Donald Stewart. The research used in the article appeared to be mostly attributable to Donald Stewart. Admiral Eller had tried to confirm some of the key sources before the article was published but had no luck.

On May 23, 1963, the *Constellation* was designated a National Historic Landmark built in 1797. At the official ceremony Robert E. Michel, the newly appointed chairman of the *Constellation* Committee, declared that the "Yankee Racehorse" article completely authenticated the ship and that the ship's origin was "beyond controversy." Donald Stewart continued under the employ of the committee as custodian, supervisor, and "captain" of the ship.

On June 17, 1964, a workman certified that:

> While driving up spikes in the underwater body of the Frigate *Constellation* I drove up one in the keel and it came through the keel on the other side. Mr. Stewart noticed a mark "GNY" near the neck of the spike and asked me to remove it. He asked me to remove another spike near the bow and one near the stern so that we could compare each one. As I removed the one near the stern I noted that it was very worn and had been turning in the hole through the keel. Both spikes were rubbed clean and the second spike had a mark of W-12 which Mr. Stewart told me meant Washington Navy Yard and the date 1812.

This was a remarkable discovery, allowing that the ship was actually built in 1854.

In 1966, the Maryland legislature held hearings to examine the controversy over the age of the ship. Various documents were reviewed and statements made. Donald Stewart testified, "She is today the oldest ship in the world continuously afloat and the last authentic piece of Maryland built maritime Americana."

The authenticity of the ship was settled. The Maryland Legislature pronounced, "Whereas, certain testimony was presented...which established beyond a doubt the authenticity of the U.S. Frigate *Constellation* and the acceptance of such authenticity by the United States Department of the Navy, United States Department of the Interior, and the Maryland Historical Society...." Donald Stewart was ecstatic. His paycheck would continue.

Howard Chapelle had been researching the controversy for some time. He was getting closer to the real problem. In February of 1967, Chapelle reported that he was

> ...beginning to put evidence together on paper and the *Constellation* becomes more and more unbelievable. Childish forgeries of evidence are evident time after time. It is hard to believe adults would attempt such a silly thing, particularly F.D.R. Must have busted a mental rivet but he kept the stuff in his files!

Chapelle knew the truth but still hadn't zeroed in on the source of the problem—Donald Stewart.

In 1967, Howard Chapelle had visited the Naval Training Station at Newport, Rhode Island, as he heard that some records on the *Constellation* were stored there. He was suspicious of these records as they should have been already stored in the National Archives. He found an interesting document there, which the committee had cited. It was dated 1904 and addressed to a Captain W. W. Meade. Chapelle found that there was no such Captain Meade listed in the Navy Register. He also found a document dated 1918 commemorating the death of a Charles E. Davis. This document indirectly referred to Davis as having worked on the "rebuilt" *Constellation* at Norfolk in 1853 rather than the building of a new one. Chapelle thought the document reeked of forgery, so he sent it to the FBI for analysis. Their report said that the document had been typed on a Royal Elite typewriter sometime after June, 1950. The files of the *Constellation* Committee grew larger.

In mid-October 1968, Admiral Eller's office received a phone call from someone who identified himself as a Stephen Brayden and stated he was responsible for transcribing documents in the 1940s at the Naval War College related to the *Constellation*. He said that these were subsequently destroyed by fire in 1946. Eller did not take the call, but upon learning of it, he attempted to locate this "Stephen Brayden." Past employees could not recall such a person. He even found out that there hadn't been a fire at the War College, but rather at the Naval Training

Station. When questioned, the officer in charge of that station prior to that fire said there were never any documents there related to the *Constellation*.

Admiral Eller hired Lloyd A. Olsson, one of his most dedicated historical researchers, to find as many original documents as he could related to the *Constellation*. One of the most important documents, and one that offered some of the most convincing proof, was a photostat copy in the *Constellation* files of a letter dated April 30, 1795, from David Stodder, the man in charge of construction of the *Constellation*, to Timothy Pickering, Secretary of War. This letter outlined Stodder's plan to deviate from the original approved plans of twenty-six inch frame spacing (1797) to thirty-two inches (as measured today and as built in 1854). This letter would destroy any present day naval architect's argument for the 1854 origin. This letter was not typed but appeared to be written in 1795 as represented. Leon Polland had been convinced as to its authenticity: "The wording and language in the...document is that of David Stodder.... This letter most certainly takes its place as one of the most important in the archives of the *Constellation*." Stewart, to enhance the contents of the letter, said that the Navy would burn its unwanted ships, not dismantle them as put forth by Howard Chapelle. Stewart also implied that he had research that proved that the original construction plans of the *Constellation* as well as the "pre-cut timber frames" were lost in a ship that had sunk off Cape Henry, Virginia, in the spring of 1795, forcing Stodder to redesign the ship at the last moment.

Lloyd Olsson segregated documents provided by the *Constellation* Committee into those that were "suspicious" and those that on the surface were not. He categorized nine documents suspicious for either being altered or complete fabrications, in spite of the fact that some bore the National Archives stamp. None of these documents bore notes as to who had placed them in the *Constellation* files.

Admiral Eller still remained loyal to the 1797 cause. He then retired in early 1970. Without Eller, the Naval History Division now seemed to be leaning toward Chapelle's contention that the ship was built in 1854.

Stewart stepped up his lobbying efforts and gained commitments from then Maryland Governor Marvin Mandel. The restoration of the ship would parallel that of the decrepit Baltimore waterfront.

Stewart branched out to other fronts. He resurrected the Maryland Naval Militia in 1967 using as authority Governor Spiro Agnew's offhand remark that the Militia should reorganize. Mandel appointed Stewart to the honorary rank of captain in December of 1969.

In August 1969, he also formed the Maryland Sea Service, Inc. as a cadet training organization under the Naval Militia. These two organizations were now receiving donations and government surplus. "Captain" Stewart, through these nonprofit organizations, took control of a number of vessels. In 1972, he convinced the Navy to donate a World War II submarine, the USS *Torsk*, to the Militia. He was now using the title "Rear Admiral and Chief of Staff, Military Department, State of Maryland."

These vessels were used to train cadets and also were exhibits where admission was charged. All of these ventures put Stewart under scrutiny. Baltimore city officials were becoming more leery of him. The new mayor, William Donald Schaeffer, had been in the city's government since the arrival of the *Constellation*. In 1973, Stewart and his organizations were investigated by the State. They found no mishandling of funds other than poor record keeping. They did find an inordinate number of high-ranking officers that were believed to have been commissioned by the now Rear Admiral Stewart. These appointments were deemed illegal, and it was noted that the certificates of appointment for Stewart and six others bore the signature of Governor Mandel, but they appeared to be a "facsimile." The report of Colonel E. Smiley to General Warfield of the Military Department, dated May 11, 1973, was preceded three days by Stewart's resignation notice to Warfield in which he gave up his "permanent rank" as captain and requested a discharge from the Militia. This resignation was on Naval Militia letterhead with the title "Rear Admiral" preceding his name at the top.

But even with this resignation, Stewart apparently did not give up his rear admiral status. On June 5, 1973, nearly a month after his resignation, Stewart wrote to Captain Thomas M. Taylor in Miami,

Florida, submitting his application for a license to operate steamship motor vessels. This letter was issued on letterhead from the "Port of Baltimore Sea School Maryland Sea Service, Inc., Rear Admiral Donald F. Stewart, Chairman." He wrote:

Dear Captain Taylor:

Please find enclosed my application and check for a limited license of 3,000 Gross Tons as this is the largest tonnage I have ever commanded and would not qualify, I feel, for unlimited tonnage. About 95% of my sea time has been aboard and in command of public and or foreign vessels from square riggers to destroyers. My current flagship is the famous old 'Constellation' and she has been under my command since 1957. Last year I commanded the Soviet Sail Training Ship 'TOVARISHCH' within our limits as she was our guest for a two-week visit and I was responsible for her within the Chesapeake area. I have likewise sailed aboard such ships as Danmark, Sorlandet, Viking, Nippon Maru and my record spans to 1945-47 when I was a student at the very same City of Baltimore Sea School which I now direct. I am currently Chief of the Office of Disaster Control Afloat, COMNAVMIL-Chesapeake (Commanding Officer-Naval Militia) and also C.O. of the Baltimore Naval Brigade-Harbor Patrol and Security Operation. The U.S.C.G. informs me that because of my public service ship commands I would be forced to start at the bottom up and have years at sea (sic) to obtain a license which is crazy when I currently captain and command USS Torsk, MV Defiant, MV DuPont, MC Delphinus and am about to receive for the sea school a 2,700 ton training destroyer from the navy.

Sincerely Yours,

Donald F. Stewart—RADM

Encl: Captain's Commission

That year he released a print of the *Constellation* that bore a striking resemblance to Montague Dawson's work. He copyrighted his print and claimed trademark of the word "Constellation" under Stewart & Co., Ltd. The proceeds were to go to the restoration project, but either he didn't sell any or the funds weren't transferred.

The next year, he acquired the *Five Fathom* lightship and set up the Atlantic Ship Historical Society. This society, as Stewart claimed, was founded by Theodore Roosevelt and Henry Cabot Lodge as the Nautical Research Society in 1885 and, according to Stewart, merged with the Atlantic Ship Historical Society at Cape May, New Jersey, in 1960. His articles of incorporation made no mention of this, however. The articles stated it was incorporated July 6, 1977, as a nonprofit 501(c)(3) by his wife, daughter, and himself. He and Captain William Atkinson, a sixty-one-year-old highly respected merchant marine captain whom Stewart had lured into friendship, had the *Five Fathom* towed to Baltimore. With it came the Atlantic Ship Historical Society, which basically became a family-run business with his wife and teenage daughter acting as directors as well as his friend, Captain Atkinson, and another man named Henry Mitchell. Stewart, with his tax-exempt status, began to collect donations from individuals seeking tax deductions. Baltimore officials became chagrined as he expanded his new ventures, but hoped they might bring increased tourism to the waterfront that was being rehabilitated.

Donald Stewart had started out at seventy-five dollars a week with the *Constellation*. By now he had amassed an amazing collection of nautical artifacts, books, and antique weapons. He even had the binnacle, which is the compass housing, from the USS *Constitution*, the sister ship of the *Constellation*. When questioned about his good fortune, he said that he had inherited some prime property in Miami from his father, but Stewart said it was "personal and private" and refused any further details.

In July 1975, John Lyman published an article in the magazine *Sea History*. In the article, he meticulously analyzed data provided in the book, *The Constellation Question*, authored by Polland and Chapelle, and put forth that the present *Constellation* was built entirely new in 1854 by using Polland's own data or data that he had seen and overlooked.

Lyman felt that Chapelle had been badly treated by the Smithsonian and was determined to bring to the public's attention the "amazing documentation that has begun to clutter public archives related to the rebuilding of the *Constellation* in 1854."

Dr. Lyman's critique of the *Constellation Question* had been published in *The American Neptune* in January 1972, where he commented that, "Perhaps the historic ship has found its way into the hands of a band of confidence men, who have not hesitated to invent false documents that support their position, nor even to plant forgeries in public archives...." The only "confidence man" was Donald Stewart. One of his most injured victims was Leon Polland. Polland apparently trusted Stewart and accepted him as valuable to the team. This was in spite of the fact that he had been observing bizarre behavior in Donald Stewart and was aware of his wild exaggerations and telling of untruths. Polland even caught him with a rubber stamp bearing the words "National Archives Copy."

Leon Polland resigned on July 18, 1975. He suffered a massive stroke in 1980, which left him totally debilitated for seven years, until his death in 1987.

In spite of the controversy that was swirling about Donald Stewart, no one looked directly to him as the source of the forged documents. He had an air of cherubic innocence, accented by his portly physique and his large eyes which would easily communicate the unspoken question, "*Who, me?*"

And when needed, he could give a believable answer to any question asked.

The Baltimore Sun interviewed Stewart about the *Sea History* article. Stewart said that in three weeks he would be receiving from London a letter from the "Greenwich Naval Museum" dated 1858 from John Lenthall (the 1854 *Constellation* builder) to Oliver Wendell Holmes. Holmes was the author of *Old Ironsides*, a poem about the USS *Constitution*, sister ship to the *Constellation*. Stewart said he had "partial notes" from the letter, which he read to the *Sun* reporter:

Unlike the Constellation, which was rebuilt in 1853, we

cannot rebuild the existing Constitution. In the case of the Constellation, which was not drafted from the Humphrey plans, she was of a sufficiently modern design to retain 34 percent of her original timbers. Her hull frames were twice the thickness of those of the Constitution, which preserved more of the original ship. Constellation was of sufficient strength to lengthen her by 12 feet and modernize her.

Stewart also "noted" that Franklin Roosevelt was the last person to request the letter at the "Greenwich Naval Museum," in 1914.

John Lyman heard of the remarks made by Stewart in *The Baltimore Sun*. On September 30, 1975, he wrote to the National Maritime Museum in Greenwich and requested a copy of Lenthall's letter. The museum wrote back and confirmed that there was no such letter and that Donald Stewart had made no such request. Lyman gave this information to the Robert Erlandson, the Sun reporter, and said that his friend, Stewart, owed him an apology and should explain himself to the Sun's readership. Erlandson then wrote to the Roosevelt Library to see if they had a copy of Lenthall's letter as proposed by Stewart's so-called research. The library could not find any evidence of the letter. Erlandson followed up with a letter to Lyman about his conversation with Stewart related to his findings at the Roosevelt Library. Stewart had told him that he had made a mistake. He said that the Lenthall letter was not at the Roosevelt Library but at the Greenwich Museum in England within the Royal Archives of the Navy. Stewart said that and had ordered a copy of the photostat copy that he had seen there the previous December.

Then, on October 29, Lyman advised Erlandson, after hearing this latest attempt by Stewart to bamboozle the reporter who had no knowledge of the role and function of the archives in England, that the Royal Navy maintains no archives of its own and that the British Public Record Office was the archive for such documents.

Lyman was now seeing a disturbing pattern. Archives go to great lengths to prevent theft of documents, but are almost defenseless to having fabricated documents planted on them. Howard Chapelle had already exposed such a fabricated document planted in the National Archives with the help of the FBI. Lyman was now becoming overwhelmed that one was purportedly coming out of England.

Lyman suggested asking Stewart for a reference if he wanted to expedite the issue. It was later discovered by Lyman and Erlandson that the Greenwich Museum was not established until 1934 and that they did not collect American letters. Stewart made no public presentation of his long-awaited documentation. He resigned from the *Constellation* shortly thereafter.

Stewart had plenty to keep himself busy. With the lightship, he opened up a museum in Baltimore Harbor that he called the Baltimore Maritime Museum and the Baltimore Seaport operating under his Atlantic Ship Historical Society.

But by 1977, the Museum was not staying afloat with gate receipts, so Stewart had a new idea. With his nonprofit corporation, he could get permission from state and federal officials to explore for shipwrecks and sunken treasure.

He never forgot the article he had read back in 1949 about the Spanish galleon *La Galga*, the *Ocean Bird*, and the unidentified Spanish ship lost off Ocean City evidenced by coins washing up on the beach. This article was written by Raymond Thompson, who had done only a cursory review of other written articles about shipwrecks. Unknown to Thompson, the name *Ocean Bird* was not the real name of the ship he described. It was, in fact, named the *Hawk*. *Ocean Bird* was the name handed down by the local residents who had been reminded of this disaster over the centuries by the captain's gravesite on the mainland. The *Hawk* was a schooner sailing from Havana to Philadelphia and was carrying a load of sugar. Everyone perished. The *Hawk* wrecked in the vicinity of present day Eighteenth Street in Ocean City. Details of her loss are found in the *Gazette of the United States and Philadelphia Advertiser* dated January 21, 1799. People who confuse the imaginary *Ocean Bird* with the wreck of the *Hawk* name William Carhart as the captain of the *Ocean Bird* even though he was actually captain of the *Hawk*.

The 1949 *Sun* article provided the inspiration for Stewart's plan to hunt for sunken treasure. The unidentified Spanish ship described as being lost in 1820 greatly intrigued him. The mention of gold coins made this shipwreck a priority.

He found that the coins, all dating 1820 and before, were discovered on the beach in the vicinity of Fourteenth Street, Ocean City. What Stewart did not know, or perhaps hoped that the public would not know, was the fact that American ships of this period carried Spanish money. Spanish coins were as common as American mint coins and were accepted as legal tender until 1857. The Spanish two *real* or "two bits" was the same as our quarter. Eight reales, or "piece of eight," was a silver dollar. The coins had been put on display in the Ocean City Lifesaving Museum located on the boardwalk just north of the inlet. In Stewart's mind, this ship would be easy to find knowing that the coins were confined to only a few blocks of oceanfront. He had read that a number of ships from the Spanish fleet of 1715 lost in southern Florida had been found by simply swimming out to the reef from where coins had been found on the beach.

All Stewart needed was some money and equipment to accomplish this end. But he also would need permits from the government. Stewart devised a stratagem to get in the front door.

He had all he needed to fabricate a compelling story about a ship that he called the *San Lorenzo de Escorial*. From his own library shelves, Stewart pulled books on Spanish colonial history, treasure, shipwrecks, and even *Misty of Chincoteague*, the children's classic on the legendary wild ponies that roamed Assateague Island. Like a chef preparing a pot of stew, he selected flavorful morsels from each.

From his knowledge of *La Galga* having an Irish captain named Daniel Huony, he put another Irishman, named Pedro Murphy, on board as the pilot who would become the sole survivor. In 1949, he had also read articles in the *Sun* about the Cocos Island treasure said to be buried on that Pacific Island in 1820. From that, he borrowed a little history and a lot of the treasure, which included a solid gold statue of the Virgin Mary. From a narrative of the famous wreck of the *Grosvenor*, East Indiaman, lost on the east coast of Africa in 1782, he borrowed the description of the ship breaking in two on a reef and the severed bow dropping the survivors safely on the beach. He also incorporated the ordeal of their overland march to civilization. From *Misty of Chincoteague,* he borrowed the author's fictional premise that the horses on Assateague came from a Spanish ship called the *Santo Cristo* destined for the mines in Peru and wrecked on Assateague. Stewart blinded the horses for his story and said the *San Lorenzo* was carrying ninety-eight of them that had come out of the mines of South America. He directed readers of his story to the fact that the present wild herd on Assateague descended from these *San Lorenzo* horses.

And then to subliminally impart truth to the whole story, he placed the sole survivor, Pedro Murphy, under oath as he recounted the shipwreck a year later before the investigating tribunal:

> The testimony I am about to give, I give freely and swear before Holy Mary, and as a member of Holy Mother Church is truthful and to the best of my recollections.

His last act, after reviewing his masterpiece for typographical errors, was to affix his claim of copyright. Stewart was ready.

On June 6, 1977, Stewart wrote to Mr. Thomas F. Norris, Jr., superintendent of the Assateague Island National Seashore. He identified his Atlantic Ship Historical Society as an educational and scientific nonprofit corporation dedicated to the preservation of maritime history. He went on to say that:

> We are about to start Project SEA (Ship Exploration and Archaeology) and would like to obtain permission to carefully study and interpret the shore wrecks on the island. I worked the Keys for several years and laid out galleons from the keel to the first futtocks at Marathon and am quite familiar with construction and fastenings on ships dating from 1400 AD to date.

He said that he hoped to identify any vessels found with records in the Library of Congress and foreign archives.

Superintendent Norris responded on June 17:

> We are eager to utilize your expertise in this field. However, since we are unfamiliar with the subject, I have forwarded

your letter to our Regional Office of Archaeology and Historic Preservation for comment and guidance. The staff looks forward to reading your hypothesis of the origin of Assateague ponies in the Baltimore Sun on June 26.

On July 22, Stewart wrote to Norris:

I just wanted to drop you a line to let you know that the article on the *San Lorenzo de Escoral* [sic] will be released this Sunday in *The Baltimore Sun*. I mailed off the application to the archaeologist at the National Park Service and if approved I plan to organize our search and interpretation in October. We completed a magnetometer air and photographic search over Assateague from 5,000 and 10,000 feet on Sunday July 3, 1977 and are just now blowing up the films. I have records and documentation on 39 ships sunk or ashore at Assateague and a check of the custom house records from Norfolk reveal an additional 67 ships lost off the Maryland-Virginia Coast north of Cape Charles and in the bay.

The story of the *San Lorenzo de Escorial* appeared in the *Sun* on Sunday, July 24 in the magazine section. The article was passed around between Mr. Earl M. Estes, acting superintendent of Assateague Island National Seashore, and other staff members. They were stupefied. The story described in vivid detail how Donald Stewart discovered references to the ship in the Archives of the Admiralty in London in 1974 and then followed up with extensive research in the Archivo General de Indias in Seville, Spain. There he said he discovered the declaration made by Don Pedro Murphy, the pilot and sole survivor of the *San Lorenzo*. Stewart described spending a week with a "special camera" generating hundreds of feet of microfilm.

Earl Estes and his staff read on as Stewart described a fabulous treasure in gold and silver coins and bars, jewels, and a statue of the Virgin Mary and a baptistery, both of solid gold. The treasure was alluring to the park staff, but it was his description of the blind ponies that swam ashore from the wreck that fascinated them the most. It appeared as if Donald Stewart had solved the mystery of the origin of the wild ponies and that they did, in fact, come from a Spanish ship as the popular legend had suggested.

On August 1, Superintendent Estes wrote Stewart about his Baltimore *Sun* article:

> The staff was intrigued by your pony origins article, which appeared in *The Baltimore Sun* on July 24. Your account appears to be well documented. Chief of Interpretation, Larry Points, wonders if it would be possible to send a reference list of the source material for this historic account. We would like to forward this source material and your article to the Service's Chief Historian for review. If he gives the account his support, the Interpretative Unit will naturally give it full exposure.... The mention of treasure in the pony origins story naturally has sparked some interest among other individuals.

Stewart did provide "source material" for his story of ponies and treasure and the *San Lorenzo*. There were eleven pages of typed transcript numbered three to thirteen. There appeared to be two missing pages. The eleven pages included a fictional account of a nonexistent British Navy ship, which surveyed Assateague in 1771, and which Stewart used to document that there were no wild horses on the island at that time. He also provided another fictional report of a survey from 1826 written by a "Henry Lloyd" which described "45 small horses no larger than a hound, many appear to be blind." There was also a repeat of Pedro Murphy's testimony with another reference to the Archivo General de Indias in Seville. This was different from the newspaper article as it gave the latitude and the depth of water of the wreck, only it was redacted and unreadable. He gave no clues as to how any of this could be verified. The Park Service, eager to put forth this fascinating story, erected a wayside exhibit outside the visitor's center on Assateague which described the *San Lorenzo* story. The exhibit proclaimed, although with some reservation: "Recent research suggests that horses came ashore from the Spanish wreck, *San Lorenzo*, in 1820."

This statement was tempered with the official position of the National Park Service, provided by Mr. Edwin C. Bearss, chief historian for the National Park Service. Mr. Bearss had previously refused to give credence to the shipwreck legend. His position was that these horses were descended from those left to roam in the 1600s by English settlers. The U.S. Department of Interior later published a full account of the *San Lorenzo* in its handbook on Assateague Island in 1980, where it proclaimed, "The ship probably responsible for transplanting the ponies was a well-armed merchant named the *San Lorenzo*, according to recent research." *National Geographic* gave a brief account of the *San Lorenzo* in its June 1980, issue as well.

By late October 1977, Stewart got the go-ahead to begin his excavation of an old hulk he called the *Ocean Bird* lying on the beach near Old Sinepuxent Inlet about ten miles south of Ocean City Inlet on Assateague. In December, he returned with a film crew to document his "discovery" of artifacts.

The Park Service was amazed and intrigued. This old hulk that they had seen stripped bare by storms and later covered over with sand

Assateague Horse Exhibit at the National Park Service
Headquarters, Berlin, Maryland. 1984. *Photo by the author.*

numerous times was now yielding artifacts. Stewart filed a written report with the Park Service where he described his research in the ship:

> The detailed sheet on the "Ocean Bird" supplied by Greenwich in 1959 documents the facts and the dimensions supplied by the wreck itself…. It was discovered that all of the measurements taken…matched those of the Irish immigrant ship "Ocean Bird." The packet was lost on the night of January 2, 1799 in a blizzard that swept the coast. The luckless ship was attempting to enter the Delaware when a violent nor'easter swept down the coast and she grounded on Fenwick Shoal. She was demasted and then was broken free of the offshore shoals to be again swept down the coast to her final resting place, just inside old Sinepuxon Inlet on Assateague Island.

Stewart listed the artifacts saying they "found" a brass English button, some lead weights that were sewn into greatcoats "to keep them from flying in the wind," a two-pounder cannonball, a huge copper key, pewter buttons, a silver four-bits piece and numerous other metal objects, "all of which were of the period of the loss of the *Ocean Bird*." The Park Service did not know that there was no such ship as the "Ocean Bird."

Stewart took the opportunity to plug his pony story in this report. He referred to seeing the horses during his excursions:

> They are provided with apples on each venture to the island, by the museum staff and have become friendly. As various shipwreck sites are checked they roam over and watch the activities of the group. The small horses have been on the island since the wreck of the Spanish Frigata San Lorenzo de Escoral [sic] in 1820.

With his story of the origins of the Assateague ponies and his apparent interest in historic preservation, the National Park Service was eagerly cooperating. With his permit, Stewart was now free to scour the beaches with his metal detector clear down to the Virginia border some twenty miles from Ocean City. He set out hoping to find artifacts from *La Galga*.

In 1977, Albert Alberi, a diver and attorney from Virginia Beach, Virginia, was researching *La Galga*. Like many, he had read about the shipwreck in Dave Horner's *Treasure Galleons*. Following the bibliographical notes in the back of the book, Alberi found that the ship lay in Maryland, not North Carolina as suggested by Horner. This clue led Alberi to the Maryland Archives in Annapolis where he discovered the letter written by Captain Daniel Huony to the governor of Maryland pinpointing the *Galga's* position as two ship lengths inside of Maryland. He and his father wanted to know more so they contacted the officials at the archives to see how to go about getting additional information. The archive staff had been familiar with Donald Stewart's interest in old ships, so they told the Alberis to go see Stewart at the *Constellation*. This they did. Stewart was very coy in his discussions about *La Galga*, but he impressed the Alberis with his apparent knowledge. Albert Alberi told Stewart that they had documents from the Virginia Archives about the salvage of the ship by the locals. Stewart not only wanted those documents, but he wanted to discourage the Alberis from looking any further. He felt lucky that his would-be competition had unwittingly disclosed themselves.

On February 6, 1978, Stewart wrote Albert Alberi from aboard the *Five Fathom* Lightship on Atlantic Ship Historical Society letterhead. Stewart said in his letter that he had compiled a list of over six thousand shipwrecks along the Delmarva coast. He said that he obtained the original documents on the 1750 fleet in 1949, and by 1951, he had completed his research. He went on to reiterate some of the common knowledge on the fleet. He recited information on each ship, and when he came to *La Galga*, he said:

> Cargo—80,000 8 real pieces registered and salvaged by the master. 2300 contracted reals—also salvaged, 25- 69.71 lb. bars

of silver—also salvaged 23 tons of Mahogany for the Royal Palaca (sic) at Madrid—salvaged by shipwreckers—restitution made to the master by a merchant of Snowhill. The ship was totally stripped of all goods for a period of one month before being swept five miles up the Maryland Coast in the storm of October 3, 1750. Location—¾ mi/ off Assateague Island— ballast pile and iron 16 and 24 cannon located by Donald F. Stewart. April 5, 1967—Salvage Contract with Spain for 20% (King's Share—Maryland—30% and the Atlantic Ship Historical Society—50%).

He went on in his letter to say he favored strict government control of shipwreck sites and that artifacts should never be placed on the auction block. And he continued:

We do plan to publish and because we have so much material that is documented we know that we will make some enemies, especially of authors who have written books on sunken ships that contain many pipe dreams. The problem seems to be that research stops when only one or two documents are found as evidence. In the case of *La Galga*, the Maryland-Virginia line has been reset four times since 1750 and that wreck was swept even further north by another storm.

And to compound the Alberis' confusion, he said that the wreck had been surveyed by a "Mr. Lloyd George" as being 2.6 miles north of the boundary line. Then the ship was swept more than seven miles north into Maryland by the later storm. "From the position of the wreck," he added, "it is evident that she capsized when she hit bottom—all great guns shifted to one side."

Stewart signed his letter "Donald Stewart—Director—Wreckmaster— Project 'SEA.'" He added a postscript, "Do you have the departure date for the three repaired and remasted ships from Norfolk? This is the only piece of information that I lack in the files. They arrived at Cadiz on December 23, 1750."

Because it appeared that Stewart had found the wreck years earlier, Alberi sent the SEA director his research since it appeared that he was too late in his own quest for *La Galga*.

To enhance his base of operations, Stewart towed his Lightship Museum from Baltimore to the harbor in West Ocean City, Maryland, and with the blessing of Worcester County, he set up a ticket booth and opened the ship for tourists in the summer of 1979. He still pursued his treasure hunting on Assateague. The *Maryland Coast Press* in Ocean City published on November 1, 1979, an article about his success: "Rare Coin Found On Assateague: May Confirm Pre-English Visitors."

In the article, Stewart is quoted as saying that the coin he found was one of one hundred struck, and it was hard to estimate its value, but he guessed that it was left by the Spaniards whom he said had visited our shores in the late 1500s. The coin's front side featured the profile of Pope Gregory XIII and the date "1572." This incredibly lucky treasure hunter would also "find" a bronze coin from the Roman period A.D. 218-222. The Smithsonian analyzed the coin in March 1980. The findings of the curator of numismatics were, "I do not believe that the coin was lying on the beach too long; the patina would look quite different if it had."

The Lightship business failed in 1979, and Stewart made the decision to sell it. Gate receipts were not worth the effort to keep it open. He and his society prospered, however, as donations in equipment kept coming in. He received a black four-wheel drive Jeep Cherokee which became his personal vehicle. The number of small craft under his control increased.

Stewart also had to find a new home to rent because his present rental was being sold. He went into Rick Firth Realty located in Ocean Pines across the bay from Ocean City. At Firth Realty, he met Robert Firth, an energetic and over-hyping salesman, who knew how to put the right spin on a sales prospect. Firth, a pilot and an adventurous sort, happened to have a book about sunken treasure sitting on his desk. Stewart acknowledged the book, and they struck up a conversation about shipwrecks. Stewart let on that he was deeply involved in the subject and that his Atlantic Ship Historical Society was seeking grants to go after a Spanish shipwreck named *La Galga*. Stewart also told him of his vast experience in maritime history and his years as director of the *Constellation*. Firth wanted in.

Firth said that he had a friend named Raymond Cardillo in Baltimore who was an admiralty attorney and that his younger brother, Rick, would also be interested. Robert said he envisioned setting up a limited partnership or corporation to raise the required capital. This was exactly what Stewart was looking for.

They had a meeting on March 31, 1980, to finalize their plans and the name "Subaqueous Exploration and Archaeology, Ltd." (SEA, Ltd.) was agreed upon. Stewart told them of millions in registered silver, and Robert Firth started quoting the then current price of silver at over fourteen dollars an ounce, which was double that of the previous year. Robert quickly envisioned a corporation that would later explore the world seeking sunken treasures and making film documentaries. They structured the limited partnership in such a way that the investors would have no vote over the affairs of the business. Control would remain with the "Founding Four."

The excitement was unbearable. Anxious to get started, Robert Firth then placed an advertisement in the *Wall Street Journal* seeking investors. The ad ran a single day and that was all that was needed. Immediately investors started lining up.

CHAPTER FIVE
The Race for the Greyhound

It was Monday evening, April 28, 1980. I called the number listed in the *Wall Street Journal* ad and got Robert Firth, the public relations man for SEA, Ltd. and pretended to be an interested investor. He explained that a man named Donald Stewart was responsible for the project.

"Have you found the wreck yet?" I innocently asked.

"No, but we know where it is!" responded Firth confidently. "Stewart has found coins on the beach in front of the site."

I expressed my concern over the state government getting in the way, and he made it clear that they were dealing with Maryland and did not expect problems. Without realizing it, he told me that they believed *La Galga* lay north of the present Maryland-Virginia line.

I phoned Greg about our new competition. We concluded that they were just getting started and had not yet actually "found" the wreck yet. Still, this new development changed things. Stewart had found coins from the wreck two miles north of where I expected the wreck to lie. And the fact that we now had competition added stress to our partnership. I was determined to beat Stewart to the wreck.

That Friday, Greg brought his wife, Mary Ellen, and his two boys, Matthew and Conrad, to Chincoteague. After our camp was set up, we were off to explore the island and the public beach on Assateague Island. On Saturday, the wind kept us from going outside the inlet, and Sunday it was more of the same. Anticipating roadblocks like this, we shed our frustration and enjoyed the beach.

This was repeated again the following weekend and the next several weekends until Memorial Day. Springtime on the Atlantic is always windy.

Meanwhile, Robert Firth sent me an article from the *Maryland Beachcomber*, dated May 16, 1980, which carried a story about an unnamed Spanish warship being sought by Stewart and SEA. The story said that the ship's cargo had a current valuation of $30-40 million and had registered on board 4,250,000 pesos in gold, silver, gemstones, turquoise, copper, animal skins, red dye, and various other commodities. There was a drawing depicting the wreck lodged against a large sandbar with the bow thrust up in the air and the stern totally submerged. The rendering, which had been done by Stewart, also showed the remains of the wreck submerged and totally buried in the sandbar within the first year.

The article stated that Stewart had copyrighted the story of this ship and the fleet she sailed with. It included a sidebar stating that SEA was seeking investors at $2,500 per share. After reading it, and comparing my notes from Victoria, my researcher in Spain, I was not sure we were looking for the same ship. The descriptions of treasure certainly did not jive with my copy of La Galga's register. These doubts gave me some relief.

With the article, I received an announcement that there would be a meeting of prospective investors on June 14, at the Ocean Pines Yacht Club. I planned to attend without disclosing my real interest.

The following Friday, Memorial Day weekend, Greg and I returned to Tom's Cove Campground. We put the boat in and proceeded to the inlet. The weather conditions weren't promising so we decided to mag (tow the magnetometer) an area several miles south of latitude 38° since it was remotely possible that the area could contain the wreck. After several hours of magging, we saw the numbers climb steadily on the LED readout on the magnetometer console.

"Greg, take a look at this!" I said.

Greg leaned over from the helm to see for himself. "Wow! It looks like some cannon!" he exclaimed.

I started dancing. "It's definitely a wreck!" I proclaimed. "Turn around and let's get a marker buoy in the water!"

I knew it was a wreck, but could it be La Galga? Could it really be this easy? With the precise directions given by Captain Huony, I realized it could, but this was well south of latitude 38°. We wasted little time suiting up. I dove in with the metal detector and almost immediately began getting hits. I dug with my hands, but couldn't get deep enough. I surfaced and told Greg that we needed the water pump set up with the jetting nozzle. Greg rapidly put the hoses and pump together while I descended with the nozzle. I lay there and waited for the familiar rush of high-pressure water to come barreling down the fire hose. It wasn't long before I was blasting away at the bottom and located some metal protruding from the sand. I blasted some more and found that this was no ancient wooded ship, but a steel hull that had been dynamited level with the bottom.

Disappointed, I surfaced.

Greg pointed to the sky and said, "Look at that. We gotta go."

While I was down, the wind had picked up, and the skies turned gray. I had to agree.

On the way in, I described what I had found. The adrenaline rush was now long over. Although we were disappointed, we were satisfied that our procedures worked and that we were surely capable of finding *La Galga*. Sunday was a blowout so we sat on the beach with a cooler of beer and discussed our strategy. I then headed back to D.C.

On Saturday, June 14, I pulled into the parking lot at the Ocean Pines Yacht Club in Berlin, Maryland, for the SEA investors meeting. I couldn't help but notice the black Jeep Cherokee parked out front with a license plate and stick-on sign that said "PROJECT SEA." I gulped. This operation seemed first class and was certainly a lot more prestigious than what Greg and I had going.

The meeting room was brimming with the excitement of the other

In the beginning. Greg Sutliff on left and the author on right. *Photo by Mary Ellen Sutliff.*

participants as they milled around the room and viewed the display table. There were Spanish coins called pieces of eight, some small cannonballs, a brass belt buckle with an enameled Spanish coat of arms, and other artifacts said to have been found on the beach in front of the wreck site. There was even a bronze swivel gun with the tag, "Swivel gun found from wreck site."

Also on the table were copies of a stock prospectus for SEA, Ltd. I grabbed one and sat down to read it. It repeated a lot of what I had read about the project in the May 16 *Maryland Beachcomber* article and listed the background on Donald Stewart. This man had an impressive résumé. He had studied archaeology at the University of Havana, participated in shipwreck salvage in Florida, and had been director of the *Constellation* in Baltimore for twenty years. He even had been dubbed a Knight Commander of Malta.

The prospectus described a unique relationship with the Atlantic Ship Historical Society, Inc., which, in return for providing equipment, personnel, expertise, and certain shipwreck records, would get twenty percent of the net proceeds.

Although *La Galga* was not mentioned by name, it was clear that this was their shipwreck. Stewart described the 1750 fleet without naming any of the vessels or giving dates. Of greatest interest to me was reference to the bronze cannon and the $40 million estimate of the value of the cargo on board. Also contained in the prospectus was a fleet manifest that told of gold, silver, and jewels far beyond that described in the documents I had. The narrative about the wreck included a description of the ship hitting a sandbar, which exactly matched the drawings in the *Maryland Beachcomber* article I already had. He was describing things that Victoria and I had not yet seen. In the prospectus Stewart also gave an account of how he had documented a ship named the *San Lorenzo* that was the source of the wild ponies of Assateague. He also described another Spanish ship called the *Juno*, which he said had foundered on Fenwick Shoal off Ocean City in 1802.

I looked up, and in the corner of the room, I saw a short heavy-set guy with graying-blonde hair who was talking in a loud voice. Somehow I knew it was Donald Stewart.

The meeting was called to order, and I took a seat and listened to the presentation. Rick Firth opened the meeting as president and then introduced the other principals. His brother, Robert, stepped up and described the business details and the goals of finding multiple shipwrecks. He explained that, after their initial success of finding the wreck, they would probably be spending a lifetime hunting and salvaging treasure from other shipwrecks.

Raymond Cardillo, an attorney from Baltimore, described the legal aspects and the benefits of having the Atlantic Ship Historical Society, Inc. as a partner. This historical society was controlled by Donald Stewart and possessed a non-profit status with the IRS. They would be assured of getting the required permits. Stewart also introduced a man named Bill Bane, a retired Navy SEAL and owner of a marina called Bayside Boatel in West Ocean City. He looked the part with his graying hair and dark tan. His barrel chest showed he was still in top shape. Bill Bane was a member of the advisory board of the historical society and would be providing technical help to the operation.

Stewart was next. I listened intently as he spoke.

"First, I would like to thank you for coming today. I have spent most of my life researching shipwrecks here and in the archives of Spain and England and have identified several treasure ships off the Delmarva coast."

The audience remained motionless as Stewart paused and surveyed the room.

"SEA, Ltd. was formed to salvage an eighteenth century Spanish man-of-war documented to be carrying a king's ransom in treasure. This will be our first target. If we are as successful as I believe we will be, SEA plans to pursue more treasure-laden ships that sit in our own backyard. Some of these are virtually unknown to other treasure hunters. For security reasons, we are not providing names or locations at this meeting."

The audience was squirming and smiling. I was captivated.

Stewart continued describing in detail how the ship wrecked and that he believed that the majority of her treasure was still safely stored in the stern section, which was in deeper water and inaccessible to the local salvagers. This was exactly how he portrayed it in the *Maryland Beachcomber* article and the prospectus in my hand. Stewart then dropped another bomb. "I have had the records of this fleet locked up in the archives in Spain where they are located, by a General in the Spanish Army whom I have known for years. I took this precaution to keep other treasure hunters from competing with us. Without these records, they can't."

My heart sank like a rock. Here I was paying someone in Spain to go looking for records that had been removed and locked up.

Stewart went on to talk about *La Galga* (without naming her) and the fleet. He told us that the wreck had caused quite a commotion on the Eastern Shore and that the captain had even managed to get two girls pregnant while he stayed in Snow Hill, Maryland. With details like this, it was obvious to me that he had done a huge amount of research. I certainly had no knowledge of this.

Stewart went on to tell the crowd, now unable to sit still, that even though they had not yet started, an Ocean City contractor had already invested $20,000 and they expected the shares to sell quickly. Pointing to the artifacts on the table, he explained that with his federal antiquities permit, he had found them on the beach and in shallow water in the suspected area of the wreck site.

The meeting adjourned, but no one left as they remained to talk more with Stewart, the Firths, and Cardillo. Stewart was occupied, so I approached Raymond Cardillo. He was very slightly built and smoked his pipe while we talked, projecting an air of false sophistication. I soon saw an opening with Stewart, so I excused myself and approached him.

"Mr. Stewart, I was fascinated to hear you say that you had these records locked up. How did you do that?"

"After I located the records, I knew that if someone else found them they could locate the wreck. I have an old friend, a retired general, who was able to have the records pulled and separately locked away. They'll stay that way until we're finished."

As I went to my car, I wondered how I could compete with a group that had this much expertise, clout, and certainly now, working capital.

I returned home discouraged and wrote to Victoria in Spain:

> I met with my competitors this weekend and found that they have been to Spain and somehow got an official to freeze the records related to the Galga. They are definitely looking for the same ship. He also has the cargo manifest. This vessel appears to be loaded with much gold, silver, turquoise, jade, and precious stones. He has not found the wreck yet and I also found he is looking in a spot different from the site I am investigating. Since the records appear to be frozen, I think it wise to discontinue research in Spain. The man's name is Donald Stewart of Ocean Pines, Maryland. Please send me your final report and bill.

I discussed all of this with Greg. We decided that because there was a great deal of money at stake for whoever could locate *La Galga* first we would press on. I telegramed Victoria and told her to ignore my last letter and to proceed with her research. She was going to another archive in Simancas north of Madrid, which looked promising. Victoria went on to locate a few more documents relevant to *La Galga* and a lot of interesting information about the other ships of the fleet and accounts written by their captains, but unfortunately there was no account from Captain Huony. Her research added nothing more to guide me in locating the wreck. Victoria surmised that Huony's report had been lost. But this was of no real concern to me now because Stewart had unwittingly told me where the wreck was.

Greg and I went to Chincoteague that next weekend. We were plagued with setbacks and mechanical failures. We did not get to the Maryland-Virginia line until Saturday, July 12. The *Maryland Beachcomber* article portrayed a sandbar lying off the beach with deeper water behind it. On the NOAA chart there were two sandbars lying about a quarter mile off the boundary fence. We went to the northern one first as it was on the Maryland side and coincided with Stewart's description in the *Beachcomber* newspaper article SEA had given me. We set the magnetometer over and began our search patterns.

We found nothing there so we moved to the sandbar on the Virginia side. The magnetometer did not register anything so after awhile we decided, instead of running parallel to the shore, we would run east, away from shore, and go over the sandbar. We used the recording depth finder to monitor the rise in the bottom, which would tell us when we were over the bar. On one pass, the magnetometer registered a small reading as the sensor head passed over the top of the shoal. We repeated this procedure many times from different directions, each time getting the same result. We placed marker buoys in the water so we knew where to dive. As we retrieved the magnetometer, the wind began to pick up. We waited to see what would happen, but it only got worse. The markers were pulled, and we headed home.

This site had looked extremely promising because it coincided with Stewart's description of the wreck. Our plans were to dive and dig the next day, but the weather didn't cooperate. Greg and I both had become quite frustrated with the constant setbacks, but with the mag readings on the shoal in the immediate area where Stewart had found the artifacts, we were certain that the search would soon be over.

The next weekend, we returned to the site, and the magnetometer failed. And this was on top of being fogged in the day before. I dove anyway, but had no success. Another weekend lost and Greg was ready to snap. I was more optimistic.

"Look Greg, if this was easy, everybody would be doing it," I insisted.

He didn't say anything as he was still trying to contain himself.

Greg took the magnetometer home to Richmond to attempt repairs.

He called me Wednesday evening. "Hey, this damn thing is still not working. I've tried everything. No need to go this weekend," he said. His tone of voice suggested there might not be any more weekends.

"Greg, we're too close to quit now," I said. "Plan on going. I will be at your house tomorrow morning to pick up the mag and take it to Massachusetts and get it fixed. I can be back at Chincoteague sometime Friday night."

Greg started to protest, but he knew he couldn't change my mind.

"Well, I guess I'll see you tomorrow," he said half-heartedly.

The next day, I drove to Richmond to pick up the magnetometer and turned right around and headed north for Taunton. I entertained myself with visions of excavating the wreck and recovering tons of treasure. I would soon be resigning from that desk job I had grown to hate.

I arrived early that Friday morning and got a few hours sleep in the car. I had called ahead to Jack Fisher and told him I would be there when he opened and that I had to have the mag repaired while I waited.

That night, after a thousand miles and little sleep, I arrived at Tom's Cove Campground at 10:00 p.m. and found that Greg had dutifully arrived and set up camp. He did not bring his family this trip. This was a bad sign. I could tell that Greg was over it. It didn't concern me that much since I knew we would be on the wreck tomorrow and that would certainly bring him around.

The next day, we made it out to the site and set up on the hit. I found nothing with the detector. We set up the pump, but it broke so I couldn't dig. On the way in, neither of us said much. I knew that Greg had reached his end.

That suspicion was soon confirmed when I called him in the middle of the week and he had an excuse for not going to Chincoteague. I told him I was going anyway, so I took a girlfriend. I did not dive that weekend but at least I was able to continue magging the adjoining area. The only other reading obtained was a small contact in close to the beach from the sandbar.

The next week, Greg called to inform me that he was definitely to be counted out, but he would leave the boat at Chincoteague for now if I needed it. I told him I understood. If he wasn't hauling his wife and kids to Chincoteague every weekend, then he was away from them. If I had been in his position, I wouldn't have lasted this long.

Over the next few weekends, I took friends along only to continue magging. There would be no diving because I needed competent help. The weather cooperated, and we had pleasant outings, but no other targets were located.

The summer was almost over and I had no partner, no results, little money, but I still had a passion for the hunt. I truly believed that the wreck was for me to find and I had to preempt Stewart. I could not let it go. I was convinced that there was a fortune lying on the ocean bottom and that perhaps I had already found it buried in the shoal described by Stewart. But what could I do about it? Greg was out. Could I find another partner? Should I set up a company and sell shares like SEA? Stewart was certainly close to starting if he hadn't already. These questions nagged me all of the way back to Washington that Sunday.

I would not sleep well that night.

CHAPTER SIX
In the Enemy's Camp

On Monday, August 25, 1980, I called the number provided in the *Wall Street Journal* ad for SEA, Ltd., and they gave me Donald Stewart's home phone number. I needed to find out where they were in their hunt for *La Galga*, and I was open to the idea of approaching Donald Stewart and telling him what I had been doing. I knew that in addition to *La Galga* he planned to search for other treasure ships, so the thought of joining forces with him was very tempting.

That evening I made the call, and Stewart was quite surprised to hear that someone else had been out there looking for his shipwreck. I told him of my research and that I couldn't find any account from Captain Huony or record of a significant treasure. He laughed and said I wouldn't because those documents had been locked up. I went on to tell him of how the magnetometer had detected a hit on top of the shoal just south of the Maryland-Virginia border. He was very intrigued. Stewart put the phone down and retrieved a chart of the area, and then we resumed the conversation:

"Do you see the two lumps lying off of the Maryland line?" I asked.

"Yes, I can see where you are," said Stewart.

"On top of the south shoal, I got a magnetometer hit," I said. "It seems to correspond to your description in the *Beachcomber*."

"No kidding! That is very close to where I found the artifacts!" Stewart's excitement and reaction gave me an adrenaline rush. "Look, can you come down here? We have a lot to talk about!"

"How about tomorrow?" I tried not act too excited.

"Tomorrow's out, but can you come down Wednesday? I'll take you to dinner at the Ocean Pines Yacht Club," Stewart said.

Wednesday was fine with me. I left work early and drove to his house on Ivanhoe Ct. in Ocean Pines. I brought my file with me so I could show him the amount of work I had already done.

We sat down for a few minutes and got acquainted. He said his wife and two kids were out of town. He didn't display the pompous air that I had witnessed at the investor meeting earlier that summer. He was quite charming, and I couldn't help but notice his boyish demeanor, which belied his age of fifty-three. Whatever negative impressions I had carried with me soon evaporated.

Over dinner at the yacht club, he held me spellbound as he described the many shipwrecks he had researched and how many Spanish wrecks were lying along the Eastern Shore. I nursed a couple of beers while he sipped coffee and chain smoked cigarettes. He said he didn't drink.

I sat entranced as he described his research on HMS *De Braak*, a British warship reputed to be loaded with Spanish treasure when she overset and sank in 1798 off Cape Henlopen, Delaware. Stewart told me about a Spanish galleon named the *Conquistadore* that wrecked in 1641 in Accomack County and that was part of the fleet that sailed with the *Nuestra Señora de la Concepción*, a treasure ship that had been found only two years before in the Caribbean by Burt Webber from Pennsylvania. I was amazed. He said he had written an article about it in the *Maryland Beachcomber* recently and would show it to me after dinner. There was also a wreck called the *Juno*, a Spanish warship that he documented had wrecked on Fenwick Shoal in 1802. That too, was just off Ocean City. I was familiar with this ship because previously published accounts had placed it well offshore when she sank. Stewart also told me about a Spanish ship named the *San Lorenzo*, which was not only carrying a fortune in treasure, but was also carrying some small horses that had swam ashore, becoming the forefathers of the wild ponies of Assateague Island today. He said that the National Park Service had recently recognized his research, which he showed me in his copy of the *Assateague Island* handbook. There were two pages about the *San Lorenzo* which not only repeated Stewart's account of the wild horses but also stated that the ship had wrecked with a considerable treasure.

Stewart's experience as director of the *Constellation* and president of the Atlantic Ship Historical Society told me that he had credentials that I would be privileged to associate with.

Stewart said that he hadn't been diving in awhile as he had put on a lot of weight, but was having a wet suit custom made and couldn't wait to get back in the water. After dinner, he drove me to the Worcester Country School and showed me a small cannon that he had salvaged off Assateague in 1960 from a privateer.

Back at his house, he produced a typewritten letter that he said was a transcription of Captain Huony's report, one that I had certainly looked for and Victoria had been unable to find. It was a letter from Captain Huony addressed to the Marqués de Ensenada, dated February 1751, from Norfolk, Virginia. In his letter, Huony said that he had had to abandon treasure worth eight million pesos and that he had wrecked at latitude 38° 2′ north. Captain Huony also said that 200 swivel guns had been salvaged from the wreck by the locals. Stewart explained that the guns had been part of the cargo. I remembered the fleet manifest described in the SEA prospectus referring to 500 swivel guns. At the bottom of the letter, there was a reference, "Libro 38." I asked him about this, and he again informed me that the original had been locked up by his friend who was a general in Spain. He also explained to me that I only had the Havana manifest and that his copy of the Veracruz manifest documented the treasure on board. I knew that *La Galga's* manifest was only thirty pages long. This was very small compared to the manifest of the *Nuestra Señora de Los Godos* that had sailed with *La Galga*. Her manifest was over two hundred pages. And then *La Galga's* manifest did not mention the mahogany that was well documented as being on board. The bottom of the letter was signed, "Daniel Mahoney." Stewart said that Mahoney was his real name, not Huony. I readily admitted my mistake since I had seen other variations of his name in English reports.

"By the way, would you like to see an old survey chart of the coast?" Stewart said.

"You bet!" I replied.

Stewart returned with a copy of a very simple looking chart, which had been reproduced on a blueprint machine. He explained that the chart had been prepared in 1752 by a British survey vessel. The chart showed various shoals and inlets along the coast of Assateague. Some had names like "Man O' War Shoals" and "King William Shoals." My eyes scanned to the area of the Maryland-Virginia line.

"Look here!" I said as I pointed to the chart. "See there! It's those two lumps I was telling you about! And look, there is a wreck symbol on it!" It was positioned opposite a point named "Spanish Point." "That is where I had the magnetometer reading!" I said.

Stewart rubbed his chin. "I'll be darned. It looks like you have something there. I think you may have found it!"

From all of the things he had shown me, I felt that investing in SEA would be a sure thing. I asked him if there were any shares left, which he verified that there were a few remaining. Luckily, I had brought my checkbook. I wrote a check for $2,500 for one share of stock.

On my way back to Washington, I realized how fortunate I was to have met up with Stewart, a former treasure hunter, maritime historian, and possessor of many secrets. Secrets that would make me rich.

SEA had just acquired a boat they named *Bloodhound*, but did not have a magnetometer or a diver yet. Before I said goodbye to Stewart, I gladly volunteered to dive and bring my equipment as soon as he

Donald Stewart. *Photo from SEA files.*

needed me. We set a date for Monday, September 8, 1980, to go out and dive the shoal.

I arrived at the Bayside Boatel operated by Bill Bane, one of the SEA investors. The marina was at the base of the Rt. 50 bridge in West Ocean City only minutes from the Ocean City inlet. I found the *Bloodhound*, a thirty-four foot wooden cabin cruiser, which had just been painted but still showed its apparent age and poor condition. SEA had paid $6,000 for it. On board besides Stewart were Captain William Atkinson, a retired Merchant Marine captain, member of Atlantic Ship Historical Society, and a vice president of SEA; Robert Firth, vice president of SEA; a diver named Alan Elzey; Bill Bane; and Richard Cook. Cook was the initial investor I had heard about earlier that summer who had put in the $20,000. Unfortunately, but to no surprise, the weather did not cooperate so the trip was cancelled until the following weekend.

The next Saturday we had the same crew. I was besieged with questions from them as we motored the twenty miles down the Assateague coastline. I found that Rick Cook was the most enthusiastic of them all. Rick was in his early forties and had recently separated from his wife. Apparently enjoying his new freedom, he kept everyone laughing with his jokes. I think he was on an adrenaline high. Just the thought of searching for sunken treasure made his intense blue eyes dance in his head.

We arrived at the site over the shoal and set the magnetometer overboard. It did not take long for us to relocate the mag hit I had found previously that summer. Everyone on board was going crazy. Elzey and I donned our diving gear, and I carried my metal detector as we plunged over the side. I anxiously began sweeping the sandy bottom. Nothing registered, so I figured that whatever had been detected by the magnetometer must be deep in the sand, which was all the better, I thought. That way there might be more treasure confined to one spot. We had no ability to dig so Elzey and I climbed back onto the *Bloodhound* and reported to the crew.

When we returned to the dock, word quickly spread that not only had another treasure hunter joined forces with SEA, but we had located likely targets on the first trip out. Potential investors, who had been sitting on the sidelines, now were eagerly writing checks for stock. I suggested to Stewart that he get a more powerful magnetometer and gave him some sales literature from Varian Electronics in Toronto, Canada. That Monday the board authorized $25,000 to purchase the device. The Varian had much greater sensitivity and a faster sampling rate. Readings could be taken three times a second if needed.

Rick Cook offered to put me up that weekend. He wanted to talk treasure hunting and about the management of the corporation. He and other investors were already getting concerned over the management structure and how the spoils would be divided. SEA had a so-called "management team" comprised of the four founders: Rick Firth, Robert Firth, Raymond Cardillo, and Donald Stewart. These four were general partners of the limited partnership. The actual investors had no vote. From the beginning, this structure showed potential for abuse. In addition to any salaries they could choose to pay themselves, they would receive twenty percent of the net profits.

This "no vote" concept started to concern a great many of the investors, who now totaled thirty-three. Whenever any investors met, they would invariably want to discuss that issue.

Every weekend I would travel to Ocean City to go out on the *Bloodhound* and continue our electronic searches for *La Galga*. Within two weeks, Stewart started directing the search toward the *San Lorenzo*, which he said was wrecked in the vicinity of Fourteenth Street in front of Ocean City. If the wind did not permit the long run down to the Virginia line, we would go north of the inlet and work that area, which only took about fifteen minutes from the marina. The prospect of finding not one but two or more treasure ships prompted the investors to organize and hold a meeting in order to express our concerns to the SEA management team.

During the last weekend in September, a meeting was organized and held by Rick Cook to get a consensus among the investors to make demands upon the management team to get to work and clean up the mess that was starting to appear. Many investors came, and they took the opportunity to meet one another. Rick Cook's wife, Delphine, came to find out what had happened to the family nest egg and to take notes, even though they were separated. From this point on, the effort to change the structure centered on investors coming up with money to buy out some of the management team. It was apparent to me that from the beginning that the Firths had seen this venture as mostly a publicity grab that might enhance their real estate business. It was thought that they might sell out.

I continued to come down on weekends, and Rick Cook let me stay with him. This was the only way I could afford to commit to every weekend.

It now became obvious that we needed the more powerful magnetometer that we had ordered and we needed the ability to move large amounts of sand. The only search activities being conducted were on weekends when I came down. Because of the weather, the search team needed to be available seven days a week in order to accomplish anything. The board started pushing Stewart to get the search activities organized. Those of us who went out on the *Bloodhound* started to realize that Stewart was not too sure of himself in his function as project director. Stewart had been drawing a paycheck since July at an annual rate of $30,000 a year. Not much had been accomplished since then.

We overlooked all of this, however, because he was the one with all of the knowledge about the wrecks. Stewart now realized he needed help. He asked me to join the team full time as assistant project director, reporting to him. This was a difficult decision to make. I had a good paying job in Washington but nonetheless was becoming bored with it. I was also single and had no responsibilities. I was so convinced by what I had seen and been told by Stewart concerning the treasure that there seemed to be little risk. I accepted the job making only half my existing pay and only a promise of six months employment. After that, it would be reviewed. I knew that six months was more than enough time to locate *La Galga* and begin salvage.

I kissed goodbye my office on the top floor of the Dodge Center overlooking Georgetown, my health insurance, and retirement plan. There would be no more fancy lunches in my favorite watering holes around town. My parents thought I had lost my mind. For the first thirty years of my life, I had been trained to believe that a coat-and-tie job was to be my life's work. But the voice inside me said it was time to go. Greg Sutliff, my long-time friend and former partner, thought I was a traitor but then quickly realized that he was the one who had opted out and knew me well enough that it was something I had to do. He wished me well.

On October 14, I gave two weeks notice to my employer, Psychiatric Institutes of America. Everyone in the office knew what I was about to do because I wore shorts and sneakers to work that day, instead of the customary coat and tie. Now that I'd made the plunge, it actually felt good. Life was about to begin again. I had just turned thirty-one.

On the first of November, I drove my rental van to Ocean Pines and moved into a house I had leased on Ocean Parkway. Bill Bane and his teenage son, Chip, were there to help me unload. Both of them had already become good friends and were having me over for dinner, where we would discuss treasure hunting and his fascinating past as a Navy SEAL and CIA operative. Bane was in his early fifties, had chiseled features and a warm grin that matched his friendly demeanor. Bill had joined the Navy when he was seventeen and had seen action at the end of WWII in the Philippines. He was a member of the Underwater Demolition Team and was invited to join the SEAL team when it was founded. After that he had joined the CIA, and retirement brought him to Ocean City, where he took over the Bayside Boatel.

Moving to a resort put me into culture shock after coming from a big city. Ocean City was nearly deserted in the wintertime. My busy social life was a thing of the past, although like DC, there was no shortage of bars.

Though winter was approaching, we would now begin working in the ocean almost daily. Most of our trips were out in front of Ocean City to look for the *San Lorenzo* and a Spanish schooner called the *Santa Clara*. Stewart told us that she had been driven ashore in 1798 in the same area as the *San Lorenzo* and was carrying a lot of money. Spanish coins had been found to that date. We mostly towed the magnetometer, but some targets found were unable to be identified because of the depth of sand.

Being out on the boat was a great change from the stuffy office environment. As far as the cold, I would adjust.

In the first week of November, the new Varian magnetometer arrived. It was a V-85 airborne console unit with a marine sensor head. We now could do more effective surveys as this unit had a paper chart recorder as well as a numerical readout. By this time, we decided that the trips to the *Galga* site would have to wait until a larger, more seaworthy boat could be hired. November was bringing more northeast winds, which would often keep us ashore for days at a time.

Now that I was on the job, Stewart would call me almost nightly to talk about our project, but sometimes other things as well. It seemed as though he enjoyed talking with me more than with his own family members. It was often difficult to get him to end the call. I would sometimes have to quit talking and endure what seemed like minutes of silence before he got the idea that the conversation was over. He would then just say, "Well, see you at Ellodie's."

Ellodie was the owner of *Skipper's Roost*, a little grill and coffee shop at the top of the hill from the Bayside Boatel, our base of operations. It was here that we would meet every morning to get something to eat and plan the day. If the weather was bad, we might be there for hours.

SEA had hired a deckhand and jack-of-all-trades named Donald Parks. He was a skinny, wiry guy, with a pony tail and a shaggy beard, which made it hard to tell just how old he was. I reckoned he was in his late thirties.

Our usual crew now consisted of me, Stewart, Parks, and many times Richard Cook. It looked to me that he hunted for any excuse he could find to avoid his construction business and go treasure hunting. Bill Bane would also stop in before opening the marina. It was here at Ellodie's that Donald Stewart held court. He loved to tell stories of his past treasure hunting days in the Florida Keys diving with Art McKee, a legendary treasure hunter in the 1950s. He described, in detail, the silver bars and coins salvaged from the *capitana* of the 1733 fleet, *El Rubi Segundo*. His experiences with renovating the USS *Constellation* in Baltimore were equally interesting. Strangers loved to listen in.

Whenever someone came in that we did not know, Stewart would raise his voice so that they could hear what he was saying. Stewart loved

Cadiz 19 de Julio de 1785.   408

A las ocho de esta noche ha entrado aqui procedente
de la Havana con 52 dias de navegacion el navio
del Rey Santiago la España con los Caudales y
efectos que expresa la nota — adjunta y que
se transportaron en dicha Havana al citado bu-
que de la Fragata de S M la Santa Rosalia
que los havia conducido de Vera-Cruz

    Recibidos en Vera-Cruz de Cuenta de S M

    2.973,252 pesos fuertes en plata

    36 barras de Oro que valen 41608 pesos fuertes

    811 marcos de plata

        Idem en la Havana

    10,700 pesos fuertes en plata

  Recividos en Vera Cruz de cuenta de particulares

  200345   pesos fuertes en Oro

  4707,471   id. en plata

  161   Candelleros de Oro

  1448   Arrobas de Grana

        Idem en la Havana

  44073   pesos fuertes en oro

  328495   en plata .

Register of treasure aboard the frigate *Santa Rosalia*, 1785. Document from the *Papers of the Continental Congress*, National Archives, Washington, D.C.

to tell stories and entertain people. It was here that Bill Bane first met Stewart and heard his stories of sunken treasure and was introduced to the story of *La Galga*.

Stewart's laugh was a loud cackle, usually followed with "Oh Christ!" Then he would start coughing as his laughter dislodged nicotine from his lungs. If the weather was bad, sometimes he would sit in there by himself waiting for lunchtime to arrive rather than go home like the rest of us.

I had worked out an arrangement with my past employer to do consulting if needed. They soon called saying they needed help. SEA released me for a few days so I went back to DC in mid-November. Before I left, Stewart called me and asked that, if I had time, could I go by the Library of Congress and research several ships. He listed the *Three Brothers* 1775, *Faithful Steward* 1785, *Adeline* 1824, *Cornelia* 1757, and the *Santa Rosalea* 1788. He said all of these vessels had wrecked along the Maryland-Delaware coast and might be of interest. I recognized them as being from Robert Marx's *Shipwrecks of the Western Hemisphere*.

My first evening after I arrived at the Library of Congress, I proceeded to the alcove that contained the volumes of the *Naval Records of the American Revolution*. I was familiar with this work; it was well indexed and I hoped to find something on the *Three Brothers*. I made a wrong turn and found before me a collection that I had not used before called the *Index, Papers of the Continental Congress 1774-1789*. Within minutes, I had found something on the *Faithful Steward* and the *Santa Rosalea*. For the *Santa Rosalea* there was an entry for 1785, not 1788, and it was spelled, "Rosalia," not "Rosalea" as Stewart had given me. The reference was to an extract of unknown origin and recorded on microfilm at the National Archives. When I reviewed it, I found it was written in Spanish, but I could easily see that this document was describing huge amounts of gold and silver. I did not understand the narrative though, so I consulted a Spanish dictionary and attempted a translation.

The first line I translated as, "By the eight who have just arrived....." This, in fact, said, "At eight o'clock tonight she arrived from...."

My erroneous translation led me to believe that this might be referring to shipwreck survivors. When I returned to Ocean City, I gave the document to Stewart as well as my shoddy translation. Stewart did not show much of a reaction, in fact he said that he did not think it relevant. I didn't give it much thought after that.

By day, our magging and diving operations continued with nothing from a shipwreck turning up. The nightly phone calls from Stewart continued. Stewart became more and more dependant on me. I was the only diver and ran and coordinated the magnetometer searches. All he did was steer the boat. At night, I would go to Bill Bane's or head over to B.J.'s On the Water, a popular bar and restaurant at Seventy-fifth Street bayside, owned by Gene Parker, one of the SEA investors. Gene was always there and anxious to hear about our progress out on the ocean. I usually related that we continued to get magnetometer readings that appeared to be scatter patterns from shipwrecks, but no artifacts had yet been uncovered. There were also more and more days that we did not go out because of the weather.

The stockholder issues magnified. But in mid-November after hearing more and more about the *San Lorenzo* and the *Santa Clara* and SEA's ongoing effort to locate them, I purchased another share of stock, even though nothing had been found nor had anyone gotten their initial stock certificates yet. There was also much consternation over the board's plans to have a second stock offering and dilute our respective share in the company. But the board, and especially Stewart, were concerned that we would soon run out of money, and they did not want to let that happen.

On November 17, Robert Firth sent each stockholder a letter as to the status of our ocean explorations and of the new stock offering. He said that he had hoped some "incontrovertible evidence" would be recovered before the weather prevented further diving. Cardillo was now actively pursuing a salvage permit from the State of Maryland for the two Ocean City shipwrecks. The State was telling him that they might be keeping most of any artifacts saved. This became a subject of great concern. SEA's Virginia Beach attorney, Albert Alberi, came down to meet with Stewart so I agreed to put him up at my place. When Stewart brought him by, he also brought the letter from Captain

Mahoney he had shown me at our first meeting.

Albert Alberi was a few years older than myself. He was very methodical and deliberate in his speech. I was surprised to hear that he had personally researched *La Galga* in the Virginia archives and that he had seen confirmation of the 200 swivel guns that had been salvaged and mentioned in Mahoney's letter that Stewart had showed to us. This greatly reinforced my belief in the project. Albert started talking about investing in SEA.

To keep the operation moving in the winter months, SEA contracted with a long-liner docked in the West Ocean City commercial harbor. George Topping and Bob Miller owned and operated a sixty-foot, Harker's Island-built fishing boat called the *Original Jackson*. These two had a successful swordfish and red crab business that slowed in the winter months, and they were glad to get some "easy sea duty," as Captain Topping would say. The *Original Jackson* had an eighteen-foot beam and a huge working deck, enabling us to load a large air compressor on board to operate the air lift. This device greatly improved our ability to excavate.

With the new magnetometer, we were now locating many "hits" or targets in front of the Ocean City beach in the area of the *San Lorenzo* and *Santa Clara*. There were also reported coin finds on the beach that bore out the dates for the *San Lorenzo*, 1820, and the *Santa Clara*, 1798. Stewart showed us examples of these coins that he had found on the beach over the years. The excitement grew among the investors and the board. *La Galga* was now taking a backseat to the Ocean City wrecks.

In December, Raymond Cardillo recommended to the board that SEA hire co-counsel and file claims to the Ocean City wrecks in federal admiralty court. Stewart had added two more ships to our list of targets. He said that the *Santa Rosalea* wrecked on the northern part of Ocean City around Eightieth Street and a British privateer called the *Royal George* loaded with captured Spanish treasure had wrecked in 1789 in the Fenwick area close to Delaware. Stewart said that he had heard reliable accounts of Spanish coins being found in these areas.

From this point on, Cardillo consulted with admiralty attorneys in Baltimore and even called David Horan with Treasure Salvors in

Top left, Rick Cook in the *Buccaneer* pilothouse. Right, the *Buccaneer* off of Ocean City. Bottom left, the *Original Jackson* off Ocean City. Bottom right the clam dredge drops spoil on deck for examination. *Photos from the SEA files.*

Key West. On January 9, 1981, Cardillo informed the board that the contemplated admiralty claims were imminent. He and the Baltimore attorneys were now working out the details. In his memo to the board, however, he expressed a looming concern. He had hoped that some concrete evidence would have been recovered in December that would have lent added impetus to our claim.

On January 13, SEA filed suits in the federal district court of Baltimore. These complaints expressly stated that SEA had found the vessels "through the expenditure of considerable money, time, expertise, and effort." The cases were then handed to Judge Norman P. Ramsey, who had just arrived on the federal bench the year before. Judge Ramsey, a highly skilled defense attorney, had vast experience

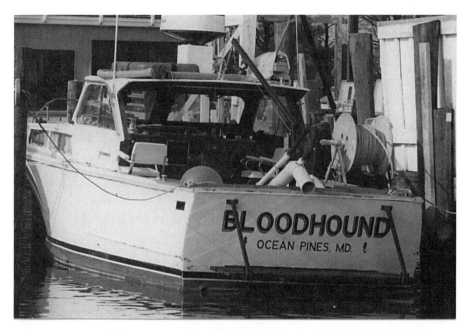

The *Bloodhound*, SEA's survey boat at Bayside Marina, West Ocean City, Maryland. *Photo by Ned Middlesworth.*

Donald Parks gets ready another marker buoy as we set up an area to be surveyed with the magnetometer. *Photo by Ned Middlesworth.*

The Varian magnetometer with the strip chart data recorder. This unit cost $25,000 in 1980. *Photo by the author.*

Donald Parks, top, and the author, below, transferring equipment from the *Bloodhound* to the *Buccaneer*. *Photo by Ned Middlesworth.*

in political corruption cases and was a confidant to many Maryland officials. He had served as Maryland's deputy attorney general for two years. And later in 1971, he was instrumental in getting the current mayor of Baltimore, William Donald Schaeffer, elected for the first time. Afterwards, he was appointed as president of the school and fire boards. His last position before his judgeship was chairman in the prestigious law firm of Semmes, Bowen, and Semmes.

In Ocean City, the filing of the admiralty cases was kept quiet and not discussed outside the board meetings. The discovery crew, as we called ourselves, continued with the mag surveys.

Now that we had the *Original Jackson*, we were able to go back to the *Galga* site and do elaborate magnetometer surveys. The Varian magnetometer unit had a paper graph output, which enabled us, with the help of the LORAN positioning unit, to record magnetic targets that we detected and then prepare anomaly maps for evaluation. We were still looking on top of the shoal, directed there by my magnetic hit I had found the year before, which coincided with Stewart's description of the wreck. Excavation of this site was now top priority.

Someone had come up with the idea of using the cage of a clam dredge lined with rat wire to drag the bottom to look for artifacts. We hired the *Buccaneer*, a clam boat operating out of West Ocean City and captained by Dale Brown, to do the job. In early January, we dragged the area on the shoal where the mag hits were located and seaward of the same shoal in the hopes of snagging a coin or even a ballast stone. We had not magged inshore of the shoal yet, so our focus was on the sandbar, still directed there by Stewart's depiction of the wreck.

With the clam cage, we got a great assortment of shells and some undersized flounder, but no artifacts. Morale was sinking. The expenses continued to mount. Mel Fisher's slogan, "Today's the day," was seldom used. The treasure ships continued to elude us.

Attitudes would soon change. It was a morning like all of the others when we met at Ellodie's, drank coffee, looked at the weather, and planned our day on the *Bloodhound* if we were lucky enough to get out. It was the third week of January and freezing cold outside.

"Where in the hell is puss gut?" Bill Bane groused. Rick Cook, Bill

Bane, and myself were wondering where Stewart was. He was usually the first one there. Bane was frustrated over our lack of success and was growing tired of Stewart's tall tales. His unflattering nickname for Stewart was no doubt a carryover from his Navy days. Cook, on the other hand, was enchanted with "Cap'n Good Guy," as he called him. He and I were still focused on the treasure.

Suddenly, Stewart's black Jeep Cherokee came zooming into the parking lot and slid to a stop on the loose gravel outside. He slammed the door and rushed in nearly out of breath and carrying some papers in his fist. He was dressed as usual in his khakis and white cable-knit sweater. He also was wearing a big grin on his face. Stewart sat down and pushed a typewritten paper toward me which he said he had just taken down via telephone from a friend in London who had found it in the British Public Record Office. I carefully read it:

> B.P.R.O.
>
> In January or early February 1785, a Spanish frigate belonging to the King of Spain named *Santa Rosalea*, sailing from Havana, Cuba, to Cadiz, Spain, via Philadelphia entered the Capes of Delaware and found them blocked by ice which pierced the ship's hull, so the captain headed south for Norfolk, Virginia, but started leaking badly. She ran for the beach and jettisoned her 40 cannon as she went, and struck a shoal lying south and inshore of the shoals of Fenwick. She remained here for two days while the passengers and crew tried to reach shore. Only nine survived. The ship later broke up and during the months of March and April 1785 over 500,000 pesos washed ashore from the Delaware Line two miles south. The Santa Rosalea was carrying over 17,000,000 pesos consigned for the King of Spain and the new mint at Philadelphia. The survivors went to Philadelphia where they returned to Spain that summer.

At the bottom was a reference to the admiralty section of the BPRO.

"Stew, this is incredible! It looks like that document I found at the National Archives was relevant!" I exclaimed excitedly. Bane and Cook looked at me for an explanation. They barely needed one based on my reaction. As they read the letter, I explained to them that I had found an inventory of the treasure on board this ship in the National Archives. And the letter Stewart brought in was telling us that she was lying off Ocean City. If there was any doubt about getting rich, it evaporated now.

Several days later, I was told that the U.S. marshal would be coming down to "arrest" the Ocean City shipwrecks. This is a formality in an admiralty proceeding where papers are attached to the ship to bring it into the court's jurisdiction. Our wrecks were underwater, which dictated special circumstances.

Stewart told me to prepare waterproof buoys to be set in the bottom with anchors for three sites. We used two-inch PVC pipe and attached small Danforth anchors with several feet of chain to one end of each. Then there was a heavy line attached from the chain to the buoy. That way, it would float and could be seen at the surface. We engraved "S.E.A., Ltd." and our phone number on each and then painted them florescent orange. They were complete except for the end caps, which would be installed after the court papers had been inserted.

On Wednesday, January 28, 1981, a deputy U. S. marshal named Charles Rowe came on board the *Original Jackson*, and we set off to "arrest" the shipwrecks with the court papers installed in the marker buoys. In admiralty court cases, the vessel is served with process and the papers are usually affixed to the wheel-house door. Our treasure wrecks were broken up and submerged, which necessitated the waterproof buoys.

Stewart, our mate Don Parks, and myself were also aboard. Stewart had thought ahead and also instructed me to have a sandwich platter brought along to take care of the crew and the deputy marshal.

We headed north from the inlet; Stewart was beaming.

As we came up on Eighteenth Street, Stewart barked, "Stop here!" Captain Topping replied, "Where do you want to set this, Captain?

"Directly off Eighteenth Street," Stewart commanded.

As the *Original Jackson* was setting her anchor, Stewart proclaimed, "We are arresting the *San Lorenzo* and the *Santa Clara* in the name of SEA, Ltd.!" He acted as if he was on stage without a sound system. We all chuckled as I began putting on my dry suit.

Stewart inserted and the court papers in the tube and sealed it with glue. Parks readied the high pressure water pump, and I got the rest of my scuba gear on and jumped in the water with the marker. After I dropped to the bottom, the water pump was started, and I proceeded to sink the anchor deep into the sand. I left several feet of chain exposed so the anchor could be relocated if the buoy were to break free. I was back on deck in ten minutes.

The *Jackson* pulled anchor, and we motored farther north to Eighty-fourth Street to repeat the arresting procedure for the *Santa Rosalea*. I huddled in the cabin to get warm. Stewart was talking to Captain Topping, and I noticed the next set of papers sitting on the table that were ready for the buoy. I was curious about what an arrest warrant looked like so I picked up the papers and started to read. Stewart snatched them from me and said that I was not allowed to read them. I thought it odd, but figured it had something to do with court rules or something.

After setting the buoy, we moved north to 138th Street and repeated the diving and arresting procedure for the *Royal George* and then returned to port. Deputy Rowe said he had a great time and wished that all of his assignments were as interesting as this. He left and went back to Baltimore to file his process return. I wasn't sure about any of this. We had now laid claim to four valuable shipwrecks which I new nothing about. But I knew I wanted to increase my stake in SEA. After the ships were arrested, I bought three more shares of stock. I emptied my retirement account and to pay for the third share, I borrowed the last $2,500 from my brother, Phil. I was looking forward to early retirement.

Part of the court process involved putting a legal notice in *The Baltimore Sun* advising the world that SEA had now laid claim to the *San Lorenzo*, *Santa Clara*, *Santa Rosalea*, and the *Royal George*. It was anticipated that the State of Maryland would probably step in and assert some form of claim, but Cardillo and our attorneys felt we would likely prevail. Cardillo personally felt that these claims would give us a lot of leverage when negotiating permits with Maryland.

In spite of the cold weather, we continued our survey work off Ocean City. We were preparing a magnetic map of the entire bottom covered by the admiralty claims. With this map, we could then locate the most promising sites to excavate. When ships break apart, they leave a trail of debris that will consist of iron fittings, cannonballs, etc. Whenever the chart recorder would show a pronounced spike, we always envisioned a cannon or ship's anchor.

On April 9, the Attorney General of Maryland filed an appearance in the admiralty claims, arguing that these shipwrecks were property of the State of Maryland. The State questioned the fact that SEA had not recovered anything and couldn't be salvors in possession of the wrecks. Our Baltimore attorneys had to defend that point and others related to the State of Maryland's claim of sovereign immunity.

SEA's corporate makeup was now changing. Rick Cook had organized the shareholders effectively enough that an agreement had been reached between Rick Firth and Raymond Cardillo to sell their stake in the management team. This included their ten percent of the net profits. One of the investors named, Vince Bredice, took it over so that the people who invested cash would get a vote in the corporate affairs of SEA. Rick Firth and Cardillo stepped down off of the board. This left Stewart and Robert Firth as the only original founders remaining as directors. Rick Cook became president, Vince Bredice replaced Cardillo as secretary-treasurer, and another investor, John Mathisen, filled an open director seat. Some of the investors suggested that I be put on the board, but for some reason Stewart strongly opposed the notion.

The SEA corporate office was moved out of Rick Firth realty building to the Bayside Boatel. The investors of SEA were very pleased with the changes. There were other notable changes. Rick Cook was now back with his wife, Delphine, and he persuaded her to start keeping the SEA books. Besides being attractive, she was a very efficient and intelligent woman, who after assuming responsibility for the books, started to question some of Stewart's expenses. She complained to Rick that it looked as if Stewart was getting reimbursed for personal items. Rick ignored it. She made no bones that she didn't like Stewart. She even insisted that I start keeping a log of our daily activities.

The spring weather brought increased diving activity as well as the usual northeast winds. There was much going on. The State of Maryland responded to our admiralty claims in federal court. The State claimed that the wrecks were State property, and without permits, we were precluded from diving on any of them. Sometimes the Maryland Marine Police would follow us out of the Ocean City Inlet to monitor our activities. When they were present, no diving was done.

Stewart had another wreck for us to find. He found a piece of eight on the beach in Bethany, Delaware. He reported that his research showed a Spanish ship named the *Principe de Asturias* had wrecked in the area in 1717 carrying treasure from the salvaged 1715 fleet in Florida. He also directed our search to Fenwick Shoal to look for the *Juno*, which sank in 1802. Stewart had previously published a story about this wreck in the *Maryland Beachcomber*. Other published accounts had placed the ship well offshore in deep water, but Stewart said he had located a ship's log that gave a survivor's account of the wreck placing it on Fenwick Shoal.

That spring, our attention became refocused on *La Galga*. We had talked with a woman named Juanita Clements who owned a vacation home on Assateague just north of the fence at the Maryland-Virginia line. Her house was the only one still allowed to be occupied on the national seashore. Her ownership had predated the formation of the national park in 1962. Mrs. Clements said she had found Spanish pieces of eight predating 1750 along the beach near her house on the Maryland side of the fence. Her coin finds were further proof that our shipwreck lay nearby. They appeared to further corroborate Stewart's version of the wreck.

As a seaman, Stewart was proving to be less than competent. He was only fifty-four, but his weight made him awkward and clumsy. Earlier in the year, a marina owner had found him sprawled and wedged in the companionway of the *Bloodhound*, unable to extricate himself. He lay there for over an hour until he was heard yelling for help. That May, he stepped through a partially open engine room hatch and injured his leg, which put him in the hospital for nearly a week. While he was laid up, he prohibited anyone from taking the boat out. He said that he was the only one with a captain's license, and insurance regulations required him to be on board.

We were so convinced that our mag readings on the shoal were related to *La Galga* that we consulted with Albert Alberi in Virginia on how to go about making a claim. He advised us to set a marker on the bottom, similar to what we had done for the Maryland admiralty cases and then maintain constant activity on the site when the weather permitted. On May 24, we went to the site without Stewart because he was still in the hospital. Another investor, Roy Davenport, took his boat, and Bill Mays, chief of police in Berlin, acted as witness, and we set a marker buoy above the bottom, but invisible from the surface.

The following week, the Varian magnetometer failed and had to be shipped to Canada for repairs. This put us way behind.

Stewart got out of the hospital and made it to the investors' meeting scheduled for June 6 at the Ocean City Convention Center. Rick Cook made an upbeat presentation as to our successes and our future plans to salvage, and then made the necessary plea for money. Stewart reinforced the potential for recovering a vast treasure in the ships to which we had claims. He also assured everyone that we were proceeding on *La Galga* as well. At the meeting, Stewart and I also reported on our finding a wreck at Seventy-ninth Street only a few weeks before.

That was a memorable day. We were looking for the *Santa Rosalea* and were magging close to shore. The recorder of the magnetometer registered a very large hit which got everyone's attention. We circled the boat and attempted another pass when the boat lurched. The sensor head of the magnetometer had snagged something on the bottom. I quickly suited up, and after entering the water, I followed the cable to its end, expecting to find it damaged. Fortunately, it wasn't, and to my surprise there was a shipwreck lying across the bottom. I immediately surfaced and yelled to Stewart and Parks that there was definitely a wreck below me. I returned to the bottom where I was able to swim along the keel for some distance as I examined more of the wreck. There were a substantial number of ribs and planking visible. I found a large iron ring firmly attached to something which appeared to be an anchor. In my mind, I replayed that cold January morning at Ellodie's where I had read the fantastic story of the loss of the *Santa Rosalea* and her millions in treasure. I fanned the sand along the keel, looking for coins, but I had no luck. I did retrieve some brass and copper spikes, which caused a lot of excitement back on the *Bloodhound*. But then Stewart frowned. He said that this looked like a more recent wreck. He later identified it as the Italian bark *Quattro* that had wrecked in 1887, and was easily identified from the lifesaving station records. At least the investors now had something old they could finally put their hands on.

On June 12, we set off to dig the shoal at the *Galga* site with a twelve-inch hydrolift we had built. It was like a huge vacuum cleaner that was powered by the large diesel water pump on the clamboat, *Buccaneer*. The mag was still in Canada, so we attempted to set up using LORAN bearings, but it became clear that our numbers did not match up with Captain Brown's unit on the *Buccaneer*, so we resorted to using line of sight and the depth finder.

Captain Brown lowered the hydrolift to the bottom and started the water pump. We could tell by the water hose that led from the deck to the hydrolift that something was wrong with the water pressure. After awhile, I dove to the hydrolift and disappointingly found nothing. The hole was only three feet deep. The water pump would have to be repaired. I also realized we were wasting our time without the mag to pinpoint our excavation.

On June 16, we returned to the site and used a large coil, towable metal detector that I owned and went inshore and got some hits. When I dove with the hand-held detector, I was unable to locate anything. We decided to dig anyway, so I got in with the six-inch airlift and started dredging. Nothing was found. Sharks moved in to see what was going on. Sharks and near zero visibility don't mix, so I got out.

On June 24, the mag arrived, and we tested it off Eighteenth Street to make sure we were back in business. All we needed now was for the weather to cooperate.

We returned to the *Galga* site and magged some of the adjoining areas. More hits were located. But bad weather and Captain Brown's clamming schedule kept us away until July 7 when we took the *Bloodhound* back and I dove on the shoal with our new Aquapulse metal detector. I detected faint readings, which told me that something was deep in the sand.

That next Saturday, we arrived at the site on the *Buccaneer* with the hydrolift. Captain Brown had repaired his water pump, and we were anxious to see another demonstration of our dredge's capability. We had previously left a small buoy in the water to mark the spot so set up was easy.

I was in the pilothouse giving Captain Brown instructions on setting up the dig when Stewart waved us off the anchorage.

"Tell Captain Brown to set up thirty-two feet east of the marker," he said.

"But what about the marker?" I protested.

"Listen, I had a dream last night, and it said that we needed to dig east of the marker," Stewart insisted.

There was not much I could say as he was the project director. Up to that time, he mostly let me decide matters of diving and targets. I think that he wanted this to be "his day." Donald Parks rolled his eyes and shook his head, but he kept his mouth shut. He had seen Stewart throw a tantrum before.

The boom lowered the hydrolift to the top of the shoal directed by Stewart's "vision." The pump was started, and we could see that hydrolift performing as expected as the water turned brown while the twelve-inch pipe disgorged large volumes of sand.

The pump was shut down and I donned my scuba gear, descending along the black water hose, carrying the Aquapulse detector until I saw the hose disappear over the rim of the hole. The dredge pipe was not visible. I had expected to see a bowl-shaped crater with sloping sides, but the dredge had opened a vertical shaft ten to fifteen feet across. I could not see the bottom because of the suspended silt. I cautiously descended, scanning the sides of the shaft with the Aquapulse. I found bottom at about ten feet and the monster dredge asleep. As I looked up toward daylight, I could see sand starting to pour in from the top. Fear triggered a flashback to a frightening nightmare.

I was sixteen and I was with Greg Sutliff, my former partner. It was a warm spring day and Greg and I had decided to go swimming below Bosher's Dam in the James River above Richmond. It was just above this dam that Greg and I had excavated our first treasure of Civil War cannonballs. We stood atop the rock wall on the north side of the river overlooking the ten-foot dam that spans about a quarter of a mile. On dry summer days, hardly any water goes over it. During floods, it's barely visible. This day, the spring rains had raised the level of the river somewhat, which should have served as a warning to us. Oblivious to the potential danger, we descended ten feet down the rock wall and studied the cascading river as it poured over the dam. The roar of the water pounding the rocks below was deafening. Greg hollered that he would go first. He let go and jumped into the white water as we had done many times before. He came up laughing so, of course, in I went. The cold roiling water was exhilarating; it took only a few seconds before we realized that we were in trouble.

In normal conditions, we would have been only be waist deep in the water and could have easily gotten a foothold on the slippery rocks. Now we were neck deep and unable to stand or swim. We both started yelling for help. My state record in the breaststroke was of no use now. There was so much air in the turbulent water that no amount of pulling or kicking could get us out. The waterfall caused a vortex, which would alternately pin us to the rocks on the bottom and pop us up into the roaring foam. I thought we were going to die.

I came up gasping and saw that Greg had pulled himself up on an exposed rock. He was ten feet from me, exhausted. I could see in his eyes that he knew he couldn't help me. As I struggled to breathe, I flashed back to when I was four—drowning in a swimming pool. It took years for me to get over my fear of the water and learn to swim. Now, I was drowning again

I went down for the last time, visualizing the headlines telling of horrific death. I wouldn't be the first to drown here. I was sucked under, and everything went black.

I was stunned back to consciousness when I was slammed against a large boulder. Reflexively, I lunged for the rock and managed to hold on. It was just big enough to afford me protection from the life-threatening river. After a few minutes, I was able to pull for shore fifty feet away. Greg climbed the river bank behind me, and we lay there heaving and coughing.

Presently, my mind began to clear. "God could have surely had us," I had said to Greg, and that day I wondered to myself why He hadn't.

As the sand continued to pour in over me, I wanted out of this death trap on the bottom of the Atlantic. It dawned on me that there was no backup diver topside. If I was buried here, it was here that I would probably remain. I kicked for the top and exited the hole. Pausing at the edge, I peered in. Before I had left, I satisfied myself that there were no metal objects to be found.

Around the perimeter of the hole I could see blackened sand similar to the black sand you see on beaches. Concentrations of it can give off a magnetic disturbance that will register on the magnetometer. There were mineral deposits in the sand shoal, which gave off a thirty-gamma reading and rose and fell with the contour of the bottom. There was no shipwreck in this shoal as Stewart had led us to believe. We were now back to square one on *La Galga.*

Back on deck, Stewart drew my attention to another boat inshore of us.

"What are they doing over there?" he asked.

I wiped the brine out of my eyes to get a good focus. "Stew, it looks like they are diving, and it looks like they are watching us. I think we've got competition," I moaned. "They're in the area where we got hits with the towable metal detector," I pointed out.

On the way back to Ocean City, we decided we better get the mag into that area. We had not gone that close in on our previous magging trips, always focusing on the shoal. We wondered now who our competition was.

Instead of immediately returning to the *Galga* site, Stewart directed us again to Eighteenth Street off Ocean City. Besides myself and Stewart, Cook, Parks, and Captain Bill Atkinson were aboard.

With the mag overboard, we started our search pattern. The numbers started to climb on the LED readout. I focused on the strip chart recorder and then it went crazy. The recording stylus slammed back and forth in the housing, and the numbers were all over the place. Rick Cook exclaimed we had a "wang-wang," a word that had become part of our vocabulary and used whenever the recorder went off the scale. We repeated the run with the same result. I suited up and dropped to the bottom with the Aquapulse and soon found an elongated object under the sand. After surfacing and reporting the find, everyone topside anticipated something big. With the jetting nozzle, I exposed the target and felt a round metal tubular object that I had thought was a cannon. After I blasted out about ten feet of the object, I found it was a sewer pipe. We later found a number of others that had been dumped for twenty blocks several hundred yards off the beach. They were good for an adrenaline rush, however.

We returned to the *Galga* site, and we expanded our search with the magnetometer. We found what could be described as a debris trail inside the shoal. On July 30, I dove on some inshore hits located in the area where we had previously noticed the dive boat. Here I found some black fused conglomerate. To me it looked like it had been burnt, so I attributed it to the "boiler" wreck, which was just north of the boundary fence about a third of a mile away and close to the beach. This wreck was documented on the charts. We thoroughly magged the area where we had seen the dive boat working months before. There were some small magnetic concentrations, but there was not enough to suggest that it was *La Galga*.

The summer wore on, and when the *Bloodhound* was not in for repairs or the weather not cooperating, we would go wherever Stewart's whims dictated—one day to Delaware, another out in front of Ocean City. If the Maryland Marine Police were following us, we always went to Delaware. There was still no decision from the federal court in Baltimore as the State of Maryland was still arguing its case.

By August, I was getting frustrated. With so many targets, I felt that we should be finding something. Stewart gave no explanation why the *Galga* site was being ignored. I was now very suspicious. I had learned that immediately after my first visit with him, he approached the board in early September of 1980 and suggested that SEA hire Albert Alberi to represent SEA in Virginia. This meant that he really did not know where *La Galga* or the boundary line was. We never looked in Maryland waters as he had originally planned. He had focused entirely on the magnetometer reading I had found on the shoal the summer before with my partner Greg, hoping that it was our wreck. He also had my copy of *La Galga's* register that said she was not a treasure ship and directly contradicted his representations that she was. It now seemed that he didn't want to find *La Galga* because if no treasure was found, he would be exposed.

I decided to write my researcher in Seville to see if she could find anything on the *Santa Rosalea* and the *Principe de Asturias*. I received Victoria's report dated September 23 the following week. She confirmed the spelling as "Rosalia," and said that it appeared that neither ship had wrecked, as they were both documented as still sailing several years after the dates Stewart had indicated they were lost.

Later, I would find out more about the saint herself. St. Rosalia was born around 1132, daughter to Count Sinibaldo and Mary Guiscard, a descendant of Charlemagne. Her father had taken part in an anti-royal plot and was killed, and his property was confiscated. Rosalia then consecrated her life to Jesus Christ and lived as a hermit in caves at Mt. Coschina near Bivona and at Mt. Pellegrino near Palermo. She inscribed on the cave wall, "I, Rosalia, daughter of Sinibald, Lord of Roses and Quisquina, have taken the resolution to live in this cave for the love of my Lord, Jesus Christ."

Rosalia died in the cave. She became the patroness of Palermo, Italy after her bones were discovered by a hunter on July 15, 1625. Later that year, an epidemic of the plague struck Palermo. Rosalia's relics were carried in a procession through town, causing an immediate end to the scourge. Another miracle would seal her association with mariners.

In 1668, an account was published in Madrid witnessing the rescue at sea of Marcisco Morilo, the owner of a large ship returning from Palermo with a cargo of wine. As the ship neared Monte Pellegrino outside of Palermo, Morilo asked the crew and passengers to recite an *Our Father* and an *Ave María* to St. Rosalia. Shortly after they sailed out of Palermo, Morilo encountered a fierce storm and everyone on board feared for their lives. The waves became ever more furious, the night was dark, and there was no possibility of help from the shore to save his crew. Morrillo took from his pocket a small relic of St. Rosalia and asked everyone to join him in prayer. With tears in their eyes, they all pleaded to St. Rosalia for deliverance. Out of nowhere, a small boat appeared and took them from their distressed vessel and to the safety of shore. They gave thanks to God and to the saint in a mass which Morilo quickly organized. Since that time, it is common for sailors to pray to St. Rosalia during a storm or when there is fear of attack by pirates. A large marble statue of the saint, which could be seen many miles away, was later erected on Pellegrino facing the sea. She became a brilliant, noble, and celestial beacon.

Charles III, King of Naples, became King of Spain in 1759 after his half brother Ferdinand VI had died. He donated a statue of St. Rosalia to the people of Palermo. It was only during his reign that ships were named *Santa Rosalia*. He died on September 13, 1788. Every year in Palermo, she is venerated for three days, July 13 to 15.

As I noted Rosalia's death as September 4, 1166, and the later celebrated feast day, I immediately recalled that this was the same day that that *La Galga* hit the offshore shoal and came safely to anchor, postponing her loss until the next day. *Was this a coincidence?* I thought back to the wrong turn that I had made at the Library of Congress the year before that led me to the 1785 reference. The feeling I had then was the same as when I had pulled one book out of fifty from of the Maryland Archives series to find Huony's letter which had given me the location of *La Galga*.

It was time to confront Stewart with the Victoria's findings on the *Santa Rosalia*. When I did, he deftly sidestepped the issue, saying that he appreciated my help but reminded me that Victoria had been also unable to find other documents related to *La Galga* that he had. Stewart

I believe I can answer why there is so little information available on your Santa Rosalea -

note: from "Naval Tracts" Lt. George Pratt-R.N., documents removed from the Record Office- Department of State, Washington City- August, 1814 and transported aboard the "Seahorse" frigate after burning that place.

" One letter from the Minister Plenipotentiary to the U.S. Department of State dated Cadiz- 27.11.1788 relating to the salvage of the merchant ship "Santa Rosalea" by the fishing folk south of Cape Henlopen."

References by Harold Underhill to the attached article -.

Habana Records- Ship Losses, Musco Maritimo- Barcelona
Armada Españolas- Biblioteca Nacional- Madrid   -

Note- Ref: 1788 Spanish merchantman "Santa Rosalea" Captain Pardenus from Havana to Baltimore wrecked south of Cape Henlopen. (Spanish Shipwreck List)-Madrid Museo Naval - this is probably where Robert Marx got his information in Shipwrecks of the Western Hemisphere.

Document presented by Donald Stewart to the SEA board to support his claim for the "Santa Rosalea." Compare to Marx: "Year 1788. Spanish merchantman Santa Rosalea, Captain Pardenus, sailing from Baltimore to Havana, wrecked near Cape Henlopen but some of her cargo saved." Note Marx's source is from Lloyd's List September 16, 1788, which stated: "Santa Rosalia, Pardenus, from Baltimore to Havannah is drove ashore at the Capes of Delaware and dismasted. Part of cargo saved." Lloyd's List had spelled it correctly. Note Stewart's embellishments in this document. To further back his claim, Stewart showed the SEA board a 1788 piece of eight he said he found on the beach opposite the site he declared to be the "Santa Rosalea." He had forgotten his earlier representation that his tale of treasure began with a wreck in 1785.

was so casual in his response he nearly disarmed me as he had done in the past.

I told other investors I had some serious questions about Stewart and his shipwrecks, particularly the *Santa Rosalea*. The wrecks appeared to be made up. My allegations were made known to the board, and I told Rick Cook that he needed to do something, because after all, he was president. He wouldn't believe me. Stewart had just produced some Spanish coins dated 1788 that he said he had just found between Seventy-eighth and Eighty-first streets, which coincided with the SEA admiralty claim. He had forgotten his earlier representation in January that the *Santa Rosalea* wrecked in 1785. I told other investors whom I had considered good friends, and they did not believe me. Rick Cook's wife, Delphine, did believe me and was not surprised. On October 5, Rick Cook resigned as president, saying he was needed more in his construction business and also that his mother was ill.

Our new president was John Mathisen, so I went to him with the same information and told him there was no wreck called the *Santa Rosalea* in 1785 and there probably wasn't any *San Lorenzo* either. And if all of that were true, then most likely the treasure that Stewart had told us was on board *La Galga* was nonexistent. I insisted that he get some proof of these wrecks before we went any further. Stewart realized that he needed to come up with something. He arrived at the next board meeting and gave them a typewritten document that he insisted that I not be allowed to see. Mathisen gave me a copy anyway.

Stewart said that the records of the ship had been removed from Washington by the British when they burned the place in 1814. He was now talking about the *Santa Rosalea* that had wrecked in 1788, which he originally had me investigate the year before. This wreck came out of Robert Marx's book on shipwrecks. After investigating, I found that this ship was lost at Cape Charles, Virginia, not in 1785 as Stewart had described before and documented in the admiralty claim, but in July of 1788. Marx had misspelled "Rosalia" by making it "Rosalea." It was an innocent typographical error that had duped Stewart. He always stuck to that spelling.

Stewart knew that Marx had said that the ship was sailing out of

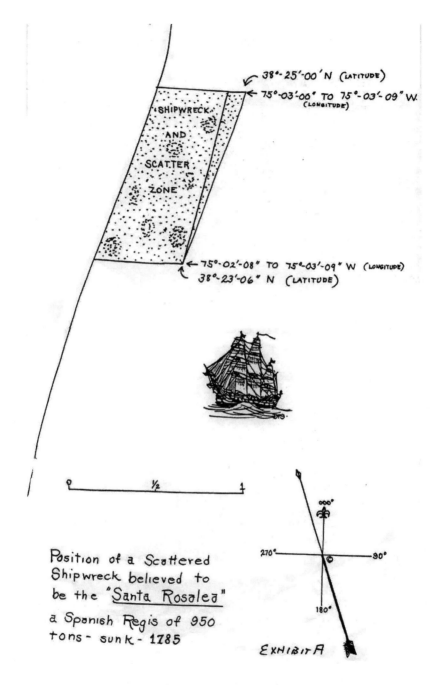

38°-25'-00' N (LATITUDE)
75°-03'-00" TO 75°-03'-09" W. (LONGITUDE)

SHIPWRECK AND SCATTER ZONE

75°-02'-08" TO 75°-03'-09" W (LONGITUDE)
38°-23'-06" N (LATITUDE)

0   ½   1

Position of a Scattered Shipwreck believed to be the "Santa Rosalea" a Spanish Regis of 950 tons - sunk - 1785

000°
270°   90°
180°

EXHIBIT A

Artwork by Donald Stewart. Notice the copyright symbol in the cross of the compass. In Stewart's own hand, the description of the "Santa Rosalea" filed as Exhibit A in Civil Action R 81-51 in the United States District Court for the District of Maryland.

Baltimore before she was lost. That would most likely mean no treasure. I later found that she was carrying a load of flour. Stewart knew that once the board found out she was out of Baltimore he would have some serious problems. In the document he presented to the board, he said that the *Santa Rosalea* was sailing *from* Havana *to* Baltimore. The opposite was true. He knew that Mathisen had no knowledge of shipwrecks, and he cleverly used Robert Marx's reference in his book to convince Mathisen that it had to be legitimate. Mathisen had no way of knowing (until I told him) that Stewart altered the Marx reference. Mathisen focused on humoring me while leaving Stewart alone. His concern was to keep the corporation afloat and then deal with Stewart later.

In November, the money ran out, and I was laid off. Mathisen asked that I stick around as he hoped that some more money would be coming in. It didn't, and I was forced to file for unemployment compensation. All of my savings had gone into SEA stock. I was broke.

I was now living at Pier Seven, a townhouse on the bay front between Seventh and Eighth streets in Ocean City. Gene Parker, a fellow SEA investor, also lived there, and he and I had become good friends. He would often treat me to dinner at his restaurant—*B.J.'s*. He said he wanted to be sure I was "eating right." What he really wanted was to talk about treasure hunting. Gene's family reached back to the seventeenth century on the Eastern Shore, and shipwrecks and treasure hunting had now captivated his imagination. I certainly owed a lot to him as he later allowed me to live at his farm next to Frontier Town in West Ocean City, since I could no longer afford rent.

Since I had free time, I started to do more research on the SEA shipwrecks. SEA now had taken yet another new direction. Since the Federal Court still had not issued a ruling on the four shipwrecks that I now realized to be fraudulent, the board was considering Stewart's recommendation to salvage a ship that all of the sport divers knew as the "*China Wreck,*" which lay in forty feet of water at the mouth of Delaware Bay. This shipwreck dated from the 1870s and had never been identified, but it was loaded with ironstone chinaware. These pieces had little value except as souvenirs to the sport diver who retrieved them.

In the spring of 1982, SEA had found a group of investors who were interested in backing this venture. They would need a boat, equipment, and divers. I told them that I was not interested and that the company would get a "black eye" for attempting to take the wreck away from the sport divers. To the credit of the board, they were trying to find a way to keep SEA afloat and protect the current investors from what was looking like a total loss of their investment. Stewart was looking for his paycheck to continue and the board was still behind him.

In February, the SEA office received a call from the state park on Assateague. They had found an orange buoy on the beach with the SEA phone number on it. It was one of our markers set the year before with the U.S. marshal, so I was asked to go get it. After retrieving it, I took it to Bayside Boatel where Bill Bane and I sawed it open. That was the only way to see which ship it belonged to. Papers inside identified it as the *Santa Rosalea* as described in the arrest warrant and complaint. I read it and was surprised to find that the complaint actually said that SEA had "found such abandoned vessel through the expenditure of considerable money, time, expertise, and effort and have present control of the abandoned vessel." And the papers clearly stated that this ship wrecked in 1785, not 1788, which was now Stewart's version. I looked at Bane and said that it certainly was true about the money and time we had wasted, but we never found anything. This explained why Stewart took the papers out of my hand the day we set the marker. I now knew that I was going to do something about all of this.

I later confronted Stewart outside the office at the Boatel and told him if he did not produce reasonable proof to back up his claims that I was going to sue him for everything he had. He looked at me nervously without saying anything. He just stood there shifting his excessive weight from one leg to the other. "You have thirty days," I said. "Then I get a lawyer!"

Robert Firth resigned from the board in April and was looking for someone to buy him out. He had been absent from the board meetings for some time. Firth had no takers on his stock. The *Bloodhound* was put up for sale as well as the magnetometer. There was not enough money to keep paying Stewart per his written contract and cover other expenses.

John Mathisen asked that I hold off on my lawsuit until the *China Wreck* project was underway. I stood down, but I did not keep my mouth shut. I was livid and told anyone who was willing to listen that Donald Stewart was a con man. By this time, I had Bill Bane, Gene Parker, and Ned Middlesworth convinced. I had met Ned the year before when he came out on the *Bloodhound*. Ned was a diver, an airline pilot, and an avid treasure hunter from Annapolis, Maryland. We became quick friends. I then contacted Albert Alberi and told him to forget about investing in SEA. We started to talk among ourselves about going back to look for *La Galga* since it was apparent that Stewart had no idea of where she lay. It was obvious that SEA was near its end.

On May 18, 1982, Stewart was boarding the *Captain Cramer* chartered to salvage the *China Wreck*. It was low tide, and with Stewart being overweight, he had difficulty getting aboard. He slipped while stepping down onto the boat, but still landed hard on his feet. He later described, "a sharp pain went from the top of my head to the bottom of my feet." Stewart claimed he was disabled and not able to work. That project was soon cancelled.

On May 21, the board terminated Stewart's contract for lack of funds. Stewart later hired Raymond Cardillo, one of the founders of SEA, to represent him in a workman's compensation claim and possible action against the SEA. Cardillo had previously agreed to represent SEA in the admiralty claims since there was no money to pay the Baltimore lawyers.

There was now some doubt among board members as to Stewart's credibility, but they all found it difficult to believe he could be a total fraud. He seemed to be such a harmless, likeable guy. He always had a convincing answer when questioned about the shipwrecks. One example of this was when we had heard reports of beachcombers finding Spanish coins dated 1821 and 1822 on the beach in front of the *San Lorenzo* (1820) site. Stewart was asked at a board meeting about them. His answer was quick and confident. He said that in 1820 they were pre-minting coins in Mexico because of the revolution. The board seemed to believe it, but our new president, Dr. Richard Passwater, still had me check it out. It was, of course, untrue. To counter my contradictory input to the board, Stewart began to portray me as someone who shouldn't be trusted. He even suggested I was stealing from the boat. The SEA investors were now divided into two camps, those who believed what I was telling them and those who remained captivated by Stewart.

When the SEA board found out that Stewart's claim might result in personal liability to them, they objected to the dual representation of Raymond Cardillo. He corrected that situation by resigning as SEA's counsel in the admiralty claims. It seemed obvious to me that he saw more money to be had prosecuting Stewart's injury than salvaging nonexistent treasure ships.

Before bringing a lawsuit against Stewart, I first had to deal with the phony shipwreck claims that had been filed in federal court. I discussed this with Albert Alberi, and being knowledgeable in admiralty law, he explained the procedure of filing a motion to intervene. I would have to undertake this myself since I couldn't afford an attorney.

On March 21, 1983, I filed a motion to intervene in the *Santa Rosalea* case at the federal court house in Baltimore. Under the rules, since I was a stockholder, I had the right to enter the litigation since the other stockholders and I could be affected by the outcome. It was short and to the point. In my sworn statement, I told the court that no vessel of any kind had been found and that the *Santa Rosalea* as described in the complaint did not wreck within the jurisdiction of the court. I told the court that this phony "claim" was being used to facilitate the sale of SEA stock and that an evidentiary hearing needed to be called. I finished by saying that "if title was awarded to the plaintiffs, such action will give legitimacy to further fraudulent sales of stock prejudicing my position as a stockholder and giving rise to further litigation."

Then, I sat back and waited.

CHAPTER SEVEN
The Hidden Galleon

In the spring of 1982, I continued my research on *La Galga*. In Spain, Victoria had not located any statements from Captain Huony about the wreck as I had hoped. It was a puzzle that would have to be solved here.

I had always felt that the ship lay in Virginia because of the document that I had found several years before that described the boundary as an east line that ended about latitude 38°. This description would place *La Galga* about a mile and a half south of where Stewart had directed SEA. The riddle left by Captain Huony was clear about one thing—he was certain he was in Virginia until early November when a survey was performed to position the wreck, shifting the boundary line and putting *La Galga* just inside Maryland.

I went to the Accomack County Courthouse on the Eastern Shore of Virginia to see what additional information I could find. At the courthouse, I located several plat books showing the Maryland-Virginia boundary. One book contained a plat dated 1943 that had been prepared for the land transfer when Assateague was taken from private ownership to the Chincoteague National Wildlife Refuge. This survey showed the approximate line in 1687 that was very near to latitude 38°. It also showed a line dated 1840 a little north of that. Both lines were well south of the present line, which lies nearly two miles north of this latitude. I also did extensive research on the owners of the land on Assateague on both sides of the line. In 1750, William Gore, who was a principle salvor of the wreck, owned the Virginia portion of Assateague. On the Maryland side, I documented the owners of the land for several miles north of the boundary. What I found was that the boundary line was inconsistent between Maryland landowners and the Virginia owners.

In Maryland, land patents, surveys, and deeds documented the line as being about a half mile south of the present line, while in Virginia there was no evidence of ownership north of the well-documented 1840 line. This meant there was an area of "no-mans-land" in between these two lines. The respective provinces had not granted this small piece of Assateague. However, Pope's Island, which lay behind this area of Assateague, had been clearly patented as Maryland territory, documenting that Maryland considered the boundary to be south of where land patents stopped on Assateague. That boundary was depicted as the 1687 line shown by the government survey of 1943. Everything still pointed to the fact that the line drawn in 1750 would be well south of the present Maryland-Virginia border.

The current boundary on the mainland had been drawn in 1668, but had been in dispute for two centuries until 1883, when a boundary commission redrew the line and set monuments. The 1668 line was clearly in conflict with Maryland's charter. The line was not a true east line as called for—it was run by a compass without recognizing the magnetic variation in the area, which was over five degrees north of east. A due east line would run a little below latitude 38°.

I knew that these differences could be ignored by expanding the ranges of the survey area in the ocean. *La Galga* would still lie in a very defined area. With this new information related to the boundaries, I was convinced that we were very close to discovery.

That spring, plans were finalized to form a new treasure hunting company with myself, Bill Bane, Ned Middlesworth, Gene Parker, Albert Alberi, and Rick Cook. I suggested the name Ocean Recovery Operations, Inc., since the acronym "ORO" was the Spanish word for gold. Everyone liked it. They all agreed that I would be the team leader since I had been the most involved in the research and exploration. Al, who was an attorney, would set up the corporation. He was also a diver who was ready to go when needed. Bill Bane could find us a boat, Gene Parker had a forty-one-foot sailboat, Rick Cook and Ned Middlesworth had time to assist in the search, and I still had my own dive gear, magnetometer, and metal detector. We agreed that no one would get paid for his time and that we would share equally in the expenses and equally in our successes. I was contributing my time and research for nothing. We all realized that if we found the wreck, there wouldn't be a lot of treasure, but it would be worth the effort.

Alberi and I had numerous discussions about the treasure on *La Galga* and where she probably wrecked. He had been researching the ship since the mid 1970s and had records from the Virginia State Archives that I had not seen. He also told me about a letter he had

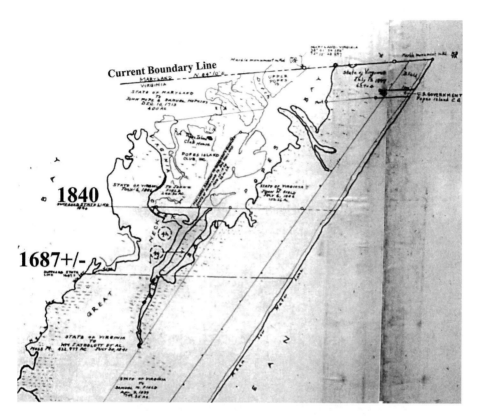

1943 plat of Assateague Island based on chain of title from the first owners of
Assateague. Located in the Accomack County Courthouse. It is part of the Nellie
Burwell tract that was acquired by the U.S. Department of Interior. Note the circles
above the 1687 line. In the deed to the U.S. Government, they indicate that the strip of
marsh was considered part of Pope Island. Plat Book #6, pp. 17-18.

received from Stewart in February of 1978. Stewart's letter contained
many factual errors about the 1750 fleet and *La Galga*. It not only
included fabricated accounts of treasure, but also simple historical facts
that he chose to distort and of which he had no real knowledge. By
now, all of this was no surprise. What did surprise me was that this
letter, written on Atlantic Ship Historical Society letterhead, stated that
he and the Historical Society had discovered *La Galga* in 1967 and had a
salvage contract with Spain. Alberi told me that he later attributed the
false statements in Stewart's letter as his way of getting to his research,
which he did, in fact, turn over to him.

One document Alberi showed me was an account by the sheriff of Accomack that described some trivial items taken from the wreck and found on a nearby island. These items included some rigging blocks, a brass scale, seven iron hoops, and two swivel guns. Alberi had given Stewart his transcription of this without a photocopy of the original. In the original document, it said "too swivel guns" for "two," but Alberi had misread it as "200 swivel guns." Given the context of the document it couldn't be interpreted any other way.

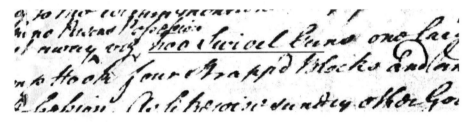

Excerpt of items from *La Galga* found on a nearby island by the sheriff of Accomack County, Virginia in 1750. *From Colonial Records, Folder 43, Virginia State Library, Richmond.*

Stewart in turn used the "200 swivel guns" in his phony letter written by Captain "Mahoney," as Stewart was apt to call him, which was purported to be in the locked-up files that were contained in "Libro 38." This letter was the same one Stewart had shown me two years before at our first meeting, and the one Alberi and I saw together when Stewart first brought him by my house. Alberi believed the "Mahoney" letter to be authentic as it was mistakenly corroborated by his own research, which we later realized was misinterpreted. Those "200 swivel guns" became "500" in the SEA prospectus. I went on to explain to him my similar situation with the *Santa Rosalia*. It was not lost on me how valuable the information was that Albert Alberi had supplied and the irony of the fact that Stewart had introduced us.

Now that we knew where to look for *La Galga*, I decided to go to Chincoteague and try to find someone who might have some local knowledge about Assateague and what might have been found on the beaches over the years. After asking around, I was directed to a man named Nat Steelman who lived on Chincoteague and was considered a good source for local history.

When I arrived at his house, he graciously invited me in. Nat Steelman was in his early seventies and retained a powerful physique from years of tonging oysters. He was soft-spoken and eager to share his knowledge of the island. His eyes twinkled as he recalled his days as a young boy and the stories his father had shared with him. He produced a map of the area and pointed to the Maryland-Virginia line: "In the 1890s, my father worked as a surfman at Pope Island Life-Saving Station just below the Maryland line," Steelman began, as he pointed with his weathered finger to the location on his map.

"When I was a young boy, my father took me there and showed me a place south of the station at the edge of the marsh where I saw some ship's timbers sticking out of the ground. He told me that they had come from a Spanish ship lost long ago, and that this is where the wild ponies had come from."

Steelman was now pointing to an area over a mile and a half south of the line.

He continued, "This lake that you see was not there years ago. The refuge built a dam by the road here, which has a valve to control the water level in the lake."

I ignored the pony story. Some published accounts of the legend I had read attributed them to a lost Spanish ship that had gone into an inlet. These facts did not jive with what I knew about La Galga. I surmised that a storm must have carried the timbers over the dunes and deposited them in the marsh. This location was consistent with the boundary lines I had documented at the Accomack courthouse.

I asked him if he'd ever heard of any Spanish coins being found on the beach. Nat Steelman told me, as his father had related to him, that there was a post about a mile and a half to two miles south of the state line where the surfmen on patrol would reset their watch clock and would sometimes meet. Nat said Spanish coins were often found there. This spot coincided with the same latitude as where he'd said the ship timbers were shown to him.

Nat Steelman said that he had read Reginald Truitt's book on Assateague, which described La Galga wrecking in Maryland. He said that *La Galga* was two miles to the north, and he made no connection with the timbers he had just pointed out and what he read about *La Galga*. I did. Steelman knew *La Galga* was north of the Maryland-Virginia line, having read it in a local history book, but he did not know where the old boundary was.

We shook hands, and I promised to let him know if I found anything.

On the way back to Ocean City, I became convinced that we could find *La Galga* the first day out. I told Gene Parker what I had learned and he went nuts. He decided to take his forty-one foot Morgan Out Islander to the site the next day. Ned Middlesworth drove down from Annapolis.

We motored the sailboat the whole way, which took about three hours. We started magging with my original J. W. Fishers unit, but the readout became unstable. Gene started cursing. I was used to it. We decided that we needed a large powerboat and a more sophisticated magnetometer.

I talked with some of the SEA board members, and they agreed to let me use the Varian magnetometer in recognition of all of the uncompensated time I had given. We could now perform elaborate magnetic surveys with its increased sensitivity and utilizing its chart recorder. The boat speed for towing the magnetometer was about five miles per hour, as it sampled the magnetic field once every second. In a four-hour period we could cover a corridor a mile long by 350 yards wide, shifting the boat's path every fifty feet. It would only take a couple of days to finally locate the wreck. Now we had to find a boat.

In the spring of 1982, I contacted Charles McKinney with the U. S. Department of the Interior. He was a manager of their antiquities program, and I had talked to him several years before. I wanted to find out about some upcoming shipwreck legislation. Charlie remembered me and told me about an organization that was being formed called the Atlantic Alliance for Maritime Heritage Conservation. It was a dual purpose organization that was going to promote maritime history, as well as fight some upcoming legislation that would give the states title to all wrecks in state waters over fifty years old. Sport divers, treasure hunters, and maritime historians banded together to consolidate their lobbying effort against the pending bill. Charlie asked me to join, and I did.

At the organizational meetings for the Alliance, I met people like myself as well as some of the recognizable names, like Duncan Mathewson from the *Nuestra Señora de Atocha* project in Florida. I also met Alan Riebe and Daniel Koski-Karell, two individuals who had worked together hunting for *La Galga*. Riebe had filed for a permit with the Commonwealth of Virginia in November of 1980 to explore for the shipwreck, but had been turned down. I found out that it was Riebe and Koski-Karell who were in the boat Stewart and I saw working the site the year before. Alan and I compared notes on *La Galga*, and he provided me with a diagram showing his interpretations of the 1750 boundary line. He said that he was giving up on the site he thought could be *La Galga* and was headed for Cape Lookout, North Carolina, to look for *El Salvador*, another ship from the 1750 fleet that was carrying treasure when she was lost. From his description, there was no archaeological evidence to make the connection between his wreck site and *La Galga*. No cannonballs were found, although he said he thought he saw one go into his airlift which wasn't recovered. His site was the same one where I had found the black conglomerate the year before. I shared with him what little I had on the *El Salvador* and put him in touch with Victoria so he could pursue additional research on his upcoming venture.

In July, Alberi called me and said he had some useful information. He had a client who had proven psychic ability and said that he had a clear vision of the wreck being buried near a grassy area in shallow water. Alberi went on to say that Bill Holloway, his psychic client, was an upstanding guy and had previously used his abilities to assist the local police. I laughed.

"Albert, you and I both know that the beach has eroded over the centuries, not built out!" I said. "This is a distraction. We need to stay on course."

"Well, I guess you're right," he said.

Bill Bane found a boat for us, a twenty-six-foot Stamas with twin engines, which he had owned but recently sold to one of his customers,

Chip Johnson. Chip generously agreed to loan it to us as he knew that Bill would make sure the boat was cared for.

Bill was always busy at the marina, so he volunteered his son, also named Chip, to go with us. He had recently finished high school and had some free time. Chip was a great boat handler and quickly learned to run the tight search patterns we needed for our magnetometer surveys. And being the son of a Navy diver, he had learned to dive when he was quite young. Chip made a 100 foot dive with his dad at age seven.

We were now ready to get back to the real search for the wreck after being sidetracked by Stewart.

Our group plugged on until October, searching the area around latitude 38°. We didn't find anything from a wreck, but we did locate recently discarded debris. We figured the wreck could be up to a half mile from the beach because of the receding beaches, but after not finding it, we just weren't sure. It was decided that the wreck must be lying very close to the beach, an area that we had not yet searched.

Just before Thanksgiving 1982, we hired the *Original Jackson* to take us out one more time. This would be our last trip—if we didn't find it we were giving up the search. Captain Topping skillfully piloted his sixty-foot boat into water that was no more than five or six feet deep. We were so close to the beach that a breaking wave almost overturned the boat. We still had no luck. It was over. I put the gear away and called it quits. I brooded through the Thanksgiving holidays, wondering what I was going to do now. I had abandoned my career in Washington, so I couldn't go back there. There was really nothing in Ocean City for me except the ocean. I was lost. At thirty-two, I should have a home, and a wife and kids, just like all of my friends. All I had was my diving gear and a $300 car. *What next?*

After returning to Ocean City from visiting my parent's home on the North Carolina Outer Banks, I decided that another trip to the Accomack courthouse might at least be therapeutic, if not revealing. I found another plat book, which I had not looked at before. The book contained a plat dated 1840 that represented a survey of land on Assateague for a William J. Aydelott and some others. It showed the area in detail that I was interested in. This survey was the basis for the line labeled 1840 on the 1943 government survey that I was already working with. It seemed now even less likely that the 1750 border could be considered to be north of this line. The plat was drawn correctly to scale, and it showed the beach to be much narrower in 1840 than it is today. If this was true, the ship most likely lay buried under the beach. If it was buried under the beach, then discovery and salvage was out of the question.

I called Alberi about my findings.

"Albert, I just found out why we haven't found the wreck. I was at the courthouse today and found a plat that not only shows the boundary line, but shows that Assateague was much narrower years ago. *La Galga* has to be buried under the beach."

To my surprise, Albert had a reason to continue.

"John, a nearly identical situation happened a few years back. Some treasure hunters who failed to find a sunken riverboat ended up finding it buried under a federal wildlife refuge. It sounds like we have the same situation here," he said.

He related a story to me of a steamboat named the *Bertrand* that sank in the Desoto Bend of the Missouri River on April 1, 1865, and later became swallowed up by the riverbank after the river changed its course. The wreck had been discovered in 1968 buried under the Desoto National Wildlife Refuge after treasure hunters had exhausted their conventional search efforts in the river. They had found a map showing that the river course had changed since the wreck. Using the map, they were able to plot the location of the *Bertrand* which put it under dry land. They then drilled into the suspected site and proved that it was there. The group then excavated the *Bertrand* with a permit from the Federal Government where they received sixty percent of the value of the cargo. The excavation was completed in October 1969 after 150 tons of cargo had been removed. On March 24, 1969, the historic significance of the *Bertrand* was recognized when it was entered into the National Register of Historic Places. A museum was built at the wildlife refuge to house the exhibit.

"Look, John, we can do the same thing! It's not over, we need to find

Chip Bane assists the author into the water. *Photo by Ned Middlesworth.*

Ned Middlesworth contemplates discovery during a magging operation in 1982.
Photo by the author.

1840 plat of *Great Neck* on Assateague for 436 and 977/1000 acres. This precise amount closely resembles the nominal amount of 500 acres described in 1696. Note Wear Bay. This document proved the coastline changes that hid *La Galga*. The north boundary is the Maryland line. The words "Due west to the Maryland line" can be seen. The south boundary line is the same as the north bounds of *Little Neck*, described in 1796 as running, "southeast across the beach to the surf." Surveyor's Book #6, p. 84. Accomack County Courthouse, Virginia.

La Galga!" Alberi demanded enthusiastically. Albert gave me a book about the *Bertrand* written by Jerome E. Petsche of the National Park Service. Albert pointed out that the National Park Service heaped praise on the discoverers of the wreck, even though their initial motivation had been finding treasure. The Park Service, however, felt that the real treasure was the riverboat itself and the cargo in her hold, not the gold and mercury sought by the treasure hunters, and that it should be displayed and protected as part of our national heritage.

Albert urged me on saying, "I have received reports that others from a dive club here are currently looking for *La Galga* and have even heard that Mel Fisher applied for a search permit several years ago. You're way ahead of everybody else."

Then I had a chilling flashback. "Albert, it looks like you need to contact your psychic friend!"

This news brightened my day even though the name of our corporation, "Ocean Recovery Operations, Inc.," no longer had any meaning. Considering the treatment afforded the *Bertrand* by the federal government, all of the partners considered it worthwhile to continue the hunt. The fact that *La Galga* appeared to be buried under the island changed more than our methods of searching for it. I now realized that *La Galga* was, in fact, the legendary ship that the locals of Chincoteague associated with the wild ponies. Documents found by Victoria in Spain made no mention of them, but she had not found any report from Captain Huony in her archival search. The documents she located gave few details about the wreck. One document had described the location of the wreck as "near some deserted islands." This description hinted at a break in the barrier, or an inlet.

It would take more than an ordinary metal detector to locate *La Galga* if it was indeed buried under the island. I contacted Geometrics, Inc., in California and found that we could purchase for a little over $5,000 a portable magnetometer, one small enough that it could be carried in a harness around one's neck and utilized a hand-carried sensor head. I certainly didn't have the money for it, and my partners didn't want to lay out a lot, so we decided to borrow the purchase price from the bank and make monthly payments. Since we were going to the bank anyway, we included enough to by the SEA magnetometer that was advertised for sale. The six of us would then contribute equally to pay the loan off.

It would be February of 1983 before the magnetometer would come in. Gene Parker had the idea of sending Bill Bane, his son Chip, and me to the Florida Keys for the month of January to do some treasure hunting. Bill had an old friend named Ernie Rickman who lived at Key West and had dived in the Keys for years. He had even helped build the old causeway. Ernie told us about some rumors of finds out on American Shoal, lying off of the Saddlebunch Keys, so we rented a house at Little Torch Key.

On my way down, I stopped at Vero Beach to meet Dr. Eugene Lyon, the historian who guided Mel Fisher's search for the *Atocha*, and the author of the book about it. Victoria had been doing some work for him and told me that Treasure Salvors had recently recovered some horseshoes on the *Santa Margarita*, so she arranged the meeting. Since Nat Steelman of Chincoteague had connected the horses to *La Galga*, I was now keen to explore the possibility.

After arriving at his house, Dr. Lyon and I discussed the project, and I told him that we now had reason to believe that there had been horses on board *La Galga* but the register failed to mention them. Dr. Lyon repeated the story that Treasure Salvors had recently found horse bones and horseshoes on the *Santa Margarita* that had sunk with the *Atocha* in 1622, but there was no archival reference to them. He went on to say that he believed that the soldiers on board were bringing them home. Dr. Lyon asked, "Were there any soldiers on board your ship?"

"Yes," I said, "Victoria documented that there were sixty of them on board."

"Then I wouldn't be surprised if there were horses on *La Galga*," he said matter-of-factly.

I thanked him for his time and left. As I continued my journey to the Keys, I reflected on my meeting with him. I had started out looking for *La Galga* in the hopes of finding a little treasure and some artifacts. Then Donald Stewart misled me for over a year, looking for what I thought would be a fabulous treasure. Now I was pursuing a legend.

Excavation of the mid-19th century riverboat, *Bertrand*, buried on the Desoto National Wildlife Refuge. 1969 © National Geographic Society.

This had become more important than any gold or silver.

Out of the month we spent in the Keys, we only dove three times on the outer reef because of the incessant winds. However, we did have a great time spearing fish and catching lobster on the inner reefs and carousing in Key West at night. Bill Bane entertained us with tales of his Navy SEAL team and some of his experiences that he could tell with the CIA. Bill was part of UDT Teams #2 and #21 at Little Creek, Virginia. When the SEALS were formed, he was called to be an instructor at the Navy's Underwater Swimmers School in Key West. After two years, the CIA recognized his skills and pulled him in.

I learned that I was diving with a man that actually helped develop the science. As Navy divers, he and the others pushed the limits in depth and decompression, which helped refine the decompression tables we use today. He also participated in the Navy's first testing of Jacques Cousteau's Aqua-Lung. Bill Bane, as always, proved to be a first-class chef and served up some fantastic food, usually the fish and lobster we had caught that day. In spite of the diving, I was putting on weight.

We had fun, but I couldn't wait to get back to Assateague. While we were gone, Albert Alberi had been trying desperately to get in touch with me. Unable to reach me by phone, he wrote a letter on January 15 that was waiting for me when we returned from the Keys. Albert said he had taken a copy of Captain Huony's letter found in the Maryland Archives and a copy of a chart of the Assateague coast and presented them to his psychic friend, Bill Holloway, for him to "divine." Albert had told him nothing else. To Albert's surprise, he pointed to an area close to Ragged Point, which was more than two miles south of the present line. Albert was quite amazed, and so was I when I read Albert's letter. He also included a map showing his notations on the location. Holloway said he would be willing to travel to Ocean City when we needed him.

Albert D. Alberi. *Courtesy of the Alberi Family.*

As soon as the portable magnetometer came in, we set off for the area we had delineated for the wreck. Gene Parker, Bill and Chip Bane, Ned Middlesworth, Rick Cook, and I made several trips to the site. Our routine was to drive Gene's Jeep CJ down the Maryland beach, which was part of the Assateague Island National Seashore and controlled by the National Park Service. We would arrive at the Virginia line where there was a fence that separated not only the two states, but the National Seashore from the Chincoteague National Wildlife Refuge. From here, we would walk down the beach to the approximate latitude and search from the edge of the surf westward.

Metal detectors aren't allowed on federal property, but we justified using the magnetometer because it doesn't send out a signal to detect metal as traditional detectors do. It is merely a receiver that registers the intensity of the earth's magnetic field. When iron is present in the field, the reading will change on the magnetometer. Regardless, we were not disturbing anything by digging. Our methods were totally non-intrusive. But then we knew this logic might not fly with the rangers so we kept the mag out of site until it was needed.

I had considered applying for a permit but realized that I would be met with two scenarios: one, they probably would laugh when I said that the ship was buried under the island, or two, they would take our research up to that point and run with it themselves. In either case, I would be forced to give up information that had taken several years to assemble, and bureaucratic red tape would have put the project off for many months with no guarantee of government cooperation.

After looking on the beach with no luck, we then focused on the area west of the dunes. Again, we found nothing. The farther west we searched, the more unlikely it seemed that we would find the wreck. But as we eliminated areas, I knew we were getting closer to the wreck.

As we moved westward, we came to the edge of the lake, or waterfowl impoundment, that Nat Steelman had described the year before. I had surmised that this lake area had been the oceanfront centuries ago. Most of Assateague consists of rolling dunes with at least scattered bushes or trees, but this area was once a great barren sand flat which was evidence of a rapid outgrowth of the beach. To the east of the lake toward the ocean was a heavy growth of kink bushes and brambles, and then the dune line. To the west of the lake were some marshes and pine forest. Beneath the lake were the old sand flats depicted on the 1840 plat.

I now looked in the area where Nat Steelman had seen the timbers as a boy. This was east and south of a ridge that ran from behind the beach southwesterly toward the woods on the west side of the lake. A road was built along this ridge. We got a small reading, but saw no timbers. The area was otherwise clean. This led us to the next obvious conclusion: the wreck must lie beneath the lake. But this posed another problem. How could we survey the lake? To accomplish this, Chip Bane and I used his Boston Whaler to tow a canoe over from the mainland where we entered Virginia Creek, towed the canoe to the dam, and then portaged it over. Now we could do search patterns much like we did in the ocean. We skirted the east side of the lake and started working west. We quickly found that the water in most places was only two feet deep and the bottom was hard sand. We also realized that we were literally sitting ducks out on the lake. Here we were, six miles from the mainland with a canoe in the middle of the wildlife refuge carrying electronic gear. We would never be able to explain that. We decided to cut that trip short and get off the lake before we were seen. Now that we knew that we could wade the lake, the canoe was no longer needed.

Nat Steelman had told me about someone else who knew a lot about Assateague. His name was Ronnie Beebe from Snow Hill, Maryland. Ronnie was a surveyor by trade, and his family had long been natives of the Chincoteague area.

In March, I made an unannounced visit to his home. After I explained to him what I was doing, and that Nat Steelman had suggested that I get in touch with him, he agreed to invite me in. Beebe was a little reserved at first, but then he opened up.

"Here is a map of the area we have been searching in," I said. "I have seen a plat at the courthouse that suggests that the beach has built way out in this area."

He oriented himself on my map and said, "You're right about that. The beach has certainly made out over the years."

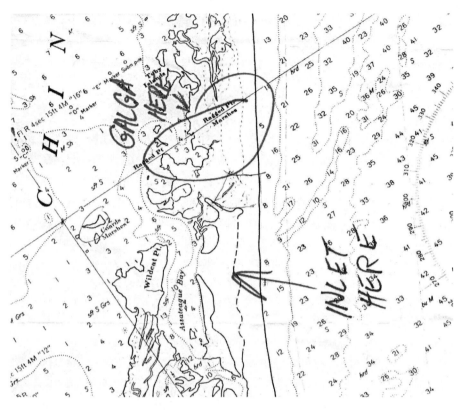

Notations on map made by Bill Holloway using his psychic ability.

He studied the map thoughtfully and then looked up at me. "You say you're lookin' for a Spanish ship?"

I nodded, "Yeah."

He continued, "I've been told since I was a kid that centuries ago a Spanish ship came into an inlet that caused it to close up in two weeks time. The wild ponies came from that ship."

Many of the people of Chincoteague in the centuries before could not read or write, so their history and traditions were passed on by word of mouth just as the Indians' were. Ronnie Beebe had said he was related to an eighteenth century Indian and oral traditions were a part of his life.

He pointed to an area just north and east of the dam, indicating where he thought the inlet was. It tied in exactly with the 1840 boundary line.

"After that time, the beach made out," he said in his Eastern Shore drawl.

"There's something else," he said as he was now warming up to me. "You see these woods on the west side of the lake? Right in here a Spanish pistol and some Spanish coins were found years ago. There was a handful—like they had been in a bag."

I did the best I could to contain myself. I felt like I was talking with Captain Huony himself.

I asked Beebe if he was related to Clarence "Grandpa" Beebe who is a main character in *Misty of Chincoteague*. He was his grand-nephew. Up until 1982, I had never associated the popular horse legend with *La Galga*. Now once again, I heard a credible story that the legend was true. Now it seemed impossible to separate this legend from the ship we were looking for. I thanked Mr. Beebe for his help. As I drove back to Ocean City, I visualized the 1840 plat. There is a marsh on the back side of Assateague just above latitude 38° today called "Ragged Point Marshes." In 1840, it was called "Horse Head Marshes."

I called Alberi and told him about my meeting with Ronnie Beebe and the similarities with some of what Bill Holloway had said. He then got in touch with Holloway and scheduled him to come to the Eastern Shore. Ned Middlesworth came down from Annapolis and joined Gene Parker, Rick Cook, and Bill Bane at my townhouse at Pier Seven. After Alberi introduced us and we all chatted for a few minutes, I got my chart out. I was dying to know what Holloway had to say. Bill Holloway was in his early forties, a jeweler by trade, slightly built with dark hair and a close-cropped beard flecked with gray. Without a turban, he didn't look like a psychic to me.

"Bill, before we take off, could you outline the area on my chart?" I asked.

He stared at the chart briefly and then pointed to the area of the dam. Taking a pen, he then drew a rectangle on the chart starting at the dam and then south along the edge of the woods, then extended the line east more than halfway across the lake, and then north running parallel with the west edge of the lake. When he finished, he had drawn a rectangle equivalent to about a half a square mile. I was surprised at

Aerial photo taken by the author of the wreck site area in early 1983.

how accurate his assumptions seemed to be. Latitude 38° went through this area.

"This is still a large area. Can you narrow it down?" I asked, trying to contain my excitement.

Without hesitating, he tapped the pen in the northwest corner of his rectangle.

"It's right in here."

Then he added something else. He told me that another ship that was with *La Galga* had wrecked off the south end of Assateague. I told him that would be the *Mercedes*, which had run ashore north of Cape Charles, fifty miles south of Assateague. He insisted he saw a ship with *La Galga* off Tom's Cove nine miles to the south. I ignored it. After all, psychic impressions are not always accurate.

After the Jeep ride through the national park to the Maryland-Virginia line and a two-mile hike into the refuge, we arrived at the dam. Holloway stood on the road that crossed the dam and looked out over the lake to the south. We were now standing in the northwest corner of the rectangle he had drawn earlier on my chart. The rest of us stood back, careful not to distract him. Holloway pointed south across the lake, "This used to be the oceanfront," he said. "The wreck is definitely right out here." And then he said he saw horses jumping in and swimming ashore. "No more than fifteen."

We spread out. I had the magnetometer on and entered the water at a shallow spot closer to the ocean and proceeded to wade south, holding the aluminum staff that supported the sensor head; the console was secured to my chest. I did my search patterns, walking in north and south directions for about a half an hour, totally focused on the LED readout. I heard someone yell my name and looked off to the west and saw Holloway standing on a point of marsh over a hundred yards away. He asked me if I had gotten any thing yet, and my response was that I had not, the readout was steady.

"Come this way, come toward me," he yelled. I changed course and worked my way toward him.

"Got anything yet?" he asked.

"No, not yet," I said.

"Keep coming," he said.

A short distance later: "How about now?" he asked.

I saw the numbers start to change. "Yeah! It's climbing!" I shouted. I kept moving toward him. The numbers continued to climb and then faded off.

"You just walked over a piece of it," Holloway said rather matter-of-factly.

I could tell by the relation of the distance I had walked and the numbers on the readout that whatever it was, it was probably ten feet or more in the ground and probably a larger mass, like a section of the ship with iron fastenings. This was the first meaningful anomaly we had thus far detected on land. Everybody was amazed.

As I walked closer to Holloway, the bottom dropped off, and I couldn't proceed any farther. It appeared that the water was over my head, so I backed off. I was now close enough to him to carry on a normal conversation. He explained again that I had gone over a piece of the wreck and that there was more to find somewhere close by. I continued working the area with no results, but ever mindful of the drop-off which was probably what remained of the old creek and inlet.

We left Assateague all keyed up. After many days of plodding through briars, branches, mud, and cold water with no results, we finally had a significant magnetometer reading. His demonstration was uncanny. Holloway said he had no doubt that we would find it now. It certainly seemed like we were close. On the way back up the beach we stopped at some timbers we had seen that had been recently exposed. They were situated very close to where Alan Riebe had been seen working two years before. There was a rib and what appeared to be a piece of planking which Holloway examined. He said that these were from *La Galga*. It was over a mile north of the lake. I used the magnetometer to scan around the area and got nothing. If it was from *La Galga* I surmised it must have washed there after the ship broke up in the later storm. I was getting a little confused over Holloway's contradictory impressions. It did not seem likely that a piece of the ship would be found this far north because of the prevailing currents. We still needed to find the main part of the wreck.

There would be more trips into the refuge with no results. We looked as far north as an inlet feature 900 yards south of the border and north of the general area that Holloway had directed us to, logging many miles on foot. Each time we came out of the refuge, we were exhausted, but still undaunted. We even magged the shallow waters of Pope's Bay using the marine magnetometer. I was totally convinced the beach had radically changed since 1750 and that the wreck must be under the island. I felt it was only a matter of time.

One day, Gene Parker and I went down to explore, and he had insisted on bringing a shovel. I told him that if we found the wreck it would be unreachable. He brought it anyway. After looking for a while with no results, a thick fogbank rolled in. The visibility was so bad that we couldn't see where we were going, so we made our way over to the beach and walked along the surf back to the Maryland line. Gene stopped to dig something out of the beach, and I went on. I was not far from the fence when a ranger in a patrol vehicle pulled up next to me. I hadn't seen or heard him coming. He jumped out and came over to me and looked at the magnetometer I still had strapped to my chest.

"What are you doing out here and what is that thing?" the ranger asked impatiently.

"I'm down here studying inlet formations, and this thing is a magnetometer and not a metal detector," I stated nervously. "I'm not digging for treasure," I added.

"Then what is your friend doing carrying a shovel?" he asked.

I had no answer.

The ranger, appearing frustrated, said, "I don't know what you are up to, but I suggest you get a permit. Since that thing is not turned on, go ahead and leave. But I don't want to see you down here again with that thing."

Shortly after that incident, Gene called me and said that he had been called by the refuge manager in Chincoteague, who demanded to know what was going on. Apparently, the National Park Service on the Maryland side had been observing Gene's Jeep being left parked on the beach on a regular basis, so they took his beach access permit number and identified him as the owner of the vehicle.

We decided to continue the search, but we had to be more careful. We would park the jeep behind the sand dunes at the fence and be sure not to be seen with the magnetometer. Gene and I went back down for another look. Besides the magnetometer, I carried my camera. If we got caught, we could easily say we were on a picture-taking expedition.

On the next trip, I was looking in the marsh just north of the dam. Chip Bane and I had previously searched part of this area by water, but we had been driven away by a freakish hailstorm. Gene was in the woods across Virginia Creek poking around. Suddenly, he let out a yell. There was a Chevy Blazer coming up the trail from the south. I was completely exposed. I dropped the mag in the marsh and kept walking toward the dam and the road where the Blazer had just passed. I had already been seen, but Gene had not. The Blazer continued across the dam, and his view of me was now blocked by trees, which I took as an opportunity to run for the dam and catch up with Gene. The Blazer had rounded a bend in the road and stopped. He couldn't see us, and we couldn't see him.

Gene and I then strolled along the road, acting as if nothing was out of the ordinary. We came up behind the Blazer and found it with the door open and a young ranger crouched behind some bushes peering out over the marsh I had just left. He didn't know we were behind him.

Not sure how to introduce ourselves, I simply said, "Hey! You looking for us?" The startled ranger shot to his feet and demanded to know what we were doing. I pointed to the camera and said we were taking pictures of some old inlets. He asked if that was our Jeep parked up at the fence, and of course, we admitted it. I asked him if he wanted his picture taken, but he declined. He did offer to give us a ride back to the beach if we were leaving. We said we had gotten enough pictures, so we accepted. Gene and I thanked him for the lift, waited until he was clear out of sight, then returned to get the magnetometer I left laying in the marsh. Fortunately, it was still there. Gene and I went to Chincoteague the next day and met Dennis Holland, the refuge manager, and discussed the requirements for a permit. I told Gene that there was no way we could show our cards yet on *La Galga*. We came up with the idea of admitting to searching for the lost pirate treasure of Charles Wilson that had been widely popularized in tourist literature.

A letter was reputed to have been found in England in the late 1940s written by Charles Wilson himself, which gave the directions:

Gene Parker with a ship's timber on Assateague opposite the site located by Alan Riebe. *Photo by the author.*

To my brother George:

There are three creeks lying 100 paces or more north of the second Inlet above Chincoteague Island, which is at the south end of the peninsula. At the head of the third creek to the northward is a bluff overlooking the Atlantic Ocean with three cedar trees growing on it, each about one and one-third yards apart. Between the trees I buried in ten iron bound chests, bars of silver, gold, diamonds, and jewels to the sum of £200,000 Go to woody knoll and remove the treasure.

Charles Wilson.

This story has never been authenticated, and there is no proof that Charles Wilson ever existed. Some have said that real estate developers put this out when lots were being sold on Assateague prior to the establishment of the national park in 1962. Ned Middlesworth had made numerous trips in previous years in search of it. Our group had already made several forays in the hopes of finding it. Gene and I settled on disclosing this part of our island explorations and leaving *La Galga* out of it.

At this meeting, I explained that we were trying to identify where the old inlets were, which would then hopefully lead us to where the treasure was buried. This was certainly true. Our secret was that a forgotten inlet contained the remains of *La Galga*.

This seemed to make sense to the refuge manager, and he accepted my explanation. But he said we needed a permit from him, and before he would issue that permit, I would need a contract from the General Services Administration in Washington. This contract would spell out each party's responsibilities and the division of treasure. I told him that I would make the application. On March 31, it was filed. The government was slow to respond.

Rick Cook insisted that we go back into Maryland waters to search for the wreck. He refused to accept the fact that the shipwreck appeared to be buried somewhere under the island and totally ignored my findings in the Accomack courthouse related to the boundary line. He even called the other members to persuade them that the search should be directed back to the ocean. After another fruitless search in the ocean, we all agreed that if Cook wanted to continue looking in Maryland waters, then he was free to do so. He was still convinced that Stewart knew more than we did on *La Galga*'s location. His obsession with the fictitious ships that SEA had searched for also increased. He never accepted the fact that Stewart had made it all up. I later found out he was still communicating with Stewart and informing him of our activities. We let him out of our partnership. Cook went on to form Alpha Quest Corporation and organized his own search for the wrecks. He and his wife parted ways for good later that summer.

The frustration had set back in. Ned and I had made numerous trips to Assateague in May. The weather was much warmer, which brought out the flies, ticks, and mosquitoes. They were so bad that we were forced to wear pith helmets with netting over our heads. This reduced the bites and prevented us from inhaling them. We ignored the aggravation, for it seemed that we were awfully close. But nothing had happened since Holloway had been with us. I would call him after each of our forays and tell him what had happened. Holloway had said on more than one occasion that he "saw" me walking over it. In fact, he said that I would find a piece of the wreck sticking out of the ground. I mentally retraced my footsteps, but I didn't see it.

Because of the heat and the possibility of exposing ourselves to the rangers, we altered our game plan a little and went in the late afternoon. We would make the run in Ned's Blazer as it wouldn't be recognized like Gene Parker's Jeep CJ. Ned would also bring what he called his "treasure chest"—a cooler of beer. This remained in his Blazer for the trip home. We'd made several trips to the area that Ronnie Beebe had fingered as an old inlet just above the 1840 line, but with no results.

One day I was down at the lake alone. I waded in where I had the first day with Bill Holloway and progressed south. As usual, the water was so dark that I couldn't see the bottom. I tripped over something. This had never happened before because the bottom was clean, hard sand. I backed up until my feet struck the object again. Then I reached down and felt a wooden timber sticking about six inches out of the bottom. It was square, not round. I looked back toward shore and noticed that I was only twenty-five yards from where Nat Steelman had indicated he

The author wading in the lake. *Photo by Ned Middlesworth.*

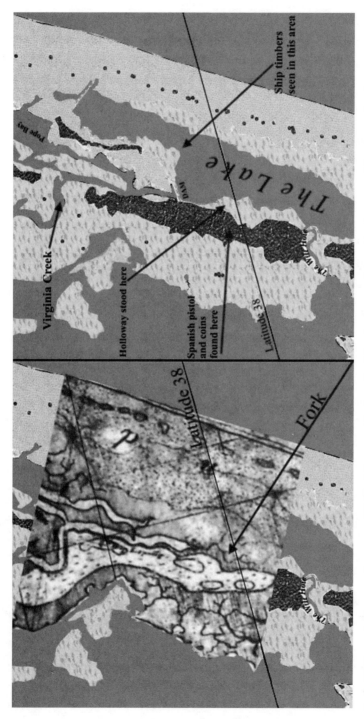

Left. 1859 overlaid on modern map. Right. After considering all of the data consolidated in these graphics the author knew *La Galga* had to be in the fork and that he had only been over a part of it earlier in the year. *Illustration by the author.*

had seen the timbers as a boy. I, of course, was quite excited, but that was all I'd found. There was no magnetic reading.

It was now June, 1983. I was sitting at home looking at an aerial photograph and comparing it to modern topographical maps, an 1859 topographical map I had recently found in the National Archives, and the 1840 plat. In my mind, I recalled what Ronnie Beebe had said about the ship going into an inlet and it later closing up. We had already searched the area that he had indicated was the inlet with no result. The 1859 coast survey map showed that the feature Beebe thought was a former inlet did not exist in 1859; it was the result of later storms.

The solution had been staring me in the face for some time, but I just hadn't seen it. The 1840 plat had a feature called "Wear Bay" which coincided with the lake area today. The definition of a *weir* is an "obstruction placed in a stream to divert its course, a dam." At the end of Wear Bay, as it was spelled in 1840, was a pronounced dead end, and in 1840, it was not far from the ocean. I also observed that the course for Virginia Creek had radically changed between 1840 and 1859, probably due to storm overwash.

From my research, I learned that place names usually have meaning. When I looked at Virginia Creek I wondered if it was called this because when one entered from Maryland, it would carry them the short distance into Virginia. Probably so, I reasoned. Also coincidental with the end of Wear Bay on the 1859 chart was a fork at the end of the creek or bay. I wondered what had caused the creek to split in two. And then immediately to the west of the western fork was a pronounced deviation in the old dune line. This was evident on the 1859 chart as well as the modern topographical map. In fact, the road from the south followed this contour. It was in this immediate area that Ronnie Beebe said the coins and pistol had been found. Latitude 38° ran right through the precise area.

I recalled the statement Sheriff Scarborough had made when he described the wreck. He said that there were many thousands of pounds worth of mahogany that could be gotten "before the ship bursts with the sea and *sinks into the land*." This statement took on a whole new meaning.

I called Ned in Annapolis.

"Ned, I know where it is! You can see it from the air!" I exclaimed.

I explained my logic and pointed out that we never had searched that area. When I waded the lake, I was always precluded from walking that far west because the water got too deep. I never believed that the wreck would lie that far to the west, but it was only a hundred yards or so from the mag hit located with Holloway's direction. After Holloway's visit, I was focused more to the north to coincide with the 1840 line and Ronnie Beebe's interpretation of the inlet. Although I had been impressed with Holloway's demonstration, I was not convinced the wreck was in this exact location until now. The charts and photographs said it all. I also remembered something else. Rick Cook had told me months before that he had received information that, years ago, before the creek was closed by the modern dam, oystermen had tonged up artifacts that appeared to be from an old ship. Cook told me that it was his opinion that they had washed in from the Spaniards' campsite. But then he was still looking for the ship in the ocean waters of Maryland.

As Ned and I rode the thirteen miles of Assateague toward the Virginia line, we reviewed all we had learned leading up to this day as his Chevy Blazer bounded along and dodged the invading surf. We agreed that all of the pieces of the puzzle seemed to finally come together. It looked like this was going to be the big day. Although we were also getting ready for litigation against Stewart, we never mentioned his name. We were totally focused on our elusive quarry, a lost Spanish warship named *La Galga*.

We arrived at the boundary fence and parked behind the dunes. As I retrieved the magnetometer from the back, I noticed Ned had remembered his treasure chest, his cooler of beer. I looked forward to celebrating later.

Ned and I went directly to the dam, crossed the creek, walked down the road to the contour in the old dune line, and proceeded to the spot where I remembered Holloway had stood. There was tall, dense sawgrass over the whole area, but on the northern section a path had recently been cleared by refuge personnel. I used the aerial photograph to guide me to the spot. The magnetometer started fluctuating before I got to the water's edge. When I looked at the deep water spot that I had stopped at that day with Holloway, I figured that I must be standing in the fork of the old creek and the mound I was on must be part of the wreck.

I returned to the road in the woods adjoining the marsh and told Ned what I had found. There was not much celebration as the reality of it all finally set in. There was nothing more we could do. To excavate this site, a cofferdam would have to be constructed and then the water, sand, and mud pumped out. After that was done, the government would require that the site be returned to its original condition. This looked like a multimillion dollar job.

As Ned and I walked along the road and the beach toward the Maryland line and his Chevy Blazer, we said little. We both shared a sense of accomplishment, which made us smile, but there was some sadness as well. The hunt and our adventure were over. For us, to realize any real fulfillment for all of our hard work and sacrifice, the wreck would have to be excavated and that depended on the federal government.

As we drove out, we drank our victory beer, but it didn't taste as good as it should have.

I decided to put together a research paper that would describe in detail some of the historical research and fieldwork we had undertaken. I hoped that with the release of this paper it might be possible to generate interest from the federal government or some organization like National Geographic. It might also help some other treasure hunter that wanted to look for *La Galga*. If we were correct, then it would save them a lot of time and money. If we were wrong, then perhaps my report would help somebody find the wreck elsewhere. I also decided not to release the news until the end of the year because of the legal preparation I was undertaking to go after Stewart.

Middlesworth and Parker still wanted to pursue Wilson's treasure, so I filed a follow-up letter in early September with the GSA. On September 28, Walter McAllestar, acting associate director of the Fish and Wildlife Service, wrote to Mr. Jack Williams of the GSA. In his letter, he advised that, before any permit was to be issued, we would have to supply to the refuge manager evidence, "stronger than rumor or legend," that a treasure did actually exist.

On October 13, I met with the refuge manager, Dennis Holland, and his two assistants. I was told that I needed to prove the existence of Charles Wilson's treasure and provide a precise location. They told me that the information would be kept in Mr. Holland's drawer. If this information was not provided, I wouldn't be issued a special use permit, and without this permit, GSA wouldn't give us a contract. Holland assured me that my information would be safe and marked "confidential" and would be excluded from the Freedom of Information Act. He also informed me that a refuge employee would have to accompany us on any searches and we would be billed for his time. I clearly understood their position, thanked them for their time, and left.

Since we did not have any historical documents that proved that the Charles Wilson letter was real, we weren't sure what to do, but we still wanted to pursue it. It looked like we had probably reached a dead end

From left to right, the author, Ned Middlesworth, and Chip Bane on a "Woody Knoll." *Photo by Charles Wilson.*

with government.

In early December, I turned my attention back to *La Galga* and mailed my research report on the wreck to state authorities in Maryland and Virginia, congressmen from both states, historical societies in both states, the Smithsonian Institution, National Geographic, the Fish and Wildlife Service, and Dennis Holland at the wildlife refuge. I also gave a copy to *The Baltimore Sun*. This release caused a chain reaction of events. Television stations and newspaper reporters wanted interviews. Bob Leary from the *Wilmington News Journal* in Wilmington, Delaware, contacted me for an interview. He also contacted the Fish and Wildlife Service in Chincoteague for permission to take photos at the wreck site area. They agreed and actually drove all of us to the site in a van. The driver was the ranger who had stopped me on the beach earlier in the year. That story appeared on the front page New Year's Day in 1984.

Other papers carried the story, and *The Virginian-Pilot* of January 4 featured an article written by Lawrence Maddry about *La Galga's* discovery and Holloway's involvement. Bob Leary of the *News Journal* saw the story and then called me and asked why I had not told him about Holloway. I explained to him that we wanted the government officials to focus on the verifiable facts that had led us to the site since some people would tend to discredit the discovery just because a psychic was involved.

Leary, fascinated with this new angle, contacted Holloway and *The Virginian-Pilot* reporter and rushed another story into the *Wilmington News Journal* on January 9. He'd heard firsthand about my initial reluctance to have a psychic involved and Holloway's thrilling account of the ship breaking her anchor lines and drifting into an inlet. Holloway recounted to him his vision of small horses, no more than fifteen, swimming ashore from the wreck. He also added that he believed there were three chests that were on or near the wreck that contained "silver—some gold, some artifacts, but mostly silver." Leary then interviewed Lawrence Maddry who had investigated several of Holloway's previous predictions. Maddry told him that there was usually someone who could verify his past psychic prophecies, as when he saw President Reagan being shot just before it happened.

The publicity faded quickly after that.

On December 29, I wrote to GSA to follow up on our permit for Wilson's treasure. I wanted now to make a clear distinction between the rumored pirate treasure and the wreck site of *La Galga*. I reinforced that we had no intention of digging in the wreck site area. The government, of course, stuck to their guns over the requisite proof that Wilson's treasure was real before any permit would be issued. I was now seeing what would've happened if I had applied for a search permit for *La Galga*. If they didn't believe upfront that *La Galga* could be buried, I would have been refused a permit.

In January, I received letters from many of those who had been sent the report. John Broadwater, senior underwater archaeologist for the Commonwealth of Virginia, said,

> I enjoyed talking with you at the Conference on Underwater Archaeology in Williamsburg earlier this month and I enjoyed even more reading your excellent report on the *Galga*.
>
> It is very apparent that you've spent a great deal of time on your research and the location you have predicted sounds very plausible. I think you are to be commended for devoting so much energy to the research and for sharing that research with others.
>
> The discovery and identification of *La Galga* would be a very significant achievement and would solve a mystery that has interested a great many people. I'm not sure what actions you have taken toward pursuing your investigations, but if I can be of any help, please let me know. I would like to keep in touch with you and Al Alberi on this matter and would be happy to meet with you to discuss your plans and to assist you if possible.

S. Dillon Ripley at the Smithsonian said,

> Your belief, based on location of anomalies detected by a proton magnetometer, that this vessel's remains lie within the Chincoteague National Wildlife Refuge, is particularly

significant. It would ensure federal protection of the site pending a careful archaeological survey.

Although the documentation indicates that the *La Galga* wreck was extensively salvaged in the 18th century, its site, when effectively established, may indeed yield significant artifacts illustrative of mid-eighteenth century military and maritime technology.

With these kinds of responses, I fully expected to be contacted by the federal authorities to ask for further information and assistance in evaluating the suspect site.

But I didn't wait for them. With Broadwater's offer to assist, I wrote to him on February 6. I pointed out that since the federal government discourages private initiatives in shipwreck exploration, it would be a good idea if he obtained the necessary "search only" permit so that our group could make the demonstration with our magnetometer. I encouraged him to initiate this step and said I was willing to do all that I could to assist in making the demonstration. I copied the refuge manager, the director of the Fish and Wildlife Service, the consulting archaeologist for the National Park Service, and the archaeologist for the State of Maryland. I heard no response, so eight months later, I wrote to Mr. Robert Jentzen, director of the U.S. Fish and Wildlife Service. I reminded them of the significance of the wreck and asked them if they intended to evaluate the site. I again offered our group's assistance in any contemplated evaluation.

On September 28, Mr. Walter Stieglitz, historic preservation officer for the Wildlife Service, informed me that they "had no plans to pursue investigation of possible shipwreck sites" and that the area of the suspect site was "closed to the public." This was not entirely true as hunting is allowed in this area every year. (The only thing we ever killed in there were flies and mosquitoes.) He did say that if there were any future land-altering activities in this area, he would keep the possibility of a wreck site in mind. The historic preservation officer had forgotten about the requirements of the National Historic Preservation Act of 1966 and President Nixon's Executive Order No. 11593, Protection and

Wreck-hunters, from left, are Chip Bane, Amrhein, and Bill Bane.

Photo from the *Wilmington News Journal*, January 1, 1984. *Courtesy of the Wilmington News Journal.* Left to right. Chip Bane, the author, and Bill Bane.

Enhancement of the Cultural Environment, which he signed in 1971. The order clearly stated that agencies should administer the cultural properties under their control in a spirit of stewardship and trusteeship for future generations, and ensure that sites and objects of historical or archaeological significance are preserved, restored and maintained for the inspiration and benefit of the people. The order also stated that such sites be located and inventoried for consideration for the National Register of Historic Places. The *San Jose y las Animas*, one of the ships that sailed with Captain Huony in 1733 and was lost in the Florida Keys, was placed on the register in 1975. I was hopeful that *La Galga* would soon get the same recognition.

But the historic preservation officer told me that if I wanted the site verified I would have to do it myself and I would have to get the necessary permits. The requirements of the permits dictated financial resources we did not have.

When I had first filed the report, I expected the federal authorities to swoop down on the wreck and run with it. In 1975, the federal government, in a very open and underhanded fashion, had attempted to seize the *Nuestra Señora de Atocha* from Mel Fisher after significant treasure was recovered and positive identification was made. They spent a small fortune fighting Fisher all of the way to the Supreme Court, ultimately losing. But they failed to show up this time. They knew there was no treasure involved.

Inside the Wildlife Service they were scratching their heads. First I was talking about Wilson's treasure with no supporting historical data, and now I was talking about *La Galga* and giving them all of the details and references to documents in Spain and survey information showing the all-important boundary, and a survey showing changes in the island itself. Ed Moses, director of District 5 and overseer of the Chincoteague refuge, wrote a memo to Walter Stieglitz:

> At the risk of sounding like I distrust everyone, I seriously believe the switch from Pirate Wilson's treasure to the La Galga by Amrhein is a subterfuge to get permission to use his 'Geometrics 856 portable magnetometer' on the refuge under

the guise 'preparing a detailed magnetic map necessary to evaluate possible test excavation sites' of La Galga. In reality, I believe he'll be trying to locate the pirate treasure he alleges to be there!! He's been totally thwarted in his efforts to get a contract with GSA on Wilson's treasure. Now he's generating all kinds of publicity and credible agency interest in the La Galga, a wreck that has been recorded as being 'extensively salvaged in the 18th century (from Smithsonian letter)

Guess we'll have to wait & see what develops.

Apparently, it was beyond the government's comprehension that a group of dedicated people would commit themselves to locating a shipwreck that had only historic value, was clearly in the public domain, and had no promise of financial reward.

The government took no steps toward verification of the site. It would have only cost the government several thousand dollars to do a magnetic verification, even factoring in bureaucratic inefficiency. I offered to make the demonstration for free. This is something they should have pursued. After all, the government has been claiming all ancient shipwrecks for themselves. This potential site was sitting under their own land and was going to be kept from public view. They ignored the literature which described the legend of a Spanish ship being responsible for the wild horses on the refuge. Instead, they would stick to their official position that the horses descended from abandoned stock of the colonists. The National Park Service historian, who had prepared the historical background report on Assateague Island, acknowledged the existence of *La Galga* in his report, but refused to entertain any connection of the famous legend with this shipwreck.

The summer of 1983 was one of many changes. For me, the search was over. It would be the last time that I would dive for the next fifteen years. For others, the pursuit of treasure was not over. Rick Cook and Alpha Quest Corporation were still looking for *La Galga*, the *San*

Lorenzo, and the other Ocean City wrecks. They hired archaeologist Daniel Koski-Karell to help them in their search.

By then I knew that Stewart's *Santa Clara* was in fact the American schooner called the *Hawk* that wrecked January 5, 1799. I would soon find the real origin of the *San Lorenzo* coins. It wasn't a Spanish ship, but an American brig called the *Samaritan* that wrecked in 1830.

The Spanish coins that were housed in the Ocean City Lifesaving Museum, and that were often referred to by Stewart, were real and certainly pointed to a shipwreck. But it was not Spanish. Later discoveries of coins on the beach pushed the date beyond 1820, the date Stewart attributed to his *San Lorenzo.* Some coins dated 1821 and 1822 came to light in 1981. By 1985, that date had gone to 1826 when Richard Cook had told me of other coin finds. To demonstrate the popularity of these coins in American commerce, an article in the *Baltimore Clipper* of October 31, 1839, said that around 1820, Spanish dollars were as common as American half-dollars were in 1839. Spanish coins passed as legal tender in the U.S. until 1857.

While at the Worcester County Library researching land and genealogical records for a reproduction sea chart I was working on, I had an unnerving experience. Before me were the field notes and survey transcriptions of a Mr. William Pitts, who had died only a few years before at the age of ninety-three. I had met Mr. Pitts back in 1981 and interviewed him for his local knowledge of coin finds and shipwreck legends. Pitts' notes included the transcription of John Henry's survey notes from the mid-eighteenth century for Worcester County. I had used these records before in analyzing the boundary line question. I had previously seen a roll of microfilm in the cabinet for the *Snow Hill Messenger and Worcester County Advertiser* for the 1830s and thought that it might be interesting to review for shipwrecks, but I was there for other research. As I studied Pitts' notes, something kept telling me to get up and get the microfilm. Finally, I gave in and put Pitts' notes on hold. I loaded the film, and within minutes, I found reference to a shipwreck. Just below the article was more news, news of the accidental death of William Pitts, the great-great-grandfather of William Pitts the surveyor:

DISTRESSING.

Was wrecked about five or six days ago, on the beach near Phoenix's Island in Worcester county, Md the brig Samaratin of Newburyport, with a cargo of mahogany and die wood. Hands all lost. Six of them were found along shore. She came on shore without masts or rigging.

William Pitts, son of Doctor John R. Pitts of Berlin, on Thursday last, whilst attempting to drive oxen to a cart, they became unruly, and upset the cart, and it unfortunately fell on him. He died about an hour after the occurrence, saying he was going to live with his pious mother who died a few days before.

From the *Snow Hill Messenger and Worcester County Advertiser*, December 6, 1830. *From microfilm at the Worcester County Library, Snow Hill, Maryland.*

Just above the article on William Pitts was posted news of the loss of the *Samaratin*. The cargo of mahogany and logwood told me the ship had come out of the Caribbean.

In the *Boston Columbian Centinal* of December 15, 1830, more information was found:

> Brig Samaritan from Honduras via Havana for New York was driven ashore on Sinepuxent Beach about December 1, 5-6 persons lost, said to be loaded with mahogany and hides.

This description was consistent with a ship that could be carrying money as cargo, possibly owned by a wealthy passenger leaving Mexico after their civil war in 1829, but not necessarily a large amount. Another demonstration of American ships carrying Mexican dollars or pieces of eight can be found in the *United States Gazette* of February 20, 1827, which described a land convoy carrying money from Mexico City to Veracruz that was to be loaded on board the *Eliza, Cato,* and *Rose* of Philadelphia, money that was destined for the Philadelphia mint. If one of these ships had been lost at Ocean City, Donald Stewart would have given it a Spanish name.

Although *La Galga's* discovery was behind us and her future uncertain, my adventure was by no means over. It was now up to me to finally expose the monumental fraud that had been perpetrated on the citizens and several governments of the United States related to the imaginary ship called the *San Lorenzo de Escorial* and her mythical connection to the wild horses of Assateague Island.

CHAPTER EIGHT
Cast Away in the Court
of the Admiralty

T here have been numerous discoveries of historic shipwrecks in the last forty years, many made by treasure hunters. Some ships had carried large amounts of treasure and others were of historic interest only, such as those related to the American Civil War.

The finders of these vessels all have at least one thing in common— the respective states where the shipwrecks were found would always rush in to claim them for themselves.

The most famous treasure find and resulting litigation was that of the *Nuestra Señora de Atocha*, a ship which wrecked off the Marquesas Keys southwest of Key West, Florida, in 1622. The *Atocha*, with twenty-seven other ships, left Havana, Cuba, for Cádiz, Spain, loaded with gold, silver, jewels, and other valuable New World commodities. The fleet met a severe hurricane dispersing the ships; the *Atocha* struck a reef that ripped open her hull causing her to sink and scatter her remains over many square miles of ocean floor. In 1971, Mel Fisher, who had searched for the *Atocha* for three years, located the first artifacts and commenced salvaging her scattered treasure and artifacts.

Fisher had a contract with the State of Florida that gave him seventy-five percent of the items salvaged and the State twenty-five percent. This arrangement had worked in the past with other treasure hunters.

Every one of these shipwreck discovery cases had something extremely significant in common. Something was actually found and brought up. In the SEA cases, not only was nothing found, but false statements had been made that something had been found, and the very identities of the "shipwrecks" were fabrications created by Donald Stewart and his Atlantic Ship Historical Society.

I waited patiently for Judge Ramsey, who was hearing the three SEA cases, to call for a hearing on my accusations of stock fraud, and more importantly the nonexistence of the *Santa Rosalea*. I was certain that he would.

On April 19, 1983, nearly a month after I had filed the motion to intervene, I received a copy of a letter addressed to Judge Ramsey from Ms. Judith Armold, assistant attorney general for the State of Maryland. She was forwarding a copy of an opinion handed down in the *Whydah* case, a pirate ship found at Cape Cod, Massachusetts, and that state attorney general's memorandum on jurisdictional issues. That business aside, she brought up my motion to intervene.

She said that my motion to intervene included "very serious and important allegations" about SEA and its officers and directors. That being said, she told Judge Ramsey that these allegations didn't bear on the jurisdictional arguments that the State had put before the court. She also argued that since these wrecks were state property, the federal court had no jurisdiction to entertain a suit against the State and were barred by the Eleventh Amendment. Ms. Armold did not grasp the fact that if my allegations were true, there was no state property present. But Ms. Armold made no objections to my right to intervene and said that "should the Court determine that further proceedings may be had in these cases, Mr. Amrhein's allegations would appear to merit serious consideration."

I felt reassured that the attorney general's office would be with me when the court came down on Stewart. It looked like Stewart's day of reckoning was near. But as I would soon find out, this would be the last time Ms. Armold would even hint that these allegations "merit serious consideration." The letter seemed almost routine at the time, but in hindsight it laid out to Judge Ramsey the extremely narrow path he was expected to walk. That is, ignore me and pretend there were actually four historic shipwrecks lying off Ocean City, Maryland.

Just prior to the State of Maryland entering the litigation, they asked for an extension of time to file their answer. It was granted, and before they filed, the state archaeologist, Tyler Bastain, contacted a Dr. John Harvey of the Johns Hopkins School of Medicine in Baltimore, who had knowledge of what was going on inside SEA. He was a friend of Bill Bane, stockholder and board member of SEA. Dr. Harvey had worked with Bill at the Navy's Underwater Swimmers School in Key West in the early 1960s. Dr. Harvey reported back to Maryland's archaeologist on April 7, 1981:

> I have personal knowledge of Mr. Stewart's overtures and misrepresentations to me that I brought to your attention a year ago. My investigation of his reputation at that time reinforced my negative impression of him; thereafter I had no further interest in his projects, until you wrote to me and I called my friend [Bill Bane] in Ocean City last week.
>
> Following that call, I reviewed a lot of documentary and conversational material about the proposed salvage operation. I will be pleased to share with you (or agents of any state or federal government) information, observations, and opinions that I have developed. In fact, I hope that competent authorities will respond to what I perceive as an incompetent operation that may well be laced with deception to the point of criminal fraud as defined from a variety of legal angles. My personal position is that of concern.... I see it being run by a man who, from my personal observation, I believe suffers from paranoid schizophrenia or from a neurosis that has palpable features of well-compensated paranoid schizophrenia.

Two days later, the State filed its first appearance and answered the claims of shipwreck discovery. They asked that the cases be dismissed on several legal points, but primarily it was the issue of jurisdiction. Their first argument was that the shipwrecks were property of the State, and they were immune from suit. The second was that discovery of the shipwrecks was merely alleged, and therefore the court did not have admiralty jurisdiction. The State never asked for an evidentiary hearing, which had there been one, the cases would have been dismissed before any decision would've been made as to ownership. The court could have, on its own motion, called for such a hearing but it did not.

For the next five months, SEA and the State traded jurisdictional arguments while the discovery team continued looking for the make-believe shipwrecks. Judge Ramsey, appearing to be narrowing in on the issues, ordered oral arguments set for October 21. Raymond Cardillo took over as sole attorney of record representing SEA and Atlantic Ship Historical Society. He had been thoroughly briefed by the corporate attorneys so that he would be prepared. At the hearing, the court led the parties to believe that a decision favorable to the plaintiffs would be forthcoming in a matter of days. Cardillo later recounted to the SEA board,

> This was made obvious by the fact that the Court had limited the State to seven (7) days within which to file post-hearing briefs; and the Court's statement to the effect that when the State appeals [his] decision nothing would be left undecided.

On October 29, 1982, the State submitted a supplemental brief. The State now seemed quite on the defensive. Apparently, Judge Ramsey was considering precluding the State from raising as a defense the obvious deficiency in the SEA complaint that nothing had been recovered from a wreck. The State said that it would be improper for the court to prevent them from "raising established principles of salvage law to defeat the Plaintiff's claims." The State then directed the court to a very important concept of admiralty law:

> ...this Court, sitting as a Court of Admiralty, would be obliged to apply settled principles of admiralty law and to recognize the deficiency of the plaintiffs' allegations. Since this deficiency goes to the heart of this Court's subject matter jurisdiction, it is a deficiency that cannot be waived by action of the State. The parties cannot confer on this Court subject matter jurisdiction that it does not otherwise possess.

What the State was saying was that on the face of the record, no shipwrecks had been discovered. Therefore, if there were no shipwrecks, there was no "subject matter" to create admiralty jurisdiction. There has to be a ship involved. To demonstrate the indispensability of this principle, one need only look to the *Titanic* and the *Central America* shipwreck cases decided in recent years. Those seeking these shipwrecks did not seek protection of the admiralty court until they had some tangible evidence of discovery. In the case of the *Central America*, it was merely a lump of coal retrieved with great difficulty from 8,000 feet of water. The salvors already had sidescan sonar images and a location, but they needed an artifact to perfect their claim. Otherwise, any treasure hunter or archaeologist who wanted a shipwreck could come into court, lay claim to the ocean bottom, and prevent others from salvage even though a vessel had not yet been found and no service rendered to a wreck.

But this would be the last time the State would admit to this critical deficiency. They wanted the question of ownership decided before any shipwreck was to be found. They wanted a legal precedent to use against the "evil-doers," the rapacious treasure hunters. They wanted equitable stature with Florida, Massachusetts, and Texas as they had dealt with treasure hunters. They wanted all shipwrecks for themselves. If the cases were dismissed because nothing had been found, they would have to wait another day to test their ownership theories.

So henceforth, Ms. Armold, for the State of Maryland, directed Judge Ramsey to focus only on the state's sovereign immunity, making it the primary threshold, and to look away from the allegations of no shipwrecks and fraud and the fact that the court had no subject matter jurisdiction to evaluate the state's claim of sovereign immunity. *"Judge, please proceed without an evidentiary hearing."*

In early April, I decided to do some sleuthing on Stewart in Baltimore. I dropped by the *Constellation* riding at the Pier One at the end of Pratt Street in the Inner Harbor. I walked onboard ship and went to the gift shop and office. There, I inquired if anyone was familiar with Donald Stewart. A woman, who obviously knew him, suggested I go over to the Star-Spangled Banner House Museum and see a Mr. Hugh Benet. This I did, as it was just up the hill from the *Constellation*.

When I arrived, I was directed to Mr. Benet's office, where he invited me to sit down.

"How can I help you?" he asked.

"I'm here to ask you about Donald Stewart."

Benet, a man in his late fifties or early sixties, gave a stifled laugh. "What kind of trouble are you in?!"

I explained to him my SEA experiences and Stewart's purported association with the *Constellation*. I told Mr. Benet that I was preparing to sue Stewart for fraud.

Benet then explained to me that Stewart was a dubious character and had been forced out of his so-called "directorship" of the *Constellation*. In Benet's words, Stewart was really just an office manager, but he was well known for his self-promotion as director of the ship.

Benet told me about the book called the *Constellation Question* that detailed an FBI analysis of a forged letter that was believed to be attributable to Stewart. He described a file that he had on Stewart that documented his phony captain's credentials, as well as a report from the State of Maryland about his activities with the State Naval Militia and his self-appointment as admiral. He also had several newspaper articles about Stewart. Benet suggested I go back to the *Constellation* to interview a particular employee about Stewart, which I did. Back aboard, I heard a rather humorous story about how Stewart had removed the life ring from the wheelhouse of his *Five Fathom* lightship and was seen painting the words "RMS Titanic" on it, no doubt a poor attempt at converting it into a valuable artifact.

By the time I left Baltimore, I was left with the impression that Stewart's reputation as a con artist was well known around the docks and among city officials.

Several days later, I received a package with copies of all of this material and a pledge from Benet that he would help out if needed.

On Sunday, April 24, a month after I had filed my motion to intervene, *The Baltimore Sun* featured on its front page these headlines: "Search for Treasure off Ocean City Is Shipwrecked on Rocky Finances."

Mary Corddry, the *Sun's* Eastern Shore bureau chief, had interviewed me at length, as well as Dr. Passwater, Stewart, Judith Armold with the State attorney general's office, and other investors. Stewart, to support his tales of treasure, offered the fact that Spanish coins had been found on the beach. The article also printed my counter-argument that said that the presence of Spanish coins do not necessarily mean that there were Spanish shipwrecks off the Ocean City beach since the coins passed as common currency at the time. The article went into some detail on the *San Lorenzo* story and Stewart's claim of possessing hundreds of pages of documentation that proved its existence. Mrs. Corddry even detailed Stewart's claim of treasure on the *San Lorenzo* for the readers. The paper also displayed a map of the coast of Ocean City that delineated the areas for all four shipwrecks. The *San Lorenzo* was clearly shown in the area between Tenth and Fourteenth Streets of Ocean City. The world now knew where to look for the so-called *San Lorenzo*.

When Mrs. Corddry confronted Stewart with the fact that my researcher in Spain could find no reference to the ship, he responded that she "must have been looking in the wrong archive." Stewart took the opportunity to connect his fictitious *San Lorenzo* with the wild Assateague horses by telling the *Sun* reporter that the *San Lorenzo* was also known as the *Santo Cristo*, the name given the mythical ship in *Misty of Chincoteague*. Stewart even admitted to the paper that the shipwrecks had not been found yet. And for the *Santa Rosalia*, the paper made it clear that records proved she was safely in Veracruz, Mexico, when Stewart claimed she was lost off of Ocean City. Mrs. Corddry also contacted Ms. Judith Armold and asked her why the State had not pressed for a decision. Her response was quite revealing: "I guess it was not believed that if anything was down there it would be worth a lot." Without thinking, she acknowledged that based on the State's information they had doubts of the ships' existence and of representations by Stewart that there was treasure involved.

The question that entered my mind then was, "Where did she get her information to base this assumption, and just as importantly, when did she get it?" Perhaps she had walked on board the *Constellation* and asked questions just as I had. It was only a little over a mile from her office on West Preston Street. It seemed to me at this point that the State of Maryland did not believe Stewart's representations made to the court and should have been backing me up. I became more confused as to what were the real motivations of the State of Maryland. It was troubling indeed. In my legal research, I found that if an officer of the court has reason to believe that fraudulent evidence has been presented to the court, that attorney or officer of the court is duty bound to alert the court of the fraud.

SEA scheduled its last meeting of stockholders for Saturday, April 30, and invited Stewart to attend. Stewart never showed up. SEA voted to dissolve and the board decided to "throw the ball in Stewart's court." The future of SEA was in his hands. All he had to do was prove what had already been played out on the front page of the *Sun*. In a telephone interview with the *Sun* that evening, Stewart said, "I'm going to throw it right back at them." In the local paper, Stewart's wife said he was too distraught to talk with reporters. She proclaimed, however, "Wait until his book comes out and we'll see who's right."

At that last SEA meeting, I explained the depth of my research related to Stewart's fraud to the investors. I also made it clear that if these ships were real, as he described, we did not need his research to locate them. The locations were now a matter of public record, as well as their alleged valuable cargo. The precise search areas were defined in the admiralty complaints and now, thanks to the *Sun*, the locations were known to hundreds of thousands of people. The locations were not needed, but rather proof that Stewart really had information that these ships truly existed and were actually located in the areas that had become public knowledge. Otherwise, I had said, we were all wasting our time and money.

At this point, Stewart had nothing to gain by withholding his sources. It made no sense for him not to state some verifiable source that would back up the shipwrecks he described. To further illustrate the point, he had published a very detailed account of the Spanish frigate, *Juno*, which he described as foundering on Fenwick Shoal in 1802 and published in the *Maryland Beachcomber* on May 22, 1981. If that story were true, all any treasure hunter would need to find that wreck would be to follow that story and go out to Fenwick Shoal with a magnetometer, which lies only five miles off of the north end of Ocean City. Years later, two treasure hunting companies would claim they found the *Juno* in two separate but unrelated locations from the one Stewart "gave freely" to the world.

The *Sun* published a follow-up on May 1 describing the efforts of the SEA investors and board of directors to get Stewart to prove the existence of the ships or the corporation would dissolve within thirty days. Judge Ramsey had still not taken any public or official action on my motion. I then reasoned that perhaps he thought it odd that I would attack one shipwreck as fraudulent and not mention the others. This, of course, was logical. On May 4, I filed a motion to intervene in the *San Lorenzo* case, which also included the *Santa Clara* because they both were described as being in the same location. The *San Lorenzo* story was quite easy to pick apart because Stewart had published so many details that could easily be contradicted. His fantasy about the Assateague horses was dismantled. The *Santa Clara* and *Royal George* were two shipwrecks that Stewart had given little information on, other than the years that they wrecked: 1798 for the *Santa Clara* and 1789 for the *Royal George*. These dates had only been verbally represented by Stewart. I knew that his only source for the *Santa Clara* was that Spanish colonial coins dating from that period had been found on the beach. By then I'd established that the American schooner, *Hawk*, had wrecked there in January 1799, on a return trip from Havana to Philadelphia. The *Hawk* would have had some 1798 coins on board that fit neatly into Stewart's *Santa Clara* hoax. This ship's identity as the *Hawk* was easily proven because her captain, William Carhart, was buried immediately opposite this site on the mainland in the area now known as Captain's Hill. The loss of the *Hawk* had also created the misidentity of the *Ocean Bird*, another of Stewart's frauds.

I also, to no surprise, found nothing on the *Royal George*. To intervene in that case, I would have to prove a negative, that is, the ship does not exist just because nothing could be found in the archives. Stewart could dance around that one. But disproving the *Santa Rosalea* and the *San Lorenzo* was easy because of the trail he had left. No one would believe the other two if it was proven that the *San Lorenzo* and *Santa Rosalea* were made up. So with this information, I now specifically said in regards to the *Santa Clara* and *San Lorenzo* that they "are not wrecked

Tombstone of Captain William Carhart of the schooner *Hawk*, Captain's Hill, West Ocean City, Maryland. The *Hawk* would become Stewart's *Santa Clara*. *Photo by the author.*

vessels and do not lie in the jurisdiction of the court. Documentation is available that proves the particulars of these vessels are fabrications," and that Donald Stewart had full knowledge of these facts and was using this "claim" to sell stock.

With this reasoning behind the second motion to intervene, I was again certain that Judge Ramsey would call an evidentiary hearing. But still, nothing happened.

Dr. Richard Passwater, now President of SEA, had had numerous discussions with me about Stewart's shipwrecks. SEA was now in the process of dissolution. Dr. Passwater had little doubt that I was correct, so he wrote to Judge Ramsey on June 13 and expressed the views of the current board of directors:

> The Board of Directors of S.E.A., Ltd. have been aware of Mr. Amrhein's motions since shortly after their filing. Mr. Amrhein is calling for an evidentiary hearing.... SEA not only makes no objection but hopes that the court will call such a hearing. The present Board has no knowledge of anything associated with the above referenced shipwrecks having been discovered as sworn to in Mr. Cardillo's Affidavit and Complaint of January 13, 1981, and January 22, 1981. In fact, the only persons claiming knowledge to the existence of the wrecks is the Atlantic Ship Historical Society and its President, Mr. Donald F. Stewart, and Mr. Raymond Cardillo. At this point, the Board of SEA, Ltd. is interested in knowing the truth as we are sure the court must be. Therefore, we strongly recommend that an evidentiary hearing be held to review the representations of Atlantic Ship Historical Society and its President, Mr. Donald Stewart, and Mr. Raymond Cardillo before any final decision be made. Meanwhile, we are at the disposal of the court.

Judge Ramsey had to have seen the last two articles in the *Sun* and known that SEA was finished. But he still made no decision on my motions to intervene. The only original party left standing was the State of Maryland and Stewart's Atlantic Ship Historical Society, which had always remained silent. The State hadn't communicated with the court since October the year before.

On May 18, I received a letter from the attorney general's office, but it wasn't from Judith Armold. Mr. K. Houston Matney with the Division of Securities said his office was aware of my allegations of securities fraud and invited me to get in touch with Mr. Jeffrey Chernow, and bring whatever evidence that I may have. I got in touch with Mr. Chernow, and on November 13 we met, where I submitted copies of the SEA stock prospectus and other promotional information. The prospectus clearly stated that *La Galga* was carrying a huge treasure. Stewart had listed the fleet's inventory as being over 30,000,000 pesos divided amongst the seven ships of the 1750 fleet. I showed him the May 16, 1980 *Maryland Beachcomber* article that specifically said *La Galga* was carrying 4,250,000 pesos and had a current valuation of between $20 and $30 million today. I explained to Mr. Chernow that this article had been handed out with the prospectus. I also pointed out in the prospectus that Stewart had claimed to have had extensive salvage and archaeological experience from 1949 to 1956. And then, I gave him proof that Stewart had actually worked as a clerk typist at the B&O Railroad from 1950 to 1956. I also gave Mr. Chernow the translated manifest of *La Galga*, which showed her to be carrying little treasure and included the statement, "This is not a treasure ship." The State did nothing until February 1984, when Mr. Chernow called Stewart in to discuss the prospectus. Stewart said he had never seen it before. The State dropped its investigation.

The year 1983 was drawing to a close and still nothing happened. By this time, I had gotten my case together and was prepared to file suit against Stewart, Atlantic Ship Historical Society, Cardillo, and the Firths. I found a law firm in Baltimore, Turnbull, Mix and Farmer, which had been recommended to me as a firm that would probably be willing to take the case. Out of the thirty-three investors, eleven, including me, were ready to sue. The ones who did not sign on refrained for various reasons. Some were friends of Stewart's. Some still wanted to believe Stewart; therefore, they didn't want to believe me. And there were some who knew they had been had, but didn't want the hassle. These people were, however, great "cheerleaders" who wanted us to succeed. It really troubled me that two of the investors had invested to hopefully gain a windfall for their handicapped children. Their hearts were certainly in the right place. For me, even though I had lost everything, I knew that I would recover.

On about January 18, 1984, I'd heard that a decision had been made in the admiralty cases. I called Dr. Passwater the next day to see if he knew anything, and he informed me that he had received the court decision issued by Judge Ramsey on January 10 from Cardillo and had assumed that I also had been sent a copy by the court. He related to me that the court gave the fictitious shipwrecks to the State of Maryland and denied my motion to intervene. I could not understand why the court had not contacted me. I called the clerk's office to request a copy of the opinion, which I received on January 20, and I read the opening lines with disbelief:

> Approximately two hundred years ago, three ships, believed to be carrying a king's ransom in gold alter plate and other riches, sank in the Atlantic Ocean after being battered by a fierce hurricane. The remains of these vessels and their cargo are currently submerged under an undetermined amount of sand off the shore of Ocean City, Maryland.

And later in the opinion, Judge Ramsey said,

> Plaintiffs and the State of Maryland agree, and the Court so finds that the defendant vessels and their cargo are situated off the shore of Ocean City, Maryland. The Court further finds that the defendant vessels and their cargo are within the territorial jurisdiction of his forum.

When he addressed my motion to intervene he said,

> Neither plaintiffs nor the State of Maryland have filed responses to Amrhein's motion. The Court denies Amrhein's

motion to intervene

And to justify his denial:

> Amrhein's claim of stock fraud is collateral and largely irrelevant to the thrust of the original action; that the adjudication of Amrhein's claim would unduly delay and complicate the adjudication of the controverted rights of the original parties and the State of Maryland; and the applicant can adequately protect his rights by instituting a separate proceeding.

He refused to address my sworn statement that there were no shipwrecks and SEA's admission of this fact. He made no mention of my sworn allegation that documentation was available to refute the very existence of the defendants in the case, the *San Lorenzo* and the *Santa Rosalia*. And his statements about actual treasure being aboard these make-believe ships cannot be supported by any part of the court record.

The court dismissed the cases because the State had a "colorable" claim to the shipwrecks, which meant that the Eleventh Amendment would bar these proceedings as they were suits against the State of Maryland. This colorable claim was an indirect way of saying the make-believe wrecks belonged to the State. And to reach that conclusion Judge Ramsey *had* to make the statement, "The Court further finds that the defendant vessels and their cargo are within the territorial jurisdiction of his forum."

The Baltimore Sun featured a story about the decision which included pictures of Judge Ramsey and me. The reporter reiterated my statements that none of the vessels had been found and specifically the *San Lorenzo* "never existed" and was a fabrication created by Donald Stewart, the former director of the USS *Constellation*.

I called my attorney, Doug Sachse, in Baltimore. He said that I would need an admiralty attorney to handle any appeal I would contemplate. Not knowing what to do, I called David Horan, Treasure Salvor's attorney in Key West, for advice. I had previously met Horan at a meeting of the Atlantic Alliance for Historical Preservation. He told me how to notice the appeal and gave me a ten-minute cram course on an *in rem* admiralty action. He explained that in this type of action you are suing a thing rather than a person, so the defendant is the ship itself and that there must really be one. A salvage claim resembled a mechanic's lien where the salvor can claim compensation from an owner for services rendered in rescuing the distressed property, but, he explained, there must in fact be some distressed property and something that in fact needs to saved. These were jurisdictional prerequisites that would need to be met before a federal court could entertain a case in admiralty.

On Saturday, January 21, 1984, I mailed my notice of appeal to the district court, which was received and docketed on Monday, January 22. The clerk at the court of appeals mailed me a form called an "informal brief" which was used when litigants represented themselves without an attorney.

On January 27, the investor suit was filed in the Circuit Court for Worcester County, Maryland, situated in Snow Hill, against Donald Stewart, Atlantic Ship Historical Society, Inc., Raymond Cardillo, and Rick and Robert Firth for fraudulent and negligent misrepresentation in the sale of SEA stock. This was the same little town that Captain Huony and his crew marched to back in 1750.

I realized that the federal court's opinion was very damaging to my fraud and negligence suit that we had just filed. I also realized that I had no money for an attorney, and it would be difficult to get the other plaintiffs to contribute. Doug Sachse had agreed to take the fraud suit on a contingency basis, but could not assist me with the admiralty cases. It was apparent that I would have to go it alone and hopefully consult an attorney when the opportunity arose. I set off to the law library at the Library of Congress and began studying case law and treatises on admiralty law. My research expanded into the *Federal Rules of Civil Procedure*, and into jurisdiction, fraud and negligence theories, and even constitutional law. What I was preparing for now was more serious than any college exam I had ever crammed for. Fortunately, my previous job in Washington had trained me not only to interpret a comprehensive set of government regulations, but also to write papers on the corporate position related to these regulations while it dealt with certain government agencies. But at the time, what I did not know was who I was preparing to go up against. It was not Stewart or Cardillo, but the Office of the Attorney General of Maryland and Judge Ramsey himself.

I reread Judge Ramsey's opinion. There was no factual basis for his conclusions. It was if he really hadn't read what I said in my motion to intervene at all. There was enough contradictory information about Stewarts's lies in the *Sun* to anger any judge who was hearing the case. When SEA filed no official response to my sworn statements that no shipwrecks were present, Judge Ramsey had enough then to call an evidentiary hearing or dismiss the SEA suit on that premise alone. Dr. Passwater's request by letter for an evidentiary hearing, although not part of the official public record, certainly should have cleared up any doubts in the judge's mind. Although Dr. Passwater's letter was not sworn testimony, Judge Ramsey certainly knew which way he would testify if an evidentiary hearing were called.

On February 6, I wrote the judge a letter. I reiterated the obvious facts that there were no shipwrecks, that all we found was junk, and that the identities of the wrecks were fabrications. I then asked him why he stated in his opinion that they were real, had been found, and were worth a "king's ransom." And I pointed out that for some reason he also failed to copy me with the court's opinion addressing the denial of my motion.

On February 15, Judge Ramsey replied short and sweet:

> Since you have appealed, it would be utterly inappropriate for me to engage in any discussion or debate with you concerning my Opinion in the captioned cases.
> Very truly yours,
> Norman P. Ramsey
> United States District Court Judge

I thought to myself that he was probably correct about not discussing the case because of the appeal, but I also knew that he was going to get another opportunity to redeem himself.

In preparation for my appeal, I would research and write my brief during the day, and in the evening Delphine, my fiancée at the time, would type and edit for grammatical mistakes. I asked for and received an extension of time to file my brief. My appeal brief was then filed March 27. I explained to the court of appeals that the district court had sent me an untimely notice of its opinion, which was my reason for being a day late. I also wrote a detailed memorandum on the district court's abuse of discretion. This is what I had to prove to overcome a denial of permissive intervention. I pointed out that not only had the court abused its discretion in denying my motion to intervene, but the court also abused its discretion by proceeding to a conclusion, knowing that nothing had been found. Simply put, the court selectively chose to accept part of the record while ignoring other parts.

On March 9, Judith Armold, for the State, filed a motion to dismiss my appeal. She raised two issues. One was that I filed one day late and failed to ask for an extension of time as required by the court rules, and second, any appeal would be moot and could serve no purpose. She directed the appellate court's attention to my statement that there were no shipwrecks but she said that this had nothing to do with the Eleventh Amendment issue. She never could understand that if there were no shipwrecks, there was no state property at stake, and therefore the State had no standing to make the Eleventh Amendment argument. She did not, however, address my contention that the particulars of the shipwrecks were complete fabrications, i.e. fraudulent. It was always her strategy to make me look like a disgruntled investor who was angry just because no shipwrecks had been found.

When the State of Maryland appeared for the first time in the SEA admiralty suits, it filed affidavits by J. Rodney Little, State Historic Preservation Officer and Director of the Maryland Historical Trust, and Tyler Bastian, State Archaeologist. In Mr. Little's affidavit, he elaborated on his years of experience in the fields of historic preservation and underwater archaeology. He said his staff also had individuals with specific training, experience, and expertise in the field of underwater archaeology. Mr. Little went on to swear,

> That if the Plaintiffs' beliefs concerning the identity of the Defendant Vessels are correct, the vessel may be of great historic significance; it will apparently have survived unmolested for many years and may therefore contain invaluable historic and scientific information, which should be preserved for the benefit of the people of Maryland and the United States.

Mr. Little held a unique position. His job as State Historic Preservation Officer has certain mandates from the federal government. The law directs individuals in his position to inventory all historic properties in cooperation with government agencies, private organizations, and individuals. In its 1983 annual report, The Maryland Historical Trust stated: "Listing and documenting all of Maryland's historic properties has been a central goal of the Trust from the beginning."

Tyler Bastian, the state archaeologist, testified that he searched for record of a permit application from SEA, Ltd. He acknowledged that he knew of SEA's activities and sent Raymond Cardillo a permit application in October of 1980. Tyler Bastain made no comment on the investigation he had done on Donald Stewart and SEA the year before. Both of these state officials had to have been aware of Stewart's *San Lorenzo* since it was first published in *The Baltimore Sun* in July of 1977.

On April 17, 1984, Ms. Armold for the State filed her response and went on the attack:

> This appeal is evidently motivated by the Appellant's unhappiness with the District Court's resolution of the legal issues raised by the State. The Appellant apparently fears that the Court's decision will affect exploration and recovery activities that he may wish to conduct in Maryland waters. He seems to be concerned about the implications of the District Court's decision for any similar case that he might institute in the future.

The assistant attorney general was trying to preserve the lower court precedent for the same reason that they said I was in opposition to it—

that the decision could be used against treasure hunters in future cases. As long as there was no evidentiary hearing, the State could portray me to the court and the media as a disgruntled investor who had lost money in a treasure hunt. But if an evidentiary hearing were called, the State would surely lose its precedent and its own expertise in maritime history would be called into question. Obviously, the State and Ms. Armold felt it necessary to reaffirm their clean hands in the matter, for they further stated:

> For purposes of its motion in the lower court, the State assumed the truth of the plaintiffs' allegations, even though the State has never had knowledge on which to base an opinion as to the truth or falsehood of those allegations.

The State of Maryland was now trying to persuade the Court that even though over three years had gone by since the filing of the suit and six years since they became aware of the *San Lorenzo*, they were still insisting that knew nothing about the *San Lorenzo* or any of the other alleged wrecks. It was unfathomable that J. Rodney Little, Director of the Maryland Historical Trust, was not interested enough to investigate the *San Lorenzo*. But Ms. Armold apparently knew more than what she was telling the court. She apparently had forgotten that the year before she had told the *Sun* paper that it, "Was not believed that if anything was down there it would be worth a lot." By that statement it appeared she did know the truth, especially since she was contradicting Judge Ramsey's statement in his opinion that the vessels had been found and were believed to be carrying a "king's ransom" in treasure. The State always led the court to believe that the State believed that the vessels were real. Ms. Armold also had forgotten that the State had argued vigorously on October 29, 1982, prior to my entry into the case, the relevancy of my own later argument about the lack of proof of shipwrecks:

> Since this deficiency goes to the heart of this Court's subject matter jurisdiction, it is a deficiency that cannot be waived by

action of the State. The parties cannot confer on this Court subject matter jurisdiction that it does not otherwise possess.

The State was playing both sides of the issue.

When news of the State of Maryland's victory over SEA circulated among the historical and archaeological community, it was lauded as a great triumph for historical preservation. This was clearly demonstrated in the quarterly newsletter of The Society for Historical Archaeology dated March 1984:

> The State of Maryland has received a very favorable decision in a treasure salvage lawsuit.... The judge specifically declined to follow some of the terrible precedents set by the Florida and Texas treasure hunting lawsuits. This case is highly significant in terms of the prospects of preservation of historic shipwreck sites instead of their destruction through commercial exploration.

Had they only known the truth. Their exuberance was a result of their blind disdain for treasure hunters that "destroy" shipwreck sites. This popular notion, spread by academic and government archaeologists, is based on their contention that treasure hunters bring up artifacts without properly recording their location or provenience on the bottom. This recording needs to be done so that each artifact's position can be analyzed in relation to other surrounding artifacts. In this way, an accurate picture may be developed of the entire site. Provenience is a buzz word used by archaeologists, particularly when criticizing treasure hunters. The situation in Maryland was ludicrous. Maryland officials were now insisting that four make-believe shipwrecks remain in the public record as if they were real. The importance of artifact provenience was thrown out the window.

Knowing Mr. Little's responsibilities and that of the Maryland Historical Trust, I paid their office in Annapolis a visit on September 11, 1984.

I found the staff very friendly and ready to answer questions. (I didn't tell them who I was.) They produced the archaeological inventory map covering the Ocean City area. I looked up and down the entire coast and could not find any notations for shipwrecks. I did see some outlines drawn on the mainland areas that extended out into the water. The staff member informed me that the dotted lines indicated a suspected site for Indian habitation, but it had not been verified. I told him I had read in the newspaper that there were some old shipwrecks found at Ocean City. He matter-of-factly said, "They are not really there." I, of course, told him that they knew this because of me. I did not need to see any more, so I left.

When I logically examined the latest findings, I came to two conclusions. One, if the State had made no investigation concerning the alleged wrecks, they probably would've been included in the State's inventory as mandated. Second, if they had done an investigation, they would have *easily* found, just as I did, that the shipwrecks were fabrications. The State wouldn't include shipwrecks they believed to be fabrications in the State's inventory. These shipwrecks were not in their inventory.

The next day I sent a letter to Mr. Tyler Bastian with a copy to Mr. Little and Ms. Judith Armold telling them of my findings and asked for someone to please verify the State's procedures for recording reported archaeological sites. I pointed out that the federal court had previously declared on December 21, 1983, that the shipwrecks do lie off Ocean City, Maryland, and had historical and archaeological value within the meaning of Maryland's Natural Resource Code. I also pointed out that the State of Maryland made no objections to these findings. I never received a response.

The "guardians" of our historical heritage, the very ones who argued the importance of the position of a single artifact on an archaeological site, were now allowing four fabricated "shipwrecks" to be inserted into the maritime history of Maryland. They were happy to let them remain in the public record as if they, in fact, existed. But the State knew they didn't exist. And now the taxpayers of Maryland were paying for a costly defense to uphold Judge Ramsey's opinion, which would never have been issued but for Stewart's fraud.

September 1984 was a memorable month. Delphine Cook and I were married on the 29th. We were both looking forward to getting this shipwreck business out of our lives. By now *La Galga* was clearly on the back burner—the federal government was content to ignore it. My only interest was to deal with Stewart's fraud related to the treasure he claimed to be aboard her. That was the reason SEA had been formed in the first place.

There were now greater responsibilities. I was also stepfather to Delphine's seven-year-old son Shane. To Delphine's credit, she supported me in my legal efforts because she realized it was something that had to be done.

Before the Fourth Circuit Court of Appeals decided my case, Stewart and the other defendants in the fraud suit filed a demurrer with the Worcester County Circuit Court, asking that the case be dismissed. They claimed that the plaintiffs, including myself, couldn't litigate the issue of the existence of the ships because the federal court had found in the SEA cases that the *San Lorenzo* and the other shipwrecks were real and were, in fact, carrying a king's ransom and were in fact located off Ocean City, Maryland, within the jurisdiction of the federal court. They recited verbatim the erroneous language Judge Ramsey used in his opinion.

This made me realize that Stewart and Cardillo had formidable allies with Judge Ramsey and the State Attorney General now representing their interests. I felt as if the walls were caving in around me. The legal system was not what I had expected. It was like being mugged in an alley only to escape and run to a policeman for help, but then being robbed and beaten by him as well.

On May 21, the Fourth Circuit Court of Appeals dismissed my appeal because I had filed one day too late. Nothing was said about the merits of my case. I called David Horan in Key West for advice. He said that he was coming to Ocean City, Maryland, on June 14 for a symposium on the SEA cases, which was part of the Maryland State Bar

Association's annual meeting. The topic was called "Treasure Salvage at Sea—Is There Gold off 9th Street, and Who Owns and Controls It Under State, Federal and Admiralty Law?" David Horan was going to present a paper arguing against the proposed Abandoned Shipwreck Act, which was going to give all historic wrecks within the three-mile territorial limits of the states to each respective state. He said I should drop by, and we could talk then.

I arrived at Convention Hall the morning of the meeting. The session started at eleven, and I was a little late. I walked in and went to the registration desk where I picked up a program. The receptionist noticed that I wasn't wearing a name tag and asked if I was an attorney. I said that I wasn't, so she said that I wouldn't be allowed in. I knew that protesting would draw too much attention to myself, so I thanked her and pretended to leave. I glanced back and found that she wasn't looking so I quickly turned a corner where I found a stairwell and scrambled to the second floor. There, I located the conference room by the sign on its closed door. I quietly opened it to find the room darkened to accommodate slide presentations, so I slipped in and took a seat. Looking around, I recognized Horan up front and Tyler Bastian, Maryland's State Archaeologist, who was speaking. There were quite a few people there, but no one from SEA.

Bastian was apparently talking about the shipwrecks when someone in the audience interrupted him and said that there were allegations that these shipwrecks were not real. He avoided the question. Judith Armold took the podium next. It wasn't long before she was asked the same question from the audience about the wrecks. She brushed it off.

I couldn't sit still any longer. I looked around, took a deep breath, and stood.

"I'm John Amrhein and I can tell you for sure that these wrecks do not exist. This whole thing is a fraud!" I blurted. "I can prove it!"

There was pandemonium. Up front, a man stood and shouted back to me, "Amrhein, don't go anywhere, I want to see you!" I had no idea who he was or what he wanted. The meeting ended soon after that, and I was rushed by several reporters. It was the reporters who had been asking the questions. While they were interviewing me, Judith Armold approached, introduced herself, and politely said how glad she was that I could make it. I told the reporters that I found that statement hard to believe, and furthermore she didn't want to hear what I had to say. I took the opportunity to tell her in front of them that this whole thing was a complete fraud and she knew it. Then I walked away to find Horan.

He was in the hall talking with the gentleman who had stood up earlier. When this fellow saw me, he said out loud, "Amrhein, you've been had!" He obviously wanted everyone to hear him. He then introduced himself as David Owen, an admiralty attorney from Baltimore, who happened to be from Semmes, Bowen, and Semmes, the same firm where Judge Ramsey had once practiced. He also told me he had been past president of the Maritime Law Association of the United States. He went on to say that a travesty of justice had occurred in Ramsey's court. He was obviously very aggravated and emotionally involved with the court's findings. Mr. Owen explained to me that he had been researching and writing a law review article criticizing Judge Ramsey's opinion and that he was following everything that I had been doing. "Amrhein, I am proud of you, you're right on track, keep it up!" I told him I was exploring the idea of a new motion. He offered to send me a copy of his article as soon as it was out.

On June 27, Judge Dale Cathell in Worcester County Circuit Court heard oral arguments on the demurrer to strike certain counts from our fraud suit because of Judge Ramsey's findings. One of these was the defendant's insistence that I could not raise the issue of the vessels' nonexistence since Judge Ramsey said that the *San Lorenzo* and the others did exist, even though they knew they didn't. One of the counts in our complaint said that our SEA stock was worthless because of the fraud. Stewart's attorneys argued that the stock was worthless because Judge Ramsey gave the ships to Maryland.

On August 6, Judge Cathell ruled, "The ships have been determined by law to be present as represented." Thanks to the Maryland attorney general's office, the issue of the existence of the ships had never been litigated. This was a huge blow to our case.

On August 30, I filed a motion to vacate the judgment dismissing the complaint and denying my motion to intervene with the federal district court. I was asking the court to vacate its judgment of its denial of my motion to intervene because the court's jurisdiction was acquired by fraud. I also pointed out that there must be a real case or controversy, not a hypothetical one.

SEA, for a second time and although defunct, wrote a letter to Judge Ramsey saying that they did not object to my motion. But the State of Maryland did.

Ms. Armold now argued that I had no standing to bring this motion since I was not a party. And I was not a party because the court had denied my motion to intervene and that I had tried to appeal that decision but I was a day late. Catch-22. She never addressed my argument that this was not a real case but a contrived one.

On September 17, Judge Ramsey denied my last motion on the grounds that I was not a party to the lawsuit. He ignored that part which related to my motion to intervene.

I appealed. In addition to submitting my required brief, I petitioned the Fourth Circuit Court of Appeals to permit me to appear as an *amicus curiae* or "friend of the court" in case the court ruled I had no standing. As a friend of the court, I wanted the opportunity to demonstrate to the appeals court the fraud that was perpetrated in the lower court since the lower court (or the State) obviously didn't care.

Now the State attacked my request to appear as amicus curiae:

> Any fraud of which the plaintiffs below might be guilty would not taint the District Court's judgements and, accordingly, there is no need to make the Appellant an Amicus. The State has no knowledge concerning these claims; however, the State believes that, even if the claims are true, they would not taint the District Court's judgements. Certainly the State participated in the lower court proceedings in good faith, and the Appellant does not suggest the contrary.

The State's contention that they had "no knowledge concerning these claims" was indeed troubling in light of the fact that the State had an obligation to investigate these "archaeological sites" and include them in the State inventory. The fact that they were not included was an admission that the Maryland Historical Trust knew that they were a hoax. In addition, when Ms. Armold told the *Sun*, "I guess it was not believed that *if* anything was down there it would be worth a lot," further indicated that the State knew what was going on. These facts were in direct contradiction to what the State had sworn in court on April 17, 1984, that it "assumed the truth of the plaintiffs' allegations, even though the State has never had knowledge on which to base an opinion as to the truth or falsehood of those allegations."

In my brief in answer to these latest statements by the attorney general's office, I chose not to accuse the State of bad faith. Rather I chose to point the court toward the fact that they had prior knowledge. I submitted a copy of Dr. Harvey's letter to Tyler Bastain, which drew attention to the fact that the State was not operating in the dark. They had been alerted to the questionable character of Donald Stewart before they ever entered the litigation. His affiliation and conduct aboard the USS *Constellation* in Baltimore Harbor was most likely known to them as well. I pointed out that the State was always hesitant to give full faith to SEA's allegations. I also directed the court to consider the following legal precept:

> It is not only the right, but the duty of an attorney of the court, if he knows or has reason to believe that the time of the court is being taken up by the trial of a feigned issue, to inform the judge thereof.

I also described to the appellate court my visit to the Maryland Historical Trust and documented the fact that the state had not inventoried the shipwreck sites as required by law. I also told the court that I received no response from anyone from Maryland when I questioned this failure. I reiterated that my sole purpose of intervention in the first place was to protect my interests in the fraud suit.

After filing this latest appeal, I realized that Judge Ramsey had never docketed a formal order denying my motion to intervene; he merely said in his opinion that he intended to. When I checked the *Federal Rules of Civil Procedure*, I found that such orders are of no effect until docketed. This meant that all I had to do was inform the district court (Judge Ramsey) of its (his) mistake, get the order docketed, and then file my appeal. This time I would not be a day late.

On December 3, I filed my motion requesting the court to issue its belated order of denial. Once my order denying my motion to intervene was entered, I would then be appealing for the court's abuse of discretion.

I went on to inform the appellate court that my interests could not be protected in another court since the lower court's erroneous findings were now being used against me and the other plaintiffs in Worcester County.

When I filed both motions to intervene, Atlantic Ship Historical Society made no response. SEA unofficially responded by letters to Judge Ramsey. The official record of the case does not include that correspondence. On the record, no exception was taken to my sworn allegations. And consistent with my allegations, the State had previously pointed out to the court that no objects from the shipwrecks had been recovered or verified. I pointed out to the court that this lack of response could be construed as an admission of my allegations under the *Federal Rules of Civil Procedure*. And to make things even clearer to the court, I pointed out that if Cardillo had originally acted in good faith, he would most certainly have conducted an investigation on his own into my allegations of the fraudulently contrived shipwrecks and responded to the court with his own findings. It appears that all he did was "circle the wagons" with Stewart and wait it out.

I argued that being shut out of both courts was a denial of due process. And in closing I said, "Where the court has to weigh the conflicting doctrines of putting an end to litigation as opposed to the doctrine of equity and fair play," a previous court had stated, "We believe the truth is more important than the trouble it takes to get it."

On December 12, the State of Maryland, in its effort not to waive its Eleventh Amendment protection, appeared "specially," not to argue any Eleventh Amendment issue, but to urge the court to deny my motion to docket the belated orders and enter them *nunc pro tunc*, meaning "now for then." In other words, they wanted to show the date of denial as the same date of the opinion so that I would have no right to appeal. Ms. Armold said I had previously appealed and lost and shouldn't get a second chance. She needed to be reminded that since my first appeal was a day late, there was, in reality, no appeal of law or fact. And of course, there was no order to appeal from. She was wrong again.

Ms. Armold went on to challenge my allegations of fraud on the court. She said, "The State has no knowledge concerning Mr. Amrhein's allegations of fraud." Ms. Armold continued, "Any falsity in the facts alleged in the complaints would clearly have been exposed by the normal adversary process, if those facts had been placed at issue and had been material to this Court's decision." She had forgotten that the State was the only one who could place those facts "at issue" until I came along. As far as materiality, Judge Ramsey acknowledged that threshold when he stated unequivocally in his opinion that the shipwrecks existed.

On December 17, Judge Ramsey denied my motion to correct the record. His stated reason was that he had not heard from the court of appeals on my motion to amend the record there.

On December 22, I filed another motion to enter the orders of denial but pointed out that the court should wait until we both heard from the court of appeals. On January 18, Judge Ramsey denied my request again without hearing from the court of appeals.

In Worcester County, Judge Cathell issued his ruling on the latest demurrers to our amended complaint. He refused to accept the defendant's arguments that I and the other plaintiffs had no case because the shipwrecks do exist by virtue of Judge Ramsey's opinion. Our fraud suit would proceed and discovery began.

In March of 1985, David Owen sent me his law review article criticizing Judge Ramsey's opinion in the SEA cases. It was published in the *Journal of Maritime Law and Commerce*, April, 1985. As I read, I found that the thrust of his arguments were very close to my own. His thesis was that the suits were properly dismissed but for the wrong reason. Mr. Owen stated that "on the face of the complaint" the court lacked jurisdiction because there was nothing salvaged, there was no evidence of a shipwreck.

After thirty-three pages of analysis, he summarized his own legal conclusions on Judge Ramsey's opinion:

> What *Subaqueous* [SEA, Ltd.] amounts to is, in legal effect but most assuredly not by design, an advisory opinion to the Attorney General of Maryland. It is elementary that a federal court has no power to render such an opinion.

And he cited the Supreme Court to back up his conclusion.

Doug Sachse was elated with this development. The defendant's attorneys had invoked the doctrine of "collateral estoppel" which means that once an issue of fact has been determined in one court it need not be tried in another. David Owen's law review shot holes into Stewart's perverted defense.

It was not until April 26 that the court of appeals handed down its decision. The court denied my motion for leave to appear as amicus curiae to demonstrate the fraud perpetrated in the district court. They also denied my motion to vacate Ramsey's judgment since I was not a party to the case. I was not made a party to the case because Ramsey did not want an evidentiary hearing. My only recourse to establish standing in the case would be the Supreme Court. There was one ray of sunlight; one glimmer of hope. In a footnote, the court of appeals noted that the district court had failed to set forth in a separate document the court's denial of my motion to intervene as required by the *Federal Rules of Civil Procedure*. Thus the time to appeal had never begun to run. "If Amrhein is so disposed, he may file a new notice [of appeal] from that order." I felt at least partially vindicated, as it proved the violations of basic civil court procedure made by Judge Ramsey. But it was not over.

As soon as the records were returned to the district court, the State of Maryland, in direct contradiction to the ruling of the Fourth Circuit Court of Appeals, filed another motion, "strongly urging" the district court to enter the orders as effective on the earlier date of December 21,

1983. This would prevent me from filing a valid appeal even though the appellate court said the time had not started to run. I was forced to respond.

On June 7, besides including all of my previous jurisdictional arguments, I challenged the State's standing to file its latest motion. I pointed out that the State's claim of ownership and sovereign immunity were based solely on the truthfulness of the plaintiffs' complaints. As expected, Judge Ramsey ignored me.

In July of 1984, I had written to Mr. Edwin Bearss, Chief of the History Division for the National Park Service, to inform him of our pending fraud suit. I explained to him that Stewart had represented to the SEA investors that the National Park Service had accepted his *San Lorenzo* story. I copied him with my analysis of the *San Lorenzo* hoax and the numerous facts that were clearly refuted and left no doubt that the entire story was a fraud. Mr. Bearss wrote back on July 19 after reviewing my findings. His letter was most informative:

> Thank you for your documentation of evidence which refutes claims by Donald Stewart on the *San Lorenzo* shipwreck. Having checked records at the Port of La Habana, we have been aware of the inadequacies of his story for some time.... The previously published Assateague handbook does give a broadened account of the report submitted by Mr. Stewart. While this makes colorful reading, the story is apparently not supportable.... I have been informed that a first revision to the handbook will take place early next year, and at that time all reference to the *San Lorenzo* story will be deleted.... The employees at Assateague Island have discounted the research of Donald Stewart since the later part of 1979.... It is indeed unfortunate that at no time did any potential investor approach the seashore staff for a discussion of the issue. Had that been done, an account of Mr. Stewart's problems with material would certainly have been divulged.

Immediately after filing my June 7 brief, I realized I needed to get evidence of Stewart's fabrication of the *San Lorenzo* and other shipwrecks into the record in front of Judge Ramsey since it was obvious that Judge Ramsey was not going to call an evidentiary hearing. The latest ruling of the court of appeals opened the door for me to introduce the actual evidence of Stewart's fabrications. The ruling of the appellate court implied that the record was still open and subject to amendment. But I would have to submit the evidence before Judge Ramsey officially denied my motions to intervene.

Discovery had started in Worcester County so it was no longer necessary to hold back what I had. I filed a motion to amend my original motion to intervene in the *San Lorenzo* case and attached my report and analysis as to why this shipwreck was clearly a fabrication. I also included the letter from the National Park Service. This move would make it extremely difficult for Judge Ramsey to continue to ignore the truth. If he overlooked the statement of the National Park Service historian, he would become a willing accomplice to fraud in his court.

I mailed my motion to amend on Monday, June 10, and it was received by the court the next day and docketed by the clerk. The State of Maryland filed no response.

Judge Ramsey had known since late April that he was required to issue the order of denial as directed by the court of appeals. Finally, on Friday June 14, I received Judge Ramsey's denial of my motions to intervene, but something didn't seem right. On the order, the place for the day was left blank when it was typed, only the month and year typed in. The order was dated the tenth by a handwritten notation. This in and of itself was of no real concern, but the envelope to me was dated Wednesday the twelfth, two days after the record said Judge Ramsey had signed it, and one day after the court had received my evidence. According to the rules of civil procedure, the clerk of court is supposed to mail court orders immediately. (This certainly makes sense because some poor litigant could end up a day late with his appeal.)

There were more irregularities. The court docket for the *San Lorenzo* case did not show my motion to amend the pleadings. It was put in the *Santa Rosalea* file. Also the clerk certified the mailing date of the order as Monday, the tenth, yet it wasn't postmarked until the Wednesday, the twelfth. I wrote to the clerk, pointed out the discrepancy, and asked for an explanation. I received no response so I wrote to Judge Ramsey as well. The required copy was also sent to the Maryland attorney general. I directed Judge Ramsey to the contents of the exhibit that blew apart the *San Lorenzo* hoax. This included the admission by the National Park historian that the *San Lorenzo* was unsupportable in the historical record. In my letter, I pointed out that neither the State of Maryland nor Stewart and his historical society had responded to this latest evidence. Their silence could only be construed as an admission of the facts. Further, I argued that since no one objected to the evidence, he could proceed without prejudice. I told him that because there was provable fraud it was still within his power to review the evidence and that "This thing has become a fraud on the whole world." In any event, I was forced to concede: "I understand that the court received the motion the day after the order denying my motions to intervene became effective." But, I reminded him that, once again, there was an open motion that he needed to address. This was the second time I needed to remind the judge about basic rules of court procedure and to properly dispose of a motion. He received the letter July 12, 1985.

On August 5, he responded:

> I have received your letter concerning your motion to supplement pleadings. As you noted, that motion was not received until after the orders denying your motions to intervene became effective. I accordingly denied the motion to supplement as moot on July 12, 1985 by sidenote.

Maryland remained silent and accepted the fruits of Stewart's fraud. They had a precedent to use against treasure hunters. And the truth about the wild ponies of Assateague Island was going to be kept out of the official record. Once I saw what had happened with the dates on the orders, I decided that I would not appeal the motion to intervene. If I appealed, I could not call the evidence I had just submitted to Judge Ramsey to the appellate court's attention since the record showed it had been received one day after Judge Ramsey's order of denial. For over two years, I had tried to get the truth entered into the district court admiralty proceedings but was road blocked by either Maryland's attorney general or a recalcitrant judge. *But why?*

When I'd first filed the motions, the idea had been to force Stewart into federal court, hopefully in front of an angry judge. Now, every time I moved the court, Maryland's attorney general was, in effect, rushing in to Stewart's defense. If an evidentiary hearing were called, I would more than likely be faced with the attorney general representing Stewart's interests, which would only make my case more tenuous in Worcester County. I realized that discretion was the better part of valor.

I would not appeal. Rather, I thought it best that these cases should stay just as they are. Years in the future, the record would speak for itself. I also knew that some day this case would go before the highest court in the land, the Court of Public Opinion.

CHAPTER NINE
Rosalia's Revenge

"Umbram fugat Veritas"
—Out of darkness truth

Part of my attack on Stewart included a claim against him in small claims court for an underwater metal detector he "borrowed" from Garrett Electronics. Stewart had always told me where the detector had come from, and I found that in 1983, he had filed an insurance claim stating it had been "stolen." He kept the money for himself. I contacted Mr. Garrett to see if he had received either the detector or any money from Stewart. He said he had not heard from him for several years. Mr. Garret had agreed to sell me his rights in the detector for one dollar so I could then (hopefully) sue and recover the detector or its value. To support my case, he sent me the bill of sale. I also got statements from the insurance agent regarding the money Stewart had received. I figured this little demonstration into Stewart's character would be beneficial later. I had successfully filed a small claim for a debt owed to me, so it seemed simple enough that an attorney would not be necessary. I also didn't expect that Stewart would get one or even show up.

On court day, March 21, 1984, Bill Bane accompanied me to the District Court of Worcester County in Snow Hill, and was there to testify on my behalf. Judge Robert Horsey from Somerset County was on the bench. I saw Stewart stroll in with someone I did not know, and Bane muttered, "Oh no!" I asked what was wrong, and he identified the man as Steve Smethurst, apparently Stewart's attorney. Smethurst needed no introduction. He had a reputation as a smart, hardball attorney. He had represented my fiancée, Delphine, in her recent divorce. I took a deep breath and collected my thoughts.

My case was called, so I approached the bench and advised Judge Horsey that I was proceeding without an attorney and begged his patience. He was very polite and said that I could do whatever I liked. I figured I'd better take the stand and state my case before I called Stewart. This I did, with no objection from Smethurst, and after stepping down, I called Stewart to the witness stand. Smethurst jumped to his feet and, while pointing at me, proclaimed, "This man is an interloper, judge. He has no right to be here!" As I tried to speak, Smethurst told the judge that my letter and bill of sale from Garret gave me no right to be there. Horsey, as if on queue, looked down on me and demanded, "What gives you the idea you could come in here like this!?" Before I could return an answer, the red-faced Horsey slammed his gavel down and said, "I find for the defendant, case dismissed!" I immediately huddled with Bane, and we heard Stewart let out a roar of laughter, "Wait until the big one!"

Now I was really pissed off. Stewart had a right to be arrogant and confident. The federal court had ignored my sworn allegations, the letters from the SEA board, the front-page headlines in *The Baltimore Sun* that clearly exposed his fraud, and then it awarded his make-believe ships to the State of Maryland. He had a willing accomplice with the Maryland attorney general's office doing all they could do to avoid an evidentiary hearing. And thanks to the antics of the attorney general, Stewart was feeling invincible. I felt like I was pinned to a wall. This was going to be a tough fight.

In June of 1985, there were more shipwreck "discoveries" in the news. A company had been formed in Delaware, called the Indian River Recovery Company (IRRC), which had filed admiralty claims in federal district court for the District of Delaware for six shipwrecks on May 24. News of this had come to me by a young attorney named Peter Hess from Newcastle, Delaware. Peter was not only an admiralty attorney, but also an avid diver who had been following my efforts in the SEA cases. He called me to express his concern about what was going on in Delaware. IRRC was not only laying claim to the *China Wreck*, the last salvage effort of Donald Stewart, but also to a shipwreck named *Santa Rosea Lea*, and four others named *Adeline, Cornelia, Faithful Stewart*, and *Three Brothers*. I told Peter I was familiar with all of them, particularly the *China Wreck* and the "*Santa Rosea Lea*," as they had described it. The names of all of the ships hit home. They were the exact same five ships Stewart had asked me to research in November of 1980. I then told him about Stewart's foolish idea to have SEA salvage the *China Wreck* and my own experience with the *Santa Rosalia*. All six wrecks had one thing in common—Donald Stewart was interested in them.

As we talked, my suspicions that Stewart was involved in this grew stronger. It also was not lost on me that a third spelling for the ship named after the little saint of Palermo, St. Rosalia, was now in play. The misspelling had made it traceable to only one place, Robert Marx's *Shipwrecks of the Western Hemisphere*. Stewart had already clearly demonstrated his source for the *Santa Rosalia*, and I had already made it clear to him and his attorneys that I was using the misspelling of the ship's name to demonstrate how Stewart fabricated his story. I knew Stewart was clever enough to realize that a third spelling of *Santa Rosalia* presented to a jury would create confusion and doubt. Stewart had lit a backfire to bolster his defense.

IRRC had been formed by Harvey Harrington, who had just the year before discovered the wreck of HMS *De Braak*, a British warship that was overset and sank just off Cape Henlopen at the mouth of Delaware Bay on May 25, 1798. Most of the people had drowned, including James Drew, the captain, whose body had washed ashore and is now buried at Lewes, Delaware. Wild rumors of treasure being aboard were spread because the *De Braak* had recently captured a Spanish prize. Over the centuries, there had been several attempts to locate and recover treasure from her. The latest was by a corporation called Sub Sal, Inc., which Harrington worked for. As to the actual existence of treasure, that question was put to rest by Howard Chapelle in 1967 in an article he coauthored in the *Smithsonian Journal of History*. His research failed to produce any record of treasure on board.

Stewart had a great interest in the *De Braak*, and when he had formed SEA the *De Braak* was on his list of future targets. In 1955, Stewart had been hired by the Zwaanendael Museum in Lewes, Delaware, to research the *De Braak*. Added to his research of the ship was a bit of contrived material with dead-end references. But like most everyone who meets Stewart, the museum was taken in by his confident demeanor. The museum had accepted all of his work as factual. His research was filed and made public to anyone interested in the shipwreck. Harrington would had to have seen it.

Unfortunately, something Harrington did need to see had disappeared. On October 7, 1980, a red vinyl notebook containing newspaper clippings about past efforts to locate and salvage the *De Braak* had been reported missing. Things that were in the vicinity of Donald Stewart had a habit of disappearing, or materializing out of nowhere, namely artifacts and historical documents. Two months previously, Stewart had published an article in the *Maryland Beachcomber* describing a treasure on the *De Braak* that included seventy-seven tons of copper ingots. Stewart also claimed that he could prove the ship was buried under the beach.

When Harrington and his company, Sub Sal, Inc., announced that they had discovered the *De Braak* there was some skepticism. Those doubters were soon convinced when a gold ring was retrieved from the murky waters surrounding the wreck. It bore the inscription, "In memory of a belov'd brother, Captain John Drew, Drown'd 11 January 1798." Its discovery nailed down the *De Braak's* identity. The ring's authenticity was later verified by Christie's Trusts, Estates and Appraisals. Why Captain Drew was not wearing it the day he drowned is anyone's guess.

Nearly $3 million was spent raising the hull and bringing artifacts to the surface. Harrington had claimed in 1984 that the ship was worth from $5 million to $500 million dollars. This was apparently taken from treasure books, which seldom are based on documented facts. The recovered treasure only amounted to about six hundred gold and silver coins.

The future of Sub Sal began to sink like a scuttled barge. Investors were bailing out, and employees were quitting or being fired. A savvy and well-to-do New Hampshire businessman named L. John Davidson took over the operations of Sub Sal. Davidson soon became leery of Harrington's abilities, and after learning of his efforts to find other shipwrecks while on Sub Sal's payroll, fired him.

The *Santa Rosea Lea*, as Harrington described her, was one of them. On May 24, 1985, he swore in his verification filed in federal court that in the month of April, 1984, he had "located the abandoned wreck of the *Santa Rosea Lea* and proceeded to salvage a portion thereof." Similar statements were sworn to for the other wrecks.

Peter Hess told me that he and a large group of sport divers had formed *Ocean Watch*. This organization had also filed a claim to the *China Wreck* to keep the wreck open to sport divers. He needed someone knowledgeable in shipwreck research to look into the other cases. I told him that I was certainly up to speed on the *Santa Rosalia* and would be glad to attempt intervention in the Delaware court cases, which I did on July 1. In my motion, I went through all of the arguments for the prerequisites of admiralty jurisdiction, namely that there must in fact be a vessel and something must be saved. I also outlined the history of the *Santa Rosalia* that wrecked July 23, 1788, at Cape Charles, Virginia, carrying a cargo of flour, and explained that it was the same one mentioned and misspelled by Marx and misplaced in Delaware.

The attorneys for IRRC filed a response to my motion on July 22, and argued against my intervention. They stated:

> From the application it is clear that the applicant is concerned that the sunken vessel which is the subject matter of this action might be confused with the Santa Rosalia which is allegedly located off the coast of Cape Charles, Virginia. Although that concern is perhaps understandable it is not sufficient to allow the applicant to intervene in this action.

Harrington's attorneys also argued there was no jurisdictional basis to permit me to intervene. (I was not laying claim to the vessel.) IRRC's statement about the *Santa Rosea Lea* and their insistence on that particular spelling was their attempt to separate the ship from the one in Marx's book. It was clear that they were laying claim to a fictitious shipwreck. I was now involved in three different jurisdictions in cases related to three different versions of the same ship.

On August 27, Judge Caleb M. Wright denied my motion to intervene *but* ordered me into the case as an amicus curiae. He also ordered that I could file an additional brief if I chose to do so.

Wow! My first thought was that unlike the Ramsey court in Maryland, this court wanted to find the truth. I immediately set to work on my supplemental brief. I expanded on my jurisdictional arguments, and just as importantly, I analyzed the historical facts surrounding the other vessels and I proved the total lack of research on the part of IRRC. I pointed out that the *Faithful Steward* (not *Stewart*, as spelled in the complaint and in Marx's book) had wrecked in shallow water within one hundred yards of the beach, not in twenty-eight feet of water three quarters of a mile out. The *Adeline* had run ashore on Cape Henlopen in 1823, not 1824, and could not be in eighty feet of water as contended by IRRC. The *Cornelia* actually didn't sink at all but only ran on a shoal and later got off to sail for other European ports. As for the *Three Brothers*, she could have been a brig from St. Thomas lost in January 1812, under Cape Henlopen. Most likely, however, it was another name applied to the *Faithful Steward* and had no historical basis.

When I filed my last brief with the Federal Court in Baltimore on June 10, I had included the National Park Service's disclaimer of Stewart's *San Lorenzo* story written by Mr. Edwin Bearss. Under the Rules, I had to copy the Atlantic Ship Historical Society and Stewart. Upon reading Bearss' comments, Stewart became so distraught that on June 12, he fired off a letter to Edwin Bearss without consulting his attorney:

> I was appalled at the contents of your letter. It is unfortunate that you relied on a report with two missing pages, both of which contained the sources. You also apparently relied on the *Sunpapers* <u>edited</u> article of July 27, 1977 that contained many errors. Neither your staff nor John L. Amrhein pursued the sources that were properly stated, therefore, I find it quite unbelievable that a historian would make the statement you did in your first paragraph. It is disturbing that conclusions were reached without proper attention to the descriptions of the ships in the document.

Stewart didn't give Bearss the "two missing pages" and didn't copy me or the federal court with this letter. Bearss gave a copy of the letter to Charles McKinney who sent me a copy.

We submitted our witness list, which included Edwin Bearss from the National Park Service, Duncan Mathewson from Treasure Salvors, Hugh Benet from the Star-Spangled Banner House, and Victoria Stapells Johnson, who was committed to fly in from Spain. After Stewart had received a copy of Benet's correspondence to me—required by court discovery rules—Stewart fired off a letter to past and present members of the *Constellation* board. He advised them of the pending litigation and Benet's role in assisting me. He did his best to put me in a bad light and then warned them that "any ensuing publicity will not have been at my instigation, but that of a necessary response to Hugh Benet's supplied documents." Pressure was put on Benet to leave Stewart alone. He told me that he could lose his job at the museum if he testified. I told him I understood and removed him from the list.

On August 8, we demanded that Stewart produce specific documents that would prove or disprove his fabricated shipwrecks and his wild claims of a huge treasure on *La Galga*. Included in that request was our demand for the "two missing pages," which he had "forgotten" to give the National Park Service in 1977. It was through this demand that Stewart's attorneys first learned of his letter to Edwin Bearss. Copies of all discovery demanded of Stewart were always sent to the other defendants. They were now getting their first glimpse of Stewart's research and his character.

By the time I had sat for my deposition, Cardillo and the Firths were already talking settlement. Our trial date had been set for October 28. They needed to put as much distance between themselves and Stewart's testimony as they could. I had anticipated much finger pointing. Cardillo agreed to settle on September 4 before being compelled to answer his interrogatories. Cardillo had been asked to describe all historical research shown to him by Stewart and to describe the events that led to his recommendation to file the admiralty complaints. Apparently, Cardillo did not want to answer those questions.

On the morning of September 4, I went to the law offices of Adkins, Potts, and Smethurst in Salisbury, Maryland to sit for my deposition. They were representing Stewart. I took a seat at the conference table and as the stenographer was setting up, I took a shot at Stewart and his attorney, Fletcher Thompson, who was assisting Smethurst: "I just thought I should tell you that today is the feast day of St. Rosalia, and her name is spelled with an 'ia' not 'ea.'"

Fletcher Thompson smartly responded, "Big deal, our ship is spelled with an 'ea.'"

That's exactly what I wanted to hear, I thought to myself. Unknown to

Thompson, the court reporter chose the correct spelling as he recorded the testimony.

Later that day, Stewart produced the Admissions of Facts and Genuineness of Documents that we had requested of him in early June. As expected, Stewart had denied authorship of many documents of which he had been the sole author. But one document presented to him that he could not deny was an exhibit that was attached to the admiralty complaint in the *Santa Rosalea* case. It described the *Santa Rosalea* as a "regis" (this was a word that Stewart repeatedly and erroneously used for a king's ship or man-of-war) and that it had sunk in 1785. In the other shipwreck cases, Stewart did not give dates. With this admission, he was precluded now from pointing to Marx's book as his source and possibly saying he had made some sort of honest mistake. Victoria had proved that the 1785 ship had not wrecked at all. Any documents he produced now to justify its existence would be fabrications.

For three days, Thompson grilled me, trying to ascertain just what I knew, and, at the same time, discredit me as an expert witness. He wanted to show that I did not know what I was talking about and that historical facts could be subject to various interpretations. I could see the tack they were taking. When we got before the jury, he wanted to portray me as young and inexperienced in historical research and dishonest enough to steal years of hard work from this poor old salt so that I could go treasure hunting. I also knew if Stewart got in front of a jury, he could dupe them with his innocent facial expressions and body language as he lied through his teeth. After all, when talking about shipwrecks and sunken treasure, the lines between fact and fantasy can become easily distorted.

In the evenings, I would go home and work on my supplemental amicus curiae brief for the *Santa Rosea Lea* case in Delaware. Delphine would type while I dictated. Because of her, I was able to devote most of my time to the lawsuit. It certainly required it.

I could see from Fletcher Thompson's reactions to my testimony that he was now entertaining doubts about his client. I was straightforward and matter-of-fact and I did not falter. He was obviously learning things that directly contradicted Stewart's own representations to him.

And, of course, he had already seen my evidence proving that Stewart had fabricated both the *Santa Rosalea* and *San Lorenzo* and had grossly overstated *La Galga's* treasure. In my deposition, I never mentioned my appearance as amicus curiae in the Delaware proceedings, and they did not ask, but somehow I think that Thompson knew. Doug Sachse and I figured that my amicus curiae status would clearly give me credibility at trial, so we would save it for then.

At the end of the third day of my deposition, Thompson was just about through grilling me. He had been asking me questions about the *San Lorenzo*. Stewart slipped him a piece of paper on which I could see a photocopy of a newspaper article. They were both smiling. Thompson slid his chair back and walked around the conference table with the document.

"Mr. Amrhein, I want you to read this," he said with a smirk.

I immediately recognized this as *The Baltimore Sun* article written by Raymond Thompson on January 4, 1949 (See page 64). I had previously located the article at the Maryland Room of the Enoch Pratt library in Baltimore. Reference to the article had been made in the index card file saying that a copy was in the vertical file under "shipwrecks." This article described an unnamed Spanish ship having wrecked at Ocean City in 1820. It also described the loss of *La Galga*. It was this article that had inspired Stewart to concoct the *San Lorenzo* story in the first place. It was evident that the reporter's source for the 1820 date was the reported finds of Spanish colonial coins stopping at that date.

I dismissed the story, saying that Spanish coins do not necessarily prove a Spanish shipwreck and that the reporter certainly hadn't done any historical research. I also pointed out that I had discovered that this article had been removed from the vertical file. I had been forced to retrieve it from microfilm. Stewart's copy had the library date stamp on it, proving that it had come from the vertical file. I gave Stewart a deliberate stare and said it was probably missing because of him. Stewart fumbled with his pencil. Thompson returned to his chair disappointed. Neither of them was smiling any more. They had no idea that I had previous knowledge of the article's existence. The deposition ended at that point. We shook hands, and I went home knowing that the best was yet to come—Stewart's performance at his own deposition.

I finished my amicus curiae brief for Delaware and filed it on September 9. In my brief, I clearly demonstrated that IRRC had relied totally on Robert Marx's book and pointed out the errors contained within his book. These errors were not necessarily Marx's as he relied almost solely on *Lloyd's List*, a contemporary source that was not always correct. IRRC made no objection. It was now obvious that IRRC's historical research had taken no more than the time to obtain and read two pages of Marx's book. IRRC was now preparing to sell shares at $2,500 each using this valuable "research."

Stewart had told his lawyers that my reason for suing him was to get his research so that I could then go look for these ships myself. He had said he was writing a book called *Delmarva Shipwrecks* and that his research needed to be protected and not disclosed in court. His attorneys argued this point with mine. For some reason, my attorney gave in, even though they knew that protective orders were not to be used to conceal fraud, only legitimate work product. On October 8, that order was signed by Judge Cathell.

On October 10, Stewart filed his answers to his interrogatories. For every direct request for historical documents that would support his case, he invoked the court's protective order where he had given the documents to my attorney, but by court order I was prevented from seeing them. However, what was presented was characterized by my attorney as fabrications. There was one group of papers that they could not have protected. Stewart was asked to provide all of the minutes of the meetings of Atlantic Ship Historical Society directors.

After reading them, it was obvious that they had been drafted after the fact and were done so with the lawsuit in mind. They were careful not to mention *La Galga* by name, referring only indirectly to her as "the Spanish ship." And there were several statements about operating in Virginia such as "Atlantic Ship Historical Society informed SEA, Ltd. that it will not involve itself in Virginia, because it does not feel it necessary." Stewart was now trying to demonstrate that looking for *La Galga* in Virginia was all my idea and that he had nothing to do with it. This, of course, would be his explanation for why SEA had not found her. SEA had never crossed the line to work in Maryland. Every decision to hire a boat or direct the company boat into Virginia had been made or approved by Stewart. The fabricated minutes showed that Stewart was beginning to unravel.

In addition to the documents Stewart had surrendered, he made some interesting statements. He said he hadn't been a party to the representations contained in the *Wall Street Journal* ad. He said he had not found any vessels worth $100 million in gold, silver, and jewels. Next he stated that he had never represented *La Galga* was carrying cargo worth 4,250,000 pesos as published in the May 16 *Maryland Beachcomber* article and that the article was for informational purposes only and not to induce stock purchases (The ad did contain contact information for potential investors).

Stewart said he did research on shipwrecks at the University of Havana in 1948. He also stated he did research in Spain at the Archivo General de Indias in 1949 with help of a translator. Apparently, he forgot Spanish in the intervening time. His lawyer let this one get by. And for his research in Seville, Spain, the archive had kept records of visitors back that far, which showed that he had never been there before.

When asked about treasure on the *Santa Rosalea*, his reply was he did not know if there was any "real cargo on board or not," and denied showing anybody any letter about the 1785 treasure ship as he had at Ellodie's coffee shop that cold January morning of 1981.

The demand for the "two missing pages" on the *San Lorenzo* story was defended with the protective order. Neither I nor the National Park Service would get to see them. When asked to support the 4,250,000 pesos on *La Galga* as described in the *Maryland Beachcomber*, he stated that he had none. Elsewhere, he had claimed that Robert Firth and the editor of the *Beachcomber* had originated that number.

When asked to produce the letter he had shown me from Captain Mahoney (Huony) of *La Galga* during our first meeting at his house, then again in front of Albert Alberi, he had denied its existence.

He was asked to produce his captain's license. He said he no longer had it.

It was now the big day. On October 15, 1985, I arrived at Stewart's attorney's office to witness his deposition. The master of the untruth was now being compelled to testify under oath. Any lie told and uncovered here would be another nail in his coffin. He was with his wife, Vivian, and was using a cane.

Although Cardillo had been successful in getting him some money for his alleged back injury, he did not get the paycheck for life that he had hoped for. And rightly so. Stewart could be seen walking easily around his yard without his cane when he thought no one was watching. His cane was now nothing more than a prop.

Stewart's attorneys brought up the possibility of an out-of-court settlement. I told Doug Sachse, who had been representing us, that having come this far, I wanted his sworn testimony on the record. No negotiations would take place until his deposition was over. I had waited too long for this day. In his last written statement to me in June of 1982, he had said, "Your numerous threats are something to be resolved in a court of law." So, today was his day.

We had the same court stenographer that recorded my deposition the month before. He seemed as anxious to hear Stewart as did the rest of us. Sachse was relaxed and began questioning Stewart about his employment and experiences since high school rather than go for the big questions. Stewart seemed to relax as well. He brought with him some prepared notes to help him "remember things."

Stewart vividly described trips to Jamaica, Spain, Honduras, and working treasure ships of the 1733 fleet in the Florida Keys. All of these things he had outlined in the SEA, Ltd. stock prospectus. Stewart and the prospectus had failed to mention he had been a clerk typist with the B&O Railroad from 1950 to 1956, the same time frame for all of his Caribbean adventures. Sachse now let him describe all of his adventures as taking place on vacation time and those times he said the railroad had been on strike.

Sachse then walked him through his years at the *Constellation*, his so-called acquisition of the Atlantic Ship Historical Society, and the *Five Fathom* lightship and how he had set up his museum in Ocean City, Maryland.

As for the formation of SEA, Stewart emphatically swore that the

Firths had been totally responsible for that. He said that he had nothing to do with the *Wall Street Journal* ad. He also said that he had nothing to do with the writing of the prospectus. Instead he insisted that it had been done by the "Firth boys" and that he had not seen the prospectus until 1984. And the description of the 1750 fleet had also been written by them but had been based on some notes he had given them, which they incorrectly represented.

Stewart was asked about the SEA investor meeting that I had attended on June 14, 1980. Stewart, wearing his saintly expression, denied ever saying he'd had information that stated that the captain had gotten two girls pregnant in Snow Hill because he wouldn't have said such a thing in a public meeting. He also said that he'd never told anyone that he had important documents locked up in Spain.

Stewart had shown me a map the night I had first met him that had wreck symbols on it and a description of a shoal named "Man-O-War Shoal." He had said that it had been made several years after *La Galga* had wrecked. He had previously denied having such a map or chart in our demand for documents. Sachse focused specifically on this map. I had shown Sachse an article written by Stewart and published in the *Maryland Beachcomber* on May 15, 1981 entitled "The Wrecks of the Isle of Wight Shoals." Stewart had specifically mentioned a Royal Navy Chart of 1707 and inferred the existence of another dated 1752 with a shoal marked "Man-O-War Shoal." Sachse started with the setup:

> Sachse: Did you ever state to Mr. Amrhein or any of the other plaintiffs that you had a map from the eighteenth century which showed a shipwreck symbol opposite [a] Spanish Point and which also showed a King William Shoal and Man-O-War Shoal?
>
> Stewart: I racked my brain over this one. I do not recall such a map. I had a number of maps. I had a number of photographs, infrared photographs of Assateague, Ocean City; I had a number of aerial views. They were all turned over to SEA.
>
> Sachse: Have you ever seen or do you have a map of Spanish

Point?

Stewart: I don't recall such a thing, no. All right. These things were taken from SEA's office sometime in November or December. Libby Nichols was there. They had a break-in at the SEA office, and I wanted to call the State Police in immediately. Some of our records were taken too at SEA. And the Firth boys wouldn't allow, they didn't want any investigation or anything. So I just forgot about it. Libby Nichols—the secretary's husband—was a sergeant in the State Police, she didn't understand why they didn't want to call them either.

Sachse: So you don't have now any eighteenth century map with Man-O-War Shoal on it?

Stewart: No. I have an early one here, but it doesn't have Man-O-War Shoal on it. No.

Sachse: Have you ever seen one with any, with the names Man-O-War Shoal or King William Shoal?

Stewart: Man-O-War Shoal. No. Not that I can say.

Sachse had asked more questions related to *La Galga*. He produced the letter Stewart had written to Albert Alberi on February 8, 1978, on the letterhead of the Atlantic Ship Historical Society. The letter was full of factual errors, but the most outrageous statement was that Stewart and his historical society had salvaged *La Galga* back in 1967 under contract with Spain. He claimed that he had located the ballast pile of *La Galga* three quarters of a mile off of Assateague. Sachse, in preparation for the next line of questioning, had previously gotten Stewart to state that Atlantic Ship Historical Society had never done any previous salvage work on *La Galga*.

Fletcher Thompson, Stewart's attorney, grimaced while Sachse stood next to the sweating Donald Stewart, holding the letter and formulating questions. There would be no protective order to hide behind on this one. Stewart could not deny authorship, as Alberi, an attorney himself, was prepared to testify in court about receiving the letter.

In a move to protect the historical society and its officers, which included his wife and daughter, Stewart had stated that he had not been authorized to write the letter on the historical society's letterhead. He said he had no other paper available at the time because he had been aboard his lightship when it was written. He acknowledged that some of his historical facts about *La Galga* were wrong because, "I did not have my research in front of me. A lot of this was from memory, but it was written in good faith." When Sachse questioned him on each point, he could only ramble on with irrelevant details and never directly answered the questions. Stewart's attorney seemed to be squirming more than he was.

Suddenly, Fletcher Thompson blurted out, "If, and when, you get to entering that document into evidence, I object to it as well on the grounds of relevance! I object to all answers on the grounds of relevance!"

Sachse pressed him more about the letter and his claim that the historical society had salvaged the ship in 1967 and the final location of the ballast pile of the wreck. Amidst the incoherent babbling, Stewart said that he had located the site with the help of the Undersea Warfare Group and their "metal anomaly detector." Sachse moved on.

La Galga was no doubt a real ship, but not one loaded with significant treasure. Stewart had said earlier that the claims of a large treasure had come from the Firth brothers. He said that their basis for the value had been using twenty dollars an ounce as the value of silver. Stewart said if *La Galga* were carrying one million pesos in silver, it would be worth $20 million today. Previously, he had said that he had the ship's manifest, but now he couldn't produce it.

Doug Sachse asked him about Dave Horner's *The Treasure Galleons*. Horner had placed *La Galga* at Old Currituck Inlet, North Carolina, based solely on what he had read in John Potters' *Treasure Diver's Guide*, and Potter had based that assumption solely on an early report of the loss of the fleet recorded in the North Carolina archives. This report did not name *La Galga*, only that it was a Spanish ship. The truth was that an English vessel named *Goodwin* of Liverpool from the Isle of May had run ashore at Currituck Inlet. This wreck was observed by Captain Pumarejo of the *Nuestra Señora de Los Godos* when he'd anchored off there at the end of the storm. I'd had the good fortune of meeting Dave Horner at a shipwreck seminar on the Outer Banks the previous

October. He told me that he "blew that one" because he was in a hurry and had to make the publisher's deadline.

Stewart was now in a corner and obviously had believed that if he could quote from a published source, it might give him credibility. Sachse had to cover that possibility since Stewart was sure to bring that up in court.

> Sachse: Can you tell me what you got out of the *Treasure Galleons*?
>
> Stewart: What I got out of that was, to me, was a confirmation that there was a million dollars at least on the *Galga*.
>
> Sachse: Now forgive me, if I am wrong. This is the same guy that placed the *Galga* off North Carolina, wasn't it?
>
> Stewart: That's a common mistake of a lot of researchers make.
>
> Sachse: Why would you believe him with regard to the treasure, when you knew he was so far off on location of the *Galga*? The reference in Horner's book regarding the treasure, did you check that reference?
>
> Stewart: No, that was in the main archives in Seville. I did not check that. I figured he had it down so—I had enough other contemporary testimony from different people that I had to believe what he was saying there, because his confirmed what mine said. (Author's note: Horner gave no archival source for the treasure.)

On October 10, 1985, Victoria Stapells Johnson had written me a letter answering some questions specifically about the *San Lorenzo*. This letter did not arrive until after Stewart's deposition. But this is what she had to say:

> As far as providing proof that the *San Lorenzo* did not leave or arrive in Havana at any time I am pleased to tell you that the evidence from the archives confirms what we thought about the ship. I located a large bound book which listed all of the

ships sailing out from Spain to the Indies and back again for the years 1817 to 1822. In this register there was no mention for a *San Lorenzo* (de Escorial) leaving Cadiz at any time between 1817 and 1822. Furthermore there were no arrivals from Philadelphia in Cadiz during 1821 or 1822. In fact, there is only one ship which arrived from Havana in Cadiz in 1821 and this was an English brig called the *John and Anna* under William Robinson. Thus, there is no foundation for Mr. Stewart's statement that Pedro Murphy arrived at Cadiz from Philadelphia in 1821 or 1822. We can also conclude that the *San Lorenzo* did not exist.

After a lunch break, Sachse started in on the *San Lorenzo* line of questions. Stewart had previously been quoted in 1983 as saying that the reason Victoria could not find proof of the *San Lorenzo* was she must have been looking in the wrong archive. He claimed that the documents could be found in the Archivo General de Indias Annex in Seville. Victoria had already verified that there was no such building, but it became evident as the deposition rolled on that he was sticking to this defensive tactic. Sachse moved on to the *San Lorenzo* manifest:

> Sachse: Where did you find that manifest?
> Stewart: That was in the Archivo General de Indias annex in Seville.
> Sachse: There is more than one building in the Archivo of Indias?
> Stewart: In 1949, there was a main archives building and then down near the river there was a separate building that had all these records in [it], and they tell me that across the river there was a town, I can't remember the name, it started with a 't,' where they had other records stored at that time.
> Sachse: You didn't check that?
> Stewart: No. I was never in there.
> Sachse: So this manifest that we are referring to—
> Stewart: Was in this building, this old building that was

locked up. It had a big—why I remember—it had a padlock about that big (indicates with hands).

    Sachse: So that was what you refer to as the annex?

    Stewart: That's what it was referred to—annexo.

    Sachse: Where was that in relation to the general archives?

    Stewart: It was a distance away from the general archives building.

Stewart had stated at the June 14, 1980, prospective stockholders' meeting, that he had some friend who was a general to lock up records in the archives in Seville. Fletcher Thompson stepped in to help Stewart refresh his memory about that:

    Thompson: Mr. Stewart, at the meeting of investors of June 14, 1980, did you say at this meeting, do you recall saying at the meeting that documents were locked in the Archivo General Annex in Seville?

    Stewart: No, I didn't say any documents were locked up at that meeting at all.

    Thompson: And are the documents locked in the general archives or at the general annex?

    Stewart: Well, the general archives are open to the public. The locked-up documents were in the annex.

    Thompson: Annex to what?

    Stewart: The annex building or buildings, if you want to call them. Across the River, to the Archivo General de Indias.

    Thompson: And you later, it is possible that you mentioned to Mr. Amrhein that documents were locked in the general annex, is that correct?

    Stewart: I said to Mr. Amrhein and others that there were documents locked up in the General Annex. I didn't, I don't believe I even specified the Archivo General. I just said the general annex. That's all I ever called the place.

    Sachse: Do you have any knowledge as to what the San Lorenzo de Escorial was named after?

Stewart: Yes but we are getting into—

Fletcher Thompson objected because he felt Stewart was getting into areas covered by the protective order. I was asked to leave the room. Although I was disappointed, I couldn't help but smile at the stenographer as I left, because I think he knew as I did that Stewart's testimony was about to become more entertaining. Now that I was gone, Sachse brought it up again (Note: Stewart interchanged "Escoral" with the correct "Escorial" repeatedly. This testimony was recorded and obtained later):

> Stewart: Okay. The *San Lorenzo de Escoral* was named after San Lorenzo, who was the patron saint of the monastery of the de Escoral or monastery near Madrid.
> Sachse: How do you know that?
> Stewart: Well, that's even in the *Encyclopedia Britannica*. That's common knowledge in Roman Catholic church history that San Lorenzo is the patron saint of the friars of the de Escoral. It's well documented in many, many historical works.

Sachse asked Stewart numerous questions about his research in Spain, and Stewart had said that he had a man named Jorge de Guzman actually do the research. He had previously stated that he had done the research, but Victoria had obtained verification from the archives that he had never been there. Stewart said he had not heard from de Guzman in years, but they had shared a great deal of information and that de Guzman provided him with valuable shipwreck information, including the manifest of the *San Lorenzo* and the transcription of the eight hundred pages of testimony that Don Pedro Murphy had given before the "Vistadores by order of the Cortez." Sachse probed deeper because we needed to find out about the elusive "two missing pages" of references he had previously failed to give the National Park Service:

> Sachse: Do you have any of that original correspondence from Mr. de Guzman?

Stewart: No. The original correspondence was kept at the Lightship. I kept it there because we didn't have room for all that. And the fool thing leaked through the top deck. We not only lost all of the files, when we got down there was a mass of mildew in those file drawers. I had the material [transcripts] so we had no choice but to toss everything.

Sachse: I want to try real quickly go through your sources, so-called two missing pages.

Stewart: Oh, those things, yes.

Sachse: Ok. Was there any reference in any of those records to the *San Lorenzo* wrecking off the coast of Maryland?

Stewart: That came from Madrid, the private collection of the Count de Casa de Valencia.

Sachse: Did de Guzman obtain these records for you?

Stewart: Yes. He sent me the translations of these records, yes, he did.

Sachse: I guess to be right to the point, if Victoria Stapells Johnson is in Spain, and, if I want her to go inspect this collection, would she have access to it?

Stewart: I would think if she is as Mr. Amrhein says she is, I don't think she would have any trouble.

Sachse: Where would I tell her to go?

Stewart: Madrid. I would believe it's the Spanish Archives, National Archives of Spain.

Sachse: And this would include the document with Don Pedro Murphy's testimony?

Stewart: Yes. And also the newspapers of Peru from 1820. Collection of the Count de Casa de Valencia.

Stewart had forgotten he had said in his *Baltimore Sun* article that these documents were in the Archivo General de Indias in Seville, not the National Archives in Madrid. Sachse continued:

Sachse: I think that will be extremely helpful. Thank you. I want to move on.

And then without being asked:

Stewart: He did a lot of research in the basement of that place.

Sachse: Transcription of the register of the *San Lorenzo* is self explanatory. That would be in the Archive Indias?

Stewart: In the Annex.

In my deposition, Fletcher Thompson had presented a copy of the 1949 Baltimore *Sun* article written by Raymond Thompson that had described an unidentified Spanish ship wrecking in 1820. The copy shown me had come from the vertical file in the Maryland Room of the Enoch Pratt Library in downtown Baltimore. I had previously stated that it had been obvious that Raymond Thompson was only a reporter and hadn't done any historical research to support his story. I had also stated that it was odd that the article had been removed from the vertical file. Stewart had had a month to prepare his counter to my accusation. At Stewart's attorney's suggestion, Stewart began to describe his research in 1949 at the Enoch Pratt Library:

Sachse: This is the 1949 *Evening Sun* article?

Stewart: Right.

Sachse: You have already provided this under document production.

Stewart: Right. I called up Raymond Thompson and said I am really interested in these ships.

Fletcher Thompson: For the record, the article has a byline on it, Raymond Thompson.

Stewart: Yeah, by Raymond Thompson. I am really interested in these Spanish ships, *Galga*, *Greyound*, and the *San Lorenzo*. Where did you get your information? I got it from the file—that is the copy or what was in the file at the historical society, at the Enoch Pratt Library. I went to him. I said, 'Where did you get your information on the ships?' He told me that it was in the Maryland vertical file under shipwrecks. In there I found a letter from the British Ambassador landing in Annapolis in 1820 that had been transcribed by a Mr. Joseph Legg of Baltimore in 1944.

Stewart rambled on about taking this information to Spain to try and find out more about the *San Lorenzo* and *La Galga*. Later, Doug Sachse directed him back to more of his supplied documentation:

Sachse: Skipping C and going down to D, this transcription of a letter dated September 30, 1820, from Charles F. Wilmot to George Howard would be found in Enoch Pratt Library. That's where you found it?

Stewart: That's where I found it.

Sachse: The main branch or whatever you call it, the main library?

Stewart: Down on Cathedral Street. I went up there specifically to pull this material when this case started. And their whole shipwreck file was in a shambles, and eighty percent of the stuff that I went up to get hold of was gone.

Sachse: So you can't give me a precise reference where I would go down and find that?

Stewart: It was in the shipwreck file, Maryland vertical file in the Maryland Room. That's where it was. Even Mr. Amrhein, in his testimony here, verified that even that newspaper is not in there now. It's ridiculous.

Sachse changed the questioning back to *La Galga* and queried Stewart on what research he had done to establish the 1750 boundary between Maryland and Virginia. This clue to *La Galga's* final resting place was the "east line drawn to know the bounds," as stated by Captain Huony in 1750. I was still out of the room as Stewart continued to divulge "protected" information.

Sachse: Mr. Stewart, again, one of the questions I asked you previously while Mr. Amrhein was here was concerning what work you have done and what evidence you have that the

Maryland-Virginia boundary line was the same in 1750 as it is today. You couldn't answer it then. Can you answer it now?

Stewart: This was a big, big thing to try to settle, and I was as confused over this for many years. And it was pro and con, pro and con, yes it was, no it wasn't.

Stewart was now about to testify what he knew about Captain Huony's letter that described the location of the shipwreck, contained in the printed series of the Maryland Archives. On that document is a notation for the page of the original manuscript document, which was "424." Stewart was now going to add an embellishment concerning page 424.

Stewart: Then there is a reference, a little reference, page 424, on the east line. And I thought to myself, what is that reference to. So I got Harry Newman, who is an author, famous Maryland historian and genealogist, to go to the Hall of Records. And he went to the archives.

The Hall of Records is now the Maryland State Archives, previously located at St. John's College in Annapolis. Stewart had also said Mr. Newman was head of the Genealogy Department at Salisbury State University. There is no such department of genealogy. Stewart was starting to come apart.

Sachse: What Hall of Records?

Stewart: The Old Annex of the Hall of Records at Parole, Maryland. This goes back aways. Now since they have built— the main building used to be at St. John's College. I have been in there many times. But there was an annex at Parole, and one over near Hyattsville, some place, and he knew these places inside out…and he went back on the surveys, and that survey that they are referring to in this document is a survey of 1748.

Page 424 of the printed archive series is in fact dated 1748. But this has to do with an examination of some Indians at Cambridge, Maryland. Sachse then pressed him into confirming that his contention was that *La Galga* lay to the north of the present day Maryland-Virginia boundary. When asked, Stewart said that he had reached that conclusion in the 1960s without the help of Harry Newman.

Sachse returned to the *San Lorenzo*. Stewart related how he had gone to the Royal Ship Society in London, a nonexistent historical society, where he had located records on a British Navy vessel that he had said had surveyed Assateague in 1771. We had already demonstrated to his attorney that the admiralty records in England showed that this vessel had been nonexistent in this time period. Stewart had given this bogus material to the National Park Service in 1977. It was impossible for him to admit to his attorneys that he had defrauded the Park Service. Once again, his only way out was to say that my researchers hadn't gone to the right archive.

Using Stewart's documents that described his research and where it was done the questions continued:

> Sachse: Where is the Royal Ship Society?
>
> Stewart: It's in downtown London.
>
> Sachse: Again, the purpose of this, if I have someone in London and I want them to go check on a document, what do I tell them where to go?
>
> Stewart: Get a cab and ask for the Royal Ship Society Library, and they ought to take them there. If they can't find it, go to the British Museum and they will tell you where it is.

Sachse continued to review Stewart's sources. He moved on to something at the Maryland Historical Society:

> Sachse: Letter, copy of list of shipwreck vessels obtained from marine file, Maryland Historical Society in Baltimore.
>
> Stewart: Right.
>
> Sachse: Can you give me any better reference for someone like me, if I want to go find it, where would I look exactly?

Stewart: Well, if you go to the desk and ask for the marine file, they will bring it up from down in the basement.

Sachse: That will have the list of shipwrecked vessels?

Stewart: Yes. They are not catalogued. You probably have to go through the whole blooming boxes but—

Sachse: This is research that was done while you were in London at the Navy Ship Society, is that correct?

Stewart: Yes.

Sachse: Again I am not trying to be facetious, any problem finding that?

Stewart: No. That's a report—wait a minute. This is Navy Ship Society, not the Royal—that's at Greenwich.

Sachse: This is located in Greenwich, England?

Stewart: Yes.

There, of course, is no Navy Ship Society. Sachse changed the subject again to the *Santa Rosalia*. Stewart had painted himself in a corner by putting the date 1785 in the federal court papers. That ship did not wreck, but that detail did not concern Donald Stewart. He was ready:

Sachse: I am still moving to your *Santa Rosalia* research. I am just referring to your answers to interrogatories. B. Letter of April 15, 1785, Varick to John J. This is in the National Archives, correct?

Stewart: There she be.

Sachse: No problem. It indicates on the back with a stamp it's a copy from the National Archives.

Stewart: Yes.

Sachse: In Washington?

Stewart: That's right.

Sachse: Record Group 26?

Stewart: Yeah.

Sachse: C. Pilot Records of Delaware Bay and Delaware River—

Stewart: They will hand you boxes and you go through

them until you find it.

Sachse: But you can't give me any further—

Stewart: All you do is ask for the pilot records, and boy they will pull them out. They are not even indexed by years.

Sachse: D. Lloyd's of London basement archives?

Stewart: Okay. This is a gold mine.

Sachse: If you are in London, you just go to Lloyd's?

Stewart: This was in '74. I went to Lloyd's. I was told I could actually go down in there by Lord Hallen, and I went down.

Sachse: Who is Lord Hallen?

Stewart: He was the vice-president of Lloyd's of London.

Sachse: Is the Lloyd's of London basement archives open to anyone who wants to take the time?

Stewart: No, you have to get in there by special permission. They just don't let the general public in. If I had not been connected with the *Constellation*, I would have never gotten in.

After a few more minutes of questions, the deposition ended. I saw Stewart come out of the conference room, since I was not allowed in for the finale. His face was ashen and tight-lipped. His eyes showed he was a tired, beaten man. The atmosphere in the law office resembled a funeral parlor. Everyone talked in hushed tones.

Fletcher Thompson huddled with Sachse for a minute and then Doug approached me as he saw I was getting ready to leave. Doug said that they wanted to talk settlement right then so I should stick around. Their offer was terribly low, but I could tell that Doug was ready to put this behind us. Stewart's attorney said that there was little to be had, so I agreed. We would now avoid the expense of flying Victoria over from Spain for the trial. Settlement by law is not an admission of wrongdoing, but neither is it an exoneration of the charges. I wanted him to be officially found guilty of fraud, but I was content that the record showed that he was. It was over.

Stewart paid up, Firth refused, but a judgement was entered against him and later collected. On November 18, 1986, judgment was entered against Raymond Cardillo to enforce his settlement agreement. He never paid.

The story of the *Santa Rosalia* did not end here. The Delaware cases, which included the *Santa Rosea Lea*, had not yet been decided. IRRC was still selling shares for what were obviously nonexistent shipwrecks but the ongoing litigation suggested that they were in fact real.

On December 20, Judge Caleb Wright raised, on his own motion, the issue of subject matter jurisdiction and issued an order to show why the *Santa Rosea Lea* case, as well as the others, should not be dismissed for lack thereof. Nothing had been brought up to perfect a claim. He gave IRRC until February 1, 1986, to respond. IRRC made a feeble attempt to overcome my challenges. On January 29,1986, Harrington had a diver named Jonathan Farrar swear an affidavit that on December 20, 1985, he had dove on a wreck believed to be the *Santa Rosea Lea* located a quarter of a mile offshore in seventy feet of water. He said that there were timbers and encrusted objects on the bottom, and the purpose of the dive was to arrest and survey the vessel. Similar affidavits were filed for the other vessels.

The attorneys for IRRC did not respond until March 3. With their response, they included an affidavit from Harrington which among other things stated:

> In my research there have been numerous references to the *Adeline*, the *Santa Rosea Lea*, and the *Cornelia*. Since May of 1984 I have conducted additional research regarding the *Faithful Steward*, the *Three Brothers*, the *Adeline*, the *Cornelia* and the *Santa Rosea Lea* by continuing to review documents in libraries and museums....

Harrington cited several books, including Marx's *Shipwrecks of the Western Hemisphere*. He never cited any archival or contemporary sources for any of the wrecks and made no reference to the historical facts I had placed in the record related to these ships. His attorneys still insisted that IRRC had tentatively identified the wrecks as named. But they asked for latitude:

It should be noted that the Court's jurisdiction does not depend upon whether the shipwrecks are actually those five ships.... It is known that these ships went down in the area near where the wreck sites have been located.

After reviewing the affidavits and response, I wrote Judge Wright and dismantled them point by point. I observed that they probably had not found anything and that these claims were for the sole purpose of tying up ocean bottom and to facilitate the selling of stock. It was obvious that IRRC had done absolutely no additional research or at least what they could admit to. It was obvious from my documentation that some of these wrecks were nonexistent, and that Harrington's attorneys had done no independent verification of the facts. I pointed out to Judge Wright that it was in IRRC's best interest to prove the identities of the wrecks for the financial well-being of his company. I also put this question to Judge Wright, referring to the *De Braak*: "Why would anyone, who believes he has located a wreck worth $5 to $500 million, go looking for wrecks that are worthless or nonexistent?" By now, the investors of IRRC had surely lost all of their money.

I closed by asking Judge Wright to urge IRRC to provide sufficient documentation to support the identities of the ships. This apparently had some effect. IRRC filed motions related to the five ships (excluding the *China Wreck*) to change the caption of the cases. This meant that instead of the defendant vessel being the specific-named shipwreck, IRRC asked the court to name the defendant vessel in each case as "an unidentified shipwreck," but parenthetically noting that the shipwreck was tentatively identified as the *Santa Rosea Lea*.

This was done for all five ships, and for the *Faithful Stewart*, they asked the spelling to be changed to the correct word, "*Steward*." They still insisted that the brig, *Cornelia*, was lost in 1757 in spite of the fact that the *Pennsylvania Gazette* of March 10, 1757, stated that she had gotten off after being aground and full of water. The *Cornelia* was reported still sailing three years later when she cleared Philadelphia for Guadalupe as documented in the *Gazette* of February 28, 1760. IRRC also insisted that the spelling for *Santa Rosea Lea* remain the same.

This was very revealing. There were only two people who had a stake in the correct spelling of "Rosalia," me and Donald Stewart. Harrington and IRRC had no stake in the spelling. I had already pointed out that Marx was his source. He was now refusing to even spell it the same way Marx did. My notion that this was a fictitious ship was again reinforced. If they were in fact talking about the *Santa Rosalia* in Marx's book, I had proven that that ship was carrying a load of flour. There was no doubt in my mind that Stewart was involved in the background and was providing information to IRRC. I couldn't understand why Harrington wouldn't at least change the spelling to *Santa Rosalea* per Marx's book and take away some of the controversy. It seemed to me that perhaps Stewart had something on Harrington. Now I wondered even more about Captain Drew's gold ring said to have been found on the *De Braak*.

Judge Wright provided me with copies of IRRC's latest motions and asked for my advice. On May 13, I responded and warned the judge of the dangers of proceeding with IRRC in these cases. I pointed out that IRRC's continued insistence of using the identities *Santa Rosea Lea* and *Cornelia* for shipwrecks that were proven not to exist had all of the appearances of fraud. IRRC did not respond to this accusation.

Peter Hess informed me that there was going to be a hearing on the *China Wreck* on June 9 and asked me to join him. At the hearing, *Ocean Watch* testified against the court granting salvage rights to IRRC, and Harrington testified why they should be granted. At the end of the trial, a young man introduced himself to me and said that Judge Wright would like to see me in his chambers. Totally surprised, I asked how he knew that I was there, so the clerk explained that he had overheard Peter and me talking in the elevator.

I entered his chambers and introduced myself. He thanked me for coming in and got right to the point. He asked my opinion as to what was going on. I told him the whole thing reeked. It made no sense to go after a sport diver's wreck like the *China Wreck*, and as far as the other wrecks, there was really nothing to pursue. I told him this was nothing more than a scam to sell stock and pay certain individuals a paycheck. For his part, Judge Wright said that he was very concerned about what was going on in his court. He asked me if I would testify if called and, of course, I said that I would. We shook hands, and I promised to continue to monitor the proceedings.

On June 11, Judge Wright dismissed the suits against all five shipwrecks. In his opinion, he stated, among other things:

> 1. The affidavits of Harvey Harrington and others contain no indication that IRRC made any actual dives upon the wrecks prior to filing the complaints.
> 2. IRRC "located" shipwrecks solely as the result of research and investigation conducted by Harvey Harrington.
> 3. Allegations in the complaints about the existence and location of ancient wrecks based upon research and investigation alone do not satisfy the Court that such vessels actually rest at that location or exist at all.

Judge Wright, unlike the Attorney General of Maryland, refused to assume the truth of the Plaintiff's complaint when sworn contradictory information had been presented. He said that IRRC could refile should they come up with actual proof in the future. They never did. The ruling handed down by Judge Wright was exactly what Judge Ramsey should have done in the SEA cases. Instead, he awarded the make-believe shipwrecks to the State of Maryland.

In October, Judge Wright dismissed IRRC's claim to the *China Wreck*. He said that the sport divers had a right to continue diving the wreck and denied IRRC exclusive possession. My prediction made four years before to the SEA board about the futility of salvaging the *China Wreck* was proven correct.

On June 30, 1987, Donald Stewart sold his house in Berlin, Maryland and left the Eastern Shore for Herndon, Virginia. Upon arrival, he told everyone that that he had moved from Baltimore, having just retired from the *Constellation*. He made no mention of his seven years in the Ocean City area.

Donald Stewart died of lung cancer on March 17, 1996. In his obituary in *The Baltimore Sun*, his flamboyant maritime dress and his self-proclaimed title of Rear Admiral were noted. The article openly stated that Stewart had produced a series of documents that later were disputed by maritime scholars resulting in the final determination that the surviving *Constellation* was actually built in 1854, not 1797. Nothing was said about his story of the *San Lorenzo* and the Assateague horses. That story would live on.

The fate of *La Galga* and the story of St. Rosalia have become intertwined. It was the ship named after this saint that had first directed

From the book by Emmanuele Calascibetta, *St. Rosalia Antidote of the Pest and of All Contagious Evil*. Madrid 1668. It was in this same year that Edmund Scarborough drew the erroneous boundary line between Maryland and Virginia. This error would confuse treasure hunters three centuries later. "Umbram fugat Veritas" Out of darkness truth. *Courtesy of the Biblioteca National, Madrid.*

me toward the truth in the whole SEA shipwreck debacle. This part of the story really began on September 4, 1750. That was the day *La Galga* struck the offshore reef and should have been dashed to pieces in her frail condition. Had *La Galga* been lost that day, I probably would never have tried to go looking for her, because her location would have been unknown. Most likely, there would have been no survivors. That day was the feast day of St. Rosalia.

Stewart had started with the real *Santa Rosalia* shipwreck lost in 1788 that had been misspelled in Robert Marx's book. Marx's source put the wreck at the Delaware Capes. Marx elaborated further and said the ship was lost at Cape Henlopen when in fact she wrecked near the mouth of Chesapeake Bay. The shipwreck was placed in Delaware instead of Virginia, because of an error made in 1788 in England while reporting on an event in Virginia. Marx's only mistake was changing the letter "i" to an "e." This became the fingerprint in my investigation. When Stewart had sent me on a research trip in November of 1980, I had mistakenly located a reference to a treasure ship of that same name from 1785, which I'd believed had been lost. Stewart capitalized on that mistake knowing that I would back him up. Victoria Stapells Johnson later uncovered irrefutable proof that the 1785 ship did not sink. And then it was the buoy containing the federal court papers on the *Santa Rosalea* that had broken loose from its anchor to wash ashore on Assateague. It was when I read the papers found on the inside that I then came to understand the real nature of the SEA claims filed in federal court.

Peter Hess, the attorney in Delaware, recognized the *Santa Rosalia* in the IRRC cases after following the SEA cases, even though her spelling had been further corrupted to "Santa Rosea Lea." And thanks to Peter's invitation to get involved, I was given the opportunity to go before a judge who was willing to recognize right from wrong and ultimately allowed me to present the same case I was trying to make in Maryland. St. Rosalia was always there.

I would find that she was still watching over me years later.

CHAPTER TEN
Found, Refound and Found Again

In 1985, my wife, Delphine, and I had left Ocean City, Maryland, and moved to Salisbury, thirty miles to the west. The shipwreck business was over for me. Later, we moved on to Laurel, Delaware, but we were still close enough to Assateague to go fishing and camping on weekends, and keep abreast of shipwreck news from Ocean City. In May of 1989, our daughter, Madeline, was born. I was enjoying family life and drifted farther away from the thought of sunken ships and treasure. In 1992, our family relocated to the Outer Banks of North Carolina. I seldom thought of *La Galga*, and I had not been diving since the summer of 1983. But during this time, stories of shipwrecks kept appearing, bringing me back.

In 1984, while I was prosecuting my case against Stewart, I kept hearing about a continued search for the *San Lorenzo* and the other SEA shipwrecks. Richard Cook, who was SEA's former president, my former partner, and my wife's former husband, was intent on finding *La Galga* in the ocean as well as the *San Lorenzo* off Ocean City. He had opted not to join other SEA investors and me in the lawsuit against Donald Stewart. He was still a believer, and he was not alone.

Later, in March of 1986, Cook and his salvage company, Alpha Quest, had filed applications with the State of Maryland for permits to explore for wrecks off Ocean City, Maryland. According to the *Maryland Coast Press* of March 28, Alpha Quest and its archaeologist, Daniel Koski-Karell, were seeking wrecks called the *San Lorenzo de Escoral* [sic], the *Nuestra Señora de Santa Clara*, and two escort ships: one an English frigate named the *Royal George*, and the other an American brig named *Santa Maria*. According to Alpha Quest, these ships were said to be lost in a storm in March of 1829. The *Maryland Coast Press* observed that these were the same ships that SEA had looked for five years before, except for the *Santa Maria*, which was not one of them. The year of loss, 1829, was different than what Stewart had described in 1980. The reporter for the paper questioned Tyler Bastian, archaeologist for the State of Maryland, about these shipwrecks. And since my litigation with the State of Maryland was over, Bastian now freely admitted, "There has been no evidence proving those ships were in the area or were lost off this coast. I have not seen any documentation demonstrating their existence." He apparently didn't believe Judge Ramsey who clearly stated in his opinion that, "Their cargo is believed to include gold altar plate and other riches. In addition it is certainly reasonable to assume that these vessels would also contain other items representative of the culture and lifestyle of people who lived over two centuries ago."

While searching for the Ocean City wrecks, Alpha Quest continued its search for *La Galga*. Koski-Karell told Cook about the wreck that he and Alan Riebe had located in 1981, 650 yards south of the Maryland-Virginia line. Cook had already heard of several Spanish coins predating 1750 being found nearby. He was convinced *La Galga* was Riebe's wreck or at least nearby. They both were aware of my research findings on the boundary line I found in the Accomack County Courthouse that put the line that would point to the wreck nearly a mile and a half south of the current boundary. If Riebe and Koski-Karell had in fact located *La Galga* in 1981, as they wanted to believe, that location had to have been associated with an interpretation of the line farther north of what had been documented in Accomack County. Richard Cook began research into the Maryland-Virginia line at the Maryland State Archives in Annapolis.

After many months, he located the conclusive evidence he thought would prove *La Galga*'s location. It was a map dated 1868 drawn by John de la Camp of the U.S. Army Corps of Engineers. It showed the boundary line on the mainland as always being the same, and on Assateague falling a little south of the present boundary but well north of what had been portrayed in the Virginia land records. The map had been drawn for the Maryland-Virginia Boundary Commission and had been based on a previous survey done in the fall of 1858 by de la Camp and his supervisor, Lt. Nathaniel Michler.

Cook and Koski-Karell believed that they had found the solution to the elusive colonial boundary. But the 1868 map didn't solve the boundary line issues in 1868.

The Boundary Commission had been established in 1858 to settle the long disputed boundary between the two states. The Commission had agreed that the Calvert-Scarborough line of 1668 should be recognized as the boundary, but the only remnants of that line were some trees on the mainland that had been marked in 1668 whose locations were known to the local people living along that line. Michler and de la Camp were hired to retrace that line and commenced their survey on the banks of the Pocomoke River just as Edmund Scarborough had in 1668. They were able to recover thirty-nine marks over the thirteen miles to the edge of Chincoteague Bay where they stopped, just as Scarborough had in 1668, without going over to Assateague.

To the surveyors' surprise, they found that the recovered line was not a true east line as they had expected, but a line 5° 15' north of east, a variation that they proved was related to the local compass variation not recognized by Scarborough in 1668. They reported their findings to the commission, and the Maryland legislature voted to accept this line in 1860. A compromise boundary was offered to Virginia, which included adjusting the line in Chesapeake Bay southward. Virginia rejected it. Michler prepared a map of the proposed boundary in 1860 and extended the line across Chincoteague Bay to Assateague and the Atlantic Ocean on the same tangent. With the onset of the Civil War, the boundary line issue was tabled.

John de la Camp returned in 1868 under the authority of the Boundary Commission to resurvey the line and set monuments. Unlike his work of 1858, he crossed Chincoteague Bay and surveyed the shores of Assateague and was directed to some posts and a stone monument set on Pope's Island marking the boundary known as the "traditionary line." De la Camp did not take notice that this was the only stone monument on the whole line. The original line contained no such markers. To Cook, this meant that the boundary had never changed over the centuries since Calvert and Scarborough had marked the line on the mainland in 1668. But in reality, the "traditionary line" was only the theoretical line extended across Chincoteague Bay on the same azimuth as the Calvert-Scarborough line on the mainland. Scarborough had not crossed the bay to Assateague in 1668 to establish a boundary marker.

Cook's research ended here since he felt it was all he needed to prove his wreck was *La Galga*. But had he looked further in this same archive, he would have found more information on the boundary line. Direct evidence that the Scarborough line was only theoretical on Assateague at this time is found on the map of Samuel Mitchell drawn in 1846, which shows the line on the mainland as the tangential line of Scarborough while the line on Assateague is nearly two miles south of its projection from the mainland over Chincoteague Bay. The boundary on Assateague was clearly depicted as latitude 38°.

In 1865, Maryland had granted several tracts of land south of de la Camp's line in the area of Pope's Island. Lying just off the west side of Pope's Island are two islands called Toby's Islands. The State of Maryland granted a patent for the southernmost one in 1865. The year before, Maryland granted sixty-seven acres of land on Pope's Island south of the stone described by de la Camp. The surveyor at the time made no mention of its significance or even its presence. The boundary line issue was still clearly unsettled in 1868.

The Corps of Engineers finally returned in 1883 to set granite monuments, including one on Pope's Island and one on Assateague that would end the controversy. Lt. Frederick Abbot, who set the monuments, made no mention of any previous boundary marks on Assateague or Pope's Island. The stone observed by de la Camp must have been set in the years between 1865 and 1868, or was a property boundary stone that had been described in 1864, because after the work of his successor was completed, the *Peninsula Enterprise* of December 6, 1883, described the final marking of the boundary:

> The Virginia line is at present the principle topic of conversation. By the old line Pope's Island was in Maryland, the present owner buying it at special commissioner's sale sold by order of Worcester County Court. The new line runs a mile north of the old line and throws the Island, with valuable oyster grounds, in Virginia.

In Daniel Koski-Karell's account of what happened next, he vividly described how the wreck they believed to be *La Galga* was found on the first day out in May of 1987. Guided by the 1868 map, they returned to the site found by Alan Riebe and Koski-Karell in 1981 and found ship timbers, ballast stones, some pottery that Koski-Karell proclaimed was Spanish, and other artifacts. No coins were found, no cannonballs, musket balls, or other artifacts that would identify it as an armed vessel. The press had little to say about the discovery.

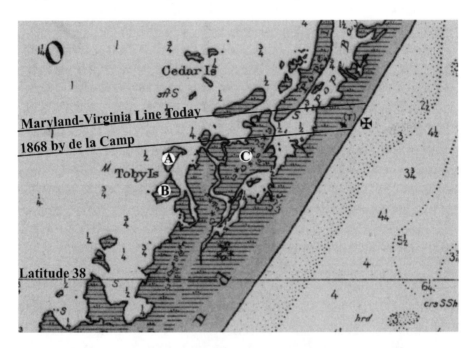

Islands "A" and "B" are known as the Toby Islands. In 1846, Samuel Mitchell's map of Maryland showed the Maryland-Virginia Boundary on Assateague as Latitude 38° even though the line on the mainland was a tangential line that would extend nearly along the present line and by extension would fall nearly two miles north of latitude 38°. These islands were considered to be lying in Maryland. Further support for the understanding of a boundary south of the line drawn by John de la Camp in 1868 is found in two Maryland patents dated 1865 for ten acres each for *Toby's Bed* and *Toby's Bed Tump* located on island "B." In 1864, Maryland granted 67 acres on lower Pope's Island at "C," These grants of land prove that de la Camp's line was not recognized as the boundary prior to 1868. It was however the line drawn across Assateague in 1711 by William Whittington. In his patent the distance from Pope's Bay to the ocean was stated as 134 poles or 2,211 feet. There has been very little erosion since then. But in direct contradiction to this, Maryland claimed all of Pope's Island. Virginia made no claim to the beach opposite Pope's Island, thus we have a "no-man's" land. See also page 141. This line however proved to have great significance. It was the line that pointed to Norfolk, Virginia where Ben Benson would file claim to his wreck in federal court. The location of the Riebe/Cook/Benson site is indicated. Chart from 1915 Coast and Geodetic Survey, the first published chart showing the Toby Islands. *Illustration by the author.*

In 1989, Cook and Koski-Karell assembled their research papers which consisted of copies of eighteenth century newspaper accounts, transcriptions of several documents from England and Spain, photographs of their artifact discoveries, pictures of coins found by a beachcomber, and de la Camp's map. The report was bound in a ring binder and they applied for and received a copyright for their work. The report made no mention of Cook's previous involvement with SEA, Ltd., with our group, or the boundary line locations documented by the federal government in their chain of title research found at the Accomack County Courthouse and in my research report in 1983. Their report, however, did include a copy of a page from my report about the shipwreck legend.

In 1990, an Ocean City tourist magazine described Alpha Quest's continued hunt for the *Santa Rosalia* and the *Santa Clara*, two of the fictitious shipwrecks named by Donald Stewart. As for capitalizing on its claim of locating *La Galga*, the article said that Alpha Quest made no attempts at a formal salvage effort. It was later stated that they had run out of money.

That same year, another story was published in *Shipwrecks of Delaware and Maryland* by Gary Gentile, a noted shipwreck diver and maritime historian. This one featured me, the story of *La Galga*, and my findings that the wreck was buried under Assateague Island. In the text of the book, he gave the latitude and longitude of the wreck, which placed it inland, although he was about a mile too far north in his calculations. His comment in 1990 was that the government had done nothing with *La Galga* after having her handed to them "on a silver platter."

Two years later, Alan Riebe published his book on shipwrecks entitled, *Treasure Wrecks Around the Globe, 900 -1900 A.D.* He disclosed the location of his *La Galga* site as "600 – 800 yards" south of the current boundary. He said that he was the first to apply for a state permit in November of 1980 but had been frustrated by government bureaucrats. Riebe pointed out that *La Galga* had been sought by many treasure hunters and historians but no treasure had been discovered. He had abandoned his effort to verify *La Galga's* location and moved to North Carolina to hunt for *El Salvador*.

In 1994, a report was issued called *An Assessment of Virginia's Underwater Cultural Resources* by the William and Mary Center for Archaeological Research and the Virginia Department of Historic Resources. The report identified three wreck locations in the Chincoteague area, one being at the Riebe/Cook site. No identification or definitive dating was reported. One of its authors, Sam Margolin of Underwater Archaeological Joint Ventures, made an attempt to locate *La Galga* in 1983 and had no luck, but a symbol was placed on his locator map indicating a wreck of some kind in the location first indicated by Riebe. The report said that *La Galga* had neither been located nor positively identified.Virginia took no further action to identify this wreck.

In late March 1997, I was in my real estate office reading the news on the Internet. A headline grabbed my attention: "Go-Ahead Given to Hunt for Booty from Two Spanish Galleons."

It was an article from *The Virginian-Pilot* in Norfolk, Virginia that told the story of a man named Ben Benson and his treasure-hunting company called Sea Hunt, Inc. that found *La Galga* just below the Maryland-Virginia line. Drawing on records from London and Spain, Benson claimed that he had found *La Galga* and that she had most likely been carrying horses that were the forefathers of the wild horses on Assateague. He based that conclusion on the fact that soldiers had been on board. Benson said that *La Galga* was a 1500-ton ship traveling with fourteen others from Havana. There was another Spanish ship he claimed to have found just off the south end of Assateague called the *Juno*, which had been lost in 1802.

As I read the story, it appeared to me that Benson's wreck was the same one Alan Riebe and Daniel Koski-Karrell had found in 1981 and again in 1987 by Richard Cook and Koski-Karrell. He seemed convinced that he had found *La Galga*. The headlines made it sound as if he had, but from what I was reading, his historical facts on the ship were off the mark. *La Galga* was much smaller than the ship he described and there were only seven ships in the fleet, not fourteen. His comments about the horses and soldiers hit home—they were the same ones I had made back in 1983 after consulting with Dr. Eugene Lyon in Florida about horseshoes being found on the *Santa Margarita*.

I was just as interested in his claim of discovery of the *Juno*. I had been following the news of the previously alleged discovery of that ship in deep water forty miles off of Assateague by Quicksilver International from Norfolk, Virginia. Historical accounts had placed that ship as much as two hundred miles off the Virginia coast when she sank in 1802. In 1981, Donald Stewart had written a fictitious account of her loss on Fenwick Shoal just off Ocean City.

In June of 1996, Ben Benson, described as a wealthy adventurer, arrived in Ocean City in his private yacht. Benson had made a fortune in timber and had retired before reaching the age of forty. His financial successes had convinced him he could become an accomplished treasure hunter. Standing over six feet tall, he was confident and self-assured. The corporation he formed was called Sea Hunt—after the television series of the late 1950s featuring Lloyd Bridges as Mike Nelson, an underwater sleuth.

As luck would have it, Richard Cook and Ben Benson apparently found each other. Cook told him of his experience and knowledge about shipwrecks along the Delmarva coast, and, in particular, what he knew about *La Galga*. Cook explained to him that he had already located *La Galga* under a permit he had obtained in 1989 (not 1987) from the State of Virginia. At the conclusion of the meeting, the two discussed the possibility of a joint venture to locate and salvage historic sunken ships along the Delmarva coast. Cook saw this chance meeting as a great opportunity, so he shared a copy of his research material on the 1750 fleet with Benson. Benson reportedly copied the material before returning it. Benson then asked Cook if he could see a copy of his permit with the Commonwealth of Virginia's Marine Resources Commission.

They seemed to hit it off. Cook took Benson down to the site he believed was *La Galga*. It was lying about 650 yards south of the Maryland-Virginia line and about seventy yards offshore in twenty feet of water. Cook told him of wooden planking, ballast stones, bricks, and glassware he had recovered and said that this shipwreck had been the source of the wild ponies of Assateague. Benson was totally intrigued.

At Chincoteague, Benson learned of an anchor being dragged up by fisherman in 1989 off the south end of Assateague. Stuck to the anchor was a pewter plate with writing on its back containing the letter "J." It appeared to spell "Jane" or "Jolle," but Benson said it could stand for "Juno."

Benson placed an ad in the Chincoteague newspaper offering a reward for information about artifact finds on the beach. Several people responded. One woman brought in twenty Spanish coins that her mother had found on the beach near the wreck site where the anchor was found.

His ad brought unexpected news. A Chincoteague resident told him of the story about an olive-skinned boy who had washed ashore on a hatch cover in the early 1800s. The boy's story was documented in the family bible of Ernestine Holston. Inside the bible was an account of a James T. Lunn, sixty, who had fallen overboard and drowned in 1913. It said that Lunn's great-grandfather was taken off a stranded ship and was so young that he didn't know his name and spoke a strange language. The islanders gave him the name of James Alone, which subsequently was changed to James Lunn. The account described the wreck as a French ship. Also found inside the Bible was a page from an Eastern Shore travel guide that related a somewhat different account on the same story. The article said that a baby had been found on the beach strapped to a plank many years ago. His rescuers named him "James Alone" because he "came from the sea alone.'"

Benson theorized that since he had seen no record of a French ship being lost, it must have been a Spanish ship. It appears that he reached this conclusion because of the Spanish colonial coins found on the beach.

In 1987, Quicksilver International from Norfolk, Virginia had begun a search for the *Juno* in deep water off Assateague Island. They were motivated by the finding of a large bronze Spanish church bell and a stern post with two bronze gudgeons that had been hauled up by a fishing boat from Wanchese, North Carolina. The find was made about forty miles east of Assateague. Quicksilver spent several years using side scan sonar to try and locate the source of the bell and stern post. They believed that they came from the *Juno* since historical accounts had placed her offshore of Assateague in deep water. In 1989, Quicksilver filed a claim to the wreck in federal court in Norfolk, Virginia.

After several years, Quicksilver claimed to have located a wreck that yielded cannon balls and other artifacts consistent with the *Juno*. They were never able to bring up irrefutable proof that they had, in fact, found it.

Benson added up the evidence. A bronze Spanish bell was found forty miles east of Assateague, which was between his wreck and the last reported position of the *Juno* some two hundred miles away. There were Spanish coins found on the beach and in the water dating to 1799, a plate with the letter "J," and an "olive-skinned boy" who had come ashore from a French or Spanish ship in the early 1800s. To him, it had to be the *Juno. But was it?*

Benson was probably unaware of the number of shipwrecks that had occurred along this coast. Many ships have been lost in this area, including another ship named the *Juno* that wrecked in the area in 1817. Until lifesaving stations were established in the 1870s that gave a complete account of wrecks, newspapers were the primary source of information on the numerous shipwrecks along the coast. Some wrecks were not reported in newspapers but found their way into other archival sources. Some were never reported at all.

Benson needed to know more about his "Spanish wrecks" so he found a researcher in Spain. It just happened to be my researcher, Victoria Stapells Johnson. She researched the 1750 fleet for him as well as the *Juno*.

From the record it appeared that Benson felt he no longer needed Rick Cook. He went ahead and obtained his own recovery permits from the Commonwealth of Virginia on March 25, 1997. These two permits provided Sea Hunt with a 75 percent reward for items recovered. The permit language expressly stated that all objects recovered "shall be the exclusive property of the Commonwealth of Virginia, with title thereto vested in the VA SHPO" (State Historic Preservation Office). Sea Hunt's investigations were to be limited to determining the significance of the wrecks in accordance with criteria established by the National Register of Historic Places. Sea Hunt was to provide daily progress reports to the State and maintain daily logs that the State could inspect at any time, including an accurate, detailed list of all items recovered. The permit spelled out that Sea Hunt's permit could be suspended and/or revoked for failing to comply with any provision contained in the permit.

The Commonwealth of Virginia had been given title to all shipwrecks in its waters by the Abandoned Shipwreck Act of 1987. Guidelines for the act spelled out numerous obligations for the states. One was to locate and identify shipwrecks and identify which ones were historic. Another provision of the Guidelines said that sunken warships or other vessels entitled to sovereign immunity remained the property of the nation to which they belonged, even though they appeared to be abandoned. The Guidelines say that a nation must specifically state its desire to abandon its vessels for them to be eligible for salvage. The Act also said that the states must protect the rights of owners of non-abandoned shipwrecks.

Sea Hunt's permits had made no mention of the vessels by name, *La Galga* and *Juno*, or even that there were Spanish vessels involved. Sea Hunt had received exploration permits the year before from the State, so the State must have known that they had granted rights to Spanish vessels. If they did not, then they were certainly made aware by *The Virginian-Pilot* headlines the day after the recovery permits were granted. It became evident that Virginia had claimed a wreck for itself that was not provided for by the Abandoned Shipwreck Act and then granted rights to Sea Hunt to recover artifacts that they claimed were the State's.

According to the Commonwealth of Virginia's Department of Historic Resources, Benson was the first in Virginia to actually receive an underwater recovery permit rather than just an exploratory one. By the time Benson had received his recovery permit in March, he said he had already expended $250,000 exploring and mapping the *Galga* and *Juno* sites.

With the permits from Virginia, Sea Hunt was free to start retrieving artifacts from the wrecks. The newspapers were now following the story hoping to be first to break with news of a great discovery. Benson was always available for interviews and seemed to enjoy the notoriety. He was not trying to raise capital like SEA and Indian River Recovery Company who were dependant on the publicity they created to raise investment. He did not need investors.

The publicity brought some unwanted reaction. News of the shipwrecks brought out voices of opposition. A nonprofit group of scuba divers called the Maritime Archaeological and Historical Society lobbied the government to stop Benson from salvaging the wrecks. They objected to Benson's right to sell artifacts and make a profit. Steven Anthony of MAHS compared Benson and other treasure hunters to "adventurers who desecrated Egyptian pyramids in searches for gold." Benson was seeing himself in quite a different light, however. He saw the story of the *Juno* and his involvement with it as compelling enough to interest Hollywood. Benson resented the article's characterization of him as a plunderer and responded, "At the end of the day, if it's going to make sense, if people are going to do this work, you have to at least break even. Anybody who goes into shipwreck hunting thinking he's going to get rich is an absolute fool."

Benson feared that the federal government or the Kingdom of Spain would assert an ownership claim to the wrecks. He was also concerned that some third parties might claim an interest as well. Benson filed preemptive salvage claims in the U. S. District Court for the Eastern District of Virginia in Norfolk. He sought to proceed under his existing contract with the State and bar any other party from interfering. Each salvage area contained approximately six square miles, even though at least in the case of *La Galga* he had an exact location in mind just off the beach. His attorney was Peter Hess, the same Delaware attorney who prompted me to intervene in the IRRC cases in 1985. Peter's admiralty law practice was now in big demand. He had worked on numerous high profile shipwreck cases including one where he had successfully gained permission for a group of experienced deepwater divers lead by Gary Gentile, a noted diver and author, to descend to the famous Civil

War ironclad, the *Monitor*. This historic ship is lying off Cape Hatteras in over two hundred feet of water. Peter, an experienced diver himself, made the dive with them.

On March 11, 1998, Benson, Peter Hess, and David Sutelan, as Virginia counsel, carried three artifacts into the federal courthouse where they had asked the court to symbolically "arrest" them in order to establish the validity to their claim to *La Galga* and the *Juno*. Presiding over the hearing was Judge J. Calvitt Clarke, Jr., a veteran in salvage cases. Judge Clarke had presided over the *Titanic* case in 1996 and later the *Central America*, a recent discovery involving hundreds of millions in gold recovered from the side-wheel steamer that sank in 1857 in over eight thousand feet of water off the coast of North Carolina.

Peter Hess was the first to address the court. He explained that there was a legal issue that needed to be decided from the beginning, that is, when is a federal court deprived of its admiralty jurisdiction by virtue of the Abandoned Shipwreck Act of 1987. Provisions of this law said that an abandoned wreck within the territorial waters of a state was property of the state and presumably removed from the federal court's admiralty jurisdiction.

Peter had stated from the beginning that the vessels may not be *La Galga* and *Juno*, but his client believed them to be. The question to be answered by the court was whether these vessels were abandoned or not. If they were abandoned, then Benson's permit with the State would be controlling. If they were ruled not to be abandoned, then Hess believed the Kingdom of Spain would make an appearance and claim the shipwrecks.

Judge Clarke asked Benson about the nature and purpose of his company, Sea Hunt. Benson explained that it was set up specifically to explore for and salvage shipwrecks anywhere in the United States. When Benson was asked about the shipwrecks, Judge Clarke was told that he had found them nearly two years ago. *La Galga* was lying two hundred feet from shore and the *Juno* was fifteen hundred feet from shore.

Benson testified that he was the sole discoverer of the wrecks and had no knowledge of anyone else bringing up artifacts or diving on them. Judge Clarke asked him if there were more than the three artifacts recovered from the two ships—to which he admitted there were none, but he was quick to emphasize that he had spent about $1 million up to that point.

Benson went on to explain to the court that they had met with Virginia officials and discussed the plan to file the admiralty claim to protect them in case someone else claimed the wreck now that he had spent so much money and effort locating them. He said he had reason to believe that it was going to happen.

Peter Hess stepped in to clarify an issue that was sure to arise: Quicksilver's claim that they had found the *Juno* forty miles away. Benson explained that the two sites were separate and neither party was working each other's site. Either one of them was right, or they were both wrong.

After hearing this, Judge Clarke wanted to know the attitude of the United States government in regards to salvage of a sovereign vessel. It was Benson's opinion that the government was against salvage and wanted the wrecks left alone.

Benson had also told the court that "various individuals" were putting a scheme together to get Spain to claim sovereign possession of the wrecks and then assign them over to the United States.

Convinced that Spain would file a claim, Judge Clarke gave the order to allow sixty days for Spain's intervention. The next day, the court entered a preliminary injunction "enjoining and restraining all persons and entities from interfering with the Plaintiff's exclusive salvage rights to the Shipwrecked Vessel(s) heretofore granted it by the Virginia Marine Resources Commission...."

On March 21, 1998, notice was given to the Secretaría General Tecnicía in Madrid of Sea Hunt's claim. On the same day, arrest of the shipwreck sites was published in *The Virginian-Pilot* in Norfolk. Benson now waited to see what would happen. Two days later, Sea Hunt put the National Park Service on notice that the court had determined that Sea Hunt's permits with Virginia were valid and that the Assateague Island National Seashore was enjoined from interfering with Sea Hunt's activities in the permitted area.

The Virginian-Pilot of March 26, 1998, headlined, "Spain Lays Claim to Shipwrecks; Maneuver Complicates Assateague Salvage Projects."

Back in Ocean City, Maryland, Richard Cook heard about Benson's admiralty claim, so Alpha Quest and Cook intervened and filed a joint claim of ownership of *La Galga* and other vessels(s) located in Sea Hunt's specified area. And because Benson used Cook's research material, they alleged copyright infringement, fraud, and bad faith and that Cook had sustained damages to the tune of $250,000. In supporting memoranda, Cook claimed he "had gone boldly where no one has gone before" to find *La Galga* and secure the VMRC permit. For the *Juno*, Cook's attorney had told the court that her discovery by Benson was "a ridiculous assertion." He offered to demonstrate to the court that the *Juno* laid outside the permitted area "somewhere off the Delmarva Peninsula" and that Cook may have already found it.

Cook needed to know more about what Benson was up to, so he hired a boat and went to his *Galga* site. News of his activities reached Benson, who quickly found out who was operating the boat and put them on notice that he had exclusive rights to the wreck and the surrounding area. Sea Hunt even sought a protective order to keep any information it might divulge to the court about artifact recoveries and locations out of the public view.

On May 11, the Commonwealth of Virginia entered the fray. Days later, Janet Reno's Justice Department showed up, not to represent the interests of United States citizens, but the Kingdom of Spain.

The court held a hearing on September 15 to look at all of the issues and open motions before it. The courtroom was filled with a wide variety of lawyers representing the Commonwealth of Virginia, Sea Hunt, Alpha Quest, and the U.S. Government on behalf of Spain.

Alpha Quest's attorney addressed the court to explain that it was Cook who had first found *La Galga* and that Benson used his research and permit filing to get his own permit from the Commonwealth of Virginia.

Alpha Quest's attorney said that his client had obtained an exploration permit from Virginia, but could go no further for lack of money. He had been actively seeking investors for the last seven years until Benson's involvement. He made further statements that Cook had been working the coast for the last twenty years and had identified several shipwrecks.

Later in the day, Ben Benson had the opportunity to tell his side of the story. Peter Hess called him to the witness stand:

Hess: Mr. Benson, when did you locate these shipwrecked vessels that have been tentatively identified as the *Juno* and *La Galga*?

Benson: In 1996 during an extensive survey that we did under a permit, a search permit issued by the State of Virginia.

Hess: And the original permit that was issued to [Sea Hunt] by the Commonwealth of Virginia, what did that provide for?

Benson: It allowed us to search in state waters, anywhere within state waters for shipwrecks.

Hess: During the time that you were conducting these survey operations, did you ever speak with an individual named Richard Cook?

Benson: Yes. I did.

Hess: And could you summarize for the court the substance of your dealings with Mr. Cook?

Benson: I spoke with Mr. Cook, as well as a number of other people, who had either worked looking for *La Galga* or had written about *La Galga*. There is quite a number of books published by people claiming to have found it as early as the '70s. Somebody claimed to have found it in North Carolina. Mr. Cook, in a book that he published, claimed to have found the site in the '80s. Another guy named John "Armahein" claimed to have found it also in the '80s in a different location. So I tried to contact each one of those people and to see what kind of data they had.

Hess: How did you find what you believe is the wreck site of *La Galga*?

Benson: Through about a 400-hour magnetometer survey that took two months to complete.

Benson described to the court how the magnetometer worked and how they would verify the magnetic targets located. He explained how difficult it was to make an identification with the amount of sand over some of the targets while using divers with probes and metal detectors. When Peter Hess asked him about how much archival and historical research he had done on these wrecks and others in the area, he said that he had spent over three years researching and currently had someone in Spain working for him. And for his investment in the research, "I don't know how many hundreds of thousands of dollars on research we have spent...."

For the next two years I followed the stories of Benson's legal problems with interest. *La Galga* was hardly mentioned while his focus shifted to the *Juno* as he believed that she was worth millions of dollars. Contemporary accounts describing the loss of the *Juno* said she was carrying about $100,000 when she sank.

The newspaper stories were so convincing, I wondered if the site found by Alan Riebe in 1981 was, in fact, *La Galga*. But when I read the headlines of *The Virginian-Pilot* on July 22, 2000, "Spain Owns Coastal Shipwrecks Court Bases Decision on 1902 Treaty," I thought that Spain probably got an empty bucket since most likely neither shipwreck was Spanish.

Although treasure hunting was no longer an active pursuit, I still enjoyed getting out on the water. That summer I'd bought a twenty-two foot Mako center console to do some fishing. It took a bit of money and several months of work to get it ready.

I was working on the boat one afternoon, and I switched on the GPS receiver for a test. I had just loaded NOAA's wreck data into it from my computer. I scrolled the electronic map up to the Maryland-Virginia line on Assateague. As I moved the cursor north, I could see several wreck symbols along the coast, and when I got near the border I saw a wreck symbol lying partially in Pope Bay and on Assateague. When I moved the cursor over it, the words "La Galga 1750" lit up to identify it. The wreck symbol was not in the ocean, but behind the beachfront, and it was a little north of the site that I had identified in 1983. While wondering how it had gotten into the database I realized that it was September 4, the feast day of St. Rosalia. *Another coincidence?*

I requested the records from NOAA that identified the names of the wrecks and sources of information contained in the data base for the GPS. In the history field in the data base it said,

WASHINGTON POST, Dec. 14[13], 1983; SPANISH GALLEON OFF MD-VA COAST IN 1750; 50 GUN FRIGATE, CARGO MAHOGANY AND TOBACCO (SPANISH ARCHIVES). WRECK ASSUMED TO BE BURIED BY MIGRATING DUNES AND SHIFTING COASTLINE. OCEAN RECOVERY OPERATIONS, INC. BACKING RESEARCH EFFORTS. JOHN L. AMRHEIN, JR. AND WILSON BANE ARE POINTS TO CONTACT. MAGNETOMETER READINGS HAVE BEEN POSITIVE AT THE SITE. SITE IS WITHIN CHINCOTEAGUE NATIONAL WILDLIFE REFUGE, U.S. FISH AND WILDLIFE SERVICE."

I'd wondered if Sea Hunt's GPS had the same information.

I always knew that someday I would write the complete story about *La Galga*. It had been tempting to dig into it when I read about Benson four years before. Friends had been sending me newspaper accounts they had read knowing they contradicted our position that the wreck was buried under the island. It was now time to find out.

In the summer of 2001, I hauled out my boxes of research and began to revisit the work that I'd started back in 1978. I also reviewed the complete court record in Benson's case. Additional research needed to be done in Spain, hopefully yielding Captain Huony's report of *La Galga* that had never been located by anybody, so I called Victoria Stapells Johnson at the last number I had from 1985. I tried several times with no answer. I thought perhaps she might have returned to Toronto where she was from, so I called the number associated with the old address she had given me. Persons living at that address did not know of her. I was fortunate, though, as the woman agreed to look up all of the people with the last name Stapells in Toronto. She gave me five phone numbers. It was not until the fourth number that I made any connection to Victoria. It was a distant cousin who had said he might be able to locate her. He and I had a short conversation, and he wanted to know where I was from. It turned out that he was quite familiar with the Outer Banks and used to live in my subdivision.

Weeks went by and I never heard from him so I wrote a letter to Victoria and sent it to him for forwarding to her. This was in late July, 2001. A month went by, and I gave up hoping that I would hear from her.

It was a usual weekday where our family got ready for work and school, and I realized that it was September 4, the feast day of St. Rosalia. I reminded Delphine that something usually happened on that day to remind me of the shipwreck. She waived the remark off and focused on leaving for work. I thought nothing more of it myself.

That evening, Delphine was going through the day's mail and tossed me an envelope. "This is for you." It was a letter from Victoria responding to my letter from July! Victoria said she was still in Seville, only at a different address. I reminded Delphine that it was September 4. She turned white as a ghost.

I called Victoria and she told me that she was quite familiar with the present situation with *La Galga* because Ben Benson had hired her to do some work for him. She said he basically got the same material she had found for me years before, so he had nothing new. I told her that I was convinced that Captain Huony's report was out there to be found.

Victoria seemed hesitant to research the 1750 fleet for a third time but agreed to help. She told me that she couldn't start until February. That was fine as I had plenty to do on my end.

Since I was dealing with the colonial period, I also had made contact with several researchers in England through the Internet.

Reopening the project was a step into the past. I felt twenty years younger. The relentless pursuit of the wreck, diving in the ocean, the forays on Assateague, the court case, all of these experiences, came flooding back.

I reviewed my notes and previous report related to the wreck and found that I had made an error. My premise for the boundary line on the mainland was wrong due to a misinterpretation of language in a deed, but the plats I had located in the Accomack courthouse still suggested that the 1750 boundary was well south of the present line.

If I was wrong about the boundary line, I realized that *La Galga* could still be in the ocean. If she was in the ocean, it most likely was the wreck that Alan Riebe had found in 1981 which was later exploited by Cook and Benson. I was certainly prejudiced against this location because it was Stewart's deception in 1980 that had drawn me to that area to begin with. I reviewed the magnetometer surveys from 1981 for the location of the Riebe wreck site. Because the water was usually only fifteen to twenty feet, our Varian magnetometer had a flotation cable which kept the sensor head off of the bottom. This not only protected the sensor, but enabled the magnetometer to "step back" and analyze the bottom area. It was important to get the overview of a potential wreck site, rather than attempting to pick specific items. A screwdriver lying next to the sensor could set it off like a cannon would at twenty feet. It certainly seemed that a fifty-six gun warship fastened with iron would leave a larger magnetic signature than the one I had mapped at Alan Riebe's site—even one that had been salvaged and broken apart. The Riebe/Cook/Benson site still did not correlate with the determination of the 1687 and 1840 lines on Assateague as documented at the Accomack county courthouse. The map that Riebe had given me showing his interpretations of the boundary line did not address the 1687 or the 1840 lines documented there. Riebe's premise was that the wreck would be found between latitude 38° and the present line. He was correct in that premise. And since he had found a wreck in this area he reasoned that it must be *La Galga*. I recalled my last conversation with him back in 1985. He had left the site to go search for *El Salvador* at Cape Lookout, North Carolina without making a positive identification of the wreck site.

I realized that I needed to start over and reexamine the boundary line question. Cook and Benson had both filed written reports in libraries, so I consulted those. Even though they both had seen my 1983 report, they both had ignored my findings related to the boundary line. There was no written interpretation on their part as to why these lines shouldn't be considered.

After reviewing the report authored by Cook and Koski-Karell in 1989, it became clear as to what had happened. Alan Riebe and Koski-Karell had found a wreck in 1981 that, based on their understanding of the boundary line, could be *La Galga*. Riebe had abandoned the site without any verification and went to Cape Lookout, North Carolina, to hunt for *El Salvador*. Cook had hired Koski-Karell in 1982 to help him locate Stewart's *San Lorenzo* off Ocean City. Through this association, Cook heard about the wreck and sought to find proof that this was *La Galga*. By the end of 1983, they both were aware of my findings related to the boundary line being located over a mile south of Riebe's wreck.

Ben Benson appeared to have relied mostly on what Cook had told him about the boundary line. Benson had made no reference to the documented boundaries in his report. He did acknowledge that the main unanswered question was, "Where was the Virginia-Maryland line in 1750?" To answer that question, he said he consulted with a retired member of the Virginia Marine Resource's Commission, who had told him about variances of the line in the Chesapeake Bay that were irrelevant to a line drawn across the Chincoteague Bay to Assateague. Benson concluded that it could be anywhere in a three-mile area. As I read this, it became clear to me why he didn't mention the documentation of the 1687 and 1840 lines. It would contradict his claim about *La Galga's* location.

In Richard Cook's report, he put forth that his wreck site must be *La*

Galga because in the 1970s, a woman named Juanita Clements who had owned a house just north of the present boundary line in Maryland had found several Spanish pieces of eight predating 1750 on the beach. Cook made Benson aware of these coins, and Benson received some updated information. In his report, he related that a piece of eight dated 1751 had been found on the beach opposite his wreck by Dale Clifton, an avid diver and director of the DiscoverSea Shipwreck Museum at Fenwick Island, Delaware. Rather than saying that this coin came from another wreck or that maybe the wreck was not *La Galga*, he stated his belief that that someone must have dropped it while salvaging the wreck. A coin minted in Mexico would've taken years to arrive in Virginia as it passed routinely in commerce. A coin dated 1751 could easily come from a wreck (or someone dropping it) many years later. But I had learned years before that Spanish coins do not necessarily mean a Spanish wreck. Neither Cook nor Benson addressed this fact. If the 1751 coin had come from the same source as the pre-1750 coins, then their premise for their wreck being *La Galga* was unfounded. From my own research, I'd found a number of vessels lost in this area that could account for the coins, and none of them were Spanish.

As I read on in Benson's report, he described how I had located the wreck on the island, "with the help of a psychic." He apparently thought that this nullified my findings of the clearly documented references to a boundary line well south of his wreck site. And as further evidence that our inland site should be dismissed, he pointed out that the federal government had shown no interest in what we documented in 1983. I was amused. He obviously had seen my report because his papers included a photocopy of one of its pages. It was the typed transcript of *La Galga's* register prepared by Victoria in 1980. At the top was stamped "Worcester Room," from the copy at the Worcester County Library. I read on and found more "borrowed research." Benson included a description of Assateague in 1826 by a Henry Lloyd. This "historical description" was, in fact, made up by Donald Stewart in 1977 and given to the National Park Service to supplement his *San Lorenzo* hoax. Benson's only source for this would have been the National Park Service who had given it to me, possibly Rick Cook, or my court files in Worcester County. Benson had even cited it in his bibliography as "Journal of Henry Lloyd, Surveyor of Dorchester County, pages 37-39" and had also included a photocopy of Stewart's document. In the first paragraph of this "journal," it says that Governor Stevens of Maryland commissioned a survey in 1826 to settle the boundary dispute between Worcester County, Maryland, and Accomack County, Virginia. The narrative says that they had five men and four mounts to carry supplies for five days travel—all of this to locate the boundary that would have been within, at most, a mile and a half of disputed territory, on a confined barrier island. An absurd tale indeed. But then Governor Stevens left office in 1825, and Matthew Smith was surveyor for Dorchester County, not "Henry Lloyd."

Benson's report outlined Cook's previous efforts in locating *La Galga*. He described Cook's research as beginning in the late 1970s. Of course he did not start on his own until 1983 after he had left our group. Prior to SEA, Cook had known nothing of the ship. But it did appear that Cook's allegation that Benson was borrowing his research was well founded. Benson acknowledged that "Rick Cook undoubtedly has done the most research and assembled the most convincing evidence to document his finds." But Benson declared that he had started his search in the summer of 1996, unaware that others had already done so in the past.

Contrary to what was being portrayed in the newspapers as a great discovery, Benson's report provided no proof as to why his site had to be *La Galga* rather than some other wreck. His belief seemed to be based on Rick Cook's belief. But the newspaper headlines were enough to convince the public that he had, indeed, found her.

There was a third report written by Cook's archaeologist, Daniel Koski-Karell, filed in the Accomack county library in 1988. His involvement with *La Galga* had actually begun in 1981 with Alan Riebe. Koski-Karell described the significance of *La Galga* as being the legendary ship that had brought the ponies to Assateague. He backed up Cook's hypothesis that the boundary line on Assateague in 1750 was a little south of the current line. He acknowledged my claim that the wreck was buried inland, but did not address the locations of the

1687 and 1840 boundaries that I had documented and of which he was aware. And for some reason, he did not mention me by name but merely referred to me as "another writer." Surprisingly, they both named *La Galga's* captain as Daniel "Mahoney" instead of Huony. Donald Stewart had always referred to him erroneously as "Mahoney."

In Spain, Victoria went to work in the Archivo General de Indias and the National Archives and Naval Museum in Madrid. She located a lot of ancillary material on *La Galga* and the 1750 fleet, but nothing that zeroed in on establishing the wreck's location or the elusive Huony declaration. Our luck soon changed. She returned to the Archivo General de Simancas on November 18, 2002. She emailed me on the twenty-third. The subject line said it all. "BINGO at Simancas."

I wanted to write to you right away to say that our trip to Simancas was INCREDIBLE. Have a look at this:

A complete description of the ship, some 68 pages dated 1733, two years after she was built in Cádiz. This includes every last piece of wood, nail, rigging, sail, and so on. With this, you could have a replica built which would be 100% accurate.

A document with the dimensions, tonnage, and number of cannons.

Various cannon lists showing that these were iron, breakdown of sizes given.

Various documents between the years 1733 and 1747 which will enable us to reconstruct her history. Up until now, the only trip we have been able to document is her last one to Mexico. The documents found at Simancas give us dates of where she was and why and many details on the ship itself.

For the 1748 trip to Mexico, a log from Cadiz to the Canaries day by day. A document detailing the position of each ship as the fleet left Cádiz…, with a color ink drawing of the convoy and merchant fleet as it approaches the Canaries. The *Galga* and the rest of the warships are drawn with a key so as to identify each ship. Another drawing which outlines the navigation route from Cádiz to the Canaries.

Her full report arrived neatly bound and bulging with documents. I found that *La Galga* had been first fitted with iron cannon. There were twenty-two twelve-pounders, twenty-four eight-pounders, and eight four-pounder cannon. She had never filled out her full compliment of fifty-six guns. The description of the ship was so specific that even small details in the construction of the launch and skiff were given. This report was based on an inspection done in 1736 at Cádiz before she sailed for Buenos Aires. Victoria documented that *La Galga* also had eight iron cannons used as ballast. If those cannons could be documented as being on board in 1750, it would disprove the Riebe/Cook/Benson site. The cannons had not been detected by previous magnetometer surveys. Another document, dated 1737, said that the ship was to have 7,388 cannonballs of different sizes aboard. There were iron rings and bolts. There were iron derricks at the hatchways. The stanchions along the gunnels were made of iron. There were nine stoves that were probably all made of iron. Although this iron would be valuable to the wreckers, some of this could have remained after the November storm. There were no large iron targets picked up in our magnetometer surveys or that of Benson, except in very shallow water next to the beach. This target appeared to be a single object or a tight cluster of smaller objects, not a hull. When we had gone over it in 1981, it couldn't be verified as especially large since the water was shallow—putting whatever iron was there very close to the sensor head. Victoria's find was valuable for the archaeology of the wreck, but I was disappointed that she had not located Captain Huony's report.

It had always bothered me that Riebe and Cook had not found any cannonballs or musket balls. In fact, it was this detail alone that had convinced me in 1981 that Riebe had found a ship other than *La Galga*. I knew that the upper part of the ship had been heavily salvaged, but that the lower sections had not, evidenced by the fact that the mahogany had remained in her hold for two months until the gun deck broke loose in the November storm. The storage lockers for cannon shot located in the stern and other tools stored below deck would have been inaccessible to the people who were salvaging the wreck. If the iron cannon ballast was still on board when she had run aground in 1750, then whatever Riebe/Cook/Benson had been working on couldn't have been *La Galga*. Again, magnetometer surveys bore this out.

It was not until February 21, 2003, that I had gotten the complete translation of the Simancas material. By this time, Victoria had had a chance to analyze her references and tell me that another trip could be worthwhile. She would go the first week in March.

On March 5, it happened. Victoria struck gold. She sent a frantic e-mail:

> In haste from the hotel internet connection..... After 20 years of looking for you, I have found the law suit on the loss of the *Galga*!!!!! An enquiry into whether Huony was responsible for the wreck, about 100 pages, various declarations by officials on board, a complete account by Huony. It was in a file on "Oficiales de Guerra, 1751-2." I will have the photocopies with me when I leave. I doubt that anyone has ever seen this, partly because of where it was filed also because there are no Simancas stamps on the documents, something which there would be if it had ever been xeroxed or microfilmed in the past. WHAT DO YOU THINK OF THAT??!!
> Back in Sevilla on Friday.
> Victoria

As I later read through Victoria's translations I'd realized how lucky I was. No one had seen these records in two hundred and fifty years, at least no one pursuing the wreck. Apparently even Spain had overlooked them when they'd searched for *La Galga's* records in the Benson admiralty case. In addition to the declarations by Huony and those of his officers, there were some water-stained documents that Huony had saved from the ship.

With Huony's own accounts and that of his officers, I was finally able to answer some nagging questions. One was the distance from shore. The accounts that had been available to me in 1980 were conflicting on that subject. One had said a musket shot from shore and another had said a cannon shot. The *Maryland Gazette* of September 12, 1750 had said a quarter of a mile. The description of the sailors swimming to shore with a line and tying it to a wrecked vessel on the beach and the account of Huony sending the barrels of bread ashore with the waves strongly suggested a distance from shore of probably less than 100 yards. And then there was the statement from Huony about being "on the border of Maryland and Virginia," but yet still in Virginia. And then what was not said takes on its own meaning. None of the survivor accounts from Huony or the Englishmen who testified about the wreck mentioned Pope's Island. It seems that if they had wrecked on Assateague opposite Pope's Island, it would have been mentioned. This fact added circumstantial evidence that the wreck lay south of Pope Island. All of this would become very meaningful in my re-evaluation of the boundary issue. And, of course, the narrative about the storm and the wreck couldn't have been written without it.

Probably the most important new fact discovered was that Huony, and several other officers, described the wreck as being "covered with sand" or "buried in sand." This clarified the statement made by Sheriff John Scarborough of Worcester County after he had visited the wreck and reported about the mahogany trapped in the hold, "There is many thousands of pounds worth if it could be got before the Ship bursts with the Sea and *Sinks into the Land*." This statement was made one week after the ship had wrecked. These two statements taken together confirmed that the ship was indeed buried under Assateague Island.

Victoria also found that the chest of gold belonging to Father Juan Garay de Concepcíon had been rescued along with most of his other possessions which he brought back with him to Spain. But I had abandoned my interest in treasure years ago when I became ensnared by the story of the shipwreck and legend it left behind.

Benson's analysis of his magnetometer surveys depicts a ship that had run aground, dropping debris starting 500 yards from shore and running southwest right up to the beach. He found some ship timbers that he said were dated as "pre-1820" in this area and described the present state of the wreck as having "no physical integrity and pieces of the wreck are scattered over a fairly large area." If anything would've been jettisoned on the way in, it would have been cannon, but they were not according to the newly discovered testimony. But then, Benson's theoretical southwest path is contradicted by his own assumption that *La Galga* had struck Winter Quarter Shoal, which is *south* of his proposed site, not *north* as would be required for a southwest trajectory. The record is unclear where she struck. Lt. Mercenaro said they were within sight of land about ten miles out when she hit the reef. Winter Quarter Shoal is about five miles off of Assateague. They were propelled towards land for two hours by a gale-force north east wind. It seems more likely she struck somewhere north of Winter Quarter and was most likely closer than the estimated ten miles.

Since determination of the 1750 boundary was still crucial in evaluating the Riebe/Cook/Benson site as well as my own, I started over on that question. I had a firm position on the 1840 line from the plat. The federal government's plat of 1943 had estimated the line in 1687 as being south of this. The surveyor had indicated a "+/-" next to it because he was unsure of its precise location. I had already determined that the two earliest patents for land on Assateague were both in 1687. The Virginia patent and later deed described the northernmost bounds as ending at the Maryland line. This line extended from "bay to sea," with no reference to Long or Pope's Island that lay just behind Assateague. This fact confirmed that the line was then south of that island. Later that year, Maryland issued a patent for Long Island to John Pope that described the entire island as being in Maryland. In 1713, a certificate of survey was issued with the same metes and bounds described in the 1687 patent and also referred to the southern end of Pope's Island as "near unto the line of Virginia." None of Long or Pope's Island was included in Virginia. The original boundary between Maryland and Virginia on Assateague was thus set and in apparent agreement between the two colonies.

The records show that the line drawn across the bay to Assateague was always a due east line rather than the tangential line as laid out on the mainland. This is strong evidence that in 1750, Maryland would have insisted on the boundary specified by its original charter whenever possible. A plat dated 1876 found at the Accomack courthouse shows the line on the mainland going through Franklin City, Virginia. This line is about seven hundred yards south of the present line. A due east extension of this line across the bay to Assateague ties in exactly with the line of 1840 on Assateague. These two plats demonstrate the confusion over the line on the mainland and one of the reasons a boundary commission was formed in 1858 to resolve the issue. The Calvert-Scarborough line of 1668 on the mainland was not run over to Assateague, making the boundary issue there separate from the mainland.

Subsequent subdivisions of land noted in the Accomack courthouse suggest that the boundary remained in this immediate area until 1883

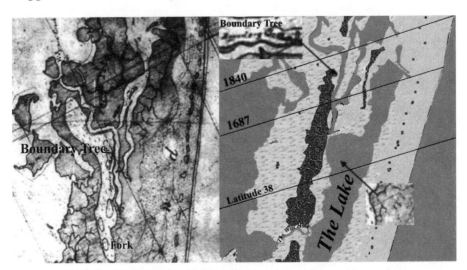

On left, 1859 Coast Survey of lower Assateague Island found in the National Archives, College Park, MD. Note the location of the Boundary Tree. This tree coincides with the southern tip of the feature shown on the 1840 survey called "Point of Pope's Island." See page 149. In 1687, all of Pope's Island was considered to be in Maryland and lying "near unto" the Virginia line. On the Virginia side, the owner had rights to Assateague from bay to sea without any mention of Pope's Island. See page 141. The southern end of this point is in line with the boundary tree. The lower insert locates the fork just above latitude 38 degrees. *La Galga* is believed to lie in or next to this fork, a remnant of a former inlet. *Illustration by the author.*

when a new boundary line was extended over from the mainland, pushing the line more than a mile north.

In 1983, I'd located a topographical map of the area dated 1859 in the National Archives. This map showed a "boundary tree" on Assateague lying between the 1840 line and the estimated 1687 line. It soon became obvious that this tree probably marked the intended boundary line of 1687 and had survived up to that time.

I needed to find out more about that tree and the underlying survey. I returned to the National Archives in College Park, Maryland. I knew that the field notes might exist for the work performed by Charles Ferguson of the U.S. Coast Survey while he had been at Assateague in 1859.

Marjorie Ciarlante of the archive staff had located some pertinent references before I had arrived. I'd found that the field notes I was looking for had not survived, which should have shed light on the source for the boundary tree, but what Ms. Ciarlante directed me to was very relevant. In Ferguson's notebook describing the signals (landmarks) erected for the purpose of the survey, there was a description of the location for the Pope Island signal. From this signal, two wrecks were noted to the south. One was 180 meters south and the other 250 meters south. With the help of a hydrographic survey dated 1850, which I'd already had a copy of, I was able to pinpoint the location of the Pope Island signal. It was situated about four hundred yards south of the present Maryland line.

The wrecks described in 1859 are most likely the one(s) located by Riebe/Cook/Benson and also the source for the timbers we'd found on the beach at this location in 1982. It did not say how old the wrecks were but they most certainly were not from 1750, or at least not *La Galga*. Huony had described *La Galga's* hull as having been cut down to the surface of the water and then later what was left, at least above water, had broken to pieces in a later storm. What was seen in 1859 was either on the beach or at least above water. Benson's archaeologist had dated the remains as "pre 1820." A vessel lost in this decade could have easily been built in this time period. *Lloyd's Register of Shipping* for 1859 lists many vessels still sailing that were built prior to 1820, and

Popes Bay (Apateague I^d

Is situated on a range of sand hills on the beach the bluff may be known by its having grass on it & is directly opposite the eastern bend of Popes Bay there are two wrecks near it from the first it is 180 Metres from the southernmost one 250 " N

Ragged Pt is seen just outside (E.) of the woods on Chincoteague Island bears SW ½ S

Hardy WNW

Big Bay Pt NW ½ N and comes between two houses on the island about a mile distant from the signal

Green Beach bears NE ¼ E !

Description of wrecks noted by Charles Ferguson in 1859. *From the National Archives, College Park, Maryland.*

some as far back as the 1780s. There was a major storm in December of 1839 where at least three vessels were driven ashore between the Chesapeake and Delaware bays. One or both wrecks referred to by the surveyor may be the result of this storm. The report of the 1839 wrecks originated in the Snow Hill, Maryland newspaper suggesting that they had occurred nearby.

In another incident, on March 15, 1852, the bark, *Sunbeam*, from Havana to Boston, drove ashore in this immediate area loaded with a cargo of sugar and fine Cuban cigars. The shipwreck was indeed a tragedy, even though the crew was saved. When the ship struck, the sea broke over her and everyone took refuge in the rigging to escape the freezing cold water. Captain Lincoln had his wife and daughter

Overlaying these three boundary scenarios on an aerial photograph clearly demonstrates the relatively narrow range of the search. Once we established through courthouse documents the 1840 boundary, we knew that the site first found by Alan Riebe was not *La Galga*. The boundary tree noted in 1859 most likely originated in the eighteenth century. After failing to find another site in the ocean and discovering from the 1840 survey that drastic changes had occurred on Assateague since 1750, we knew the wreck was buried under the island. *Photo by the author.*

aboard, and when they came from their cabin, lightly dressed, they were unable to withstand the brutal elements. Captain Lincoln held his daughter in his arms until she died, and as he tried to secure her body to the deck, a wave snatched her body from his arms and carried her away. Captain Lincoln returned to the rigging to comfort his wife, who also died in his arms a few hours later. With nothing left to live for, he too fell into the sea.

Now that other wrecks were documented to be in this exact area, it becomes a bit difficult to separate them from what Benson and his predecessors believed to be *La Galga*.

When Captain Huony was in Norfolk, Virginia, and had heard the report of the survey of the Maryland-Virginia border line, he was told that his ship was now in Maryland, not Virginia. For this new interpretation of the boundary to effect this change in jurisdiction, the line would have been moved south of a previously conceived boundary, such as a marked tree.

Captain Huony filed his first report from Norfolk, Virginia, on October 13, 1750. He informed the Marqués de Ensenada that when he landed at Assateague he was told, "We were on the island of Azetegue on the border of Maryland and Virginia." And his understanding as to what side of that line he was on is demonstrated in the title of his report: "Report of the events of the frigate La Galga from her departure from Havana to her loss off the coast of Virginia." This was in spite of the fact that his first landing on the mainland, after leaving Assateague Island, was in Maryland. Whoever told Captain Huony at Assateague that he was near the border of Maryland had a ready landmark—the southern point of Pope's Island. When Captain Huony wrote Governor Ogle of Maryland on November 12, 1750, he said he had been told that a survey had taken place that contradicted his understanding of where his ship had come ashore. He said, "The Country People, telling me She lay in Virginia, was my motive that made me write the President [Thomas Lee in Virginia]."

The site our group had located in 1983 was south of the 1859 boundary tree. This is consistent with Captain Huony's understanding of being "on the border" *and* in Virginia.

In contradiction to boundaries described in individual parcels of land, maps of the day depicted the boundary as the east line of latitude 38°, and also some maps showed it just below this latitude. So, to override the boundary tree, or any preconceived mark on Assateague, a more encompassing interpretation of the colonial boundary would have to have been considered.

There were no other "official" surveys of the boundary line determination in 1750.

The only records that could shed any light on that question are the surviving field notes of the deputy surveyor for Worcester County, Maryland, at the time, Colonel John Henry. As deputy, he reported to James Harris, surveyor general for the Eastern Shore. He was also a member of the Lower Assembly representing Worcester County in Annapolis. His notes are not a daily log but a recording of surveys performed. There is no mention of the survey or "experiment" of the colonial boundary. It seems almost illogical that he would not have been consulted, since he was a Maryland official. After scheduling out the record of surveys done with their dates, it is possible to calculate his open days when he *could have* done the survey work. *If* he were present, the survey most likely occurred between October 14 and 20. According to the log of HMS *Triton* riding in Norfolk, there was probably good weather, and no survey work was recorded in John Henry's diary. And then of course, if he were there and he did not record it in his field notes, it would have been performed *off the record*.

There is legitimate reasoning that the "experiment of an East Line" was the determination of latitude 38° or at least nearby. This line was the theoretical boundary line, at least for Assateague. The starting point of the current boundary line as well as the 1668 Calvert-Scarborough line on the Pocomoke River is just below latitude 38° on the east side of Chesapeake Bay. This position could have been calculated astronomically and then transferred to the western edge of Chincoteague Bay or onto Assateague itself. Redrawing the line across the Eastern Shore would not have been necessary. The same is true for a precise determination of latitude 38°. The difference between these two points of origin is about six hundred yards. This method could easily be used to override previous property surveys and what may have been deemed erroneous determinations of the Maryland-Virginia boundary itself.

A large quadrant or sextant mounted on a fixed frame would yield a very precise position being calculated to within one second of latitude, which is a little over one hundred feet. The 1859 chart shows latitude 38° at almost exactly as it is today. It could have been done in 1750.

Ralph Justice, a ship owner and prominent citizen of Accomack County, characterized by Huony as "Not only witness, but Actor" in the looting of *La Galga*, had presented himself to Huony in Norfolk with the news of the looting since he had left and the later survey. He had also named three men as being from Maryland who were also involved in salvaging the wreck. They were Thomas Robins, someone named "Dalason," and Daniel Mifflin, a Quaker and a prominent citizen of Virginia, not Maryland. Mifflin owned an 1100 acre plantation in Virginia called *Pharsalia* that bordered Chincoteague Bay on the mainland opposite the wreck on Assateague and adjoined the Maryland line. Virginia records document him as a Virginia resident. He also owned several tracts of land in Maryland, but those records also describe him as being from Virginia. Later, his son Warner, who became famous during the American Revolution for his antiwar and antislavery sentiments, wrote of his life on his father's Virginia plantation. Ralph Justice would have had to have known Daniel Mifflin. This misclassification may not have been a mistake.

On August 10, 1751, the Executive Council of Virginia issued the sheriffs of Accomack and Northampton counties blank summons to be served on everyone known to be involved in pillaging the Spanish wrecks. In the Virginia archives, there is a list of sixteen residents of Accomack County who were summoned to Williamsburg. Included in these were Ralph Justice who lived south of Chincoteague Inlet and William Gore who owned Assateague. Daniel Mifflin was not one of them. Latitude 38° ran through his plantation. His manor house no longer exists, but a visitor in 1903 described it as being near Franklin City, Virginia, "a fine house in its day and commands a good view of Chincoteague Bay." Franklin City is about a half mile north of latitude 38°. The fact that a prominent resident of Accomack, Virginia was at least temporarily misclassified as a resident of Maryland provides strong circumstantial evidence that the survey referred to by Captain Huony was a determination of latitude 38°. Further support for this hypothesis is the statement made by Acting Governor Thomas Lee to the Board of Trade in England on October 9, 1750, about the line on the Eastern Shore: "Our Northern Bounds are Divided from Maryland by a line drawn east, from Watkins Point; the south side of Pocomoke, on the Eastern Shoar, to the Atlantick Ocean, and ends about the latitude of 38 degrees." This statement was made prior to my estimated date of October 14-20 for the "experiment" mentioned by Captain Huony. In 1751, the map makers Joshua Fry and Peter Jefferson published their map of Virginia showing the line as due east and a little below latitude 38°. (See page 58)

On September 15, 1998, Benson and his attorneys, Alpha Quest's attorney, and counsel for the federal government and the Commonwealth of Virginia appeared in federal court before Judge Clarke in the matter of *La Galga* and *Juno*.

Most of the day was taken up with attorneys for the Justice Department and Spain making arguments for a temporary injunction against Sea Hunt to halt its recovery efforts. They said Benson needed another permit to operate his vessel close in to the beach. Peter Hess, representing Sea Hunt, pointed out that all of the government's testimony seemed to be about protecting artifacts for Spain. The government's attorneys were trying to halt the use of a prop wash deflector to excavate the bottom. They said that a trained diver needed to be in the hole as the sand was blasted away. Benson countered this saying that it was too dangerous to put someone beneath the boat in near zero visibility. The government archaeologist, who was encouraging this practice, admitted that he had never dived in this area and further clarified that he had not done any verification of the shipwreck sites. Judge Clarke said that if the government was going to represent Spain, and make the assertion that the vessels were not abandoned and therefore the property of Spain then perhaps the government would need to affirmatively establish that these were in fact Spanish warships. The government said that they were barred from diving on the sites because of his injunction of March 12, 1997. But Judge Clarke had a quick solution:

"All you have to do is come to court and say, 'Judge, we are not sure that these are the right ships. How about letting us put a diver down there to find out,' and certainly I would agree that you could do that."

Ms. Barbara B. O'Malley for the government countered, "I understand that, Your Honor. My first answer to you is if Sea Hunt with its resources has not been able to identify them, I don't think sending down one U. S. diver is going to either."

Judge Clarke replied, "But Sea Hunt has never guaranteed that these are the two ships. You are, in effect, trying to guarantee that they are these two ships, and I'm not satisfied that the court is going to give Spain the yea or nay on salvaging these vessels when we don't really know what they are."

Judge Clarke wanted to expedite the trial date. Alpha Quest agreed to a dismissal of its claims of fraud, copyright infringement, and bad faith in return for the right to litigate those issues in another court, assuming Benson would win title to *La Galga*.

Judge Clarke then questioned how the U.S. government could represent Spain against the Commonwealth of Virginia. It was the U.S. government who, in 1987, had given title to all historic shipwrecks lying within the territorial limits (usually three miles) of each state. The Abandoned Shipwreck Act, as it was called, excluded warships of other nations, however. The federal government's motion was dismissed, and they were barred from representing Spain. The court did allow Spain to enter its own claim and gave them ninety days to do so.

Spain filed its own claim on December 23, 1998, and the U.S. government filed an amicus brief the same day in support of it.

No one could say for sure that the artifacts found proved that, in fact, the *Juno* and *La Galga* had been found. When Spain entered the litigation, they merely assumed the truth of Sea Hunt's allegations. Sea Hunt's statements were based on the fact that a wreck had been found in an area that could contain *La Galga* and apparently relied on

Cook's interpretation of the 1750 boundary and the finds of Spanish coins on the beach to back it up. Spain's entire legal standing was based on the allegations found in Sea Hunt's complaint and the erroneous assertion that Spanish colonial coins were proof of a Spanish shipwreck. Archaeologists for Virginia and the United States government were certainly aware that these coins were legal tender in this country until 1857. Neither government pointed this out to Spain. To Spain, Spanish coins were identifiable Spanish artifacts, so Spain continued to do the bidding of the federal government.

Benson now had the option of saying that these artifacts were not from these ships. But if he did, then the burden of proof would again be his. Some observers in the background thought that his affirmative claims on *La Galga* and the *Juno* may have been premature. Virginia had been willing to deal with him regardless of the ships' identities—he had valid salvage permits. Benson stuck to his belief.

Spain was now invoking its prior treaties with the United States going back to 1763. The issue now was whether *La Galga* and the *Juno* were actually warships and whether Spain had expressly abandoned the wrecks. Benson, who from the onset had characterized them as warships and property of the King of Spain, now was trying to demonstrate that they were commercial vessels and not acting as ships of war. His effort was as much a game of semantics as anything else. The Abandoned Shipwreck Act used the term warship to describe a naval vessel belonging to a government. Both ships had always been characterized as property of the King of Spain regardless of their mission. Spain, in response to Sea Hunt's new characterization of the *La Galga* and *Juno* as commercial carriers, submitted hundreds of pages of photocopied archival material in support of its argument that they were warships and part of the Spanish Navy. They also said that they had not abandoned the wrecks. Spain was making an all out legal assault and had the U.S. government on the sidelines acting as head cheerleader. The U.S. government has never liked treasure hunters.

Meanwhile, Sea Hunt was forced to stop salvage efforts until the ownership questions were resolved. Its legal bills were mounting. Newspaper accounts showed that Benson was now focusing on the *Juno*. It appeared that this was where Benson thought he might realize some profit. He said he had documented that there were over 700,000 silver pieces of eight on board when she sank. Based on this assumption, Benson's appraiser had put an $83 million value on the *Juno's* contents.

There was a lot at stake. Quicksilver International, who was working in deep water on a wreck that they had claimed was the *Juno*, was certainly delighted to hear from Benson about how many millions were on their wreck. They were also relieved that Spain had not interfered with their salvage claim. But were there millions to be had by anybody? In May of 1999, Spain submitted some very convincing documentation to the court that the treasure on board the *Juno* had been transferred to the *Asia* when she arrived at Puerto Rico and before she sailed for Spain in 1802. The *Asia* had arrived safely in Havana. This information was a little late in coming, however. Quicksilver had already lost a diver the year before in their quest for the millions.

The court convened a hearing on April 1, 1999, to review motions. Quicksilver was still contending that it had, in fact, found the *Juno* in deep water forty miles off the coast. Sea Hunt again clarified for the court, with the concurrence of Quicksilver, that there were two distinct shipwrecks at stake. One of them was the *Juno*, or neither. Sea Hunt was convinced that Quicksilver's wreck was not the *Juno* because the anchor on the site had a chain attached to it, which was not used until well after 1802. Quicksilver was convinced that it was impossible for the *Juno* to travel such a great distance in the sinking condition described by the survivors to arrive at the south end of Assateague Island. If both arguments were correct then neither ship was the *Juno*.

In court, the next to appear was counsel for Alpha Quest. He told the court that they were all in court because of the successful efforts of Alpha Quest and Richard Cook in locating *La Galga*. For the record, he said that the ship laid some three hundred yards south of the Maryland-Virginia line (previous statements said 650) and seventy yards off the beach, and he said that everyone conceded that this site was *La Galga*. He went on to say that Alpha Quest let its permit lapse for lack of money, and later he'd led Ben Benson to the site and guided him in the Virginia permitting process. Judge Clarke pointed out that a salvor must show financial ability to complete the salvage. He further stated that it appeared that Alpha Quest was describing some sort of contract between Sea Hunt and Alpha Quest. Alpha Quest's attorney said that there had only been negotiations and that Cook had shared his findings and research without a formal contract. Judge Clarke was still uncertain why Alpha Quest was there.

> Judge Clarke: There is some confusion about your position. Are you seriously asking this court to award salvage rights or even ownership rights to the wreck?
>
> Alpha Quest: No, sir. We would just like a share of the finds.
>
> Judge Clarke: You just want to do what?
>
> Alpha Quest: We would just like to be allowed to have our day in court and present our evidence, and hopefully at the end of the day to be awarded some share of the finds.

The court, Alpha Quest, and Sea Hunt agreed that if Sea Hunt were awarded final rights to *La Galga*, this should be decided in another forum.

The court then moved on to review Spain's claim and Sea Hunt's new assertions that *La Galga* and *Juno* were not warships. This new and inconsistent claim seemed to frustrate Judge Clarke.

Sea Hunt argued that both ships had been abandoned, with Spain strongly asserting that they had not. The United States government weighed in and stated that its position was that the ships had not been expressly abandoned, and therefore they were not the property of the Commonwealth of Virginia. This would nullify Sea Hunt's permits with the State. Several times during the day's various testimonies, it was acknowledged that the ship's identities had not been conclusively established. The federal government would have no standing to be there if these two sites were not the alleged Spanish ships. They were cruising in very shallow water.

On April 1, 1999, the court dismissed Alpha Quest's remaining claim of ownership. Alpha Quest was free, however, to file other claims against Sea Hunt in a separate action if it chose to do so. On April 27, the court ruled that *La Galga* belonged to Virginia. Whether or not the ship was a warship was irrelevant now. The deciding issue was that of abandonment. The court said that through the 1763 treaty, Spain had expressly abandoned title to *La Galga*. The decision validated Benson's permit with Virginia. This was a small victory for him. His research showed that there was little treasure to be had on *La Galga*. The *Juno* was the prize he sought along with the millions that he insisted were still on board. But the court was less generous with the *Juno*. The court said that Spain had not abandoned the *Juno*, therefore, it remained the property of Spain.

There was one glimmer of hope for Sea Hunt. The court still needed to rule on the alternative salvage reward Sea Hunt had asked for should title not be granted. There were more briefs filed addressing this question. Faced with the possibility of paying a salvage award, Spain vehemently denied that Sea Hunt had found the *Juno*. After winning title to the wreck, Spain obviously wanted to win both ways. In supplemental memoranda, Virginia argued that since no discrete location for the *Juno* had been determined, Sea Hunt should be able to proceed under its permit to retrieve artifacts. If these proved to be from the *Juno*, Sea Hunt should be awarded a normal salvage fee.

Not surprisingly, Spain disagreed.

The last brief was filed by the federal government on June 15, and it took Judge Clarke only ten days to render his decision. Sea Hunt would get nothing. No return, no compensation for the $1.5 million dollars Benson claimed he'd spent on researching, salvaging, and litigating these wrecks. "Such is the risk inherent in treasure salvage," Judge Clarke commented. Benson was now ordered to return to Spain the salvaged *"Juno"* artifacts. He was devastated.

Benson was not alone. Some third graders from Las Vegas wrote letters to Judge Clarke criticizing his decision. One boy said, "I think you made a bad call," and a girl asked, "Why does Spane git the Ship anyway." Some in the media were taken aback by the court's reliance on old treaties. Dave Addis of *The Virginian-Pilot* posed this question:

"Does anyone else find it odd that a government so famous for ignoring 200-year-old treaties it made with its own native peoples can be so militant in enforcing a 200-year-old treaty in behalf of a long-collapsed Spanish monarchy?"

One thing was obvious to anyone who had followed previous salvage cases. This was the first time Spain had ever staked any claim to a shipwreck in American waters. It was apparently the first time that they had been invited in by the United States government. In the very high profile case of the *Nuestra Señora de Atocha* discovered in the Florida Keys by Mel Fisher and Treasure Salvors, Spain had made no claim to the millions recovered. But this case was different. It involved Spanish naval vessels and the Abandoned Shipwreck Act of 1987.

The fight was not over. Spain wanted *La Galga*, and Benson still wanted the *Juno*. They both appealed.

These cases were now drawing worldwide attention. Never before had Spain entered a salvage case over a Spanish shipwreck. The ramifications were clear. It might well preclude any salvage company, state, or the federal government from controlling or salvaging a Spanish shipwreck in United States waters. Amicus briefs were filed by Columbus-America Discovery Group, the company headed by Tommy Thompson who had just recently discovered and salvaged the *Central America* containing hundreds of millions in gold. Other salvage companies, including Treasure Salvors, Cobb Coin, Intersal, Enterprise, Quicksilver International, Deep Sea Research, and even the State of North Carolina, weighed in with their own amicus briefs. It would now be up to a panel of judges in Richmond, Virginia to decide the fate of Ben Benson and the wrecks he wanted.

The continuing saga of *La Galga* headlined again in *The Virginian-Pilot* of May 1, 2000: "Shipwreck's Story Will End in Court—Spain, Virginia and Treasure-Hunter Argue over Sunken Ship off Assateague."

Benson was sweating it out at Sea Hunt's headquarters in Chincoteague, Virginia. His case was the next to be decided in Richmond. He couldn't have predicted that what had started out as a little adventure would turn into an underwater nightmare. He told the reporter of *The Virginian-Pilot*, "If I had it to do over again, I would never have stopped here."

In late July, the Fourth Circuit Court of Appeals rendered its decision. The court upheld the lower court's decision that the *Juno* still belonged to Spain. And as for *La Galga*, the court reversed the lower court's decision and said that the Abandoned Shipwreck Act of 1987 preserved Spain's right to the ship, absent an express abandonment. The court found no express abandonment. The court quoted from the 1763 treaty: "It is moreover stipulated, that his Catholic Majesty shall have the power to cause all of the effects that may belong to him to be brought away, whether it be artillery or other things."

Benson pondered his options. There was only one. Take it to the Supreme Court. However, after considering his odds, he decided against it. "My involvement has ended. I'm never going to look for shipwrecks off the coast of the United States."

Benson sold his company to two investors, Peter Knollenberg and Joseph Birch. They decided to appeal to the Supreme Court with the Commonwealth of Virginia, but the court refused to review the case.

Sea Hunt, contrary to Judge Clarke's order of June 25, had still not turned over the recovered artifacts. What had been documented as recovered at this point were artifacts from the *Juno* site consisting of two anchors, glass and pottery shards, some iron fittings, numerous straight pins, a lead shot, a pewter button, rope fragments, a small bar of low-grade silver, a pewter spoon, and four Spanish coins dating from 1734 to 1796. The official report and inventory seemed to be devoid of any artifacts recovered from *La Galga*. The federal government continued to allow Spain to proceed with the erroneous assumption that the coins were proof of a Spanish wreck.

Sea Hunt and Virginia had stated that they were happy to comply with the court's order to turn over to Spain all artifacts that had come from *La Galga* and *Juno*. But they now posed this question: "Which of these artifacts belonged to which ship, if any at all?" Both Sea Hunt and Virginia stated that they had no conclusive proof that either of these ships had been found. In court papers, Sea Hunt even stated, "The record is clear that the parties and the Court relied on supposition, conjecture, and speculation when referring to the unidentified vessels as the *Juno* and *La Galga*." No evidence to support these identities was ever received or solicited by the court. This statement upset Spain, which then responded that this was quite contrary to Sea Hunt's sworn statements made at the initiation of the suit.

Sea Hunt claimed that it had found a total of twelve wrecks in the *Juno* area and that the artifacts were interspersed. They said it should be up to Spain to prove which artifacts had come from Spanish ships.

Spain not only wanted the artifacts, but the specific locations of the wrecks and artifact discoveries. This was troubling to Sea Hunt. They stated that Spain could use this information without rewarding Sea Hunt and salvage the wrecks themselves.

As for *La Galga*, her location was already part of the record. This had been provided by Alpha Quest in its claim filed July 24, 1998: "650 yards south of the Maryland line and 70 yards off Assateague Island in twenty feet of water." Sea Hunt never denied that this was the same site that they had "discovered" in 1997. Years earlier, Alan Riebe had documented this location with papers filed with the Commonwealth of Virginia.

The court was forced to hold more hearings. On March 2, 2001, Virginia testified that there were not enough artifacts recovered to make a positive identification of the shipwrecks. Counsel for Sea Hunt was quick to concur: "We are not in a position to confirm for *in rem* purposes that the ships are in fact those of the *Juno* or *La Galga*." Spain still demanded to know the locations. Virginia stated:

> We want to have control of our underwater land when we get through with this, except for the area in which the LA GALGA and the JUNO lie. But the weakness of that exception is, nobody knows where that is.

Spain used Sea Hunt's own flimsy evidence against them. For the *Juno*, Sea Hunt had presented Spanish coins as evidence of a Spanish ship and a list of shipwrecks known to Sea Hunt as having been lost in the area. The list included twenty-seven shipwrecks from *La Galga* in 1750 to the steamer *Wicomico* lost in 1907. Spain cleverly pointed out to the court that according to Sea Hunt's own list, there were only two Spanish shipwrecks in the area, *La Galga* and *Juno*, therefore the Spanish coins must have come from these wrecks. The coins found had come from the alleged *Juno* site, therefore Sea Hunt had found the *Juno*. This premise contradicted Spain's own archival documents that had given the location for the *Juno* as many miles off shore, nowhere near the southern tip of Assateague.

No coins had been found on the site alleged by Benson as *La Galga*. Spain relied on two pieces of information to support their claim to her, and Benson's premature identification of the site as *La Galga*. Spain was aware of the documents in the Maryland archives giving the location of the ship, which it submitted to the court. Just after wrecking, Captain Huony had been told on the beach that the wreck was in Virginia. After talking with Sheriff Scarborough in Snow Hill, Scarborough went to Assateague to see the wreck and found people at work salvaging the ship. He wrote a letter to the governor of Maryland about his visit. In court, Spain highlighted the following from that letter:

> I went over last Saturday and told them to be easy until we had Your Oppinion but they told me the vessel was in Virginia as there was Several Gentleman with their slaves all at work from Virginia they did not regard anything said to them but the People living on the beach tell me that she lies two miles within Maryland lines.

In a footnote, Spain ignored what the "Virginia Gentlemen" had said and addressed the purported statement of the "beach people:"

> These people knew that they were subjects of Lord Baltimore. It is possible that they assumed the Maryland line to be the 38th parallel (the Northern Tip of Ragged Point).

Spain's statement that "they were subjects of Lord Baltimore" was a conclusion made without basis. And the fact that there were only "Virginia Gentlemen" and no Marylanders on the wreck was of no surprise. Huony had told the people on the beach before he left that the "Owner of the Land owned the Ship." That would have been William Gore of Virginia. Records found at Simancas, Spain, which contain Captain Huony's testimony, say that the unidentified person or persons who were on the beach when they had come ashore told them that they were on the border on the Virginia side. Apparently none of the mainlanders who had ferried them across the Chincoteague Bay contradicted this understanding as he had this perception when he arrived at Snow Hill and later, Norfolk. The Sheriff's reliance, or Spain's for that matter, on the beach people's statement might have been hasty. In 1764, Daniel Mifflin, one of the owners of the island, had characterized the people living on Assateague as "generally poor people much used to fishing and fowling. They are in general plain illiterate country people." And Scarborough did not say these "beach people" lived opposite the wreck. He only said that they lived "on the beach." Captain Huony had told Governor Ogle in his letter that "the Country People, telling me She lay in Virginia, was my motive that made me write the President [Thomas Lee in Virginia]." The question that begs an answer now is, where were these "beach people" referred to by Scarborough when the Spaniards were at Assateague? It's obvious they showed up days later. Spain and its American attorneys may have jumped to a wrong conclusion.

In 1750, the only people near the wreck appeared to be Indians. This is evidenced by Francisco Caro, caulker, who testified in London that December that it was not until the third day that an English vessel had arrived. There was testimony that some unnamed individual(s) were on the beach and had assisted them on September 6. Other testimony said they had made their way to shore in "Indian canoes." Unlike the records found for 1764, it is uncertain what English may have lived on the beach at the time of the wreck. William Gore's herdsman, William Tyndle, who lived at Ragged Point near the wreck, was away, as records showed he had died in Delaware at this same time. Sheriff Scarborough's statement about the people living on the beach suggests that they must have not been from the immediate area, or the statement itself is suspect.

There is some justification for the "two mile" statement, however, as there had been some confusion for years over the issue of the line running through Chincoteague, south of latitude 38°. Several early Virginia land patents had called for the Maryland line to run through the northern end of Chincoteague Island. The boundary tree on the 1859 map lies nearly two miles north of Wildcat Marshes at the northern end of Chincoteague. As late as June 16, 1835, a John Cullen was deposed about the line. He had said that he was seventy-nine years old and understood that "there was a direct line from Smiths Pt. [in Chesapeake Bay] to Chincoteague." Some maps of the day still showed the line this way even though they were in error.

The survey, or "experiment" as it was called in 1750 by Captain Huony, apparently hadn't convinced the Spaniards that the ship was really in Maryland. Upon Huony's return to Spain, he turned in the cargo register. The first page shows a notation dated March 2, 1751, "wrecked on the coast of Virginia." When Diego Guiral, the captain of the Battalion of Marines, petitioned for a promotion on July 31, 1752, he referred to the loss of *La Galga* on which he had served from 1740. He complained of "fatigue and ailments" he had been suffering from, "the shipwreck of the frigate *La Galga* on the coast of Virginia." No Virginia records acknowledge the wreck as being in Maryland. There is no evidence in the Maryland Archives that a survey was performed to position the wreck. There is no record in the Maryland Archives of the 1750 "experiment" other than the reference made by Captain Huony.

Spain may have made the same mistake as Scarborough had done in 1750. Since Scarborough obviously had wanted control of the wreck, he chose to ignore what both the "Virginia Gentlemen" and Captain Huony had said about the location of the wreck in favor of what he had claimed the people on the beach had said. The purpose of Scarborough's statement to the Maryland governor was to get the governor to proclaim that the wreck was in Maryland based solely on his own say-so. Scarborough made no suggestion of a survey or the need for one at that point. The records of the Provincial Council of Maryland make no mention of this survey, no mention of recovered salvaged items, money from their sale, or any correspondence directly to Spain or England's

Secretary of State by Governor Ogle. The *Maryland Gazette* was silent on the subject, which suggests that the new determination of the line was not permanent. In Virginia, President Lee documented everything in relation to the Spanish ships.

The situation may have been that Scarborough just wanted the wreck, right or wrong. As sheriff, he probably got a percentage of the recovered items if the wreck was in his jurisdiction. Such was the case decades later when the office of "Wreckmaster" was created in Worcester County.

In 1784, John Teackle, Commissioner of Wrecks of Accomack County, complained about the residents of Maryland in the neighborhood of Assateague:

> That County was held in great odium on account of the robberies Made on Wrecked Vessels. The Maryland people seem to think themselves priviledged to embezzle from wrecked vessels. They have a good opportunity for doing this as the island of Assitiaque (famous for its shoals & on which three valuable vessels have lately been stranded) lies near that state. They are furnished with information from the Island people, who are concerned in such villany.

Maryland's reckless zeal to claim wrecks for themselves extended into the twentieth century when it insisted that the *San Lorenzo* and three other fictitious ships belonged to them.

And in an interesting parallel to gain control of the wreck, Spain supported Benson's location since it was a mile and a half north of the thirty-eighth parallel. Spain conducted no additional research into the determination of that all-important line. Spain also failed to note that in Benson's report, he had acknowledged he didn't know where the old boundary line was and that the wreck could be anywhere within a three-mile area. The federal government remained silent on that issue. The truth about the boundary line was contained in its own deed of 1943 when it acquired the wildlife refuge.

Spanish coins have been found all up and down the beaches of Assateague. And like Alpha Quest and Sea Hunt, Spain relied on the existence of Spanish coins as the only archaeological evidence of Spanish wrecks. And like Benson, they ignored the fact that a coin dated 1751, a year after the shipwreck, was reported found. They were well aware of this as they had submitted a copy of Benson's initial report found in the Eastern Shore public library, which documented this fact, to the court. The federal government, knowing that these coins could have come from any wreck of this period, continued to allow Spain to operate under this erroneous assumption.

It appeared that Virginia had done nothing on its own to verify the site Alpha Quest had been working on under an exploration permit in 1989. Their 1994 archaeological site inventory positioned a wreck at this location with no identity. Alpha Quest officially proclaimed discovery in 1989 and subsequently its permit expired. Alpha Quest's activities in the area were also known by the National Park Service. It appeared that either the Commonwealth of Virginia did not think *La Galga* important enough to send a dive team down to inspect in the intervening years of 1990 to 1996, or they believed that that site was not *La Galga*. In any case, they were happy to see Benson undertake the cost of excavating the site.

Virginia told the court that Sea Hunt was under no obligation to surrender locations to the State until its permit had expired, which would not occur until April 30, 2002. The permit did say, however, that Sea Hunt's logs were always open for inspection. There was little agreement at the end of the hearing, so Judge Clarke continued the matter until March 16 and ordered that the artifacts be turned over to Virginia and Spain as joint custodians.

On March 16, Sea Hunt, Spain, Virginia, and the United States were present before Judge Clarke. The court was expecting Sea Hunt to give a final archaeological report to Virginia and Spain so that ownership of the artifacts could be determined. Sea Hunt still had reservations about this. They were concerned that Spain would resume salvage.

Judge Clarke had asked Spain if there was anything about the artifacts which would identify them as having come from *La Galga* or the *Juno*. As their evidence that the wreck was a Spanish ship, namely the *Juno*, Spain pointed to the two anchors, which were described by the Naval Museum in Spain as "the kind that these vessels were equipped with"; a button, which *could have* come from an officer's tunic; and the four Spanish coins. No one corrected or attempted to advise the court or Spain that the Spanish coins were not proof of a Spanish shipwreck as they were common currency passing as legal tender in the U.S. until 1857.

Virginia and Spain had come to an agreement that the artifacts would be returned to Spain. Virginia counsel said,

> We are not interested in the physical artifacts. We are interested in the story and the history they represent.... The problem with the two vessels, we don't know where they are. We have some locations which may or may not be the vessels.... Spain would be entitled to the *Juno* and *La Galga* if they were ever found.

Virginia expressed concern about Spain and the court proclaiming these sites to be Spanish wrecks, closing them off for good without absolute proof. The question that should have been asked was, "Can the mere allegation by Sea Hunt that they believed, but were unsure, that Spanish ships had been found be sufficient to create a real case for the Kingdom of Spain to intervene in, absent any proof from Spain that they were Spanish?" That "proof" apparently lay solely with the coins. All of the other artifacts only proved that a wreck of some kind was there. Spain was never asked to establish why Spanish coins prove a Spanish shipwreck, and neither the federal government nor Virginia opted to inform them that they didn't. If there were no Spanish ships, Spain would be ordered out of the case.

Spain now argued that Sea Hunt was still seeking compensation in spite of the federal court's ruling to the contrary. But Sea Hunt had made a compelling argument that they were not in fact seeking payment for salvage services rendered, but for the location information that they had claimed they had spent a great deal of money ascertaining. It seemed that what they were trying to say was that if no money flowed from Spain for salvage services, Sea Hunt was under no obligation to provide locations. Sea Hunt said that as long as the door was not closed on that final determination, they would gladly relinquish the locations.

The court ordered again that the artifacts be turned over on or before March 23 and that the location information be filed in open court by the thirtieth. The court rescinded Sea Hunt's permission to salvage other wrecks in the permit areas. Sea Hunt filed an appeal, which was quickly dismissed on the motion of Spain.

Spain was now forced to file another motion to compel compliance. On June 11, Judge Clarke, exasperated, ordered Sea Hunt's counsel to turn over all of the names of Sea Hunt's officers within twenty-four hours. Spain asked for sanctions against Sea Hunt and a hearing was set for July 23.

The new officers of Sea Hunt realized that the risk of financial penalties or jail time wasn't worth non-compliance with the Judge's order. They quickly worked out an agreement with Spain and notified the court on July 20 that a hearing would not be necessary. Sea Hunt acknowledged that Spain was the true owner of the ships, and Spain was satisfied that all of the artifacts had been turned over. There would be no future salvage of any artifacts from either ship. By the stroke of Judge Clarke's pen the truth about an unidentified shipwreck site dubbed *La Galga* by Alan Riebe, Richard Cook, Daniel Koski-Karell, and Ben Benson looked as if it would be buried forever. The federal government got what they had wanted.

CHAPTER ELEVEN

The Trial of Captain Daniel Huony

December 9, 1750
Cádiz, Spain

Your Excellency, I have just arrived from America and regret to inform you of the wreck of His Majesty's, frigate, *La Galga*. I have brought the report of Captain Huony detailing her loss for his Excellency, the Marqués de Ensenada," said Vicente Marcenaro, *La Galga's* young ensign, as he stood nervously before Spain's director of the navy, the Marqués de la Victoria.

Marcenaro had been dispatched to Spain on the sloop, *Industry*, October 16 from Norfolk, Virginia where Captain Huony and the other Spanish captains were waiting for passage home. The *Industry*, Captain Sam Tenant, had been destined for Lisbon, but because of bad weather off St. Vincent, Captain Tenant put into Cádiz. When he arrived, Marcenaro immediately penned a letter to the Marqués de Ensenada covering Huony's written report he had carried across the Atlantic, which he was now delivering to the Marqués de la Victoria who resided in Cádiz.

"Señor Marcenaro, we have already learned of the disaster to our fleet by reports from England and France," replied the Marqués. "His Majesty is greatly disturbed about the loss of ships and that the treasure cargos are vulnerable to the English. Thank you for your report. I will forward these to His Excellency."

Ensenada reviewed the reports of Captain Huony, the ship's purser, Joseph de la Cuesta y Velasco, and Ensign Marcenaro and thought that perhaps *La Galga* could have been saved. He knew Huony to be an outstanding officer, but in the end he had to answer to King Ferdinand about the loss of his ship. And what troubled him more was why this highly respected captain had not returned to Spain on the *Real Fénix* as he had been instructed the year before.

On January 12, Ensenada wrote to the Marqués de la Victoria to review the case. On the 25th, the Marqués de la Victoria wrote to Ensenada and informed him that he had received the copies of Huony's report of the wreck as well as that of Velasco. After reading them, he was left with some unanswered questions. Why did Huony return to Spain with

La Galga when the *Real Fénix* was his intended command, and who requested him to convoy the merchant ships? Could he have saved his ship? Why didn't he use more anchors? Did he act without consulting the other officers? What efforts did Huony undertake to salvage the cargo? These were questions prescribed by the royal ordinances that demanded answering. The director of the navy would have to wait for Huony to return to find out.

Daniel Huony was born in the late seventeenth century to Walter and Marguerite O'Huony, in Tullamore, Ireland. He, like many others who were known as "Wild Geese" that had fled Ireland to escape the anti-Catholic penal laws, had joined the Spanish navy as a young teenager. In 1714, he was a pilot, and in 1715, he had been promoted to lieutenant. He soon dropped the prefix to his last name as the Spanish had difficulty enough pronouncing it.

Huony was promoted to *teniente de navío* in 1727 and to his current rank of *capitán de navío* on August 28, 1740. After the war broke out in 1739, he was soon put in charge of the *San Felipe* of eighty guns under Don Blas de Lezo at Cartagena, Columbia. In 1741, during Admiral Vernon's siege, Don Blas, a seasoned warrior who had lost an eye, a leg, and a hand in previous engagements, died of wounds from this last battle. Huony was also severely wounded, but upon recovery, took charge as commander of the *Tierra Firme* galleons.

The war that began in 1739 between England and Spain was known as King George's War or the War of Jenkins's Ear. In peacetime, British shipping had suffered seizures and harassment in the Caribbean from the Spanish who were getting frustrated at England's arrogance in going to the Mosquito Coast of Honduras to cut logwood. Logwood was quite valuable because it was used to produce colorful dyes for clothes. The debate over what to do about Spain's aggression had gone on for years, but the last straw came when Captain Robert Jenkins of the ship *Rebecca* appeared before the House of Commons in 1738 and exhibited his ear, which had been cut off by one of the Spanish *Guarda*

Costas in 1731. The story goes that after being boarded near Havana, Jenkins was hung up by a rope with the cabin boy tied to his feet. He fortunately survived. Other members of his crew were tortured, and he was told to sail away from Cuba or they would burn his ship. After a perilous voyage, the *Rebecca* arrived in the River Thames in June. This demonstration of Spanish cruelty so inflamed the populace and common sentiment that war was finally declared on June 15, 1739. In 1744, this war merged with other conflicts in Europe that involved Austria, the Netherlands, Great Britain, and Sardinia aligned against France and Spain. The Spanish treasure ships became fair game.

The Spaniards were quick to outfit privateers from Havana, Cuba and St. Augustine in Florida to harass and seize English shipping on the American coast as well as near their Caribbean island possessions in the Leeward and Windward islands. Sometimes, the privateers boldly went ashore to sack plantations. The Spaniards had warships in the Caribbean to protect the treasure fleets and warships at home to protect the coast and the shipping in the Atlantic and Mediterranean. The British had guard ships in the Caribbean and along the American coast. Their job was to convoy merchant vessels safely home and to discourage harassment by the enemy in the colonies.

Daniel Huony's last command during the war was the sixty-gun *El Fuerte*, which he had assumed in early 1746. He captured numerous prizes while protecting the Cuban coast and port of Havana until the war ended in October of 1748. After the war, he looked forward to returning to Spain and assuming command of another ship in the navy of King Ferdinand VI. A new eighty-gun warship called the *Real Fénix* was under construction in Havana. He was led to believe that his next command would be aboard the *Fénix* on her maiden voyage convoying treasure back to Spain. But his orders soon changed. Unbeknown to him was that a warship named *La Galga* was on her way to Havana and would ultimately bring him to his trial before the navy tribunal.

September, 1747
Cartagena, Spain

The Spanish warship, *La Galga*, was lying on her side, careened, as workman cleaned her hull and made repairs in preparation for a secret mission. Capitán de Navío Blas de Barreda had received orders from Zenón de Somodevilla, known as the Marqués de Ensenada, Spain's powerful and influential minister of the navy, to take charge of *La Galga*, and he would soon be leaving with two other warships, *Léon* and *Xavier*, for Italy. The orders said to be prepared for a minimum three month's cruise. They would first stop in Cádiz before proceeding to Italy. Ensenada knew their real mission was to join a fleet of merchant ships making ready to sail for Mexico. The warships were going to take on a cargo of mercury, which was badly needed for the refining of silver. The reason for secrecy was that because of the war, mercury shipments had suffered greatly at the hands of English privateers. The three warships left on October 17, 1747, stopped in Malaga for two days, and sailed on to Cádiz, arriving November 4.

This was to be the last voyage in the King's navy for the aging warships *La Galga* and *Xavier*. The Marqués de Ensenada wanted a modernized navy and had ordered new ships built in Havana. *La Galga* was old and required constant maintenance. She was no longer needed. When they arrived at Veracruz, they would unload their cargo and take on treasure to be transported to Havana for shipment to Spain. Upon their arrival at Havana, the vessels would be sold to the Real Compañía de la Habana and serve their last years as commercial vessels.

In Cádiz, the commanders learned the truth of their mission and began readying the ships for the mercury cargo. On January 3, Captain Barreda had had a violent attack, lost consciousness, fell onto his bed, and was taken off *La Galga* the next morning. Prescribed medications gave no improvement, so a replacement was found, Capitán de Navío Don José Montero de Espinosa. By the sixteenth, Barreda had sufficiently recovered to resume command. A month later he became delirious again, but recovered in time to make the sailing of the fleet.

Spain needed cash. Their whole economy revolved around, and

depended on, treasure from the New World. The extravagances of King Philip and the Royal Family competed with the expenses of running the country and fueling an army and navy at war. On Christmas Eve of 1734, the former Muslim fortress of Alcázar in Madrid, used as a palace by King Philip V, was destroyed by a fire started by a forgotten oil lamp. King Philip ordered that a new and very extravagant palace be built on the same site, one that would be fireproof. It would require large sums of money to complete. King Philip died in July of 1746 and was succeeded by his last surviving son who ascended to the throne as Ferdinand VI.

Ferdinand, thirty-three years old, delighted in his new power after having been shunned by the court as a timid and inept prince. He had been dominated by his corpulent wife, Barbara of Braganca, since his marriage at the young age of fifteen.

The construction of the new palace was always behind schedule as choice materials and artisans were gathered from around Europe. The new queen concerned herself in the affairs of Spain. Ferdinand entertained himself with the details of the new palace while half-heartedly continuing the war.

The choice wood for the palace doors and windows was mahogany. Spain had its local variety, but Ferdinand didn't like its smell. His trusted minister, the Marqués de Ensenada, sent money and instructions to Havana that more mahogany needed to be cut immediately and shipped back to Spain.

During the war, Spanish shipping would suffer not only coming but also going to the New World. England, Spain's arch enemy, wanted the treasure above all, but they also were quite satisfied to keep the Spaniards from making it. They hunted the *azogue*, or mercury ships, which transported this valuable commodity from Spain to the New World mines. The year before, a fleet of mercury ships was intercepted off Portugal where Captain Juan Manuel Bonilla lost his ship, the *Nuestra Señora de los Remedios*, and a valuable cargo of mercury worth over a million pieces of eight.

With Juan Bonilla's loss of his valuable mercury cargo to English privateers, the mines in Mexico were in short supply. Captain Don Juan de Eques was given orders to assemble a mercury fleet for Veracruz. This time, warships would be used to escort the fleet as well as carry their own cargo of mercury.

After *La Galga* arrived, the ships were prepared to receive the mercury and other cargo. The crews and officers were selected. Don Juan de Eques would be the fleet captain aboard the *Léon*. Don Joseph Soriano, the Conde de Vega Florida, would command the *Xavier*.

Six more warships under the command of Don Francisco Liaño were added to the convoy of twenty-three Spanish merchant ships, six French and one Tartan. The fleet was loaded with 705 tons of mercury. This included 667 chests of mercury, each weighing 150 pounds, on *La Galga*. She was also loaded with fifty tons of iron in bars, fluting irons, rakes, and nails. *La Galga's* compliment of crew and officers numbered sometimes over four hundred. Provisions for their maintenance as well as chests of personal belongings were loaded: the higher the rank, the more was allowed on board.

The fleet was ordered provisioned for three months, but there was little room left for water and food for the crew. Captain Barreda, however, planned to live well as he loaded 380 barrels of aguardiente, 300 barrels of wine and vinegar, 400 bottles of good red wine, olive oil, spirits, and many assorted foods. Barreda was also carrying live animals for fresh meat: ten calves, twelve pigs, fifty turkeys, and eight hundred hens.

After the ships were loaded, Liaño noted that *León, Xavier,* and *La Galga* were riding dangerously low in the water so inspections were ordered. Francisco de Varas y Valdes, president of the Casa de Contratación in Seville, performed the inspections, and it was decided to rearrange the cargo and take some off. This greatly improved the seaworthiness of *León* and *Xavier*, but Liaño reported to Ensenada, "We are aware here that the construction of *La Galga* is deficient and that is the reason her lower deck of cannons are so close to the surface of the water. It appeared that her first battery would be of no use in combat even in calm water." *La Galga* had been one of the first ships built by Juan de Casanova who had previously served as a gunner aboard the *LanFranco*. King Ferdinand had expressed his concerns to Eques and

Valdes about the seaworthiness of the vessels and wanted it corrected. In *La Galga's* case, nothing could be done.

In February, the Duque de Sotomayor in Lisbon had gotten word that there were two English squadrons waiting for the ships in Cádiz to sail. He sent messages to the Marqués de Ensenada to warn the fleet. Ensenada himself had previously received word from Cádiz that three or four English men-of-war had been seen between Cádiz and Gibraltar. For increased protection, the warships *Sobervio*, 66 guns, *La Oriente*, 66 guns, *Brilliante*, 66 guns, *Neptuno*, 66 guns, *Halcón*, 70 guns, *Retiro*, 54 guns, *León*, 70 guns, *San Francisco Xavier*, 50 guns, and *La Galga*, 52 guns were ordered into the fleet under the command of the fleet Admiral Liaño.

The commanders of the guardships were given orders dictating their position in the fleet and the signals to be used on this trip. When engaging the enemy, they were to form a single line, with *La Galga* in the third position. Liaño was ordered to convoy the fleet as far as the Canaries and leave only the *Xavier*, *León*, and *La Galga* to complete the trip across the Atlantic. If at any time enemy ships were engaged, for security reasons the commanders were instructed to drop the Crown correspondence overboard sufficiently weighted to guarantee that it would sink. During an engagement the *Sobervio*, with Admiral Liaño, would take the lead, with the *Oriente* in the rear. The valuable merchant ships were then to be flanked with the others. In case of combat, each would assume a new position. *La Galga* would sail ahead of *León*, *Xavier* was to assume guard in the rear, then all three would fall to the leeward of the fleet.

Rumors had started to spread across the North Atlantic that Spain's great mercury fleet was expected to leave in early March. Ensenada had heard of a British man-of-war cruising nearby. He also received word from Lisbon in early February that five English corsairs set sail on January 21 destined for Cádiz to harass or capture the Spanish fleet. On February 7, Ensenada wrote to President Valdes of the Casa de la Contratación and Captain Juan de Eques and said that if this risk was confirmed, the ships shouldn't set sail. However, he pointed out that King Ferdinand was equally concerned about the mercury reaching

Mexico. This fact was to be "carefully considered and the ships must be ready to set sail immediately upon receiving word that there are no enemy ships in the area of superior strength than our merchant and armada vessels...."

When the Spanish fleet departed, they flew Dutch flags to confuse or fool any English who were lurking about. Fourteen of the merchants were bound to Veracruz, seven others were to sail on to Cartagena, Mariacaibo, Peru, and Buenos Aires. The combined value of the fleet's cargo was over five million pesos. The necessity of maintaining the production of the silver mines outweighed the risk. If the ships did not sail, King Ferdinand would have investigated the matter. On March 14, 1748, *La Galga*, with eight other warships escorting the fleet of Spanish merchant ships, cleared the Castillo de Santa Catalina guarding the port entrance. The ships left with a clear horizon.

The rumor of the preying English was, in fact, a reality. Benjamin Keene, the English ambassador in Madrid, had gotten the final word of the sailing date of the fleet from Cádiz: March 18. Keene was able to sneak a letter out through Lisbon, which was put on board the *Prince Henry*, Captain Jasper, who set out to find Rear Admiral Edward Hawke. Hawke was on board the *Kent*, in company with the *Yarmouth*, *Defiance*, *Anson*, and *Tavistock*, and had been ordered to block the expected Spanish fleet coming out of Cádiz. His cruising grounds were between Cape St. Vincent, Portugal and Cape Cantin, Morocco, on the African coast. He was also to rendezvous with Captain Cotes in the *Edinburgh* with four other English warships on this station. He missed his rendezvous after being blown off the coast by an unfortunate gale.

Admiral Hawke had previously had a chance to take *La Galga* in 1744 at the Battle of Toulon. In his first action, he was then known as *Captain Edward Hawke of the Berwick*. He was sent to Toulon, France on the Mediterranean coast in February to assist Admiral Thomas Matthews in his blockade of the French port, where twenty Spanish warships under the command of Don Joseph Navarro, the future Marqués de la Victoria, were holed up. The French were allies of Spain, but weren't officially in the war yet. The English had blockaded the port for two years, rendering the French and Spanish warships useless.

La Galga had returned to Cádiz from Buenos Aires, Argentina on March 13, 1739, and remained in Cádiz until she had received orders to sail with Navarro in November 1741 to other Spanish ports. In early February, she had arrived in Toulon under the command of Don Francisco Maldonado where she remained. *La Galga* did not enter the engagement with the English as she remained in port.

Admiral Warren had dispatched Commodore Cotes in the HMS *Edinburgh*, 70 guns, along with the *Eagle* 60, *Windsor* 60, *Princess Louisa* 60, and the *Inverness* sloop to lay off Cape Cantin and keep a look out for Admiral Hawke and the anticipated arrival of the Spanish fleet of Admirals Liaño and Eques. Cotes was positioned to intercept the Spanish fleet if they made for the Canary Islands lying off the North African coast.

At dawn on March 18, the British fleet was cruising sixty leagues to the northwest of Cape Cantin. HMS *Eagle* hoisted a signal, indicating a fleet to the northwest and fired two cannon to alert the others to observe the signal. Because of the faint light, the other ships did not react until half past six, whereupon they all tacked and cleared for action and followed the Eagle under Captain George Rodney. The *Eagle* observed the chase and hoisted a Spanish flag. He and the *Inverness* moved in and only encountered several musket shot before two of the smaller ships struck. Prisoners were brought on board, and without much encouragement, confessed the size of the fleet and the strength of their guard.

The Spanish men-of-war executed their battle plan and formed a line, keeping the merchants to the leeward and the English to windward. On board the *Eagle*, Captain Rodney signalled to the other ships that there were nine Spanish warships ahead. Rodney then rejoined Cotes, and by noon, they had taken three more Spanish merchant ships. The *Eagle* and *Windsor* were sent in pursuit of the escaping Spanish fleet, while Cotes triumphantly escorted the five prizes into Lisbon.

On March 20, *La Galga* signalled to the remaining merchants to keep

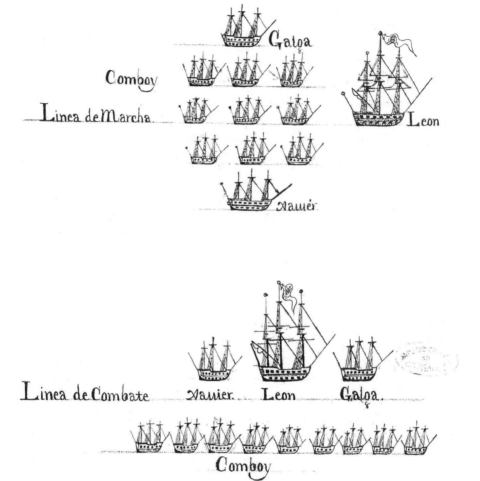

The contemplated formation of the mercury fleet of Juan de Eques as they sailed from Cádiz to Veracruz in the spring of 1748. In case of attack, the warships would form a line. This was to be *La Galga's* last assignment in the Spanish Navy. They are believed to be drawn by Juan de Eques. Diagrams from the fleet orders, Secretaría de Marina, 400-2. *Courtesy of the Archivo General de Simancas.*

leeward of the protective warships. The English were now up wind on the horizon. If the Spanish could outrun them, then Liaño could return to Cádiz with his six warships as planned. The next day, Rodney came up and hoisted Spanish colors in an attempt to fool the Spanish. The Spanish warships recognized the *Eagle* and surrounded their convoy of merchants as they continued to bear away to the west. The *Eagle* and *Windsor* realized that it was now impossible to take another ship without engaging a largely superior force, so they tacked to the windward and gave up the chase.

On March 22, at 1:00 p.m., the horizon was clear and Admiral Liaño separated from Eques fleet, and with his six warships, returned to Spain. *La Galga, Xavier*, and *León* continued on to Veracruz with the merchant fleet.

Captain Jasper in the *Prince Henry* did not intercept Admiral Hawke until March 26. Hawke, who missed the Spanish fleet and his rendezvous with Cotes, had determined that he couldn't remain on station any longer as he was nearly out of water and there were many cases of scurvy in the fleet. Two days later, he sailed for Lagos on the south coast of Portugal. But by then, Cotes was ahead of him and in Lisbon.

With the threat of the English behind them, the Spanish fleet pressed westward, and the farther south they traveled, the hotter the weather became. It was found that the supplies of water and food weren't holding up as there were nearly three hundred stowaways discovered on the three warships, and by estimation, one thousand on the merchant ships. It was decided to make for Santo Domingo on the island of Hispaniola.

On the evening of April 24, the fleet was eighty-two leagues east of the island of St. Martin when *La Galga* captured the schooner, *Dispatch,* Captain James Seller, sailing from Boston to Antigua. Her cargo proved a godsend for the crew as they seized the water and her cargo of seventy-nine barrels of fish. In the hold, they also found five hundred feet of pine plank, shingles, and stalks of walnut.

Two days later, in the evening, the fleet was now twenty-two leagues east of St. Martin when the *León* captured the packetboat, *Samuel and*

Mary, captained by Joseph Henderson sailing from Boston to St. Kitts with a large cargo of pine planks, shingles, barrel staves, and hoops. Fortunately for the hungry Spaniards, she also had twenty-one barrels of fish as well as some salted tongue.

The fleet continued on to Hispaniola and passed Santo Domingo in favor of Ocoa Bay. On May 5, they landed the English prisoners and sent them on to Santo Domingo to be forwarded to Havana as prisoners. They also landed the stowaways. There were nearly three hundred on the *Nuestra Señora del Rosario* and the *Nuestra Señora de la Concepción* alone. Some begged to come back aboard as they were too frail to make the overland trip to Santo Domingo. It was then decided to take them on to Veracruz where they would be forwarded to Havana to serve on the warships of Admiral Reggio and General Benito Spinola, who were severely lacking in crew. This obviously was not what these poor wretches had in mind when they had left Spain for a better life in Mexico.

While at Ocoa, the fleet took on fifty-seven head of cattle. After taking on water and dividing up the prize cargo, they calculated that they would still have to ration their biscuit at fourteen ounces a day per man. Their planned route was to sail from there to Grand Cayman, then south to Cabo Catouche at Yucatan, and from there to Veracruz. The captains were still concerned about an encounter with enemy ships.

The mercury fleet of Juan de Eques arrived safely at Veracruz on June 2, 1748, without any further encounters with the enemy. But when they unloaded the ships, they found that *La Galga* and the other warships had been leaking and forty-five tons of precious mercury was ruined as a result of defective bottle containers. Even the cargo of nails and iron bars was damaged.

The east coast of America was now swarming with Spanish and French privateers. One of the most successful and notorious privateers of the war was Don Pedro Garaicochea, who had come out of Havana with ten vessels and was again working the coast by May of 1748. The

English papers had forecast his arrival, as it had been reported in the *Maryland Gazette* on March 6 that Captain Owen Lloyd had brought this troubling news from Havana. This account said that Garaicochea was seen at the Havana dockyards every day, outfitting twenty-five vessels as well as his own frigate, the *Nuestra Señora del Carmen*. The ships were all going to be double-manned and ready to sail that March. By May, reports of his successes off of the Virginia coast were making the papers.

In the summer of 1748, the Spaniards became even bolder as they entered Chesapeake Bay on the Virginia coast in spite of the fact that there was usually a guardship stationed to protect the Bay. In Virginia, some of the residents in the Lynhaven Bay area inside Cape Henry fled out of fear of a land attack. The Spaniards ventured as high as Mobjack Bay north of the entrance to Hampton Roads. From that position, they could cut off shipping that might try to get under the protective guns of Fort George at Point Comfort.

October, 1748
Havana, Cuba

As the fleet of Juan de Eques had safely arrived in Veracruz, the warships, *La Galga*, *Xavier*, and *León*, were being fitted out and loaded with treasure to be taken to Havana, destined to be offloaded onto Admiral Reggio's ships, now waiting for their arrival.

La Galga and the others avoided capture by the English only months before. Now instead of capturing cargoes of mercury, the English saw their second chance to be a far greater opportunity. Word reached Admiral Knowles that *La Galga* and the other Spanish ships were planning to transport treasure to Cuba. With his fleet of six warships, Knowles was making for Havana while the long-prayed-for Cessation of Arms was negotiated. Being at sea, he had no knowledge of it. He continued with his plan to intercept the treasure fleet expected from Veracruz and hopefully reap millions while dealing a devastating blow to the Spanish Navy. His fleet consisted of his flagship, the *Cornwall*, 80 guns; the *Lenox*, 70 guns; the *Canterbury*, 60 guns; the *Strafford*, 60 guns; the *Tilbury*, 60 guns; the *Warwick*, 60 guns; and the *Milford*, 50 guns.

In Havana, the Spanish hadn't yet received word of the peace either, but had received reports of Knowles and his fleet cruising off the Dry Tortugas, eighty nautical miles north of Havana, waiting to pounce on *La Galga* and the others of the returning Veracruz treasure fleet. The governor of Cuba ordered all available warships to fit out immediately and put on board one thousand soldiers as an added defense. The situation was so precarious that the governor also ordered that every household was to contribute one hand each so that the ships could be double-manned. Havana was suffering badly from the war. There were shortages of everything. There was not enough food to adequately feed the citizens and the large number of soldiers and sailors that had convened there for the military operations.

On October 12, Pedro Garaicochea entered Havana with a newly captured prize, called the *Mary*, 20 guns, Captain Thomas Nesbit. The *Mary* had left Jamaica with sixteen other merchants under convoy of the HMS *Lenox*, 70 guns, and was intercepted by Garaicochea in the Florida Straits.

In Havana, Admiral Andrés de Reggio could only muster six warships, his flagship *Africa*, of 70 guns; the *Invincible*, under General Spinola, 70 guns; the *Conquistador*, 60 guns; the *Nueva España*, 60 guns; the *Dragon*, 60 guns; and the *Royal Family*, 60 guns. Don Pedro Garaicochea was ordered to use his own ship, the *Nuestra Señora del Carmen*, of 36 guns, upon his arrival in Havana. *El Fuerte*, 60 guns, under Captain Huony was on careen, and three more ships, the *Tigre*, *Rayo*, and *Real Fénix* were under construction.

Admiral Reggio sailed out of the harbor to intercept Knowles. Captain Holmes of HMS *Lenox*, after engaging the Spaniards in the Florida Straits, set out to find Knowles to alert him of the approach of Reggio and the Spanish fleet. Captain Holmes did so, risking a large sum of personal money he had on board as well as passengers who were urging him to proceed on to England. He found Knowles, who'd communicated the news to his fleet, and they proceeded toward the Cuban coast. The English and Spanish found each other on the morning of October 14. Both sides prepared for action, and both sides appeared to be almost evenly matched with seven ships each; the English carried more guns, but the Spaniards had over twelve hundred more men.

At 2:00 p.m., the Spaniards opened fire, but were out of range. Knowles boldly closed and both sides opened up with fierce broadsides. Shortly afterwards, the *Cornwall* dropped back, having had her main topmast and her foretopsail yard shot away. The *Warwick* and *Canterbury* were yet two hours away to the rear.

The *Conquistador* was badly damaged as well and fell back not far away from the *Cornwall*, which was busy repairing damage. Knowles launched an all-out attack even in his near-disabled condition. The *Cornwall* bombarded the *Conquistador* with her cohorn shells and set fire to the Spanish ship. Don de St. Justo, the captain, was killed.

The *Lenox* maneuvered in as the *Cornwall* dropped back and continued the bloody siege. The *Warwick* and *Canterbury* were now in position to engage the other Spanish ships that were trying to assist the *Conquistador*. The *Real Familia* fell back from the battle.

Reggio, in the *Africa*, retreated toward Havana after the *Conquistador* was taken and anchored in a small bay about twenty-five miles east of Havana, totally dismasted. The *Stafford* and *Canterbury* brought Knowles news of this, and after repairing his ship, he proceeded to take Reggio in his disabled flagship. When Knowles approached the next morning, the Spaniards abandoned the *Africa* and set fire to her rather than risk losing another ship to the English. After the Spaniards fled in their boats, *Africa* blew up.

Knowles continued toward Havana to land his prisoners, and when he arrived, he found the *Invincible* reduced to a wreck and three other ships badly damaged. As the British ships lay off Havana making the exchange of prisoners, a Spanish sloop came in and informed them that a peace agreement had been signed and hostilities had ended. Knowles sent an officer with a flag of truce to meet with the governor, who confirmed the news.

Knowles's hope of capturing *La Galga* and the other ships from Veracruz was dashed. The war was over; there would be no treasure plundered. Knowles sadly returned to Jamaica.

The second Treaty of Aix-la-Chapelle was signed on October 18, 1748. This was between France and England with Spain signing on later. It was not until February 14, 1749 that the final peace with Spain was officially proclaimed in England. Celebrations on both sides of the Atlantic were witnessed by cannon firing, rockets, parades, church celebrations, singing, bonfires, bell ringing, and other demonstrations of joy. When the *Maryland Gazette* of May 14, 1749 carried the news, the publisher had inserted the word "PEACE" on all of the margins of every page. Life would return to normal.

On January 18, 1749, after suffering long delays, the New Spain Fleet commanded by Juan de Eques left Veracruz. *La Galga, Xavier, El León, La Santísima Trinidad, San Jorge, La Concepción, San Espiridon, El Rosario, El Galgo* (French), and the *San Fernando* were now carrying treasure destined to be loaded aboard the fleet of Admiral Andrés Reggio. *La Galga* was carrying 785,203 pesos in coin, 1,356 silver marks, 1,124 arrobas of cochineal, 471 arrobas of indigo, 50 skins, 120 arrobas of carmine, and 3 chests of gifts. They arrived safely in Havana on March 6, 1749.

La Galga's cargo was then transferred to the *Nueva España*. While Admiral Reggio was getting his fleet ready for the trip home to Old Spain, he had received instructions from the Marqués de Ensenada that His Most Catholic Majesty, King Ferdinand, wanted to establish an *Esquadra de Barlovento*, or "windward squadron," at Havana. Reggio convened a meeting of the naval commanders and informed them of his orders.

"His Excellency, the Marqués de Ensenada, has expressed his concern that now that the war is over, we are fearful that pirates may lay off this coast in wait of our treasure ships," Reggio began. "The frigates *Fuerte; Vizarra; Flora;* and the packetboat, *Diligente,* are to join under the command of Captain Joseph Montero y Espinosa for that purpose."

The commander of *El Fuerte*, Don Daniel Huony, stood to object to his new assignment. "Sir, with all respect, I was under the impression that I would be allowed to return to Spain with the treasure fleet now getting ready. Would you reconsider?"

Captain Huony was highly respected by the Marqués de Ensenada, and he did not understand his change of orders. Reggio may have been getting even with Huony as he was laid up in Havana careening *El Fuerte* when he and Admiral Knowles engaged off Havana the year before and Reggio lost his flagship. Reggio had charged three other captains with deficient conduct in order to soothe his own humiliation. One was Mark Forrester, but he had been ordered to Cartagena to pick up treasure in the *Real Familia* along with General Benito Spinola in his sixty-four gun *Dragon*.

Reggio, scowling after being interrupted, continued with his instructions to Captain Huony. "Before you assume your new command under Captain Montero, your orders are to take *El Fuerte* in company with *La Galga* back to Veracruz to pick up more treasure and return here as soon as possible. The treasure will be transferred to the *Real Fénix* now being completed in the harbor." Otherwise Reggio stipulated, "Then Your Lord should not, under any circumstances, delay any further than is necessary in this port to refresh the provisions and water. It is expected that you will be able to carry this out with the utmost precision which is of so much interest in the service of His Majesty."

La Galga was now being retained as a naval vessel because the Real Compañía had decided in December, before *La Galga* and *Xavier* had arrived, that they did not want the aging warships.

Captain Huony accepted his orders but did not relinquish the idea that he would be returning to Spain. Havana was a hell hole decimated by the late war. The streets were over run with vagabonds, tricksters and free agents. Leprosy was spreading; the hospitals were over capacity. Huony would seek command of another ship and leave the *Fuerte* with Montero. His hopes for returning to Spain were now with the *Real Fénix*.

La Galga had been found to be taking on water, so temporary repairs were initiated by removing four rows of sheathing in order to properly caulk the leaking hull. There was not time for much else.

On April 14, 1749, *La Galga*, commanded by Capitán de Navío Fernando de Varela, and *El Fuerte*, commanded by Don Daniel Huony, who had the responsibility for both ships and the title General of the New Spain Fleet, set sail for Veracruz.

On April 24, Huony's ships arrived at Veracruz with a planned brief stay. Being short-handed since Reggio's fleet had taken the best men, proclamations enlisting crew were posted in Mexico City and Veracruz. The ships would be returning to Havana the first of June. While there, Captain Huony was instructed by the viceroy of Mexico to take custody of a necklace of thirty-six pearls, which was being sent at the request of King Ferdinand as a gift for his wife, Queen Barbara. The King had requested pearls the size of "garbanzos" but a search from Mexico City to California failed to produce ones of sufficient size. Huony's instructions from Ensenada were to return with them to Spain immediately and personally deliver them upon his arrival in Cádiz. The pearls were his ticket home.

Admiral Reggio sailed on May 12, 1749 from Havana for Spain with his new flagship the *Vincidore* of 74 guns, accompanied by the *Tiger*, *Invincible*, *Nueva España*, and *Grande León*, escorting ten merchant ships. In the American colonies, this event was described in the *Boston News Letter*, which said the fleet was carrying an enormous treasure of sixty million pesos. Many a former privateer contemplated the possibilities, but the war was over. Also on board were the three captains of the warships who were to stand trial for their questionable actions during Admiral Knowles' attack on Havana.

After loading the treasure and finding the needed crew, Huony, on board *El Fuerte* and in company with Captain Varela aboard *La Galga*, departed Veracruz. On the way to Havana, they met with some hard weather, straining the old hull of *La Galga*, causing her to start leaking again, only worse than before. On July 17, they arrived off Havana where Captain Varela wrote to Huony about the condition of his ship:

> During the good weather and throughout this trip, the ship has taken on four inches of water per watch and when the waves became rougher, this amount doubled. The first caulker

who has long been aboard this ship said that the ship hadn't been careened for five years, and it was his opinion that there was not enough oakum. This was evident in Havana, the sides of the ship did not have any oakum, and he did not think the ship would be able to endure any longer. I believe it is wise to anticipate this news to Your Lordship before dropping anchor in the port so that a decision can be made.

The next day, on the incoming tide, *La Galga* and the other ships came into Havana harbor and anchored at 11:00 a.m. General Benito Spinola, who had arrived the week before with the ships from Cartagena and was the ranking officer in port, received the news about her condition from Captain Huony himself. He ordered the necessary officers to check and clean the keel. Pedro de Torres, ship's carpenter, reported, "It is necessary to remove the rest of the planking, put oakum along the seams and resheath the ship, and overhaul the rest of the vessel. This is what I consider should be done so that the ship is correctly fitted."

On the twentieth, Spinola decided that, "If *La Galga* is ready at the same time as my fleet, I will take her, and if not, I will leave her behind so that the work can be executed." *La Galga's* cargo of silver bars was valued at nearly three million pesos, and some worked silver and dyes were unloaded and later put on board the *Dragon*, which had just been careened. Huony received the disappointing news that the cargo of treasure, including the Queen's pearls, would continue on to Spain aboard the *Real Fénix* without him and that Spinola was taking charge of the ship. But Huony still had hopes of getting command of the *Rayo*, a new ship of eighty guns, which was nearly completed, and thereby return to Spain with the Spinola's treasure fleet making ready to sail.

Huony later found out that the *Rayo* would not be available to him either, so he wrote to the Marqués de Ensenada on October 13, hoping to get some sway over Spinola with whom he had already requested command of the *Dragon*. But Spinola ignored his request and put Don Fernando de Varela, who had been in charge of *La Galga*, in command of the *Dragon*. But Huony was not without a ship for long. On November 1, General Benito Spinola ordered Huony to take command of *La Galga* as she lay disabled on careen at La Machina, which was located near the Governor's Fort. Huony wondered if he had not protested earlier about remaining with *El Fuerte*, if he would have been sailing back to Spain.

His new command did not sit well with Daniel Huony. He had always been given more prestigious positions. Captain Huony had no choice now but to obey orders, and if he wanted to go home to Cádiz, it would have to be on *La Galga*.

On November 24, 1749, Captain Huony stood at the Havana docks and watched the three warships, *Real Fénix*, *Real Familia*, and *Dragon*, and various merchant vessels carrying treasure and the pearl necklace for the Queen that Ensenada had instructed him to personally carry back to Spain, weigh anchor and begin their journey home. His heart sank as he heard the booming of cannons at the fort of Morro Castle as they saluted the departing fleet of General Spinola. It was now clear that his only ride home would be aboard a dilapidated ship that neither the navy nor the Real Compañía thought fit for service.

Huony's frustration increased as repairs on *La Galga* were hampered by a shortage of supplies and crew that had been confiscated for use on Spinola's fleet. Recruits from Mexico were now carrying out the work. When the ship had been unloaded and careened at La Machina in Havana harbor, her true condition was revealed. She was in need of a major overhaul, both structurally and cosmetically. She was now nearly twenty years old and had been totally neglected since her last refit in 1747 at Cartagena, Spain.

Huony was now not only irritated by the obvious delays, but was becoming concerned whether he would sail at all. Lorenzo Montalvo, Minister of the Port of Havana, had been sitting on three thousand planks of mahogany destined for King Ferdinand's Palace to finish the doors and windows, and it was *La Galga* that had been designated to carry them.

Montalvo decided it best to start shipping some of the planks out of Havana as soon as possible on other vessels so that construction in Madrid would not come to a halt.

Huony decided to write directly to the Marqués de Ensenada to complain about the recent mistreatment by General Spinola and that he was fearful that there weren't enough suitable men in Havana to properly man *La Galga* for the trip home. Huony's only hope would be to use some green recruits from Mexico.

Captain Huony was a loyal servant, however, and continued with the supervision of the careening and repairs of *La Galga*. There was much work to be done. The viceroy of Mexico sent 150,000 pesos to Havana and fortunately designated that some of it would go to the expense of the overhaul.

After six months of repairs and other delays due to weather, *La Galga* made ready to sail. She was undermanned and still barely seaworthy. Some of her rigging was rotten, but it was not replaced. With the new warships just being completed and the storehouses plundered for the sake of Spinola's treasure fleet, there was not enough material and supplies to properly refurbish *La Galga*. She was ill-prepared to go to sea. Instead of the required five great anchors used in mooring the ship in open water and three smaller kedge anchors used for harbor use, *La Galga* only had three large and two kedge anchors when she cleared Havana Harbor, August 18, 1750.

October, 1750
Norfolk, Virginia

Captain Pedro Pumarejo of the *Los Godos* sent a messenger to Williamsburg to meet with President Thomas Lee, acting governor of Virginia, to ask for permission to unload.

On September 10, before hearing from the Spanish captains, President Lee had already sent a letter to the Board of Trade in England advising them of the circumstances of the disabled Spanish treasure ships. President Lee was very concerned about the proper handling of this affair since the two countries were just putting the war behind them. He ordered an official to go out to the Spanish ships to examine their papers and inventory their cargo before any unloading would be allowed.

On September 15, word was received on board the ships that the president wanted to see both captains in Williamsburg. Pumarejo sent Don Francisco de Ortiz, his supercargo, and Don Manuel Martinez de Aguiar, master of the *San Pedro*, to Williamsburg to meet with President Lee. He would have gone himself, but the crew was now near mutiny, having had to endure the labor of keeping *Los Godos* afloat. Ortiz and Aguiar were ordered not to yield their registers except under extreme pressure, and "to inform the President of his great infidelity," hopefully disarming him so that his "greed will not lead him to any excess." Pumarejo clearly did not trust the English. He also instructed Ortiz and Aguiar to say they did not know how much treasure was on board as it was "in sealed boxes." When Pumarejo wrote the House of Trade about these events, he shared his observations of his English benefactors:

> Because greed is inseparable from these neighbors, because of their limited reasoning, and the great disobedience of our own seamen, added to the rebellious character of the inhabitants of this coast who know no justice and government other than their interest, I live in constant fear of being insulted with no other defense than Providence.

Once Huony arrived in Norfolk, he and Pumarejo worked closely together to maintain their crews. But they were both extremely nervous. Pumarejo's ship, the *Nuestra Señora de Los Godos,* was formerly the English ship, *Harrington,* built on the River Thames in 1744 and captured by Captain Huony on December 20, 1746, nine leagues east of Havana after she left Jamaica. The *Harrington* had been owned by John Hanbury & Co. of London, and her captain had been William James. She was carrying a cargo of sugar, rum, cotton, mahogany, and pimiento to London after clearing port on December 1. Huony was, at that time, in charge of *El Fuerte,* a warship of sixty guns, clearly superior to the twenty-six guns mounted by the *Harrington*. The crew of seventy-five was taken prisoner along with some passengers. An English flag-of-truce ship returned some of them to Charleston in February, 1747. Pumarejo bought the ship after it was condemned for 34,100 pesos.

Reports of the former identity of *Los Godos* circulated the docks anyway. The *Harrington* had sailed into Hampton, Virginia in July of 1746 with none other than Captain John Hunter of Hampton. Hunter was a prominent merchant and ship-owner, and his brother William was publisher of *The Virginia Gazette* in Williamsburg and a close friend of Benjamin Franklin.

On September 10, President Lee received belated word that the *Nuestra Señora de Mercedes* had run ashore in Northampton County, six leagues above Cape Charles. The report he was given said that some of the locals had plundered the wreck, taking tackle and rigging and some parcels of money. After the locals got what they could, they set fire to the hull to get inside. When President Lee heard this, he immediately issued a warrant to William Burton, the Northampton County sheriff, to take into his possession all items from the wreck that could be wrested from the looter's hands.

On October 1, 1750, shortly after Captain Huony arrived in Norfolk from Assateague and Snow Hill, he ordered Ensign Vicente Marcenaro to board the sloop, *Industry*, lying at Norfolk and preparing to leave for Lisbon, Portugal. As required by regulations, the *Industry* sailed the twelve miles over to Hampton to clear customs, but unfortunately was delayed five days because of bad weather. Captain Tenant found that some of his cargo had been damaged so the *Industry* returned to Norfolk. By October 13, Captain Huony had regained his strength and felt up to the task of writing a complete account to the Marqués de Ensenada of what had happened, including reliving his ordeal in the hurricane and the fate of the other ships. In his report, Huony said that he had had to abandon the idea of salvaging the mahogany, because even if it washed ashore from the wreck, "the cost of salvage will exceed the value, irrespective of the difficulty of finding anyone brave enough to risk their lives on such a wild beach without exorbitant compensation." As he was writing the report, he received word that the looters at Assateague had cut the hull down to the surface of the water trying to extract the iron and other small things from the ship. The mahogany was still trapped inside the flooded hold. In his letter, he complained that the excessive freight costs imposed by the English "made him tremble." Three days later, Ensign Marcanero boarded the *Industry* and left for Lisbon.

The English bureaucracy was becoming ever more cumbersome for the Spaniards. The ships were in Norfolk, but whenever they needed permission to do anything they had to petition the Council in Williamsburg, which necessitated ferrying over Hampton Roads and then travelling thirty miles over land. On October 7, Captains Pumarejo, Kelly, and Anaya petitioned for permission to auction some of their cargoes to meet expenses.

On October 8, Governor Ogle of Maryland wrote a letter to President Lee and informed him of the measures he had taken in relation to *La Galga* and enclosed a copy of the warrant he had issued to Sheriff Scarborough. His letter informed President Lee that the ship lay in Maryland within his jurisdiction and that "a strict Enquiry should be made" of those in Virginia who had taken possession of items from the wreck. He even suggested that if the King had no claim to the salvaged items, then the lord proprietary of Maryland might. President Lee did not acknowledge the letter.

Don Francisco de Ortiz returned from Williamsburg, and on the eighth, Pumarejo received permission to unload *Los Godos* and *San Pedro* and contracted with John Hunter to store the cargo in his warehouse in Hampton for twenty shillings a day. Huony dispatched two of his sergeants, Juan Ramos and Francisco Miguel Pinto, with some soldiers to guard the warehouse.

President Lee issued warrants on October 10 for the inspections of *Los Godos*, *San Pedro*, and *La Marianna* to be carried out by six citizens of Norfolk who were knowledgeable of ships. Two of them, Captain John Phripp and Captain John Hutchings, were members of the Norfolk

Council.

After the inspections were completed on November 1, *Los Godos* was found to have broken knee braces and timbers, and other parts so rotten that they needed to be replaced. The *San Pedro* was judged just too rotten to be repaired. Both ships were condemned. *La Marianna* was in better shape and was already being refitted for the trip back to Santo Domingo for which she was intended.

Huony had met with Felipe García, the pilot of the *Guadalupe*, and wrote to Captain Bonilla at Ocracoke, North Carolina on the sixteenth, assuring him that he was doing all he could to help. He hired a brig and a sloop from John Hutchings in Norfolk for 600 pesos each in which he was sending food, men, and supplies to Ocracoke as soon as they were ready.

President Lee again wrote the Duke of Bedford in England on October 14 about the Spanish fleet. When he mentioned *La Galga*, he referred to her as having been lost "on the Eastern Coast of this Colony." Apparently, he didn't accept Governor Ogle's claim to the wreck. On October 28, Thomas Lee presented a letter from Huony to the council where Huony had documented the names of those people of Virginia who had been involved in the salvaging of his ship. William Gore, who owned Assateague, and Ralph Justice, Thomas Crippen and Thomas Bonnewell, who lived just south of Chincoteague Inlet, were reported to have taken items from the ship valued at almost one hundred pounds. The council ordered them to appear at their next meeting of November 13 to answer the charges. The council met on that day, but the men did not appear. President Lee made no mention of the letter he received from Governor Ogle earlier in the month claiming the wreck lay in Maryland.

In Maryland, Governor Ogle was still taking an active interest in the wreck. He sent a letter on October 19 to Colonel Robert Jenkins Henry, sheriff of Somerset County, which bordered Worcester County to the west, to express his concerns about the outrageous conduct of the looters and their treatment of the Worcester County sheriff. He suggested that Scarborough confirm the facts with Sheriff Henry, and if they were true, ensure their appearance at the Provincial Court. If they refused to submit bail, then he was to arrest them.

Huony was having a difficult time taking care of so many men in this hostile environment. Winter was setting in, and his expenses continued to rise. Even his servants demanded extra pay. Some of those who had loyally followed him to Norfolk were now deserting to find better conditions for themselves. By November 1, he was down to ninety-three men and ship's boys. Juan Baquero, cooper, had died on October 25. Huony was also having difficulty finding suitable ships to transport the cargoes and crews back to Spain.

Between November 1 and 3, there was a northeast storm that was reported to have broken *La Galga's* hull to pieces, freeing the mahogany planks from the cargo hold where they had washed up on the beach. On about the twelfth, Ralph Justice from Accomack, who had been salvaging the wreck, met Huony and informed him that a survey had been recently conducted to determine the boundary line between Maryland and Virginia and settle the dispute over the wreck. Shortly after, Huony was informed that the wreck was judged to lie just inside Maryland as a result of an "experiment" or a survey.

Ralph Justice told Huony he had witnessed many others from Maryland and Virginia plundering the wreck. He named Thomas Robins and Daniel Mifflin and a "Dalason" as being from Maryland. Mifflin, whose property bordered the Maryland line, had been considered a Virginia resident up until the survey was done.

Ralph Justice also told him that about 200 planks of mahogany had washed up on the Virginia side and had been purchased by a merchant from Snow Hill at a very low price. Hoping to get restitution for the mahogany and items he'd heard had been seized by Sheriff Scarborough, Huony immediately wrote to Governor Ogle in Annapolis. Based on what he had been told, he reported to the governor that "by a late experiment of an East line drawn (to know the bounds) it's found, she lies within twice her length of it in Maryland."

He explained that he was unaware that his ship could have been in Maryland. He apologized for being misinformed as to the location of the wreck because he said he had relied on what the "country people" on the beach had told him. He asked that justice be done on behalf of the King of Spain and that possessors of salvaged items be allowed a customary salvage percentage and the rest returned to him. Huony seemed to acknowledge the new jurisdiction of the wreck to Governor Ogle, but made no mention of it to the Virginia officials.

Governor Ogle responded on receipt of his letter. He assured Huony that he would do all he could to recover whatever had been taken out of his ship by people in his jurisdiction. He was going to have them apprehended and advised Huony to appoint someone to receive the mahogany and other recovered effects. Huony did appoint a Virginia merchant named Peter Hog to act as his attorney in his absence. In the end, nothing was returned to Captain Huony or his attorney from the governor or sheriff from Maryland.

Winter was just around the corner and was starting to become a real concern not only to the Spanish, but also to the English. If they did not leave soon, they could be forced to stay until spring. On November 17, President Thomas Lee wrote the Duke of Bedford to update him on the Spaniards' dilemma:

> I have therefore with Advice of Council given them leave to freight Vessels belonging to his Majesty's Subjects to carry their cargoes to Europe, and I hope they will leave this Colony before the Winter Sets in too hard; they have been furnished with everything that was necessary as Friends and I hope that the good usage they have had here will occasion those Nations to Use his Majesty's Subjects well that may at any time fall into their hands.

In England, the Duke shared these communications with Richard Wall, Spain's ambassador, who was comforted by the reported efforts by the English to assist his distressed countrymen.

Virginia's Acting Governor, Thomas Lee, died on November 25.

Life in Norfolk was a hardship for most of the Spaniards. They were looked down upon by the English, as memories of the late war still lingered. The common crew especially weren't well cared for. One passenger named Pedro Vedoya on *Los Godos* would later complain that there was little food in Norfolk and that he was obliged to share his ration of half a chicken with some of the sick passengers. The twenty chickens, three pigs, and a calf that had survived the storm would only last them ten days. After that, the only way for Vedoya and his wife to survive was to buy cock-fighting hens at an excessive price from the sailors on the Norfolk docks.

On December 16, James Anthony Ullrichus, James and Adriana Van Wardts, and Jean Bousenau, captain of the French sloop *Les Deux Amis*, who were also passengers on *Los Godos*, traveled to Williamsburg to present their case before the Council of Virginia. The council not only ordered that Francisco de Ortiz take them with him when he left for Cádiz, but also ordered that he reimburse them the costs of the suit, travel expenses to and from Williamsburg, and a daily allowance. The magistrates of Norfolk were to carry out the order, which they did. On December 2, the alderman of the Common Council of Norfolk ordered Alexander Ross, vendue master, to pay out of the auction proceeds of some of *Los Godos*'s cargo, their travel and suit expenses, as well as six shillings per day, from their arrival on September 6 to the day that they departed.

When Pedro Vedoya returned to Spain, Francisco Ortiz insisted that he still pay full price for his voyage. Vedoya then filed a complaint. Some other passengers wanted a refund of their passage money and made the demand upon Francisco de Ortiz, which he refused. Francisco Ortiz insisted he couldn't be responsible for acts of God.

The Spaniards had a unique way of looking at the disaster. They attributed everything to the Almighty, and in this light tried their best to reconcile the reality of it all. Spain's Secretary of State, José Carvajal y Lancaster, wrote to Richard Wall, Spain's ambassador in London, on January 4, 1751 about the disaster:

> With great frequency the misfortune of our ships at sea is repeated, this is not news which is received with pleasure, however, it is an opportunity to give thanks to God for his measures. H.M. is well as is the rest of the Royal family. May God protect you for many years.

It was now imperative for Captains Pumarejo and Kelly to find transport on English ships if they wanted to get home. They worked independently of each other and negotiated separately. Verissimo de los Santos, quartermaster of *San Pedro*, was trying to convince the Virginia officials that he was in charge of the ship. The owners had given John Kelly responsibility for the navigation to Cartagena on the outbound voyage. Kelly was now assuming full control over the ship and its cargo, which usurped his supercargo, Manuel Martinez Aguiar who had applied directly to President Lee for help before Lee had died. Captain Kelly enlisted the help of Huony, and he chartered a ship called the *Allerton* and agreed to take Huony with him. Captain Pumarejo chartered the *Dorothy*, of 160 tons and twelve guns, to carry his cargo of treasure back to Spain.

At John Hunter's warehouse in Hampton, treasure and cargo had been stored from *Los Godos*, *San Pedro*, *La Mariana*, along with some that had arrived from the *Guadalupe* in North Carolina. It became apparent that there was no room for any of the *Guadalupe* cargo on the *Dorothy* or *Allerton*, so it was suggested to Captain Bonilla that he would need his own ship and that he or his representative would have to escort his cargo back home. Huony could be of no further assistance.

The *Dorothy* took on board 593,000 pesos in coin, 3 chests of silverware, 250 quintales of copper on the crown account, 62 quintales on private accounts, and various amounts of vanilla, dyes, sugar, medicinal herbs, chinaware, hides, and tortoise shell. In addition to the *Dorothy*'s crew of seventeen, she carried Don Diego Guiral and twenty-two others from his battalion that came from *La Galga*. Pumarejo elected to travel on the *Allerton* with Huony.

The *Allerton* was under the command of Captain James Wallace. Smaller than the *Dorothy*, she was rated at one hundred tons and carried eight guns and a crew of twenty. She had been riding in the upper district of the James River in ballast and moved down to Hampton on November 30 and prepared to take on a cargo of Spaniards and 343 bags of cocoa, 5000 pieces of Brasiletas, 21 boxes of sweet meats, 22 boxes and chests of gold and silver plate.

Huony, Pumarejo, Kelly, and the supercargo and master of *San Pedro*,

Manuel Martínez de Aguiar, traveled on this ship with eighty officers, soldiers, and sailors. Those who were fortunate enough to salvage some personal items before abandoning *La Galga* loaded them on board the *Allerton*.

The Spanish crews left Norfolk January 10, 1750, and boarded the English ships at Hampton, Virginia. Nine days later, they were underway and headed across the Atlantic to Spain. It was the dead of winter. Everything was fine until February 19. The *Allerton* was 110 leagues from Cape St. Vincent, Portugal when Captain Wallace informed Captain Huony that according to his contract with Captain Kelly he was obligated to go to Lisbon with the treasure of the *San Pedro*. Huony insisted that it made more sense to put into Cádiz because it was closer and there were weather considerations. Huony held a meeting in his cabin and took a vote. Captains Wallace, Kelly, and Manuel Aguiar all wanted to go to Lisbon, while Huony, Pumarejo, and the other Spanish officials voted to go to Cádiz.

The *Allerton* arrived at the Bay of Cádiz on February 27. Apparently with twelve soldiers and sixty-seven of his crew from *La Galga* on board, the vote was easily decided in Huony's favor. However, upon his arrival at Cádiz, Huony was not warmly welcomed.

March 2, 1751
Cádiz, Spain

Father Juan Garay de Concepcion relaxed in the plaza of San Juan de Dios, which spanned the distance between the convent hospital, La Misericordia, and the docks along the bay and harbor of Cádiz. He had arrived here the month before and was still forced to endure more inconvenience, if not hardship. Although he had found lodging at the convent hospital of his order, he was still waiting for the bureaucratic dispute over taxes and freight charges on his baggage to be settled. Upon his arrival, the *Depositaria de Indias* had taken possession of his luggage and other things that he had rescued from the wreck at Assateague Island. Out of the 4,800 pesos in gold doubloons that he had when he left Havana he arrived with 2,868. Within his bags was not only his treasure but his only change of clothes. The Depositaria claimed he still owed freight and taxes, which prompted him to file a petition for an exemption as he pointed out that he had only been on board several weeks before *La Galga* had wrecked. The Depositaria finally agreed to waive his freight charges but forced him to pay 165 pesos in taxes.

Father Garay's attention was diverted from the seagulls fighting over a dead rat when a squad of soldiers marched out onto the pier to greet a boat coming ashore. Seated in the stern was Captain Huony. Garay had not seen Huony since they were together in Norfolk, Virginia months before. Father Garay had found earlier passage on a ship to England and went from there to Spain.

When Huony climbed onto the pier he was informed that he was under arrest. He was not really surprised as he had lost a King's ship. Huony waived casually to his former passenger when he approached and, noticing the concern on his face, explained that his detention was expected as mandated in the *Real Órdenes*. The soldiers escorted him to his home in Cádiz and guards were placed at his front door. He was told he had to remain there until the investigating tribunal called him in. Huony immediately wrote the Marqués de Ensenada to let him know of his arrival and arrest.

The Marqués de La Victoria, Director of The Navy, appointed Juan de Soto y Aguilar, capitán de fragata and interim Major General of the Royal Navy, to head the investigation. Eight capitánes de navio, one of whom was the Conde de la Vega Florida who commanded *La Galga* in 1740, and the Jefe de Escuadra, Don Ignacio Dauteüille of the Spanish Navy, who commanded *El Oriente* while escorting *La Galga* past Cape Cantin in 1748, comprised the Tribunal. Dauteüille had also been Huony's commander in 1730 aboard *La Potencia*, where he had served as lieutenant.

On March 12, 13, and 15, with Huony still under house arrest, *La Galga's* officers, Don Diego Guiral y Concha, capitán of the marines; Lt. Manuel de Echaniz, second in command; Ensign Vicente Marcenaro; Joseph de la Cuesta y Velasco, purser; Juan Bernardo Mayonde, first pilot; Francisco Izaguirre, boatswain; and Gabriel Joseph Muñoz, second pilot, were deposed with the prescribed questions at the home of the Marqués de La Victoria. Each man was sworn to tell the truth before God and King and made the sign of the cross.

The tribunal wanted their version of events before Captain Huony would be questioned. The tribunal's main focus seemed to be on what had happened on September 5 when the anchor cable was cut and *La Galga* ran ashore. There was no consensus among them as to the number of cables remaining, but they all stated that their last anchor was in the water, except Velasco, who avoided the question. Ensign Marcenaro, hoping to help his captain and contrary to the facts, testified, "As we went into shore we threw over the rest of the artillery into the water and also the arms, supplies, and ammunition."

The next day the officers returned to review their testimonies and make the necessary corrections. Diego Guiral changed his testimony on the anchors. He said that only one anchor had been thrown overboard during the storm. The only exception made by Manuel Echaniz was that only one anchor was jettisoned, not two great anchors and a kedge as he had previously testified. No other corrections were made including the erroneous statements made by Ensign Marcenaro about the artillery.

While his officers faced the Tribunal, Captain Huony mentally prepared for his upcoming testimony. He contemplated the unfortunate chain of events that had placed him aboard *La Galga*. If things had just gone as planned, he would have returned to Spain the year before and revelled in the glory of the returning treasure fleet.

March 18, 1751
Cadiz, Spain

Juan de Soto y Aguilar, capitán de fragata, and the rest of the tribunal arrived at the home of Daniel Huony dressed in their best navy-blue uniforms, trimmed in gold with contrasting red lapels, their best swords and sashes slung at their waists. Their heads were adorned with powdered wigs and regulation bicorn hats. At the front door, they passed the guards and greeted the anxious Daniel Huony, who was equally dressed; and with little formality, Aguilar administered the oath to him and began with the first question: "Sir, why did you take command of the merchant ships at Havana?"

"Your Lordships, I must say that I had no superior order to sail to Spain," Huony calmly began as he stood and faced his fellow captains. "General Andrés de Reggio had ordered me to board the *Fénix*, but that was countermanded by General Benito Spinola. He ordered me to take command of *La Galga* without explanation. These orders were in writing. I was to careen *La Galga* and sail that summer and leave as soon as possible with the mahogany and tobacco. This was to assist the Royal Treasury with the already delayed shipments. I had no other choice but to follow these orders."

Captain Huony turned around, and from his table, lifted some water-stained documents. "These documents were, by the grace of God, saved from the wreck. Although the ink is blurred, you can see that I followed the orders of General Spinola and those of Lorenzo Montalvo, the port minister in Havana. I offer these into evidence."

"Captain Huony, at whose request did you assume the command of the convoy of merchant ships? Was this your idea?" Juan de Soto y Aguilar challenged.

"It was at the request of the merchant captains. I took command of their convoy, without my soliciting this and not because I had been delayed as the said captains can testify."

Aquilar continued, "Captain, during the storm did you consult with your officials and pilot about jettisoning your anchor and artillery, cutting down the mainmast, and grounding your ship? Or were these acts all your decisions?"

Huony, stiffening slightly, answered, "Esteemed sirs, I can assure you that, at these times and others, I consulted with both the Officers of the Sea as well as those of War. These were not actions of my own determination."

"How about the decision to give command of your ship to the

English captain?" continued Aguilar.

Huony paused to get his breath and reflect on the proper answer, "Honorable Sirs, the command of the ship was not given to the English captain. He only acted as a person knowledgeable of the coast due to the unfamiliarity of this area as declared by the ship's pilot. The pilot continued at his duties. The responsibility given the Englishman was done at the insistence of my officials, and was absolutely necessary, and it was decided that we were going to head for the closest port and the said Englishman was the only one knowledgeable to guide us."

Aguilar paused and allowed the scribe to finish recording the last answer, then turned and stared directly at Huony while he formulated his next question. The others on the tribunal stirred as they already knew the impending question:

"Sir. You were at anchor. For what reason did you decide to run the frigate ashore? Could you not have saved your ship? How many cables and anchors remained and what was the weather like?"

"There was no probability of saving the frigate," Huony said without hesitation as he looked away from Aquilar and faced his fellow captains. "Our last anchor was in the water with a fourteen-inch hurricane hawser. The weather was extremely stormy with rough waves and a wind traverse from the coast. The ship was in a ruinous state, completely open, without a rudder and sinking in spite of the gallant efforts made at the pumps. The ship was amongst reefs and it was evident to everyone that we were faced with the horror of death. Our only hope was to save our lives, and all agreed that the only way was run her ashore." Huony turned back to Aguilar ready to take the next question.

Aquilar could see that the capitánes were sympathizing with Huony. "Now that you are ashore, what did you do to save the artillery, weapons, and cargo?" And putting his chin in his hand and furrowing his brow he added, "What did you do for your crew, and why did you not take the suggestion to burn the ship?"

"It was unanimous, sir. All of the officials agreed that it was impossible to salvage the ship. It was full of water, and the sea continued in an agitated state, and there was a great undertow. It took three days to get everyone off and many were obliged to leave their belongings and the arms that they were ordered to take with them. The little biscuit we had the forethought to save was not enough to sustain us. It was agreed to abandon the ship and get to the mainland as quick as possible.

And as far as burning the ship, the officer who suggested we set light to what was left changed his mind since burning the wreck would only be done in time of war. Besides, our King is at peace with the English and doing this would not benefit our Master. Rather, it was hoped we would be assisted by the commander of the colony and as well, we feared resentment from the local population through whose territory we were to travel. Due to ignorance and greed, as often happens, they might have thought that the remains of a shipwreck could be claimed by them. This can all be certified to by the purser."

Huony's testimony ended after describing what had happened to the other ships in his convoy. Huony was given the chance to review his testimony as taken down by the scribe. He then certified:

> Having read the declaration and orders mentioned in this, I affirm the statements to be correct and the commands to be those which were given. And I confirm and ratify this by power of the oath sworn to declare the truth in answer to that asked and in faith of this, I sign,
> Daniel Huony

On March 22, at the home of the Marqués de la Victoria, the navy officials reconvened to render their verdict. Each one was polled and rendered the same verdict. Captain Daniel Huony was relieved of all charges and commended for his conduct. The next day the Marqués de la Victoria reported to the Marqués de Ensenada the results of the investigation and their final verdict of Captain Huony. First there was the opinion of Juan de Soto y Aguilar, who headed the investigation:

> Having seen and read the charges against Captain Don Daniel Huony in relation to her sailing from Havana, the diaries and testimonies of the army and navy officials, the ship

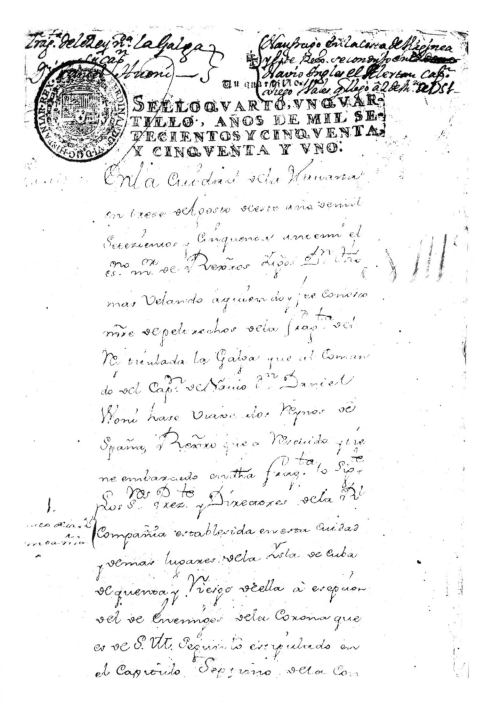

First page of *La Galga's* cargo register that was brought ashore when *La Galga* wrecked. *Courtesy of the Archivo General de Indias, Seville, Spain.*

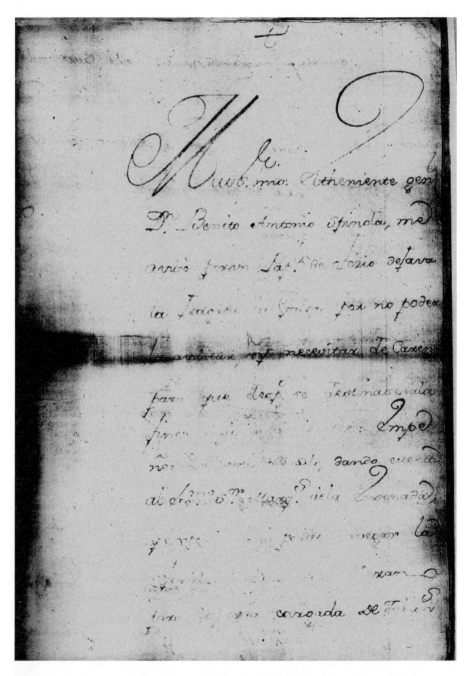

Water-stained document saved from the wreck of *La Galga* and later presented to the Tribunal as evidence of Huony's orders. *Courtesy of Archivo General de Simancas, Simancas, Spain.*

accountant and other officials and having been duly informed, it is evident that the ship should have sailed from Havana to Spain only on the express order of H.M. and not as a result of the minister. Further, in every other way the conduct of Huony is in order with that set out in the Royal Decrees in similar cases.

Signed: Juan de Soto y Aguilar, Capitán de Fragata

Then the President of the Council, the 72 year old Marqués de la Victoria, rendered his verdict:

Having seen and read the charges against and depositions presented by the Capitán de Navio on Daniel Huony in this enquiry, it is my opinion that this official has complied perfectly with his responsibilities. He has satisfied the most serious issue by having presented the letter in which he is told to come to an agreement with the Minister as regards the destination of the frigate *La Galga*.

Signed: The Marqués de la Victoria.

Captain Huony was vindicated and restored to active duty.

Construction continued on the Royal Palace. The budget for 1751 was established at one million pesos. The supplies of mahogany at Cádiz had been exhausted, so at additional expense it was brought in from Graña on the west coast of Spain. The Palace building itself wouldn't be completed until 1755, and it would take another ten years to finish the details and decoration. None of the mahogany on board *La Galga* made it to Spain. As for the tobacco, Lorenzo Montalvo at Havana was told, "This has been a considerable loss because both the snuff and leaf tobacco promised to be of superior quality and not in such limited amounts as in other years." The Real Compañía was advised to "exercise patience in the face of this setback…because these accidents at sea are incurable."

Back in Virginia, *La Galga* was not yet forgotten. Sheriff Thomas Parramore of Accomack had interrogated many residents of the county in the hopes of recovering items from the ship. Most of the items had been sold off by the sixteen individuals proven to be involved. Parramore had found on an island not far from the wreck two swivel guns, some iron hoops, a pair of brass scales, and other assorted items that had been left there by an unidentified looter.

The council held October 23 in Williamsburg had originally summoned Ralph Justice, William Gore, Thomas Crippen, and Thomas Bonnewell from Accomack to appear and answer for their salvage activities. They failed to appear as ordered at the next meeting, but the council was made aware that there were many more implicated.

On August 10, 1751, the council issued the sheriffs of Accomack and Northampton blank summons to be served on everyone known to be involved. The sheriffs were also instructed to go ahead and auction off what they had remaining to cover the mounting expenses of the sheriffs and Huony's attorney, Peter Hog.

In Northampton County, Sheriff Burton had auctioned the items he'd recovered from looters of the *Mercedes* on March 6 and realized only two pounds, fifteen shillings, and sixpence. Later in September, the new sheriff, Custis Kendall, auctioned the sails for ten pounds, eight shillings, and sixpence. This was not enough to cover Peter Hog's expenses of recovering the sails from the wreck and then managing the Spaniards' affairs in Northampton County.

In Accomack, the sheriff's auction brought in seventy pounds, two shillings, and fivepence. Sheriff Parramore and his deputy, William Beavens, hauled the sixteen plunderers over to Williamsburg to appear before the council. Many of these were prominent citizens and plantation owners. After they were examined, the council was able to extract another twenty-two pounds out of them that they had previously failed to report. After that, it was found that Thomas Bonnewell still had some items he had concealed, which brought in another two pounds, four shillings, and fivepence.

The council awarded the sheriffs five percent of the proceeds and gave the looters, including Bonnewell, ten percent to be divided amongst them. Their travel expenses to Williamsburg were reimbursed. Peter Hog failed to record receipt of any money or mahogany from Maryland. After the accounting was completed in 1752 by Deputy Beavens of Accomack, there was only eighteen pounds, one shilling, and six pence left after paying Peter Hog his balance due of twenty-five pounds, thirteen shillings, and two pence. Not much for two ships that had once belonged to the King of Spain.

1752
Cadiz, Spain

On the recommendation of the Marqués de La Victoria, the Marqués de Ensenada ordered Captain Huony to take command of the newly built *Princesa* and *Galicia*, both of seventy-four guns, on May 29, 1752. His first mission was to escort two merchant vessels en route to the Indies out beyond St. Vincent, Portugal. After successfully completing this assignment, he returned to Cape Finisterre, where he received orders to patrol the coast from Cape St. Vincent to the Straits of Gibralter. Huony was happy as he still had the respect of the Marqués de Ensenada.

By 1753, Huony was in charge of the *San Felipe* of seventy guns and in October he sailed into Ferrol, Spain. Here he was greeted with news of the death of Cosme Alvarez who had, until then, been the commander of the *Departamento de Ferrol*. Huony, being a senior commander, took over Alvarez's position temporarily. In June 1754, he was named officially as the commander of Ferrol, Spain, a position he much appreciated as he was now on equal footing with General Benito Spinola who had been appointed Commander of Cartagena in February of 1753. Spinola was the one who had ordered him to stay behind and take charge of *La*

Galga in 1749.

In 1755, Huony became *jefe de escuadra* and in 1760, was promoted to *Teniente General* of the Navy. He remained in Spain from that point on.

Don Daniel Huony never married. He gave his life to Spain and to the sea. On June 14, 1771, at half past six in the afternoon, he died at Isla de León, just east of Cádiz. The next day he was buried with full military honors. He was then laid to rest in the Franciscan convent and hospice.

The following day, a funeral mass was celebrated in his honor where 2,026 additional masses were announced in his name. Huony's only heir was his nephew, George Lysaght, who was present when he died and was living with him up to that time.

The day after Huony died, an inventory of his estate was ordered by the officials to be taken by Richard Butler and Edward Gough, old friends and merchants residing in Cádiz. They decided that this unpleasant chore was not required, however, as his nephew was present and over the age of twenty-five. The necessary documents were then signed and George Lysaght inherited Huony's "fortune," which consisted of, "furniture, clothing, papers and correspondence, precious objects, and money."

In Spain, Don Daniel Huony is all but forgotten and little more than a footnote. He was memorialized in *Galeria Biográfica de Los Generales de Marina, 1700 a 1868,* by Vice Almirante D. Francisco de Paula Pavia, published in Madrid in 1873. Pavia described him as "an able sailor, a brave military man, and an honest official."

In America his name is known only to a few, but his ship is remembered, not by name, but by legend, to millions.

CHAPTER TWELVE
The Legend

C hincoteague Island was first patented in 1670, and only a few hardy souls set up residence on this seaside island of about six thousand acres. The shore across the bay of the same name was referred to as the mainland. This is the peninsula known as the Eastern Shore that borders the east side of the Chesapeake Bay in Maryland and Virginia. For centuries this peninsula was all but cut off from the western shore of the Chesapeake Bay, as the only way to travel there was by boat or an extremely long land journey around the head of the bay. It was not until 1868, when a railroad was built from the steamboat docks in Salisbury, Maryland to the new resort of Ocean City, Maryland, at the northern end of Assateague Island, that regular travel to the Eastern Shore took place. Almost a century later, a bridge that would accommodate vehicular traffic was built from Annapolis across the bay. Many residents of the Eastern Shore opposed its construction, as it threatened their simple and unhurried way of life.

The residents of Chincoteague were as isolated from the mainland only a few miles away as the "mainlanders" were from the western shore. They were a hardy and self-reliant people, much like the wild ponies that made them famous. Years ago, their chief occupations had been fishing, hunting and tending their little gardens. The healthy climate and slow pace created above-average longevity. The early residents of Chincoteague were not only self-reliant but self-taught. Many could not read nor write as fishing and farming did not require the disciplines of a formal education. And if they weren't related to each other, they still knew everyone as if they were.

No one paid much attention to Chincoteague except for the salty oysters that were harvested from the shallow flats washed by the tides. These were transported by sea to the lucrative northern markets beginning in the 1830s.

Before the Chincoteague oyster became famous, the island was also known for its roundup of wild horses that ranged free on neighboring Assateague Island. This roundup has been celebrated since the early 1800s with a great festival and attended by many from the mainland.

As fathers and mothers taught their children the basic skills of producing food and keeping house, they also conveyed stories of the lives of their ancestors and the chance happenings that come from living by the sea. One of the traditions passed on to younger generations was that the wild horses that they were all familiar with had come ashore from a wrecked Spanish ship.

Probably the first recorded version of the shipwreck legend was published in *Scribner's Monthly* in April, 1877. In this article, entitled "Chincoteague. The Island of Ponies," a tradition was retold about a vessel carrying horses that wrecked upon the south end of Assateague and that crew were carried to the mainland by the Indians where they found their way to early settlements. This tradition is very similar to that recounted by Marguerite Henry in *Misty of Chincoteague*. In that story, just after Grandpa Beebe tells his grandchildren that the legend of the lost Spanish ship was true, he said, "Why I heard tell it 'twas the Indians who chanced on 'em first."

In documents located in the archives of Spain there are references to the crew of *La Galga* going ashore in Indian canoes on the second day after she wrecked. The Indian presence is supported by another reference saying that the English did not arrive until the third day at Assateague. These documents seem to bridge the gap between historical fact and recorded legend and bear remarkable coincidence to the wreck of *La Galga*.

In previous centuries, the horses on Assateague were known to be much smaller than the mainland variety and the shipwreck legend seemed to explain why these horses were different. As time went by, others, who were not as familiar with the legend, attributed their inferior size to neglect by their former owners. They believed that inbreeding within a small herd and a poor diet of marsh grasses was to blame. The horses are a bit larger today than their forbearers were in the early 1800s.

The earliest eyewitness testimony as to the size of these curious creatures was given by Henry A. Wise, a former governor of Virginia. A statement attributed to him and reported in the 1840s described the horses:

> There has been, since long before the American Revolution,
> on the islands along the sea-board of Maryland-Virginia, a
> race of very small, compact, hardy horses, usually called beach
> horses…. They are very diminutive, but many of them are of
> perfect symmetry and extraordinary powers of action and
> endurance…and [one] was yet so small that a tall man might
> straddle one and his toes touch the ground on each side.

Henry A. Wise was born in 1806 in the town of Accomack fifty miles from Assateague. His knowledge of the horses on Assateague most likely came from his grandfather, John Cropper. John Cropper's grandfather was Coventon Corbin, a prominent citizen of Accomack who lived just across the bay from Assateague and immediately south of the Gore family who owned the Virginia portion of Assateague. Although Wise did not mention the shipwreck legend, Coventon Corbin was involved in the salvage of *La Galga*. He owned property on Chincoteague and his son George owned land behind the sand hills on Assateague across from Chincoteague Island.

Henry A. Wise's term of "beach horses" was commonly used during his time to differentiate them from other horses because of their size and value. In the early 1800s, these horses were considered inferior to regular horses and lesser values were placed on them. In 1805, Jonathan Watson, the great-grandfather of Victoria Watson Pruitt, owned six horses on Assateague called "island horses," which were valued at $40 apiece while his other horses were valued at $75 and $80. In 1796, he had purchased 500 acres on Assateague adjoining Ragged Point from the Gore family and used this location to pasture horses and cattle.

Assateague was used as a pasture for grazing horses, cattle, and sheep from the beginning of English habitation on the mainland. In 1689, when Maximilian Gore purchased from Daniel Jenifer the 3,500 acres comprising the entire Virginia portion of Assateague, his deed gave him title to "commodities of pasture" already there. This most likely was cattle, sheep, and hogs, but it may have included some horses.

There were no horses on Assateague prior to the English settlements in the latter 1600s. Some tourist literature, however, will say that horses have roamed the island since the sixteenth century (1500s) but this is simply a writer's misapplication of terms which then was repeated too many times.

The cattle and horses that were on the island had value and were well cared for, and were bought and sold in normal commerce. Horses and livestock would be ferried over to the island and some would be ferried back for the use of the mainlanders. There seemed to be a regular infusion of new blood into the island stocks. Through the centuries, when owners of the island died, their wills and estate inventories left vivid descriptions of the horses as to each one's sex, color, and sometimes age and value. It is from these records that their history can be told. In the early 1700s, the records show that the horses did not get classified as "beach horses" to separate them from larger horses. The values placed on them appear to be the same as any others. And there was never a term used for "beach cattle" or "beach sheep." The use of the island as a pasture is clearly shown by the name of tracts that were first granted such as "Winter Pasture," "Winter Quarter," and "Towers Pasture" on the Maryland portion of Assateague. These horses and cattle were continuously at risk from the forces of nature and extreme weather and when animals were lost they would be later replaced. The worst recorded storm ever to hit the island of Assateague was in October of 1749. The complete record of loss is not available but the *Maryland Gazette* of October 18, 1749, said that 400 to 500 cattle and sixty horses were drowned in the area of present Ocean City. Only one horse survived. A fifteen-foot storm surge had covered the island. Wills and estate inventories of those owners of the island who predate this storm show only a few horses on the island after this dramatic event. New horses and cattle were brought over.

In 1782, the Commonwealth of Virginia instituted a real property tax as well as a personal property tax on slaves, horses, cattle, and wheeled carriages. From these records the history of the Assateague horses resumes. It appeared that the largest concentration of horse management on the Virginia portion of Assateague centered around the area of Assateague immediately opposite Chincoteague and behind the sand hills.

In 1764, George Stewart purchased 150 acres in this area from the Daniel Gore, whose family had owned the island since 1689. By 1782, he owned more horses than any other in Accomack County with thirty-two and was in control of an adjoining 500-acre parcel belonging to the heirs of James Smith. The source of his horse stock is unknown, but it is from this same area of Assateague that the Spanish shipwreck legend becomes embedded with three families who would then inhabit and raise horses in this area.

In 1794, George Stewart's son James sold his interest in Assateague to a John Lewis. Lewis in turn conveyed his interest in Assateague and 32 horses to his son Isaac in 1818. In 1796, Jonathan Watson bought 500 acres north of Lewis on Assateague called *Little Neck* from Thomas Teackle Gore. Besides cattle and sheep, he had horses on Assateague. His great granddaughter, Victoria Watson Pruitt, would later record her belief in the Spanish shipwreck legend as the source of the horses. In 1797, Joshua Whealton purchased 175 acres on Chincoteague directly opposite the sand hills. He and his descendants would later raise horses and through intermarriage with the Lewis family would own land on Assateague. The Whealton family would become one of the principal defenders of the shipwreck legend.

Another pivotal point for the horses seems to be the year 1821 when a great hurricane inundated Assateague and Chincoteague Islands, drowning many horses. The countywide loss of horses was 127. An infusion of new blood most likely took place resulting in larger animals. Values later increased. By 1835 the herd was clearly managed as private property. By the early 1900s horseraising and the legend of their origin would devolve from the Whealtons to the Beebe family.

Since no Spanish documents have been discovered that specifically say that *La Galga* left Havana, Cuba, on August 18, 1750, with horses on board, support for the legend may be found with another Spanish shipwreck, lost in another century 1,200 miles away.

On September 4, 1622, the Terra Firme Fleet left Havana for Cadiz, Spain, on that the 1750 fleet had made. The next day, September 5, the fleet was assaulted by a tremendous hurricane, resulting in the loss of the *Nuestra Señora de Atocha* and the *Santa Margarita* in the Florida Keys. This was the same day that *La Galga* was driven ashore on Assateague 138 years later.

In 1980, Mel Fisher found the wreck of the *Margarita* while searching for the *Atocha* off the Marquesas Keys. They found at least one horseshoe on board. This was recently reconfirmed to me by the staff at Treasure Salvors. The archaeologist at the time was Duncan Mathewson, who had again in 2004 described the horseshoe to me as being quite small. Apparently, the horse was similar in size to the small horses described by Henry A. Wise in the early 1800s as having been on Assateague prior to the American Revolution.

Dr. Eugene Lyon, who had done the comprehensive research on the 1622 fleet, found no reference to horses on the *Margarita* in the archives, but he felt strongly that their reason for their being aboard was that they had belonged to the soldiers who were documented as being on the ship. *La Galga* had registered fifty-six soldiers on board in Havana before three of them deserted.

Over the centuries, the collective memories about the Spanish wreck became blurred. Many knew that the origin of the wild horses were from a Spanish shipwreck. A few had been told that the legendary ship was lost in an inlet, but the location of that inlet became subject to debate as overwashes and breakthroughs from later storms created features that resembled inlets while masking others.

In the spring of 1983, I got a first-hand account of the shipwreck legend from a former resident of Chincoteague Island. His name was Ronnie Beebe and he also happened to be the great nephew of Clarence "Grandpa" Beebe who described the shipwreck legend to his grandchildren in *Misty of Chincoteague*. His ancestry in the area went back centuries. He was also a descendant of Joshua Whealton, as was "Grandma Beebe," and claimed Indian heritage through him, as Whealton had married an Indian woman in the late eighteenth century. I had been told that he knew a lot about Assateague and would be worth talking to. When I told Ronnie Beebe that I was having trouble locating a Spanish shipwreck, he knew the answer. He did not know the name or the date of the wreck, but he told me of a legendary lost Spanish galleon as he remembered being told of it from childhood. His recounting of the legend not only confirmed the origin of the horses, but he also said that the ship had entered an inlet, which had caused it to sand in within two weeks' time. I would find out twenty years later from newly discovered Spanish records that the ship was actually buried in sand within the first three days.

In 1982, when my partner, Albert Alberi, told me that a psychic had told him that the shipwreck lay under Assateague Island and not in front of it, I laughed at the idea. It was not until we came up empty in the ocean, discovered the 1840 plat of Assateague, and then had a chance meeting with a descendant of an Assateague Indian who told me about the legendary inlet that enclosed the ship, that I finally became convinced that *La Galga* was buried under the island. Finding that inlet became prerequisite to finding the ship. With that in mind, it's possible now to ignore any preconceived interpretation of the Maryland-Virginia boundary and look only at the range of possibility, that is, within the two miles between latitude 38° and the present boundary. There are only three possible locations for that inlet in this area.

When I began my research on *La Galga*, I had read in Dr. Reginald Truitt's *Maryland's Arcadia*, published in 1977, about a legendary Spanish ship going into an inlet. The wild ponies were attributed to this wreck, although the story was discounted by Dr. Truitt. I had ignored the story myself because I thought it didn't relate to *La Galga*. I had thought Truitt was associating the legendary inlet with the 1850 inlet called Pope's Island Inlet, which lay a mile and a half north of the present boundary. That was clearly outside of *La Galga's* range of probability. But after a closer reading of his book, I realized that he was talking about a feature 900 yards south of the present boundary. Truitt described a "Spanish Bar," an elusive feature not illustrated on any map. Dr. Truitt was repeating an account given him by a Reverend Paul Watson, a descendant of David Watson, the first lighthouse keeper of Assateague Lighthouse and grandson of Peter Watson who had lived on Upper Pope's Island from 1873 to 1884. Peter Watson died that year. Reverend Watson was born in 1890 and lived with his parents and grandmother in Snow Hill where he'd heard stories about the life of his grandfather as an oysterman and farmer on Pope's Island. He recounted his understanding of the location of Spanish Bar:

> Going through Pope Ditch into Pope Bay, on the far side and a little to the right, is a sand bar long-time and commonly known as Spanish Bar, and running from that point to the ocean is still evidence of a creek always said to be the remains of a one-time inlet through which, it was understood, the ship that was wrecked sought refuge.

The above description seems to be describing the location between Upper Pope's and Lower Pope's, or Pitt's Island, as it is called today. These two islands are separated by an unnamed "ditch." Additional comments given by Dr. Truitt refer again to Spanish Bar: "There is a wading place on the end of his island, not far from Spanish Bar where he drove to the ocean front to gather and cart driftwood."

What is compelling about this account is that an inland feature is being associated with the Spanish wreck. Truitt, born in 1891, also recounted that Captains Alva Powell and Frank Mumford, both born in the mid-nineteenth century, had been told since childhood that horses escaped from a wreck on Spanish Bar.

Modern maps clearly show a small creek opposite this "ditch" on Assateague that appears to be a remnant of a former inlet, but this feature was quite different in 1859. The overlay in images on page 352 suggest that this area is most likely an overwash influenced by water flowing in and out of the ditch of Pope's Island. If *La Galga* had entered this location, the Spaniards would have sought the protective cover of Pope's Island. In 1751, during the court martial of Captain Huony, the Spaniards made no mention of Pope's Island in their testimony. When the English prisoner, Captain Edward Ford, sent a message back to the ship for Captain Huony, he said, "We're on the island of Azetegue on the border of Maryland and Virginia." And it was from Assateague that they departed for the mainland.

Part of our 1983 field work on Assateague included the area described by Truitt and no targets were located. But eliminating areas of possibility were just as important as searching probable areas indicated by historical research.

During my meeting with Ronnie Beebe, he had pointed to a spot he'd thought was the legendary inlet (See page 354). The feature he indicated was just above the boundary line of 1840. It seemed at the time to be a very likely location. We explored this area with the magnetometer in 1983 with no magnetic anomalies detected. Comparisons with the map of 1859 and today show that what Beebe thought was evidence of an old inlet was not there in 1859.

Over twenty-three years have passed since we went to Assateague that day with Bill Holloway, the psychic introduced to us by Albert Alberi. Since then, more facts have come to light that explain what happened.

Holloway had indicated on a NOAA chart of the Assateague coastline the area he believed the wreck to be in. It was in the lake area that I had already searched to some degree. He guided me over a magnetometer contact and proclaimed that I had gone over a piece of the wreck. My path was then blocked by deeper water. I assumed that what I had located was just a piece of the wreck and the main body of it was probably some distance away. This prompted us to search in other areas, which included the inlet features described by Truitt and Beebe, with no success. I never returned to the spot we detected that day for further analysis. Part of the reason for searching outside of his predicted area was that he had some conflicting "visions" that day on Assateague. He had described another ship being with *La Galga* and wrecking on the south end of Assateague. I knew this to be incorrect. He also stopped at the timbers sticking out of the sand opposite the future Riebe/Cook/Benson site and declared that they were part of *La Galga*. This was in direct contradiction to his vision nearly two miles away in the lake area where the magnetometer indicated the wreck to be. These contradictions troubled me at the time, even though he had

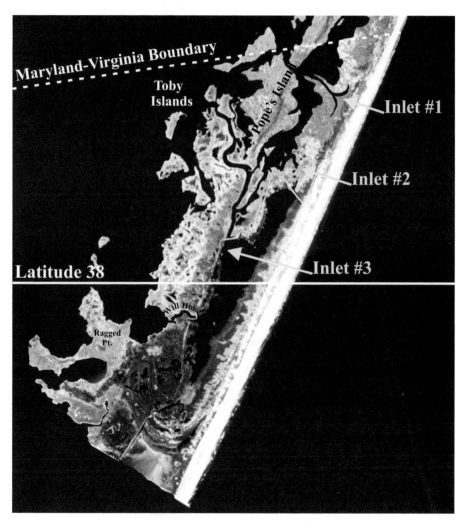

LANDSAT infrared image of Assateague Island. Within the two mile range of search there are only three locations for a former inlet which holds the secret of the hidden galleon. *Illustration by the author.*

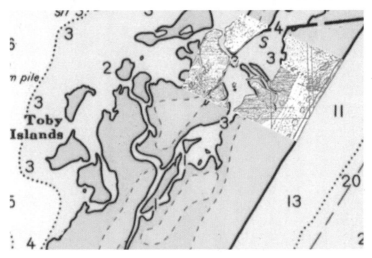

This is the inlet described in Reginald Truitt's book as the legendary inlet. It lies about 900 yards south of the present boundary line and has clearly evolved since 1859 as seen on the top right with 1859 superimposed. In 1859, there was no trending of water toward the ocean. The trending evolved after 1859. There does appear to be evidence of a pre-1859 overwash subsequently eroded by the southerly flow of water in Pope's Bay, followed by another overwash after 1859 and moulded by the ebb and flow of water through the "Ditch." The Ditch separates Upper Pope's Island from Lower Pope's Island also known today as Pitts' Island. The hurricane of 1933 was most likely responsible for the changes in this feature as it is today. The Pope's Island Lifesaving Station logs reported that there was extreme overwash during the storm

and most of the buildings had been moved off of their foundations. The Ditch was cut through after 1713, as it was not mentioned in the first survey of Pope's Island. But nonetheless, Truitt's description would put "Spanish Bar" south of this feature. In 1751, the Spaniards made no mention of Pope's Island in their testimony. Had they wrecked here they would have sought the protective cover of this island. When the Englishman, Edward Ford, sent a message back to the ship for Captain Huony, he said, "We're on the island of Azetegue on the border of Maryland and Virginia." Magnetometer surveys in this area produced no results. Any extension of the Calvert-Scarborough Line falls north of this feature. *Photos and illustrations by the author.*

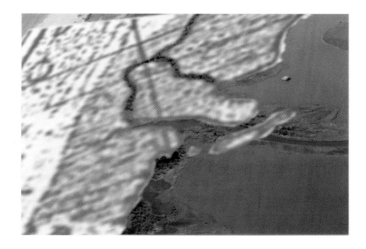

Candidate #2. This "inlet" lies another 1,000 yards south of the inlet depicted on pages 352-3. Ronnie Beebe told the author in 1983 that he believed that this was the inlet that trapped the legendary Spanish galleon. At the time it appeared that he was right because the 1840 boundary line was positioned exactly for a perfect match.

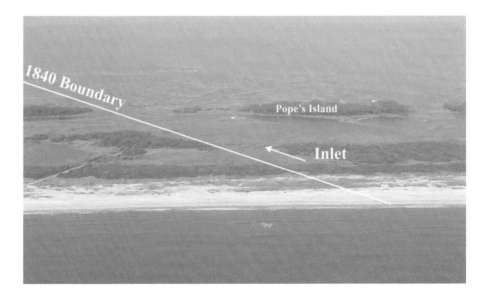

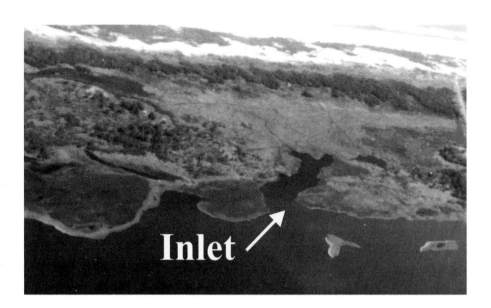

However this area was magged with no success. The yellow overlay is from a 1972 NOAA chart. The dark brown is from the 1859 topographical map drawn by Charles Ferguson. The inlet feature indicated by Ronnie Beebe to the author in 1983 was nonexistent in 1859. *Photos and illustrations by the author.*

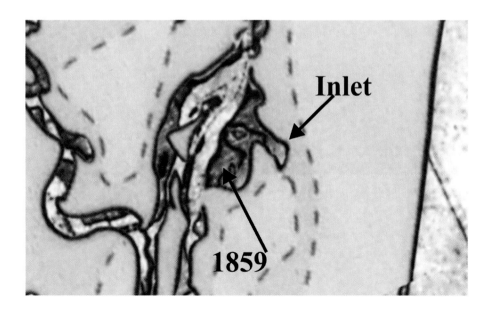

Aerial view of entire search area. *Photo by the author taken 2006.*

This 2006 photo of area contains *La Galga*. Her remains lie within the square. You can see the outline of the creek beneath the water. To the left of this area the author was told in 1983 about a Spanish pistol and Spanish coins being found in the woods. A little to the right, the author found a timber sticking out of the bottom which coincided with information he received from a Chincoteague waterman whose father worked at the Pope Island Life Saving Station in the 19th century. In the creek, some artifacts had been tonged up years ago. Magnetometer readings taken in 1983 are further proof that the hidden galleon is buried in this location. *Photo by the author.*

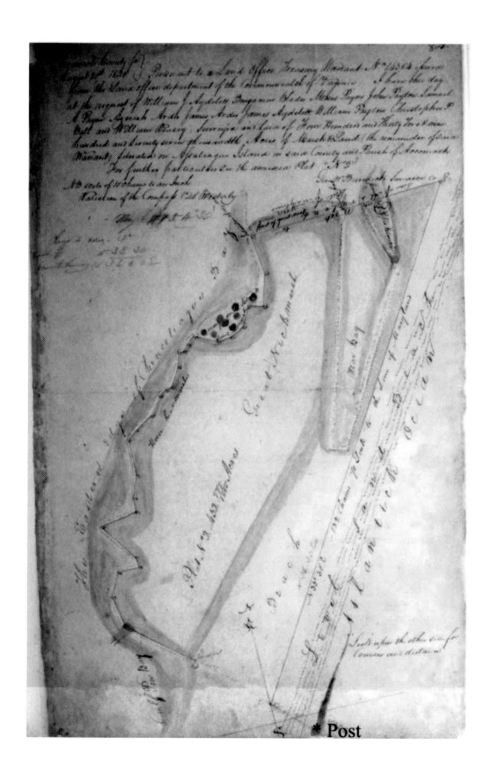

* Post

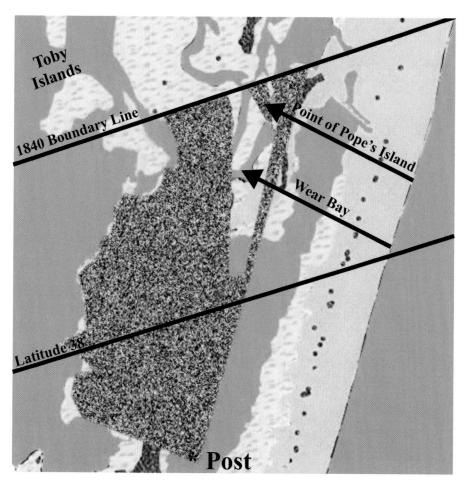

The 1840 plat, left, and its outline, right, overlaid on a map of Assateague. Wear Bay was inundated and overwashed after 1840. The eastern edge of the shaded area was the high water mark in 1840. The features inside the bay could only have been formed by flowing water. It was not until 1897 that land was patented east of this tract to the ocean. The lower right corner of the shaded area coincides with the northeast corner of *Little Neck*, which was described in the 1796 deed from Thomas Teackle Gore to Jonathan Watson as "at the surf." Watson was the great grandfather of Victoria Watson Pruitt. See also page 357. The south bounds of *Great Neck* is the north bounds of *Little Neck*. The Toby Island just above the 1840 line was patented in 1865 by Maryland. *Illustration by the author.*

This 1939 photo shows the Ragged Point area just south of the area shown on the bottom of page 361. The line of the eastern edge of the 1840 patent has been extended. At Will's Hole water once flowed in an east/west fashion centuries ago. Sand accretion brought an abrupt end to that process. This feature most likely took its name from William Tindall who is believed to have lived at this location in 1750. The recurved beach ridges which document a former ocean front blend in with a newer accreted beach. *Photo courtesy the National Archives, College Park, Maryland.*

TOP. 1983 photo taken by the author in late summer. The lower water level and blooming algae painted a perfect picture of the remains of the old inlet that had remained invisible to us during our search. *Photo by the author.*

BOTTOM. 1939 aerial photo taken before Assateague was acquired by the U.S. Fish and Wildlife Service. The future dam is indicated. Note that the creek ends at the line marking the eastern limits of the 1840 patent. This was the former high tide line and is evidence of a rapid outgrowth of the beach. The end of the creek trends toward the ocean. This feature could only have been produced by water flowing to or from the ocean. This area was known as the "Levels" in the nineteenth century and was a sand beach. Water continued to flow around the wreck until years later when the accreted sand halted this process. In 1840, this water feature was called "Wear Bay." A Wear or Weir, is an obstruction in a stream which diverts its course. *This photo courtesy the National Archives, College Park, Maryland.*

The wreck site looking south. *Photo by the author.*

TOP: At the dam looking north over Virginia Creek. BOTTOM: Looking south. This water impoundment has hidden valuable clues to the wreck's location for the last fifty years. This dam places the wreck outside of navigable waters and outside of the federal admiralty court jurisdiction and the Abandoned Shipwreck Act. *Photos by the author.*

Virginia Creek looking south. From the vicinity of the Boundary Tree.
Photo by the author.

Believe it or not, this is the former sandy beach where Captain Huony and his soldiers and sailors gathered after leaving the wreck. A Spanish pistol and some pieces of eight were reported found in these woods long ago. *Photos by the author.*

View of the lake looking east. On September 5, 1750, this was a raging ocean. *Photo by the author*

J. HOLYLAND,   PHOTOGRAPHER.

William J. Aydelott and his wife, Eleanor, 1878. Aydelott was the grandson of Benjamin Aydelott who in 1770 had acquired one hundred acres on Assateague from the Gore family who had owned the land opposite the wreck in 1750. This one hundred acres may have encompassed the wreck site of *La Galga*. In 1840, he founded a partnership with ten others and acquired 880 acres on Assateague that had reverted to the Commonwealth of Virginia. See page 358. This land patent encompassed the wreck site. Aydelott later became a Boundary Commissioner from Maryland and was instrumental in having the boundary moved north from the line documented in his patent. Aydelott's son-in-law, D. J. Whealton, was an uncle of Ronnie Beebe who had related the legend of the hidden galleon to the author in 1983. *Photo courtesy of the Maryland Historical Society.*

led me to a magnetic contact—something we had not found before. It is only now that the conflicts can be understood. The ship he saw with *La Galga* was actually the *Juno*. It, of course, wrecked in 1802 and not 1750, but this so-called "Juno" was with *La Galga* in Benson's admiralty case. The location he indicated off the southern end of Assateague correlates exactly with Benson's wreck. And the timbers we had seen on the beach had come from the site that Benson had claimed in court to be *La Galga*. Today I can only wonder if this is just a coincidence or more proof of Holloway's ability. But we need not rely on a psychic to tell us where the wreck is. The only question left to answer is, *was this area a former inlet?*

Using computer graphics to overlay the 1840 plat on Assateague and cutting out the area of Wear Bay, we find a remarkable window into the past. Instead of only water as found in 1840, there is evidence of storm overwash after that time, which proves that this area had been formerly much closer to the ocean, and that the sand that had poured into the bay was molded by flowing water—water that travelled from Pope's Bay, which then found an outlet to the ocean. From July 10-12, 1842, a northeast storm raged like a hurricane at Assateague and was probably responsible for these changes.

The 1859 topographical map (see pages 166 and 276) clearly shows that the years between 1840 and 1859 were quite evolutionary. By 1859, this area of Assateague was much like it is today. But the area east of the 1840 patent (see page 358) was not granted by the Commonwealth of Virginia until 1897. The last strip of accreted beach east of this was patented in 1919. In 1983, when I was analyzing the 1859 chart, I did not have the benefit of Huony's testimony. But now a closer analysis can be made. He described the lifeline to the beach as having been fastened to *La Galga's* bow. That of course proves that the bow was closer to the beach than the stern. This theory is validated by the fact that the stern, by description, appeared to be in deeper water and farther from shore. With the predominant current travelling from north to south along the beach, further propelled by northeast winds, a strong current of water would have been funnelled around the ship's bow toward the beach. This could have scoured the beach in front of the wreck. The 1859 chart shows a pronounced deviation in the old dune line opposite the split in the creek. This deviation was certainly caused by flowing water as it is directly related to the course of the west branch of the creek. The creek split at the end of Wear Bay: a weir is an obstruction in a stream to divert its flow, and for water to flow, there must have been an outlet and that was the ocean.

I made another interesting discovery as I poured through my old research. In a box of pictures, I found an aerial photograph of the wreck site taken after we had located the wreck. It was a color slide I had not seen since the late summer of 1983. The hot dry weather had caused two things to happen. The water level had dropped in the lake, and the algae had bloomed in the shallower water, factors that gave a dramatic presentation of old features of the island in the lake area, namely the creek bed, which was what had remained of the old inlet. This feature had been hidden for many years because of the lake created by the dam. In photo on page 361 the creek bed is plainly visible. The eastern branch reaches toward the ocean. If only I could have had this picture when I was walking the lake, I could have done a thorough job with the magnetometer. At the time, when I stepped into deeper water, I didn't know where it ran. The picture I had previously used in 1983 to evaluate where to probe with the magnetometer had been taken in the winter (see page 158). The features of the old creek were not visible from the air at that time. When I compared the former photograph with my recent discovery, I realized that I had misjudged my target on the last trip to Assateague with Ned Middlesworth in June of 1983.

At the National Archives, I found aerial photos of the area taken in 1939 before it became part of the wildlife refuge and was then flooded with water. These images document the final evolution that had taken place since 1840. As storm overwash gradually filled in Wear Bay from the east, the creek became the dividing line between the beach in 1750 and the present one (see page 360).

Just south of the wreck site is more evidence of a sudden and dramatic accretion of sand. Page 361 shows a feature that is now called "The Will Hole." It looks like a former well formed creek, but it deadends on its eastern terminus toward the ocean. One can see direct evidence of beach accretion and the rapid development eastward of the beach that resulted in the closing of the former creek, which most likely was a drain from Wear Bay.

In 1796, it was called "Will's Hole," no doubt named after someone. That someone was probably William Tindall, who is believed to have lived on Ragged Point sometime before he died in 1750. The plat of 1840 notes the location of the house. Someone has lived in this location sporadically from the late 1600s to the latter nineteenth century. All that remains of the house today is a few bricks buried in the sand.

Also shown in this photograph is clear evidence of where the oceanfront was in earlier centuries. Dune ridges formed by the tides and blowing sand define the line where the ocean waters formerly flowed.

Ten miles to the north of this location are features very similar to these, at what is known as Old Sinepuxent Inlet. That inlet was said to be over a mile wide in the eighteenth century and finally closed in the first decades of the nineteenth century. Dune ridges and vegetation clearly define the outline of the beach and former inlet.

Spanish records make no mention of an inlet, but they do say they were at some deserted islets. This particular inlet actually lay north of the wreck, not opposite it. It was not presented as an obstacle to the Spaniards, thus explaining why it was not mentioned when the crew swam a line to another wreck lying on the beach. Captain Huony also described the bad undertow caused by the retreating waves, more evidence that the ship was opposite a shoreline. However, because the wreck lay in close proximity to the channel of the inlet, it triggered its closure.

In 1982, I learned of some archaeological evidence consistent with *La Galga* being in this location. Nat Steelman of Chincoteague had told me about being shown timbers from the legendary Spanish ship by his father when he was a boy. He pointed to a spot near the edge of the lake (see page 166). His father was very familiar with this area as he had worked as a surfman at the Pope Island Life Saving Station in the 1890s. The station was located just below the present Maryland line. Steelman was considered by many at the time to be the local historian since he read whatever he could find about the history of Assateague and Chincoteague. He knew from Reginald Truitt's book about *La Galga* being lost a little above the Maryland line. He made no connection between the legend he grew up with and what modern-day historians were telling him. At the time I talked with Steelman, I still thought the wreck was in the ocean and only considered the latitude of the timbers as significant. The next year, at Steelman's insistence, I met Ronnie Beebe who told me that a Spanish pistol was found in the woods opposite this area, as well as a "bunch of Spanish coins like they had been in a bag." I was then convinced the wreck was buried nearby. Beebe had told me about his great uncle, D.J. Whealton. He said that Whealton was the authority on the Spanish wreck. I would find out twenty years later who he was. In 1887, he was a member of a partnership that owned part of Assateague Island. That partnership was founded in 1840 by William J. Aydelott and ten others for the land around the buried Spanish warship.

The 1840 plat that I had found in the Accomack County Courthouse in 1982 was invaluable at the time as it not only documented the all-important boundary line but proved that the beach had been much narrower back then as well as earlier in the eighteenth century. It was a bridge to understanding earlier land records for this area. Twenty years later that plat revealed yet another story.

William J. Aydelott, the founder of the 1840 partnership that acquired the land, was the grandson of Benjamin Aydelott, who in 1770, had been willed by Daniel Gore one hundred acres on Assateague south and adjoining the then-Maryland boundary. Daniel's father, William, was one of the primary salvors of the wreck and had owned the Virginia portion of Assateague in 1750. William Aydelott's grandfather, Benjamin, had lived on the mainland just above the Virginia line in 1750 and could easily have participated in the salvage as well. These one hundred acres in 1770 appear to encompass the wreck area when considering the old coastline. The fact that Aydelott was willed the land rather than getting it by deed of sale suggests a business arrangement between him and Daniel Gore or possibly Daniel's father William.

In 1840, there were eleven partners, who had varied in age from twenty-two to sixty-one. Their occupations were farmers, shoemakers, fishermen, and a ship's carpenter. There were four sets of brothers, and they'd all lived close to one another in Worcester County, Maryland, just above the Virginia line. William Aydelott, at twenty-three, appeared to be the managing partner.

The partners had acquired this land on Assateague formerly abandoned in the late eighteenth century by the Gore family and Aydelott's grandfather. In 1840, this land was deemed to be nearly worthless. By purchasing a treasury warrant for $17.60, the partners received a patent from the Commonwealth of Virginia for 880 acres in two adjoining pieces called *Great Neck* and *Ragged Point*. The only additional fees were $4.65, and the real property taxes the first year were only 45 cents. The total price paid could have easily been paid by William Aydelott himself. This was far less than the forty-six dollars Isaac Lewis paid in 1821 for forty-six acres at the south end of Assateague behind the sand hills. It was also less than the thirty to forty-five dollars paid for "beach horses" in 1835. I noted that the survey of 1840 had come very close in acreage to the description of this part of the island in 1696 when the designations of *Great Neck* and *Ragged Point* were created. This was further evidence that proved the accretion of sand since then.

It appeared that the purpose of the partnership was raising livestock, but the records are unclear. It was obvious that William Aydelott needed trusting partners rather than working capital.

It is not known what the first years produced for the partners, but circumstantial evidence suggests a salvage attempt on the wreck buried on their land. On January 16, 1843, Moses Payne had sold his interest to the others for one hundred dollars. He'd made a nice profit. This sale may have been precipitated by the northeast storm of July, 1842, at Assateague. The sand flats and Wear Bay depicted on the plat could have easily been overrun with the sea, negating any progress of salvage. The 1859 chart of this area shows some radical changes from 1840. On September 23, 1843, Christopher Ball sold his interest for one hundred dollars to the remaining partners, and to Moses Payne, who wanted back in. Ball's one-eleventh share had also included his interest in a cow boat and bull on Assateague. On December 18, James Aydelott sold his share to the others for apparently the prescribed one hundred dollars. He too sold his interest in the cow boat and bull. All of these men made a nice profit from their original investment.

Two of them had cashed out early. What can only be inferred is that they saw no future in the endeavor, while the remaining partners did. None of these transactions mentioned horses or other livestock being conveyed. It was not until 1873 that any reference was made of joint ownership of cattle or horses when Samuel Payne had left his "partnership horses and sheep" to Ira Payne.

Before Rick Cook had left our group to form Alpha Quest in 1983, he had learned that fishermen in the early 1900s had dredged up some items that appeared to be medical instruments from the creek. This was south of where the dam is today and just north of the wreck site and within the area acquired by Benjamin Aydelott in 1770. It was at this dam that we stood with Bill Holloway as he looked south across the lake and described seeing the wreck. It was documented that on August 4, 1750, some surgeon's instruments had been put on board *La Galga* in Havana. Cook told me in 1983 that he'd believed that the items had come from the Spaniards' campsite and had washed into the creek. He saw no connection to my hypothesis that it appeared that *La Galga* was buried in a former inlet and now this creek bed. From survivors' accounts we know that everyone remained at the wreck site until they left. So if it had been the Spaniards' campsite, the wreck would be only yards away. To me, this was a valuable clue which coincided with everything else that indicated the wreck was buried in this immediate area. The fact that someone in the 1900s could have dredged up items from this ship suggests that they could've easily done so in the previous century. When Aydelott and his partners had acquired this land and creek bed in 1840, they may have been able to recover items from the wreck themselves. The exact location of the wreck would have been known by their grandfathers.

There are three interpretations of the legendary inlet. But only one of them holds the secret of the hidden galleon.

At present, the government will mention the legend of a Spanish

A scene from the book and movie *Misty of Chincoteague*. Clarence "Grandpa" Beebe relates the legend of the Spanish shipwreck and the wild ponies to his grandchildren, Paul and Maureen Beebe. In 1983, his great nephew, Ronnie Beebe, without knowing the name or the year of the shipwreck, gave the author the same account but said that the wreck was buried in a forgotten inlet. *Illustration by Tom Dean.*

galleon associated with the horses, but they then tend toward discrediting the legend in favor of their position, that the present horses owe their existence to former pastured horses originating from the seventeenth century. They appear to be unaware that the great storm of October 7-8, 1749 had nearly wiped out all of the horses on Assateague. Contemporary records show that these pastured horses were cared and accounted for. Those that roam wild today are unable to claim certain ancestry prior to 1750. However, the current *Assateague Island* handbook published by the Park Service, after dropping the *San Lorenzo* hoax, does say that *La Galga* is associated with the pony legend but then retreats saying, "no hard evidence supports this idea."

When my psychic friend, Bill Holloway, was at Assateague in the spring of 1983, he told me that he clearly saw these horses on board. His impressions, as he described them, were given to the journalist with the *Wilmington News Journal* when they were reporting on our discovery. If he is proven right in his ability to *see* the wreck, it becomes difficult to discount his vision of horses. But his psychic vision becomes a little more than a footnote when compared to the persistent legend preserved by those residents of Chincoteague, like Victoria Watson Pruitt and Clarence Beebe, who recounted the now world famous legend to the author of *Misty of Chincoteague*. Grandpa Beebe, he knew, "Legends be the only stories as is true!"

CHAPTER THIRTEEN
Uncovered

*"The story of each shipwreck is woven
    into the intricate tapestry of regional history."*
—The National Park Service.

The federal cases involving the shipwrecks labeled *La Galga* and *Juno* by Ben Benson ended in August 2001. A year later, the governments of Virginia, Maryland, and the United States undertook an archival and electronic search for sunken vessels off Assateague Island. Some of the details of this survey were reported in *The Virginian-Pilot* of August 26, 2002. According to the *Pilot*, Susan Langley, underwater archaeologist for the State of Maryland, had prepared an inventory of nearly two hundred and fifty wrecks off of Assateague Island based on archival research. She then set off with a magnetometer and a side-scan sonar to look for them. When I'd read about this, I wondered if the GPS system she used had the wreck data recorded in it as mine does. She would've seen the site of *La Galga* as being inland from the oceanfront. That certainly would've raised some questions for her survey. To double check this, she could have gone to the NOAA web site and performed a shipwreck search. All you do is fill in "LA GALGA" under vessel name, and you get the information as to the source for the wreck's position and identity. Bill Bane and this author are listed as the source. No one has ever gotten in touch with either Bill or me to find out any information about *La Galga*.

The article said that Langley's research had been going on for over a year, no doubt prompted by Benson's claims of shipwreck discovery. Carl Zimmerman, resource management specialist for Assateague National Seashore, said Langley's survey work "is a positive step after the testy court battle. The Park Service had agreed in the early 1980s to survey the island for historic resources, but never had the money to go offshore. The fight over *La Galga* emphasized the need to get on with it, and money became available recently." Zimmerman said further that "this is strictly locating areas of potential, we would hope to follow this up with some more specific surveys involving diving, but that's a little bit off in the future."

I was taken totally by surprise when I saw the following, included in the same story and related by Langley:

> The *San Lorenzo* wrecked in 1820 on the way from Panama
> to Spain with 100 small ponies that had been blinded for use
> in mines. Six years later, at least 45 were seen on the island by
> a surveyor. It's possible, Langley conceded, that at least some
> of the Chincoteague ponies came from that ship, although
> legend, a la Misty, claims that they came from a Spanish ship
> wrecked in the 1600s.

It seemed to me that Susan Langley's research on this shipwreck must have been limited to tourist literature as the source of this story dead-ends with Donald Stewart in 1977, not in any archive. The National Park Service, as promised, had deleted reference to the *San Lorenzo* in the *Assateague Island* handbook after 1984. Tyler Bastian, Langley's predecessor at the Archaeology Department, had stated in 1986 that he had never seen any evidence to support the existence of the *San Lorenzo*. I realized I needed to find out more about this research conducted by the National Park Service, and by the States of Maryland and Virginia.

I located her report at the State Historic Preservation Office in Richmond, Virginia. It was over three hundred pages and loaded with interesting information. In more than one place, I found references to the *San Lorenzo* and her fabulous treasure concocted by Donald Stewart. There was no reservation that the story might be untrue. The Park Service had taken deliberate measures after my letter to them in 1984 to remove references to the *San Lorenzo* from printed material. The wayside exhibit at Park Service headquarters in Berlin, Maryland had been changed also. Now, the long-awaited report from the National Park Service detailing our underwater cultural heritage has refloated the fictitious *San Lorenzo*.

Langley gave her source for the *San Lorenzo* as a book called *Notebook on Shipwrecks, Maryland-Delaware Coast*, by Richard Moale. Unfortunately she relied on a book that had not cited direct references to sources—only limited names of libraries and names of other books.

There were also several newspapers listed in the back of the book. There was no traceable proof of the author's shipwrecks. One paper listed was *The Baltimore Sun*, which could've been Moale's source for the *San Lorenzo*. The shipwreck list had contained names of a number of peculiar wrecks, which were not published anywhere else. Moale's book was rife with errors. One ship easily disproved was HMS *Marlborough* sunk in 1762 west of Portugal in the eastern Atlantic. Moale said it sunk ten leagues (30 miles) off the Maryland coast with no source cited. Langley included this ship in her inventory.

Another source she used was a Timothy Akers in England. Amazingly, every shipwreck I looked at up to 1767, where I stopped and he was the source, appeared to be nonexistent. His stated source was the "Preston Public Record Office," more commonly known as the Lancashire County Record Office. There he said he had located a research report called the "R. Taylor Collection of Shipwrecks off the East Coast of America." This was supposedly based on Lloyd's shipping records. Many of Akers' wrecks predate 1764 when *Lloyd's Register* begins. But this register does not contain wreck information. *Lloyd's List* which does, began in 1741. Akers listed seventeen wrecks for 1743—the most for any year. But *Lloyd's List* for 1743 did not survive. None of these wrecks could be verified in American colonial newspapers. One example was the wreck of an Italian brigantine called the *Harletta* lost in 1704. Langley quoted Akers:

> Went in aid to compatriot ship *Larino* but got into difficulties herself and beached at Ocean City just outside of harbor approach. Cargo was salvaged but ship foundered as attempts to save her failed. Capt. Giglia Arpinllio; Port: Spezia; From Spezia to Charlestown; Cargo: Wines, ports, and brandy in casks.

Contrary to this account, Ocean City, Maryland, was not founded until 1869. The "harbor approach" referred to would be Ocean City Inlet. This "harbor approach" was not created until the hurricane of 1933. Her source, being Akers, cited only the county library in England with no document, collection, manuscript, or book supporting this entry. The inventory of records at the Lancashire County Record Office failed to produce any reference to an "R. Taylor" related to shipwrecks. The library does not contain Lloyd's shipping records. Bruce Jackson, Lancashire County Archivist, after being asked about this controversy, posed the question, "Why would we have something relating to shipwrecks in America?"

Of course the most logical thing to do was to contact Akers. By e-mail, I asked him about the lack of Lloyd's records there. In his reply he failed to address that point, but he insisted that he had relied on a typed transcript from a "private researcher at the Preston Public Library." Later attempts to get verification from him failed.

Langley's local researcher, Joan Charles, who had compiled hundreds of wrecks in several books and had always listed her sources for each wreck, did not include any of these wrecks in her work, including the *San Lorenzo*. Langley made no attempt to reconcile these irregularities between these two sources.

In Moale's book, there was another shipwreck which stood out. Listed just below the "*Santa Rosalea*," was the "*Santo Cristo*." There were no particulars given, no date, no source, except that it wrecked on Assateague. The *Santo Cristo* was the imaginary vessel in *Misty of Chincoteague*. Langley chose to include this wreck, which was nothing more than a literary device of *Misty's* author, in her inventory.

Even though Susan Langley now wants us to believe that this was a real wreck, she had a very negative statement about the ponies immortalized in *Misty*: "While on the subject of myths, another one that requires debunking is that the feral ponies on the island are descendants of ponies, which swam ashore from a Spanish shipwreck. There are many variations of this myth." Within her own report she contradicted herself when she admitted that horses may have descended from Stewart's *San Lorenzo*.

Langley, apparently fascinated with Charles Wilson's buried treasure, documented that story in her report. After her investigation, she confirmed that no records could be located in London contrary to published accounts about the buried treasure. This reaffirmed my quiet belief that most archaeologists are actually latent treasure hunters.

With these distractions aside, I looked further and found material on *La Galga*. She generously supplied transcripts of several contemporary newspaper accounts describing the wreck of *La Galga* and the 1750 fleet. She'd also provided several excerpts of documents from the Maryland Archives, which had given information on the wreck at Assateague. She hadn't included Captain Huony's letter to the Maryland governor found in the adjoining pages of her source material but made reference to it. This was the letter that gave the specific directions to locating the wreck, but she did say that the wreck occurred above the Maryland line. She also stated, "Subsequent boundary delineations have placed it below the boundary. This became significant when the vessel was relocated by commercial treasure salvors in 1997."

But inconsistent with her understanding of where the wreck should lie, she made no notation on her site map for *La Galga's* location.

Although she quoted liberally from the Maryland Archives documents, Langley left out the statement from Sheriff Scarborough when he described the remaining mahogany, "There is many thousands of pounds worth if it could be got before the Ship bursts with the Sea and *Sinks into the Land.*" And another omission was the statement by Scarborough when he quoted Captain Huony who said that, "The Owner of the *Land* owned the Ship." Although Sheriff Scarborough didn't realize it, he was vividly describing the location of the wreck to those in the future who would choose to find her.

Nowhere in the Langley report will you see my name mentioned. Yet in her "References Cited" at the end, she acknowledged examining files at the Chincoteague National Wildlife Refuge and its regional headquarters. Within those files, you will find my 1983 report on the location of the wreck as well as numerous newspaper articles about it. Their presence in these files was verified through a Freedom of Information request I'd made in 2003. What other sources were examined but not considered for inclusion in her report is unknown, as they are not disclosed.

In her report, there was one paragraph that was not included within the body of her documentation on *La Galga* that most assuredly had related to the wreck. A former National Park Service employee named Mel Olsen and a resident of Chincoteague named Tom Reed had given a description of what they'd believed was *La Galga's* final resting place. They described the exact spot I'd pinpointed in 1983. In Langley's words:

Another consideration, is a possible wreck near the north end of Old Fields Pond on U.S. Fish and Wildlife Service administered lands. The pond was created by the USFWS when it built water control systems to dam some of the old channels. At times of extreme drawdown, a mast may be seen protruding from the mud. The present road runs over this causeway and local lore has it that the bow of this vessel rests under a clump of trees on the west side of the causeway, and the mast is 800' south of the water control port in the dike (the port is at 38° 00' 14.96"N 75° 16' 28.10") between the port and the four poles protruding from the water. Mr. Reed insists that this is the genuine *La Galga*, which is also referred to as 'Gagla' or 'Greyhound,' and all are believed to be different vessels by local residents. He believes that Sea Hunt, Inc. is looking at a different vessel. He also told the author that the diameter of the mast is relatively small implying that this is the upper portion and that the remainder of the vessel would be significantly below the mud. While this bodes well for preservation, it would entail a great deal of costly effort as the area is relatively remote and the vessel would be well below the water table. Also, unless the vessel broke up, it would be enormous if 800' separate the bow and one mast; prohibitively large to transit that waterway. Mr. Reed permitted the author to photograph a bottle and two coins that came from the vicinity of the reported bow area many years ago.

This account had, of course, captured my attention. It is hard to say what this "mast" is but it is in nearly the exact spot that the remains of *La Galga* are believed to lie. And the reference to the bow being 800 feet away fits nicely with the records recently found by Victoria describing the lifeline being run from *La Galga* to another wreck on the beach. Magnetometer readings were obtained in this location. It has to be two separate vessels as the largest vessels of this era were no where near 800 feet long.

Since I was at the State Historic Preservation Office, I looked for my own report of 1983 which I had given John Broadwater, the state's underwater archaeologist at the time. It was nowhere to be found.

In January of 1984, I had met with John Broadwater, discussed my research on *La Galga,* and my reasoning on her location. His statement to me was that the discovery and identification of *La Galga* would be a very significant achievement and would solve a mystery that has interested a great many people. He was aware that just the year before Underwater Archaeological Joint Ventures had failed to identify *La Galga's* location in the ocean even though they knew it would be in the vicinity of the Maryland-Virginia border and were directed there by the permit application of Alan Riebe. Even if the location proposed in my report was given the status "unverified," the report would still provide valuable anecdotal evidence until such verification took place. There would be no reason not to file the report. I was left with only two questions. Was it lost or was it "unfiled"?

I then consulted the maps for Accomack County which inventoried the county's archaeological sites. Documented in *An Assessment of Virginia's Underwater Cultural Resources* published in 1994 is an unlabeled site at the location worked by Riebe in 1981, Underwater Archaeological Joint Ventures in 1983, and Cook in 1987-89. This report said that *La Galga* had neither been located nor positively identified. This was the site that would become Benson's future *La Galga.* Based on Langley's statement that treasure hunters had relocated the wreck in 1997, I'd expected to find notations and a site number for *La Galga* at this ocean location. There was no notation for *La Galga,* or for any wreck at the Riebe/Cook/Benson area in the ocean. There was none for *La Galga* on land either. But there was one for the *Juno.* The site form for the *Juno* summarized the State's opinion on that alleged discovery: "[It] was thought to be the location of the Spanish shipwreck, *Juno.* There is no evidence that the site is *Juno*."

Virginia's records contain no site form for *La Galga* and no site indicated, yet there was one for the *Juno*. I could not find any rationale for this inconsistency other than that the State knew that *La Galga* was not at this location.

The Virginia Code says the Director of Historic Preservation shall "Identify, evaluate, preserve and protect sites and objects of antiquity which have historic, scientific, archaeological or educational value and are located on state-controlled land or on state archaeological sites or zones." The Virginia Code specifically authorizes the Department of Historic Resources to obtain its *own* permit "to preserve and protect or recover any underwater historic property." The State's responsibilities are mandated by the National Historic Preservation Act of 1966. The lack of a site form for *La Galga* was consistent with statements made in the Benson case that *La Galga's* location is unknown. The lack of a site form suggests that either Virginia does not know where *La Galga* rests, they know it's under federal land, or they don't want anybody else to know. But that would be inconsistent with the many other valuable archaeological sites clearly documented with site forms.

At the end of the federal litigation over *La Galga*, Sea Hunt stated, "However, as a result of the lack of evidence presented by both parties, the Court was forced to render an opinion that is based on a hypothetical premise; that is, that the *Juno* and *La Galga* are actually at rest in the VMRC permit site areas." Spain argued that it was not necessary to actually locate the ships to win title. Virginia responded by saying that Spain would only be entitled to the *Juno* and *La Galga*, "*if they were ever found.*" It seems everyone had forgotten that Benson himself had testified at the beginning of the trial that "Another guy named John Armahein (sic) claimed to have found it, also in the '80s, in a different location."

On June 15, 1999, Spain submitted Benson's report on *La Galga* as evidence in support of its brief on the issue of salvage. Spain quoted from that report: "The targets investigated by Sea Hunt cannot be considered to be shipwrecks or even specific shipwreck sites." But Spain did not mention what else Benson had had to say in that same report about our previous work. In that report, Benson had acknowledged our extensive magnetometer work in the area, which led us to believe that *La Galga* lay buried on the landward side of the beach. These facts were overlooked by Judge Clarke and the media.

On September 15, 1998, Judge Clarke said that he would authorize government divers to verify the wrecks if they had asked. There is no record in this case that they ever did. One would think that, given their mandate to verify historical assets, the federal government would've been anxious to dive the purported *Galga* site. Particularly when their position was that the ships belonged to Spain and not Virginia or Benson. Their failure to verify might have been deliberate. If verification proved that the sites were not Spanish ships, they then would be obligated to notify the court of their findings. The court would've then dismissed Spain and the feds from the case for lack of legal standing, and then there would've been no legal precedent set, no government victory, and Benson would have been free to continue if he'd chosen to.

Benson never positively identified his site as *La Galga*, he just hoped that it was. Court testimony in his case reveals a great deal of skepticism from everyone as to the site actually being *La Galga*. Few artifacts were recovered, and not a single cannonball. Neither Riebe nor Cook had recovered anything that would point to a positive *La Galga* verification. The magnetometer surveys conducted by Riebe, Cook, Benson, SEA, Ltd., and our group do not point to any other candidate for *La Galga* in the ocean. If we dismiss the Riebe/Cook/Benson site, as it appears that Virginia and the National Park Service have, then *La Galga's* location can only be characterized in one way. She is buried under the island.

The federal claim filed by Benson and the resulting rulings and opinions leave legal questions unanswered. In the Benson case, there were shipwrecks found, but there was no evidence that proves that they are Spanish ships and subject to sovereign immunity. If they are not Spanish ships, then they belong to Virginia and are subject to their permitting authority and deserve proper identification.

In Benson's case, the threshold issue raised by his attorney was the question of abandonment. In 1750, Sheriff Scarborough may have documented such abandonment in his report to Governor Samuel Ogle. He reiterated that Captain Huony had stated to him that "The Owner of the Land owned the Ship." He also chose to give the wreck to the English rather than burn it to avoid hostilities. It is reasonable to assume that Huony was the legal agent for King Ferdinand at the time. In 1750, the owner of the land was William Gore. Today, it is the U.S. Fish and Wildlife Service. In all of the research I had done in England and Spain in the diplomatic correspondence, there was never any demand made by Spain for the return of anything taken from the ship. If there was any doubt about Huony's intentions, we need only look to the fact that Spain's Navy no longer wanted *La Galga* evidenced by the fact it was intended to be sold to the Real Compañía de la Habana to serve out her last days as a merchant vessel two years before. The Real Compañía rejected that notion because of her condition. None of this evidence had been presented in the Benson case. It appears that Spain did abandon *La Galga*. Since no one had died aboard the ship, Spain shouldn't be able to make any legal objection to an archaeological excavation, especially since it could be government controlled and supervised. It also appears that the federal government did not follow the language in the Abandoned Shipwreck Act. Assuming that the wreck was in fact abandoned, the government disposed of government property without adequate public notice. Furthermore, they used a forum which did not have jurisdiction over the wreck. The federal court was a special court, sitting as a court of admiralty, whose jurisdiction is limited only to navigable waters. So any ruling by an admiralty court that *La Galga* was not abandoned is null and void since the court lacked the jurisdiction to reach that decision. In Benson's case, Janet Reno and her gang of lawyers accomplished nothing. If a treasure hunter went to the *"Juno"* site contrary to existing court order and was arrested, he could offer in his defense that it is not the *Juno* and submit believable documentation why it is not. If the court would not accept this defense and continue to maintain that it is the *Juno*, that same treasure hunter could then go offshore to where the real *Juno* lies and salvage it. And as long as he can say with a straight face that it couldn't be the *Juno*, because the court says that she *in fact* and *in law* lies just off of Assateague Island, then he might get away with it. Spain might be barred from protesting.

In 1986, for the Delaware IRRC cases, Judge Caleb Wright dismissed the premature salvage claims saying that "Allegations in the complaints about the existence and location of ancient wrecks based upon research and investigation alone do not satisfy the Court that such vessels actually rest at that location or exist at all." This precedent is in direct contradiction to the findings in the Sea Hunt cases.

It appears that the court's decision in the *La Galga* suit by Sea Hunt may be merely an advisory opinion, just like the SEA, Ltd. cases which dealt with imaginary shipwrecks.

If so, the court had no power to award the wreck to Spain. *La Galga* is not covered by federal admiralty jurisdiction anyway since her remains are buried outside of navigable waters. The Abandoned Shipwreck Act, which was the backbone of Spain's and our federal government's case against Benson, only covers vessels under "submerged lands" which the act defines as "lands beneath navigable waters." It seems that this hard-fought battle by the federal government has done nothing for historic preservation but to put obstacles in the way for future generations to know the truth. Perhaps some relief from this legal perversion can be found by going back to the federal court.

Unlike Virginia, the federal government still retains my 1983 report concerning *La Galga*'s location. But was it discussed among the government players during Benson's federal case? The report verified two things, even if they chose to disbelieve the location we indicated for the wreck. Documentation showed that the boundary lines in 1687 and 1840 were well south of Benson's wreck, and the beach had built way out in this area since the colonial period and probably 1840. This would have been valuable information when considering Sea Hunt's claim. In Langley's report for the National Park Service, she had recognized that the old boundary is south of the present one, but makes no mention of where that might be or what her source is. It is clear from her report that she had been running magnetometer and side-scan sonar surveys in the area of the Riebe/Cook/Benson site but she never stated that verification or contact with any wreck had been made in that area.

In 1984, when the federal government chose to ignore our findings about *La Galga's* location, they relied on statutes that only mandated protection of archaeological sites if they are threatened by man or nature. These same statutes, however, mandated that historic sites be inventoried if nothing else. We volunteered to make the magnetic verification, but were turned down. The government never gave us a chance to be proven right or wrong. Nearly a year after our findings were made known to them, they informed us that they had "no plans to investigate." Now, documented in Langley's report, is an account by a retired National Park ranger that elements of a shipwreck have been observed in the exact spot described in our report.

With the technology of today, the site could not only be easily verified with a magnetometer, but *analyzed* with ground penetrating radar, which is capable of outlining the hull or ballast pile. Unfortunately, these techniques were not used in the National Park's survey. This is totally non-intrusive and could be done for a lot less money than what the government spent on lawyers trying to take the shipwrecks away from Benson when they didn't even know what they were.

So, what is the future for *La Galga*? What will our government do about this historical and archaeological treasure? Will they take the position that she is fine how she lies and will forever remain undisturbed? Is that what they mean by historic preservation? Or will they go ahead and dust off their own regulations, which state, "This high priority responsibility entails locating historic and archaeological resources at a level of documentation such that the resources can be evaluated for potential nomination to the National Register of Historic Places…?"

The steamboat *Bertrand*, lost in 1865, was discovered buried under the Desoto National Wildlife Refuge in Nebraska and was excavated and preserved in a museum. It is now on the National Register, as are numerous other vessels of much more recent and less significant use and origin. The Nebraska refuge is visited by 250,000 visitors a year. Assateague, boasts over three million visitors annually between the wildlife refuge and national seashore.

The discoverers and salvors in the *Bertrand* excavation got sixty percent of the finds for their effort. In the case of *La Galga*, the government could keep it all as long as Spain does not interfere. There is no foreseeable reason why Spain would object to one of their lost navy ships being placed on our National Register.

Is *La Galga* important enough to excavate and preserve? If it was worth litigating over in the first place, then it must be. In the Benson case, Larry Murphy, Assistant Program Director for the SCRU (Submerged Cultural Resources Unit) of the National Park Service, was invited to testify on behalf of the government. He laid out a strong case for careful salvage and preservation, testifying that we have "very, very little information on eighteen century Spanish maritime culture." He went on to say how the wrecks of the Spanish fleets of 1715 and 1733 in Florida had yielded very little information because those wrecks were heavily salvaged by the Spaniards as well as by modern salvors. Some of these wrecks have been placed on the National Register.

In the book *Submerged: Adventures of America's Most Elite Underwater Archaeological Team*, the author and Submerged Cultural Resources Unit Director, Daniel Lenihan, describes the feelings that he, Larry Murphy, who had testified for the government in Benson's case, and others have about for-profit shipwreck salvors, and more importantly, any archaeologist who would assist them. This attitude, and that of many other elitists, is further illustrated in *Shipwreck Anthropology* mentioned in Lenihan's book. This work documented a high-level seminar attended by noted academics and theoreticians in 1981. At this meeting the participants signed "A Statement by Seminar Participants on the Present Looting of Shipwrecks in Florida and Texas." This included an indictment of any archaeologist who worked with a treasure hunter, *even though* their only purpose was to protect, preserve, and record artifacts. In *Submerged*, Lenihan reveals Larry Murphy's characterization of treasure hunters as "treasure pukes, whose very existence he finds offensive."

This threat of "indictment" was real. In 1982, Edward Dethlefsen, a professor of archaeology and anthropology at William and Mary College, worked on the 1717 pirate ship *Whydah* at Cape Cod with a commercial salvor named Barry Clifford. Besides being a noted academic, he was also the president of the two-thousand-member Society of Historical Archaeology. He was seeing archaeologists being blacklisted, and his own society was refusing to accept research papers by anyone associated with treasure hunters. Dethlefsen was punished for his illicit relationship with the *Whydah*. When commenting on his resignation, he said, "I have since found that some of my colleagues expect me, at the risk of Inquisition, to behave like a high priest whose vested purity allows only consort with temple virgins according to a strict ritual of academic cohabitation." In Florida, the same thing happened to Duncan Mathewson at Treasure Salvors. These two were criticized for doing what other SHA members secretly dreamed of doing themselves.

The SCRU deserves their self-proclaimed elite status as they dive many hazardous wrecks, archaeological sites, and even perform recoveries in fatal diving accidents. But this elitism seems to have blinded them to their real purpose: to preserve our cultural heritage whenever possible, not when it suits them.

If the government is asked if they intend to excavate *La Galga*, they might claim that since the wreck is Spain's, they are precluded from disturbing it. They may even go so far as to say it is not part of our heritage. But that would be inconsistent with the reciprocities with other nations described in Lenihan's book. The CSS *Alabama*, sunk off France by the USS *Kearsarge* in our Civil War, is the subject of salvage by a French dive club which the SCRU went to observe.

And then there is HMS *Fowey*, a British warship that had been lost off Elliot Key, Florida in 1748. The *Fowey's* claim to fame was that she acted as a guard ship in King George's War and had just captured a Spanish merchant called the *Judas* carrying treasure before she'd slammed into a reef that would later become known as *Fowey Rocks*. A sport diver turned treasure hunter thought he had a treasure ship when he'd found it and filed a claim in federal court in 1979. There was an injunction barring anyone from diving or removing anything from the wreck pending resolution of the claim. For several years the National Park Service personnel routinely went in and recovered artifacts contrary to court order. Today the public is prohibited from the site. Not even a glass-bottom boat is allowed.

In 1990, the U.S. government, contrary to historical fact, described the wreck as a merchant vessel and property of the United States, in spite of the fact that the United Kingdom claims otherwise. It should be noted that "HMS" (His Majesty's Ship) automatically designates it as a British sovereign vessel. HMS *Fowey* is listed on the National Register as being "nationally significant." At Yorktown, Virginia, HMS *Charon*, a British Navy warship sunk during the American Revolution, lies in fifteen feet of water in the York River off Gloucester Point. In direct contradiction to the status given the *Fowey*, the government acknowledges that this vessel is entitled to sovereign immunity. HMS *Charon* only received "regional significance" in the National Register.

What will happen to *La Galga*, a warship of Spain, is anybody's guess.

Virginia had spent millions excavating an unidentified Revolutionary War period vessel that had been mostly stripped before she was deliberately sunk at Yorktown, Virginia. Without even knowing the name of the vessel, a complete and costly archaeological investigation was undertaken using a cofferdam to surround the ship, and then the water was clarified to facilitate diving and proper archaeological techniques. This unidentified vessel was placed on the National Register and ranked as nationally significant, ahead of the warship HMS *Charon*.

La Galga could be excavated the same way, but more likely the cofferdam could be pumped dry and the entire remains lifted and preserved. The returns would most likely be much greater. There is most likely a great deal of the lower hull and its contents preserved in a time-capsule state (see page 3). In 1750, after the locals had dismantled the upper deck, they would have exposed cannon and other artifacts to the actions of the sea. Once the upper deck was taken off and the sides dismantled, as described by Captain Huony in his letter to the Marqués de Ensenada in 1750, the sea would have been continuously rolling over the wreck. There were several feet of water over the gun deck. The sea would had to have been very calm to permit any significant salvage at this point. The wreck had remained in this state for nearly a month since the mahogany had not been released until the storm of November 2. When bad weather occurred, driving the looters off, some items could have been lost, either into the hold or around the perimeter of the ship to sink into the sand. Even tools used by the looters might be found.

As I place myself aboard *La Galga*, before Huony left, I see the possibility that he may have ordered the ship's bell, the soul of the ship, thrown over the side or into the flooded hold to prevent that valuable trophy from being taken by the English. This idea is reinforced since burning the ship had been considered for the same reason.

In any event, the probability of large artifact finds and unique archaeological data is high.

La Galga is significant as a wreck to be recovered and preserved for several reasons. Its age, origin, function, and the possibility of many artifacts being recovered stand out. If it is buried, as legend and as this narrative suggests, the wreck played a role in the geomorphology of the island itself. And then there is the nagging question of the legend about the wild horses of the island being descended from horses liberated from a wrecked Spanish galleon. This makes *La Galga* the primary suspect for creating this world famous legend. By default, *La Galga* becomes a truly historic and significant shipwreck not to be ignored. This is where Susan Langley and I agree. *La Galga* deserves recognition on our National Register. But under the nominating guidelines, the ship's location must first be verified.

There is some hope that the verification anticipated, but not yet done, by the National Park Service survey will soon take place. Recent developments have directed government agencies to become more proactive in historic preservation.

On March 3, 2003, President Bush signed Executive Order 13287 called, "Preserve America." This order commands in part:

Each agency with real property management responsibilities shall, by September 30, 2005, and every third year thereafter, prepare a report on its progress in identifying, protecting, and using historic properties in its ownership and make the report available to the Council and the Secretary. The Council shall incorporate this data into a report on the state of the Federal Government's historic properties and their contribution to local economic development and submit this report to the President by February 15, 2006, and every third year thereafter.

The wild ponies are already a factor in the economies of Accomack, Virginia and Worcester, Maryland. This is fueled in part by the shipwreck legend that is so appealing to tourists.

There is one thing for certain. The horses did not come from the *San Lorenzo* since there is no *San Lorenzo*.

Thanks to Donald Stewart, the maritime history of Maryland will never be the same. With his hoax of the *San Lorenzo*, he had hoped to go down in history as the one who solved the mystery of the Assateague ponies. And with the three other fictitious ships, he created needless litigation and confusion.

Unfortunately, today the *San Lorenzo* is now getting more attention in print than *La Galga*. Several books are giving full credence to the *San Lorenzo* story. The reason may be that the original National Park Service *Assateague Island* handbook, published in 1980, is still floating around in libraries. This is the same publication Stewart used to give himself credibility the night I met him in 1980. In addition, any author who had relied on this erroneous information and had been published also has a book floating around perpetuating the fraud. Over the last twenty years, this error has compounded itself, and continues spreading like a computer virus. The story has always been accepted at face value. On the legal front, the SEA, Ltd. cases are being cited in many other admiralty cases as legal precedent. And since the Fourth Circuit Court of Appeals did not publish its opinion when they denied my motion to vacate the judgment, related only to my motion, their ruling, "AFFIRMED," has been interpreted by many as a validation of the entire proceedings in the lower court when it wasn't. No party to the case ever appealed.

Two books have recently surfaced spreading the *San Lorenzo* hoax. One is Kirk Mariner's *Once Upon an Island: The History of Chincoteague*.

Mr. Mariner is a respected Eastern Shore historian. He, unfortunately, relied on the government publication. The latest to come to my attention is the work of Rich Pomerantz called *Wild Horses of the Dunes*. This book has many splendid pictures of the horses accompanied by some narrative, which unfortunately includes the *San Lorenzo* story.

This continued corruption of historical fact probably would not have happened if the National Park Service had put forth a public statement discrediting the *San Lorenzo* when they realized their mistake. I do give them credit, however, as they had openly admitted to me in 1984 that they knew that the *San Lorenzo* story was bogus and assisted me in my case against Stewart. If only the State of Maryland had been so cooperative. They did everything they could to bury the truth.

I fought for two years with the attorney general of Maryland and a federal judge to get the truth out about the *San Lorenzo* being a fictitious ship made up by Donald Stewart. When I submitted the damning evidence on June 10, 1985 related to the *San Lorenzo*, for some reason it was misfiled into the *Santa Rosalea* case. Today, although the docket and correspondence proves that it was submitted, it is nowhere to be found in the federal court record.

Now, having read the latest on the government survey, it appears that Maryland is still having trouble after twenty years of evaluating historical documents. It is truly ironic that Susan Langley, the underwater archaeologist for the State of Maryland, has now fallen victim to Stewart's fraud, a fraud that would've been exposed years ago, but for another Maryland employee—Judith Armold with the Maryland attorney general's office. As they say, "What goes around, comes around."

This expensive government report is now tainted with many fictional shipwrecks. Let's hope that divers are not sent down—they won't find them.

Donald Stewart did find his place in history aboard the USS *Constellation*, however. Because two separate ships had become blurred together over the passage of time, Stewart was able to pull off a number of bold forgeries. Had the truth been truly known to the citizens of Baltimore when she'd first arrived, the old ship may have

USS *Constellation* today in Baltimore Harbor. This ship was built in Norfolk, Virginia, not Baltimore, Maryland. In close parallel with *La Galga*, Maryland laid claim to a ship rightfully due Virginia. *Photo by the Author.*

been scrapped. Stewart's fraud may have bought the ship time that ultimately led to her last restoration, completed in 1999, as a sloop-of-war built in Norfolk, Virginia, in 1854.

A visitor boarding her today will hear about a case of mistaken identity, but not one word about Donald Stewart in the controversy. But like it or not, he has become as much a part of her history as any of her captains. No complete history of the 1854 *Constellation* can be written without recognizing his dubious role in her preservation and the havoc he created in political and historical circles. The *Constellation* is a monument to Stewart's fraud.

For the millions of people visiting Ocean City and the islands of Assateague and Chincoteague every year who may ask, "Will we ever get to see the wreck of *La Galga*?" the answer is simple. There are only two obstacles. One is the government. Hopefully, they will take a proactive position on its excavation or at least refrain from blocking the concept. The other is money.

Money will most likely not flow from the federal government. Too many, from all aspects of our society, are looking to our government for handouts. We will, however, see less deserving pet projects of the influential funded. Our government's idea of historic shipwreck preservation is to spend a fortune on lawyers playing games with people like Benson at public expense. This might serve individual egos, but it does nothing for historic preservation. There is one hope, however. With the popularity of the horses, raising private money for excavation, preservation, and display might be feasible.

I had no idea what I was getting myself into when I decided to hunt for *La Galga* back in 1978. It seemed that it would be such a simple matter to follow the precise instructions left by her captain. It ended up being a life-changing experience, and certainly no simple matter. I am where I am today because of *La Galga*. As I wrote about the description of the storm and the last twenty-four hours of *La Galga* at sea, I became aware of how precarious life is and the role of fate. On September 4, 1750, *La Galga* hit the offshore reef and miraculously survived twenty-five blows before getting herself clear. Each time that old hull crashed down, the probability that my daughter would be born became more and more unlikely, since the loss of the ship here would have changed the entire scenario. It could have sunk with no one knowing where she was lost. If I had not looked for *La Galga*, I would not have moved to Ocean City and married my wife, Delphine. My daughter's very existence, my own position in life, and the lives of all aboard her were spared on September 4, 1750, the feast day of St. Rosalia.

Epilogue

Cádiz, Spain
June 22, 2004

I t was 3:00 p.m., and Delphine, our daughter, Madeline, and I were sitting at the pool at the Playa Victoria hotel in Cádiz. Our week in Spain was drawing to a close and I was contemplating *La Galga's* last trip from this city over two and a half centuries before when she'd escorted the mercury fleet of Juan de Eques to Veracruz, Mexico. I looked toward the stairway and there was Victoria Stapells Johnson who had just come from the Archivo Histórico Provincial. She had just discovered the wills of Daniel Huony, *La Galga's* captain, and of Juan Manuel Bonilla, captain of the *Nuestra Señora de Guadalupe*, which had also sailed with the 1750 fleet and had been left disabled at Ocracoke Inlet. From the smile on her face, I could tell that she had found some interesting information.

Victoria opened her computer and began reading from her notes. She described the military funeral for Captain Daniel Huony of *La Galga*. She said that there was more information to get the next day and that she still had to go to the Catedral de Cádiz, which had its own archives that would provide the burial information on both Huony and Bonilla.

The four of us piled into a cab and toured the old section of Cádiz— the port that had received the great treasure fleets from the New World. It was fascinating to travel the narrow streets, no more than alleys, lined with many seventeenth and eighteenth century buildings. We returned to the archive for pictures. The Archivo Histórico Provincial is located on the narrow Calle de Cristóbal Colón several blocks back from the old shipyards. The archive is housed in a late seventeenth century building whose entranceway is sealed with a formidable wooden door, built of wooden planks and iron bolts.

We went from there to the Cathedral and photographed the adjoining church of San Diego which housed the archives of the Cathedral. It was here that the funeral of Juan Manual Bonilla, captain of the *Nuestra Señora de Guadalupe,* was held in 1759. We walked past the post office and relaxed in the Plaza de las Flores. Victoria later ascertained that the post office had been built over the former Convento de los Descalzos, a Franciscan convent. It was in this plaza where Bonilla had been buried. In the eighteenth century, it had been the vegetable garden for the convent.

We next tried to locate the Calle de Comedias, a small street where Bonilla had owned a part interest of a building occupied by some merchants. We found out later that we had unknowingly walked down it without realizing it because the name had changed to the Calle de Feduchy.

We were ever mindful that we might be passing the home of Daniel Huony or that of the Marqués de La Victoria.

The Castillo de Santa Catalina, which had guarded the seaward end of Cádiz for centuries, was our next stop. The fort dates from the end of the sixteenth century and provides one of the most beautiful scenes in Cádiz as you look across the water to the Castillo de San Sebastian—another fort that is built out on a small island and that is now connected to Cádiz by a road built over a levee.

From there, we walked to the Calle de Santa Rosalia where Victoria took a picture of us beneath the street sign. It seemed fitting as St. Rosalia had played a large role in this story. *La Galga* had been spared a horrible death on the offshore reef on September 4, her feast day, and the inadvertent spelling error of her name by Robert Marx had helped expose the fraud that had been perpetrated by Donald Stewart related to a ship named after her. This picture would have been quite valuable in my case against him twenty years before.

We had dinner together that evening and discussed the events of the day and the progress of the book. We were flying home in the morning.

Delphine, Madeline, and I had landed in Madrid the week before on Saturday, June 12. Our goal was to visit the archives and places of interest that had related to this story and to finally meet Victoria and her family.

As soon as we'd arrived in Madrid, we took a train to Valladolid to see the Archivo General de Simancas. It was in this archive that Victoria had found many valuable documents on *La Galga*, including Captain Huony's report, which she had located two years before. When we

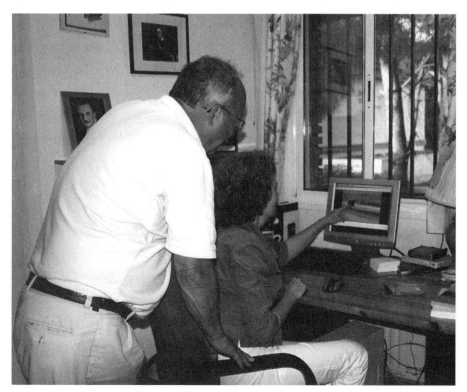

Victoria sees the wild horses on Assateague for the first time. *Photo by Madeline Amrhein*

took the cab out to Simancas, we were disappointed to find that the castle that housed the archive was closed for repairs. The castle had been constructed in the latter half of the fifteenth century as a fortress, and later purchased by Ferdinand and Isabella and converted to a royal archive by their grandson, Charles. Many of the records had been moved to the Casa de Contratación in Seville in 1785.

It still was an impressive site, even with the crane towering overhead and the scaffolding stacked against the exterior stone walls. We took the train back to Madrid and checked into the Hotel del Prado in the heart of Madrid and the museum district.

While we were there, we visited the Prado, the Museum of Archaeology, and we saw the Biblioteca National. The next stop was the Museo Naval, which contained many impressive ship models and armaments of Spain's navy covering the last five centuries. The museum also had a library which Victoria and Norma Cantu had utilized on my behalf.

The most spectacular place we visited, however, was the Royal Palace. The original palace was the Alcázar, which had completely burned in 1734. This had been a permanent residence of the Spanish kings, which had caused the little town of Madrid to evolve into the nation's capital. King Philip V had commenced construction of the new palace in 1738. His son, King Ferdinand VI, had completed the architectural work, except the staircase, which was finished in 1765 under the next king, Charles III.

In 1750, the palace warehouses received a large shipment of mahogany. Two hundred and twenty-six tons had been transported overland by ox cart from Cádiz to Madrid during August, and due to the drought and heat, 150 of the oxen had died. Still, more mahogany was needed from the Indies.

The new palace would have relatively little wood; only the doors, windows, and other trim were made of wood. *La Galga* had been carrying the mahogany planks for the construction of these doors and windows. The palace contains 800 windows and 110 doors.

The palace architect was Giovanni Battista Sacchetti from Turin, Italy. He had not only designed the palace, but supervised the craftsmen. There were nearly two thousand workers employed in building scaffolds, sculpting, plumbing, laying tile and marble, and building the doors and windows. In a separate carpenter shop, Mateo de Medina had built mock-ups of the windows and doors for Sacchetti's approval. Other than the stone walls and carvings, the most prominent feature to be noticed by the admiring visitor was the elaborately carved woodwork of the doors and windows. Even though the palace was years from completion, their installation was necessary to keep the weather out because other finish work was underway inside. The doors present today are more simplistic in design than the ones originally installed and designed by the architect Sacchetti under the rule of Ferdinand VI. When Charles III succeeded him in 1759, he removed the ornate carved doors and donated them to area churches. It might be surmised that if *La Galga's* mahogany had made it to Spain, it could have later ended up in a Spanish church.

We toured the inside and saw awesome chambers with intricate marble floors, overshadowed by domed ceilings painted with frescoes that would have been appreciated by Michelangelo. From the walls hung priceless tapestries. There were many, many works of art. Every room was different. The main staircase into the Palace was a sight to see in and of itself. The dining room, which was the former ballroom, contained a table so long that you could not recognize someone seated at the other end. When we entered the throne room, I immediately sensed the power felt by the Spanish kings as they ruled from a gilded chair flanked with bronze lions dating back to 1651. There was red velvet throughout. The Palace is truly a monument to Spain's former wealth and decadence, and a tribute to the European craftsmen who had built it.

On Thursday, we flew to Seville and checked into Las Casa de Los Mercaderes located in the old section of Seville and only a few blocks from the archives and cathedral. Victoria had suggested this hotel because it had been a former merchant house in the eighteenth century.

After we checked in, we strolled the avenue to the Archivo General de Indias located in the oldest section of the city. It was easy to find

Victoria shares her book of naval drawings done by the Marqués de la Victoria with the author. *Photo by Madeline Amrhein.*

Victoria Stapells Johnson at the National Archives in Havana, Cuba. Her research on *La Galga* also included the Archivo Historico de la Cuidad de la Habana. *Photo by Richard Johnson.*

because it was directly opposite the massive Catedral de Sevilla, built in the late fifteenth century. The cathedral is the largest in Spain and the third largest in the world, and it is here that the tomb of Christopher Columbus is located. It was a stunning sight. There were palm trees lining the street overshadowed by the huge flying buttresses that supported the cathedral walls. Horse-drawn carriages waited to carry tourists through the adjoining streets.

Victoria was in the archives in a temporary building across the street from the main archive, which was being repaired and closed to visitors. For our first meeting after twenty-four years, she suggested a rendezvous on the Plaza de Triunfo beneath the monument to the Immaculate Conception.

Since we had never met, she described what she was wearing. We were certainly easy to spot as three American tourists beneath the statue. She spotted us first, and after introductions and pictures in front of the archives, we walked to the restaurant, Sabina, to meet her husband, Richard, and daughter, Alexandra. Her son, Adrian, was away and unfortunately, could not join us.

A casual lunch was certainly an easy way to get acquainted, and everyone had the chance to get to know one another outside of the business of the 1750 fleet.

The Archivo General de Indias had formerly been the Casa de Contratación, or House of Trade. In 1785, King Charles III had decided to transform it into an archive for documents and testimonies from the New World, for documents which up until then had been scattered throughout various territories.

Victoria suggested that we join them on Saturday at their home for dinner. She wanted to show me her copy of the Marqués de La Victoria's book on Spanish ships that had proven to be a valuable guide to us both. I brought CDs with pictures of various aspects of our story.

At dinner, she surprised us with fried *boquerones* (anchovies). I had told her earlier that I had grown very fond of them. I had sampled them at a number of tapas bars Delphine and I had visited since we had been in Spain.

First, I took her on a picture tour of our project, which included a video clip from the movie *Misty of Chincoteague*. For the first time, she saw Assateague Island and the legendary wild horses galloping along the surf.

After dinner, she showed me the book of ship drawings by the Marqués de la Victoria. It was very large and somewhat difficult to handle. There were many pictures of interest, including a complete fifty-two gun warship that closely resembled *La Galga*, and many pages depicted shipboard items in detail, from anchors, cannon, and carriages to surgical instruments, shipboard furniture, and uniforms.

We said good-bye and thanked them for a wonderful evening, but we had planned our next rendezvous in Cádiz on Tuesday.

Our trip to Seville was over except for attending mass at the cathedral, which was a memorable experience. I have to admit that I was distracted by the thought that Captains Huony and Bonilla, no doubt, had attended mass here centuries ago.

After mass, we took the train to Cádiz where we checked into the Playa Victoria Hotel, which was right on the oceanfront. I was struck by the similarity of this resort area of Cádiz and to Ocean City, Maryland where my adventure had begun twenty-four years before.

Here, we relaxed on the beach, something Madeline had looked forward to, since she had been burned out long ago with Dad's history lessons. After our visit with Victoria, we returned home knowing that we would return to Spain again. It was a memorable trip.

July 26, 2006
Chincoteague, Virginia

As the rising sun silhouetted Assateague Lighthouse towering above the blue-green pine forest on Assateague, school buses were already ferrying some of the expected 50,000 spectators from satellite parking to Memorial Park to witness the 81st Annual Pony Swim. Some of the spectators came from far away as California.

I arrived shortly after 7:00 a.m. in the hopes of not only capturing pictures of the horses but also to photograph the tourists themselves and witness once again this exciting and historic event. The crowds were already heavy even though the slack tide that would signal the beginning of the swim would not happen for another three hours.

In spite of the predictions, it looked like it was going to be a sunny day as the clouds began to disperse. I was reminded of our adventure twenty-three years before by a random bite of a mosquito escaping the wet grass. Since the park was rapidly filling, I ventured south to Pony Swim Lane in the hopes of getting a close up view of the ponies as they climbed the grassy bank out of the channel.

When I arrived, I found the marsh already crowded with spectators. Others were trudging barefoot through the mud and grass to get to the water's edge in the hopes of obtaining a better view. The regional television station had their satellite truck set up and the print media photographers were plainly visible as they had already gained entrance into the corral area that would hold the horses. The conditions were not pleasant but everyone was happy and smiling, particularly the children. It was going to be a long wait so I just stood in the grass next to the pier and focused on memories of our previous exploits. Occasionally the public address system that covered the half mile of shoreline would give updates and anecdotes on the pony swim. When the announcer mentioned the legend that the horses came from a lost Spanish galleon, I smiled, but no one noticed. Finally, after almost four hours of waiting, the Coast Guard discharged a red smoke flare to signal the start of the swim and the crowd let out a cheer. Children climbed onto their parents' shoulders as they pointed to the swimming horses. The NBC news helicopter that had been circling began to hover overhead.

Two years before, I had witnessed the event but then I was lucky enough to be invited aboard one of the senior fireman's boats owned by Clarence Bowden—thanks to Guy Banks, my brother-in-law, who'd arranged it. Clarence Bowden was one of the few who were permitted entry into the cordoned area where the horses would cross. It was truly a front-row seat that only a few could enjoy. The presence and power of the horses was something I will always remember.

Many of the men and women of the fire department are waterman as were their ancestors, deriving their living from oysters, crabs, and fishing. In contradiction to their chosen lifestyle, they mount up once a year and become "saltwater cowboys."

After the swim, the ponies are paraded through town, corralled, and some are auctioned off the next day. The remaining horses are swum back to Assateague on Friday. This is truly an historic event, dating back to at least 1800. The carnival ends on Saturday, and like the early one described in 1835, local "fish and waterfowl, fried and barbecued" are almost as big of an attraction as the horses. The waterfowl has been replaced by chicken.

Although no documents have yet surfaced to prove that *La Galga* had horses on board when she wrecked, the body of circumstantial evidence suggests that it is entirely possible. The horseshoe found on the 1622 *Santa Margarita*, a ship that had made the same journey home as *La Galga* and had carried soldiers as did *La Galga*, goes a long way to bridge the gap between fact and the pervasive legend that has been told for centuries at Chincoteague Island. When one reads the extensive lading of animals aboard *La Galga* on her last trip from Spain in 1748, one can see that the ship was capable of carrying horses.

The legend says that a Spanish ship wrecked on Assateague from whence the horses came. Whether horses were aboard or not, without a doubt, the legendary ship attributed to that legend, and remembered for centuries, is *La Galga*.

With the detailed documents that have been located by Victoria in the archives of Spain, Bill Bane has begun construction of a model of *La Galga*. If it is anything like any of his other models, it will truly be a thing of beauty. For Bill, his son Chip, and me, it also is a chance to keep the adventure that started a quarter century ago alive. I hate to see it end.

It is this author's hope that *La Galga* will someday soon get her long-awaited and well-deserved recognition.

Captain Don Daniel Huony had no idea when he sailed out

of Havana Harbor on August 18, 1750 that a chain reaction of events was about to begin, brought on by the chance encounter with a hurricane that would not only sweep him and his ship far from his intended course but centuries into the future, where there seems no end to the final disposition of his fatal command.

January 24, 2006

It looks like another chapter in the story of *La Galga* is about to begin. From Newtown, Pennsylvania, news has been released that a company called Sovereign Exploration Associates International, Inc. has obtained permission from Spain to recover the remains of the wrecks found in the Benson case that were mislabeled as *La Galga* and *Juno*. The chairman of this new company is none other than Peter Knollenberg, who had bought the rights to the unidentified wrecks in 2001 from Benson. The press release said that they were applying for renewal of the recovery permits from the Commonwealth of Virginia. Knollenberg was quoted as saying,

> Our shareholders, the Kingdom of Spain, and the Commonwealth of Virginia, will all benefit from a successful recovery of the JUNO and GALGA. We view our agreement with the Spanish Government as an important vote of confidence in our ability as a private sector company to provide a public service in helping to discover and present historical information, while contributing to educational programs.

The issuance of permits by Virginia would create a unique, if not a troublesome, set of circumstances. The official records of Virginia state that the *Juno* site is not the *Juno*. Virginia does not recognize as *La Galga* the site discovered by Alan Riebe and Daniel Koski-Karell in 1981, then rediscovered by Richard Cook and Koski-Karell in 1987, and discovered again by Ben Benson in 1997. If Virginia believes there are Spanish ships present, it would behoove them to allow recovery since, according to the press release, Spain had signed an agreement for the recovery of the vessels and Knollenberg's company would share artifacts with Virginia. On the other hand, if Virginia believes that no Spanish ships have been discovered, would they then permit treasure hunters armed with a permission slip from Spain to recover and possibly distribute artifacts to Spain when they are not Spanish ships?

These questions may now be moot. As of this writing the web site for Sovereign Exploration Associates International no longer specifically mentions their intent to pursue shipwrecks called *Juno* and *La Galga*.

But the story of the hidden galleon has not ended. More is yet to come.

May 21, 2007
Madrid, Spain

It's been ten months since those last prophetic words were written. Now, the Kingdom of Spain is in an uproar. All of the newspaper and television outlets are running stories about 17 tons of gold and silver coins that had been flown from Gibraltar, a British outpost on the southern coast of Spain, to Tampa, Florida, where the treasure hunting company, Odyssey Marine Exploration, filed claim to the treasure in the federal district court in Tampa on April 9. The papers were saying that the value of the treasure was estimated at $500 million dollars. Shares of Odyssey stock surged ahead on the news. Odyssey was being very secretive about the discovery only describing it by its code name, *"Black Swan."* Odyssey had been working with Spanish authorities for over a year for rights to recover millions in treasure from HMS *Sussex* believed to have been lost off Spain's southern coast at the end of the seventeenth century. Greg Stemm, cofounder of Odyssey, said *Black Swan* was definitely not the *Sussex*, and stated that when the ship's identity was confirmed he would notify any possible claimants to the treasure. Speculation is running rampant on the ship's identity but the focus is on the *Merchant Royal* which sunk in 1641 in the English Channel.

Included in an Associated Press wire originating from Madrid about the Odyssey controversy was the reminder that Spain had won the rights to *La Galga* and the *Juno* in 2000. Both she and the *Juno* were awarded to Spain without being within the jurisdiction of the court making the award. No artifacts that can be definitely attributed to either wreck were recovered. *La Galga's* actual location is not even in navigable waters and the *Juno* most likely is in deep water many miles from the site that Virginia now acknowledges is not the *Juno*.

On May 31, Spain filed a claim to the treasure in the Tampa court represented by James Goold the same attorney who represented Spain in its dubious victory over *La Galga* in 2000. Spain made it clear in this latest filing that they had not consented to any salvage of the vessel or treasure in spite of the fact that even Odyssey did not yet know the identity of the *Black Swan*.

Sensing either weakness on the part of Odyssey or perhaps unnecessary secrecy, Spain filed a motion on June 19 to compel Odyssey to reveal specific location and identity information on *Black Swan* to the court. By doing this, they hoped to create a stronger foundation for their previous claim to the treasure. In the memorandum in support of its motion, Spain cited as precedent the Sea Hunt case where they "won" *La Galga*.

Bolstered and empowered by this decision, Spain is now boldly proclaiming, "If it's ours, we're taking it." A week later, reports were coming out of Spain that they were preparing to board Odyssey's exploration vessels if they left Gibraltar. But Odyssey stated that they were most happy to cooperate and invited Spain's inspectors on board. In spite of these assurances of cooperation, the Spanish coast guard boarded the *Ocean Alert* after she left Gibraltar on July 12 and ordered her into the port of Algeciras where the ship's crew were detained and a rigorous inspection made of Odyssey's research vessel. Six days later, *Ocean Alert* was cleared and was free to leave, but only after the hard drives had been removed from laptop computers.

The deadline for Odyssey to answer Spain's claim and motion

to disclose more information was July 23. Odyssey was granted an extension until August 6 as they claimed that Spain had forced an unexpected work load on their corporate attorneys by the seizure of the corporate vessel off Gibraltar.

August 6, 2007

Odyssey Marine not only filed their response to Spain but named Spain as a Defendant in the action seeking compensation for its unnecessary interference in Odyssey's archaeological investigations on three separate sites and the illegal seizure of one of its vessels. Within these papers, Odyssey also exposes what may be a troubling conflict of interest. Spain's lead attorney, James Goold, is the chairman and legal counsel to RPM Nautical Foundation of Key West, FL. This organization has worked closely with Spain to search for shipwrecks off the Spanish coast. Odyssey has reason to be concerned.

James Goold was the same attorney who represented Spain in the cases of *La Galga* and the *Juno*. He is the same attorney that sat in the court room and heard attorneys for Sea Hunt and Virginia tell the presiding judge that they did not know where *La Galga* and *Juno* really were. He heard the Attorney General of Virginia say that the four Spanish coins found could have come from any shipwreck. Goold then told the judge that their latest conduct was "outrageous bad faith." He was complaining that Sea Hunt should not be able to put forth such an idea after filing the claim that stated otherwise. Goold demanded the right to ask for sanctions. He was not going to let them recant. He did remind the court that apparently the only evidence of discovery of Spanish ships was Ben Benson's say-so. Like a shark circling in blood-stained waters, he became blinded and forgot that, as an attorney, he was there to seek the truth. He left court that day and decided that he would not educate himself on the use of Spanish money in American commerce long after the wreck of the *Juno*.

On March 16, 2001, the federal court in Norfolk reconvened. Goold was there to get the Spanish coins and the precise locations to the wrecks that he claimed must be *La Galga* and *Juno* since those were the only Spanish ships known to be in the area. And the four coins proved it. Virginia brought along an expert witness, Dr. Ethel Eaton, from the Virginia Department of Historic Resources, who was introduced to the court as an expert who would testify that Spain's evaluation of the artifacts as Spanish may have been premature. She was never called. James Goold chose to rely this time on Sea Hunt's research.

In the Odyssey cases, the reverse is true. Odyssey never said *Black Swan* was a Spanish ship, but Spain and its attorney are all over the wreck. There must be Spanish coins involved. As the *Black Swan* case moves to trial we, most assuredly, will hear James Goold gloat over his previous success of winning *La Galga*. But if the 2000 awards were made without valid jurisdiction, this writer suggests that these judgments are void and subject to collateral attack. If such an attack is made could Spain then sustain itself? It seems Spain has prepositioned itself for such an assault. They have loaned the artifacts they acquired in the Sea Hunt court cases to the National Park Service to be displayed at the Assateague Island National Seashore Visitor Center. Of special interest are Spanish coins. It is most likely that the visiting public will be seduced by these coins as evidence of a Spanish shipwreck even though every archaeologist employed by the National Park Service knows that these coins could come from any shipwreck from this time period. It is not known if Spain is aware of the universal usage of its former currency as late as 1857. Perhaps, given the aggressive stance taken by U.S. attorneys in the Sea Hunt cases, the National Park Service may not be able to decline the loan of artifacts. But this loan of artifacts purported to be from *La Galga* and the *Juno* is inconsistent with records at Virginia's Historic Preservation Office in Richmond. For the past 25 years they have known about this so-called *La Galga* site but don't recognize it as the actual location. The location for *La Galga* is not listed in their inventory which is required by the National Historic Preservation Act, if it is known.

If another review over the fate of *La Galga* is permitted in federal court, Spain may argue that, since seven years have elapsed, the judgment should not be disturbed. But Spain has done nothing on the two sites in the past seven years. In 2004, Spain hired Jim Goold's RPM Nautical Associates to explore for wrecks off its coast. One of RPM's research vessels is coincidentally named the *Juno*. It leaves one to wonder if Spain is so connected with a hi-tech archaeological outfit as RPM, why don't they take RPM's *Juno* to go to Assateague and excavate the *Juno*? Spain has the court order from the Fourth Circuit Court of Appeals that has already authorized such an excavation.

What's fundamental to the outcome is the truth. In an amazing reversal, Captain Don Daniel Huony may be called to testify in absentia after 257 years of losing his ship. His statement recorded in the Archives of Maryland that the "Owner of the land owned the ship" will finally be entered into evidence. The record of his court martial may be reopened to look for more evidence of abandonedment. He will repeat his testimony that they thought it better to let the English have the wreck rather than to set her on fire. Sheriff John Scarborough will reinforce Captain Huony's testimony about the wreck being buried in sand as he said, "[the mahogany planks] can be got before the ship bursts with the sea and sinks into the land." Will Spain accept the testimony of a former captain, especially one who rose to second in command of Spain's navy? Spain will cry that *La Galga* is part of their heritage. Evidence will be presented that as of 1748 the King of Spain didn't want *La Galga* anymore because of her age and condition, and it was decided to sell her. It was only because the King needed transportation for his tobacco crop and mahogany for his palace in Madrid that the decision was made to overhaul the ship in Havana. Otherwise, she most likely would have been stripped and disposed of in Havana after she returned from her last haul of treasure from Veracruz in 1749.

Any hope of revisiting the Sea Hunt cases lies with the original parties in the case. Ben Benson, the man who started it all, is no longer in a position to admit error or lack of evidence. He sold Sea Hunt, Inc. to some other investors, which then devolved to Sovereign Explorations Associates International, whatever rights he had to *La Galga* and *Juno*. He can't recant now without giving back the money he received. Sovereign Explorations has standing to ask that the judgments be set aside since the sites are in fact not Spanish and the artifacts recovered would be theirs according to the share agreement with the Commonwealth of Virginia. But would they spend money trying to recover a handful of artifacts that have no appreciable value?

The Attorney General of Virginia has strong footing to move the court in these cases. Since the shipwrecks are not Spanish and not property of a sovereign nation, the wrecks before the court in the Sea Hunt cases are clearly property of the Commonwealth of Virginia according to the Abandoned Shipwreck Act of 1987. The coins and anchor graciously "loaned" by Spain to the National Park Service actually belong to Virginia and it is now incumbent on the State to see that the true source of these artifacts are properly identified since they are going to be displayed to the public. Under the 1987 Act, Virginia has no claim to *La Galga* or the *Juno* wherever they lie, but according to their own statutes the State must "Ensure that archaeological sites and objects located on state-controlled land or on state archaeological sites or zones are identified, evaluated and properly explored so that adequate records may be made." This mandate comes from the National Historic Preservation Act of 1966 which requires the State Historical Preservation Officer to evaluate and inventory historical sites at such a level of precision that each could be considered for eligibility to the National Register of Historic Places. Historical sites include shipwrecks.

Our last hope to rescue *La Galga* could be the U. S. Justice Department who was equally as premature to enter the litigation as Benson. They had no concern to the actual ships' identities. They were there only to protect the interest of Spain over the interests of its own citizens, and to punish yet another treasure hunter. History, archaeology, and the truth were mere inconveniences, and something they easily ignored. But the federal government has the strongest standing to bring an action to set aside the judgment. They are the actual owners of *La Galga* since the wreck is buried beneath their land. It would be a wonderful show of cooperation if the Justice Department and the Attorney General of Virginia joined in the proposed action, The U.S. Government representing *La Galga*, and Virginia representing the two unidentified wrecks that clearly belong to them. The only argument Spain could make would be that there were Spanish coins found at one of the sites. This is the same argument made by a con man named Donald Stewart in the 1980's as he duped investors.

La Galga is part of our heritage. Thanks to Marguerite Henry and her book *Misty of Chincoteague,* there are millions of people all over the world who are familiar with the wild ponies of Assateague and the legend that they came from a lost Spanish galleon.

Today, there is no reason not to put *La Galga* on our National Register. There is no reason for Spain to object to this or a proper excavation and preservation program for the shipwreck. It is certain that they have no intentions of doing any archaeological investigation. On the other hand, until the rulings are overturned in the federal courts, Spain has no legal basis to object to excavation of a shipwreck on Assateague that the rest of the world will soon know to be *La Galga.* The next chapter in the saga of the hidden galleon is yet to be written.

Some of the wild horses on Assateague Island. *Photo by the author.*

Wild Assateague horses grazing on Ragged Point not far from the wreck site of *La Galga*. *Photo by the author.*

TOP: Pony swim day, Chincoteague Island, Virginia. The "saltwater cowboys" get the horses ready at the edge of the Assateague marsh. *Photo by the author.*

BOTTOM: The horses once again reenact their legendary swim to Chincoteague. *Photo by the author.*

TOP: In 1835, an observer stated, "the thousand half-frenzied spectators, crowding into a solid mass around the enclosure, to behold the beautiful wild horse, in all his native vigor subdued by man." Today, amateur and professional photographers alike rush to capture the moment the horses arrive on shore. *Photo by the author.*

BOTTOM: The saltwater cowboys drive the herd to the carnival grounds after the swim. *Photo by the author.*

The harbor entrance of Havana, Cuba, today. The Morro Castle guards the entrance just as it did on August 18, 1750 when *La Galga* cleared for Cádiz, Spain. *Photo by Richard Johnson.*

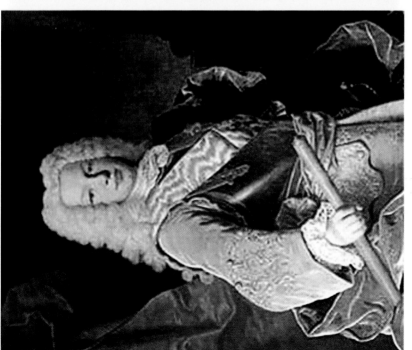

Left: Ferdinand VI, King of Spain, 1746 – 1759. *Courtesy of Wikipedia.com*

Right: Zenón de Somodevilla y Bengoechea, the Marqués de Ensenada, 1701 - 1782, Prime Minister and Secretary of the Navy. *Courtesy of Wikipedia.com.*

Don Juan Jose Navarro, the Marqués de La Victoria, 1687-1772. Captain General of the Royal Armada when *La Galga* wrecked and presided over the court martial of Captain Don Daniel Huony. *Courtesy the Museo Naval, Madrid*. He was also an accomplished artist. See Pages 2 and 425.

The statue and altar piece inside the chapel of St. Rosalia built to house the remains of the Marqués de La Victoria. In the center, there is the coat-of-arms of the Marqués de la Victoria surrounded by military decorations and symbols of victory and there is a large anchor which distinguishes the Marqués as a General of the Armada. The tomb of the Marqués was originally in this chapel but later moved to the Panteón de Marinos Ilustres. St. Rosalia was the patroness of mariners and a protector from pirates. This long forgotten fact was discovered in 2007 in a book found at the National Library of Spain and published in 1668. See page 245. *Photo by Esther González Pérez.*

LEFT. The church and convent of the Carmelitas de San Fernando in Isla León. This church dates to 1680 and contains the chapel of St. Rosalia. *Photo by Esther González Pérez.*

RIGHT. The Parroquia de San Francisco in Isla León. It his here that Captain Don Daniel Huony was buried in 1771. This baroque style church was built in 1785 to give shelter to parishioners of the Armada, although its foundations date to the hospice and school of the Franciscans built in 1765. *Photo by Esther González Pérez.*

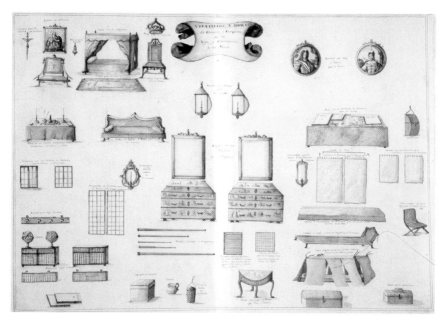

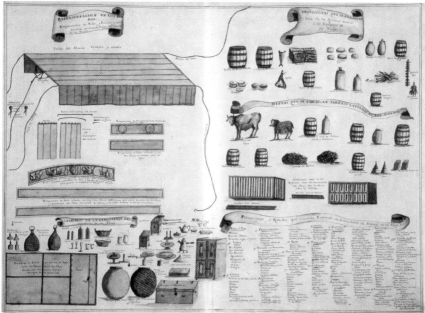

TOP Cabin Furnishings found on board eighteenth century Spanish men-of-war.
From the Album of the Marqués de la Victoria, Museo Naval, Madrid.

BOTTOM: Supplies carried aboard eighteenth century Spanish men-of-war.
From the Album of the Marqués de la Victoria, Museo Naval, Madrid.

The church and convent of San Juan de Dios, formerly known as La Misericordia when it was a hospital. This building dates from 1597 and overlooks the plaza of San Juan de Dios in Cádiz. It is here that Father Juan Garay de Concepcíon was buried after his death in 1766. Father Garay was a passenger aboard *La Galga* when she wrecked on Assateague Island. *Photo by Victoria Stapells Johnson*

Victoria Stapells Johnson at the entrance to the Archivo Provincial Historico in Cádiz, Spain. *Photo by the author.*

The Archivo General de Indias, Seville, Spain. *Courtesy of Wikipedia.com*

The Archivo General de Simancas, Simancas, Spain. *Courtesy of the Archivo General de Simancas.*

The Royal Palace, Madrid, Spain. Built from 1738 to 1765. *La Galga* was carrying mahogany for the doors and windows on her last voyage. *Photo by the author.*

TOP: Inside view of the Palace windows. *Photo by the author.*

BOTTOM: One of many mahogany doors found in the Royal Palace.
Photo by the author.

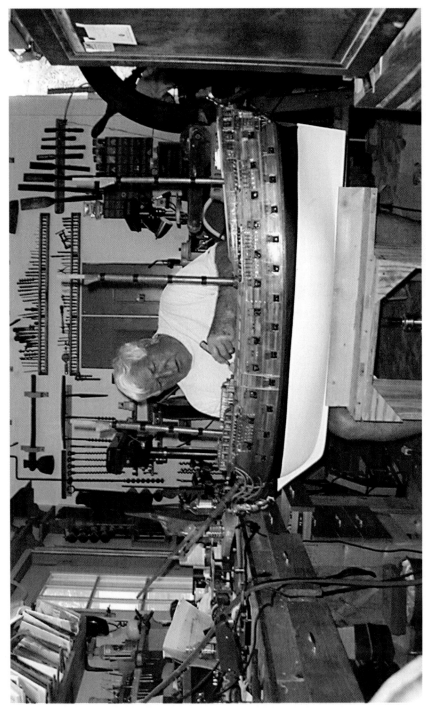

Bill Bane, former Navy salvage diver, SEAL, co-discover of *La Galga*, now a master model builder, as he looks upon his nearly complete model of *La Galga. Photo by the author.*

Notes and Bibliography

Note to the reader: Everything in this book is based on documented facts. However, the author took license in some cases to create dialogue and some scenes for the sake of illustration. Dates in the narrative have been adjusted from the Julian Calendar to the Gregorian Calendar which did not go into effect in England until 1752. Spain used the Gregorian Calendar since 1582. The Gregorian Calendar was eleven days later in 1750. Dates in the notes and bibliography are not adjusted. This is most common when referring to English newspapers prior to September, 1752.

For nautical terms see http://southseas.nla.gov.au/refs/falc/contents.html. For Spanish weights and measures see http://www.geocities.com/colosseum/Park/8386/medidasantiguas.htm.

Because of the extensive searches done in the archives of Spain, all records consulted are listed even if not used. All other sources are disclosed in each note.

Spanish Primary Sources for _La Galga_

AGB   Archivo General de Marina Álvaro Bazán, Viso del Marquès, Cuidad Real
AGI   Archivo General de Indias, Sevilla
AGS   Archivo General de Simancas, Simancas
AHC   Archivo Histórico Provincial de Cádiz
ACH   Archivo Catedralicio Histórico de Cádiz
AHCH   Archivo Historico De La Ciudad De La Habana, Cuba
AHN   Archivo Histórico Nacional, Madrid
AHPS   Archivo Histórico Provincial De Segovia
AMS   Archivo Municipal de Sevilla
APR   Archivo del Palacio Real, Madrid
BN   Biblioteca Nacional, Madrid
MN   Museo Naval, Madrid

Archivo General de Indias, Sevilla

Contaduría
784A, R.65. Cartas Cuentas de la remitido en los navíos de azogue del cargo de D. Daniel Huony remitido por los Oficiales Reales de México y Veracruz. 1738.

892 B, N.1, R.68. Cartas y relaciones de caudales remitidos a España por los Oficiales Reales de Veracruz en las flotas que se expresan. Año 1739, Comandante Daniel Huony.

1172 A. Autos y expedientes sobre presas, comisos y comercio ilícito, 1743-1765.

Contratación
2017-18. Registros de venida de Nueva España, 1749.
2476. Registos de venida de la Habana. N.2, R.1 – _La Galga_, maestre Tomás Velando, 1751.

2526. Registros de venida de Veracruz y San Juan de Ulúa. N.1 – *N. S. de los Godos,* Francisco Ortiz, maestre. 1751.

2527. Registros de venida de Veracruz y San Juan de Ulúa. N.4 – *N.S. Guadalupe,* Juan Manuel Bonilla, maestre, 1751; N.5 – *Nuestra Señora de la Soledad,* José Ventura de Respaldiza, 1751.

2625. Registros de venida de Cartagena. N.4 - *El Salvador,* maestre Juan Cruañas, 1749.

2626. Registros de venida de Cartagena. N.2, R.2 - *San Pedro,* maestre Manuel Martínez. Aguiar, 1751.

2902A. Libros de registros, 1739-83.

2918. Pliegos y Reglamentos de los Registros de Ida. N.1, R.7 - D. Luís Bernardo de Larrarte, maestre de la fragata *La Galga.* A Nueva España. 1747.

2923. Pliegos y Reglamentos de Registros de Venida. N.6, R.1 - D. Daniel Huony, Capitán del navío *San José* desde la Habana, 1733.

4729. Cartas Cuentas de los oficiales reales de Veracruz, años 1690-1766.

4759. Expedientes pidiendo certificaciones, 1750-57.

4854. Admisiones de Naos y primeras visitas, 1700-49.

4899. Asientos y Contratas para provisión de víveres, construcción de bajeles y administración de reales derechos, 1676-1777.

4927. Relaciones de oro, plata y efectos, 1701-55.

4935. Relaciones de pertrechos de guerra y mercaderías, 1747-59.

5078 - 5079. Reales Cédulas y Órdenes a la Casa de Contratación, 1750- 1751.

5157 - 5161. Cartas al Tribunal de la Contratación, 1750- 1754.

5800. Relaciones sobre derechos de Toneladas, 1671-1778.

Audiencia de Santo Domingo

292. Cartas y Expedientes de los oficiales reales, 1748-1753.

297. Cartas y Expedientes de personas seculares, 1737-1758.

326. Consultas y Decretos, isla de Cuba, 1731 – 1766.

344. Minutas de consultas y despachos, isla de Cuba, 1743 – 45.

345- 348. Minutas de consultas y despachos, isla de Cuba, 1746-1754.

366 Cartas y Expedientes del Gobernador de Santiago, 1747-1749.

368. Cartas y Expedientes del Gobernador de Santiago, 1751.

387 - 392. Cartas y Expedientes del Gobernador de la Habana, 1744-1752.

412. Cartas y Expedientes de los oficiales reales de la Habana, 1728-57.

431 – 436. Cartas y Expedientes de personas seculares, 1744 – 61.

437. Cartas y Expedientes de Sevilla, Cádiz y otros lugares que tratan de asuntos de dicha isla de Cuba, 1687-1759.

500. Expedientes y Papeles de la Compañía de la Habana, 1741-65.

548 - 549. Cartas y Expedientes del Gobernador de Puerto Rico, 1746-1759.

554. Cartas y Expedientes de personas seculares de Puerto Rico, 1730-59.

574. Puerto Rico. Expedientes sobre varias presas de embarcaciones extranjeras hechas en la isla, 1751-1761.

845 - 846. Cartas y Expedientes del Gobernador de la Florida, 1740-1759.

849. Cartas y Expedientes de personas seculares de la Florida, 1721-1756.

942. Cartas y Expedientes del Gobernador de Santo Domingo, 1744-1752.

1009 - 1010. Santo Domingo. Expedientes e instancias, 1729 -1758.

1072. Presas hechas a los ingleses: Santo Domingo, 1745-1753

1098 Presas, represalias, corsos, armadores de la isla de Santo Domingo, 1728-1774.

1130 - 1131. Consultas, Decretos y órdenes: Cuba, 1741-1753.

1194. Correspondencia oficial con los Gobernadores de la Habana, 1730 – 67.

1197. Correspondencia oficial con sus Gobernadores. 1771-1851.

1204 - 1205. Correspondencia del Gobernador de la Habana, 1743-1761.

1207. Correspondencia del Gobernador de la Habana, 1742-1746.

1219. Cartas y expedientes de Gobernadores de Cuba, 1720-1749.

1318 - 1319. Cartas y Expedientes del Gobernador de la Habana, 1747 – 1755.

1322. Duplicados del Gobernador de Santiago de Cuba, 1734- 1749.

1501 - 1502. Cuba: Expedientes, instancias de partes, 1748 – 1754.

1571 - 1572. Duplicados de cartas y expedientes de personas seculares, 1716-1759.

1812 - 1813. Cartas y Expedientes de los oficiales reales de Cuba, 1730 – 1757.

1827. Duplicados de cartas y expedientes de los oficiales reales de Cuba, 1715- 1749.

2005- 2006. Expediente de tabaco, azúcar, y otros frutos: Cuba, 1746-1748.

2009 - 2010. Expedientes de tabaco, azúcar, y otros frutos: Cuba, 1750 – 1752.

2065. Expedientes de comisos, 1747 – 1763.

2168 - 2170. Expedientes de presas, represalias, corsos y armadores, 1745 – 1751.

2197. Licencias de embarques: Cuba, 1726-68.

2208. Expedientes sobre asientos de negros, 1739-1751.

2298. Cartas y Expedientes del Gobernador de Puerto Rico, 1737-1754.

2470. Cartas y Expedientes de los oficiales reales de Puerto Rico, 1730-1776.

2513. Puerto Rico. Expedientes de presas, represalias, corsos y armadores, 1729-1771.

Audiencia de México

384. Consultas y reales decretos, 1743-1749.

385. Consultas y reales decretos, 1750-1759.

512 - 515. Cartas y Expedientes del Virrey, 1748 – 1751.

542 - 543. Cartas y Expedientes de la Audiencia, 1747-1754.

569. Cartas y Expedientes de personas seculares, 1746-51.

746. Cartas y Expedientes de los oficiales reales de México, 1730-1760.

853. Cartas y Expedientes del gobernador de Veracruz, 1742-1761.

862. Cartas y Expedientes de oficiales reales de Veracruz, 1740-1759.

1689. Cartas y Expedientes, 1742-1762.

1850. Expedientes e instancias de parte, 1749-1751.

2501. Expedientes del Consulado y Comercio, 1709-1754.

2914. Cartas y Expedientes de oficiales reales de Veracruz, 1743-1751.

2971. Registros de navíos y licencias de embarque, 1749-1752.

2979. Expedientes de flotas y incidencias, 1740-1749.

2980. Expedientes de flotas y incidencias, 1750-1756.

2998. Expedientes sobre presas, represalias, corso y armadores, 1742-1763.

Audiencia de Santa Fe

459. Cartas y Expedientes del Gobernador de Cartagena, 1736- 1759.

1012. Duplicados de Gobernadores y Comandantes Generales de Cartagena, 1738-83.

Indiferente General

8. Consultas, Reales Decretos y Órdenes: Nueva España, 1737-1758.

59. Cartas y Expedientes de personas seculares y Eclesiásticas, 1743-1759

800. Consultas Indiferente General, 1708- 1860.

1201. Cartas remitidas al Consejo, 1698-1832.

1299 - 1300. Órdenes generales, expedientes e instancias, 1749-1753

1501. Peticiones y Memoriales, 1735-1779.

1548. A. Expediente sobre el envío de caoba de la Habana para el Real Palacio, 1739-1785.

1989 - 1991. Correspondencia con el Presidente de la Casa de la Contratación. 1745 – 1747 – 1755.

2023 - 2027. Cartas y Expedientes de la Casa de la Contratación, 1741-1753.

2044. Cartas y Expedientes del Consulado de Sevilla y Cádiz, 1748-1754.
2209. Entradas y registros de las embarcaciones de América, 1700-1784.
2304. Expedientes del Consulado Comercio y dependencias de Cádiz, 1748-1753.
2345. Correspondencia y expedientes, Consulado de Sevilla, 1708-1768.
2525. Reales Cédulas sobre asuntos de Armadas y Flotas, 1583-1800.
2724. Expedientes de varios papeles sobre flotas, 1718-1772.

Escribanía de Cámara
62. Pleitos de la Habana, 1744-1745.
70 A. Pleitos de la Habana, 1749-1750.
99B. Residencia de Francisco Cagigal de la Vega, Gobernador de la Habana.
     1754 –1760.
1128C. Pleitos de la Casa de la Contratación, 1748-1749.

Arribadas
17. Oficios de José Patiño a Francisco de Varas Valdés, 1731-1733.
29 - 32. Oficios del marqués de la Ensenada a Francisco de Varas, 1747-1751.
134A. Órdenes desde el Consejo de Indias, 1729-1734.
136. Órdenes desde el Consejo de Indias, 1743-1759.
172. Cartas particulares y oficio, 1721-1753.
178B. Instrucciones y otros papeles pertenecientes a las flotas, 1730-82.
181. Reconocimiento y arqueo de navíos, 1739-1767.
270. Oficios y comunicaciones con el Gobernador de la plaza de Cádiz, 1804-1822.
325B. Correspondencia de oficio con Nueva España, 1735-1765.
368. Libro registro de aperturas de Registros y entradas y salidas de buques para Ultramar, 1817-1822.

Ultramar (Isla de Cuba)
1002. Tabacos. Compañía de la Habana, 1749-1762.

Consulados
78. (Libro) Correspondencia del Consulado de cargadores a Indias, 1750-3.
88. Correspondencia del Consulado de cargadores a Indias, 1681-1812.
204 - 205. Correspondencia del Consulado de cargadores a Indias, 1750 – 1751.
295 - 296. Correspondencia del Consulado de cargadores a Indias. Secretaría,
     1748-1754.
325 - 326. Correspondencia del Consulado de cargadores a Indias. Secretaría, 1749-1756.
347-348. Correspondencia del Consulado de cargadores a Indias. Secretaría, 1733-67.
796. Cartas cuentas representaciones de los Diputados de Comercio en México, Veracruzy la
     Habana, 1745-1754,
861. Prorrateo de la plata y frutos salvados del navío *N.S. Guadalupe* que naufragó en la costa de
     Virginia, 1750.

Archivo General de Simancas, Simancas, Spain

Secretaría de Estado
806-846, 2511-2604, 3955-3979, 6820-7040. Negociaciones de Inglaterra, 1480-1780.
5266-5351. Secretaría de Estado, correspondencia con ministros y embajadores, 1724-88.
6915, 6916, 6917, 6919, 6920, 6928, 6929, 6931, 6933, 6934. Negociaciones de Inglaterra, 1749-1756.
8133-8333. Embajada de Inglaterra, 1764-1833.

Secretaría de Guerra
313, 316, 397-1, 398-2. Infantería, 1714-1803.
559 – 565. Marina y Ultramar. Suplementos. 1713 -1790.

Secretaría de Marina
15-1, 15- 2. Oficiales de Guerra de Marina, 1751-1752.
16.1, 16-2. Oficiales de Guerra de Marina, 1753-1754.
69. Títulos, pensiones y limosnas a familias de oficiales, 1729-1770.
145. Ministerio de Marina, 1750-1751.
251, 256, 258, 259, 276. Negociado de Matriculas, 1742-1752.
303- 305, 313-318. Arsenales, 1735 – 1750.
392-432 Expediciones a Indias, 1711-1783.
438- 442. Expediciones de Europa, 1740 – 1753.
497-523. Navegación de particulares. Españoles y extranjeros, 1718-1783.
524-551. Corsos, presas, prisioneros, 1726-83
660 – 662. Estado de la artillería, pólvora, municiones y armas, 1734 – 1753.
725. Propiedad de bajeles, 1733-1772.
727. Canje y conducción de prisioneros, años 1740 - 1749.
96. Memoriales y Expedientes de Marina, años 1751 – 1753.

América
6952-7050. Nueva España. Correspondencia con virreyes y gobernadores, 1748-1805.

Archivo Histórico Nacional, Madrid.

Secretaría de Estado
2320. Consejo de Indias, 1746-1754.
4263, 4264 A-B, 4265 A-B, 4270, 4273, 4277, 4294, Correspondencia Diplomatica con Inglaterra, 1750-1763.
Sección Consejos Suprimidos – Consejo de Indias.
20197-99. Consejo de Indias. Sala de Justicia. Escribanía de Cámara. Casa de la Contratación,
21729. Consejo de Indias. Memoriales. 1744-1779
21796. Consejo de Indias. Expedientes eclesiásticos y papeles varios. 1739-1769.

Sección Consejos Suprimidos – Consejo de Hacienda.
34902. Escribanía de la Junta de Hacienda.
34127-133. Escribanía de la Junta de Haciendas.
38.519-28. Escribanía de la Junta de Hacienda.

Sección Inquisición.
4813 Exp. 57. Remisión de fondos por el Tribunal de la Inquisición de México al Consejo de Inquisición, en 1749.

Museo Naval, Madrid
Álbum de Jorge Juan, 1713-1775.
Álbum del Marqués de la Victoria: Diccionario demostrativo con la configuración y anatomía de toda la arquitectura naval moderna, 1719 – 1756.
Colección Guillen. Manuscritos 322, 1455, 1587.

Archivo General de Marina Álvaro de Bazan, Viso del Marqués (Ciudad Real)
Arsenales, 3705, 3761, 4288.
Cádiz, 8722 / 55-A, B, 8176.
Cádiz – Contaduría 8118 – 111, 112, 113.
Cuerpo General 561, 620, 713.
Histórico, 4809, 4821.
Real Órdenes 6510, 6515, 6518.

Archivo del Palacio Real, Madrid

Obras del Palacio – Administrativo

786, 787, 1027, 1028, 1029, 1116, 11117, 1416. Expedientes, planos, informes, partes diarios referentes a las obras del Palacio nuevo 1738 – 1752.
Legs. 350, Expedientes y proyectos sobre los adornos del Palacio, diseños de puertas, año 1748.
Legs. 3-5. cajas 9, 10 B, 12, 13. Órdenes, años 1750 – 1754.
Leg. 277. caja 778. Papeles diversos de la intendencia de la fábrica del Palacio, 1737 1762.
Leg. 355. cajas 1030, 1032, 1033. Partes diarios, declaraciones, y documentos relacionados con las obras del Palacio Real, 1740-1765.
Leg. 441. cajas 1260, 1263. Diario general de lo ocurrido en el Palacio Real, año 1751.
Leg. 448. cajas 1281- 1282 -1283. Diario general de lo ocurrido en el Palacio Real, año 1751.
Leg. 469. cajas 1348- 1351. Diario general de lo ocurrido en el Palacio Real, año 1750.
Leg.479. cajas 1381 – 1384. Planos sobre el estado de las obras del Palacio Real, 1738-1749.

Archivo Histórico Provincial de Cádiz
Sección de Protocolos: Cádiz y San Fernando, 1738-1772
Tomo 39. (fols. 202-220).
Tomo 1.006. (fols 19-20).
Tomo 3.645. (fols 374-376).
Tomo 3.649. (fols. 337-399).

Archivo Catedralicio Histórico de Cádiz
Tomo 16. Libros de Funerales, Matrimonios y Bautismos.

Archivo Municipal de Sevilla
Gaceta de Madrid. Nos. 8-10, 13-14 (Años 1750-1752, 1759-1760).

Archivo Historico De La Ciudad De La Habana
Tomo 27, 28.

Biblioteca Nacional, Madrid

Calascibetta, Emmanuele. *La Rosa de Palermo, Antidoto de la Peste y de Todo Mal Contagioso, Santa Rosalía*. Madrid, Bernardo de Villadiego, 1668.

Ciudad Gómez Bueno, Juan. Compendio…, pág.266-267.
Clavijo Clavijo, Salvador. *La Trayectoria Hospitalaria de la Armada Española*. Instituto Histórico de la Marina, Madrid, 1944.

Clavijo Clavijo, Salvador. *La Orden Hospitalaria de San Juan de Dios en la Marina de Guerra de España Presencia y Nexo IV Centenario de la Muerte del Santo Fundador 1550-1950* Madrid 1950 ([Tip. Artistica]).

Ciudad Gómez Bueno, Juan. *Compendio de Historia de la Orden Hospitalaria de San Juan de Dios.* Granada : Archivo Interprovincial, 1963.

Ciudad Gómez Bueno, Juan. *Historia de la Restauración de la Orden Hospitalaria de San Juan de Dios en España.* Granada : Archivo Interprovincial, 1968.

Ortega Lázaro, Luís. *Para la Historia de la Orden Hospitalaria de San Juan de Dios en Hispanoamérica y Filipinas* / Luís Ortega Lázaro. Madrid: Secretaría do Permanente Interprovincial, Hermanos de San Juan de Dios, D.L. 1992.

Vila Valencia, Adolfo. *Historia Descriptiva de la Plaza de San Juan de Dios, de Cádiz, y Sus Calles Más Próximas.* Cádiz, 1975.

Horozco. *Historia de la Ciudad de Cádiz.* 1845. Clavijo Clavijo, Salvador. La trayectoria hospitalaria.

Vila Valencia, Adolfo. *Historia Descriptiva...,* pág.70-71.

Archivo Histórico Provincial de Segovia
DH-25, (Delegación de Hacienda-Legajo 25) indexed as *"Cartas circulares del Convento Hospital de San Juan de Dios (1742-1834).*

List of other repositories and their abbreviations
LOC   Library of Congress.
NAE   National Archives of England (formerly the British Public Record Office).
MSA   Maryland State Archives, Annapolis, Maryland.
VSL   Virginia State Library, Richmond, Virginia.
WCC   Worcester County Courthouse, Snow Hill, Maryland.
ACC   Accomack County Courthouse, Accomack, Virginia.
ESPL   Eastern Shore Public Library, Accomack, Virginia.
WCL   Worcester County Library, Snow Hill, Maryland.
JRW   John D. Rockfeller, Jr. Library Williamsburg, Virginia.
SLW   Earl Gregg Swem Library, William and Mary College, Williamsburg, Virginia.
NARA   National Archives, Washington, DC and College Park, Maryland.
MHS   Maryland Historical Society, Baltimore, Maryland.
SFMM   San Francisco Maritime Museum, San Francisco, California.
EPL   Enoch Pratt Library, Baltimore, Maryland.
MM   Mariner's Museum, Newport News, Virginia.

Introduction: A Legend and a Shipwreck

Henry, Marguerite
Misty of Chincoteague, illus. by Wesley Dennis. Rand McNally, Chicago, 1947. Aladdin Books, New York, 1991.

History of Land Owners and horses on Assateague.
The first land patent on Assateague was 300 acres granted by the Maryland colony to William

Stevens. It was called *Winter Quarter*, no doubt for its intended use to pasture livestock. Successive patents were granted. The owners of Assateague also owned land on the mainland. Detailed inventories of their personal property were often taken describing the age and color of their horses and cattle. Some inventories specifically state which animals are on Assateague. Others can be inferred if they are listed in more than one place in the inventory. Inventories were ordered by the court and usually were done by immediate neighbors who were familiar with their property.

1687. In Maryland, William Stevens 500 acres called *Winter Pasture*, IB & IL #C, 265 MSA; 1687 in Virginia, Daniel Jenifer received 3500 acres for all of Assateague to the Maryland line. Patent Book #7, 563, VSL.

1689. Jenifer sold to Maximilian Gore. Deed included the conveyance of "all commodities of pasture" indicating the presence of livestock. Wills & Deeds 1676-1690, 507, ACC.

1696. Maximilian Gore willed 500 acres to his stepson James Smith, his son Daniel got remainder. Will Book 1692-1715 pt1, p. 199, ACC.

1705. *Baltimore's Gift* to William Whittington for 1000 acres on Maryland side WD, p. 500, MSA.

1708. Richard Holland et al. received a patent on Maryland side called *Bald Beach* opposite Sinepuxent Neck. DD#5 536, MSA. In Virginia, James Smith gave his four sons his portion of Assateague and to all six children "one grey mare of three years old to run upon Assateague Island and her increase till my son Thomas Smith reaches age eighteen and then to be equally divided between them." The stock of cattle and sheep in Thomas Milman's possession who lived on Ragged Point was equally divided among the six children. The children also got "privilege alike in the new pasture."

1709. Maryland issued a patent called *Spence's Lott* for 200 acres to Adam Spence, EE #6, 98, MSA. John Franklin received a patent from Maryland for 500 acres called *Assateague*, DD #5, p. 528, MSA. Margaret Towers patented 125 acres called *Tower's Pasture*, EE #6, p. 96. MSA.

1710. In Virginia, Thomas Smith's inventory gave no distinction of livestock on Assateague but seven horses and colts are listed along with other cattle. Will Book 1692-1715, Part 3, ACC. In Maryland, Thomas Purnell received a patent for 200 acres called *Adam's Fall*, EE #6, p. 99; Lawrence Reilly patented 250 acres called *Winter Range*, DD #5, p. 694; 175 acres patented to Richard Woodcroft called *The Cellar*, DD #5, p. 643, MSA.

1711. 1300 acres between *Baltimore's Gift* and Virginia line patented to William Whittington called *Assoeteague Beach*. This patent describes the "neck fence where James Taylor now dwells", EE #6, p. 291, MSA.

1712. Robert Perrie patented 170 acres from Maryland called *Pentland Hills*, DD #5, p. 778, MSA.

1713. Maryland granted 110 acres to Benjamin Aydelott called *Sand Beach*, EE #, p. 97 MSA.

1714. Henry Hudson was granted 200 acres by Maryland called *Hudson's Purchase*, EE #6, p. 99, MSA.

1719. In Virginia, Daniel Gore, son of Maximilian Gore, gave *Little Neck*, part of Assateague just below *Ragged Point* to his son William as well as 1/3 part of 500 acres bought from his step brother John Smith. Daniel's son Selby got *Great Neck* above *Ragged Point* to Maryland line.

Both sons had privileges to keep steers on Assateague. Daniel left a detailed inventory of his personal possessions including livestock. Daniel Gore's will 1715-29 pt. 1, p. 252, his inventory p. 438, 8-18-1722, ACC: 136 cattle, 40 horses, 130 sheep, and there were rams, ewes, weathers, and barrows. Selby got 8 horses, 4 cows, 2 steers, 1 bull. No distinction of livestock on Assateague. Selby later died intestate. Land on Assateague fell to his brother William.

1734. John Smith sold 500 acres of Assateague to Daniel Gore, father of William. Deeds 1734, p. 399, ACC.

1736. John Mercy owned land on the Maryland side on Assateague about two miles above the line. His inventory April 5, 1736, Will Book 1729-37 pt. 1 p. 493, ACC. One mare 10 years old, 1 mare 7 years old, 2 young horses, 16 cattle, and some outlying hogs. It does not specify Assateague Island.

1738. Hannah Hough was granted 400 acres by Maryland called *Upper Pines* EI #5, p. 172, MSA.

1744. William Marcey's will stated that 325 acres of land on Assateague and stock to be sold for best advantage of his heirs. Ten horses, 44 cattle, 23 sheep. 4 horses were identified separately, probably on Assateague. Will Book 1743-1749 pp. 132, 331, ACC.

1749. For the October Storm see the *Maryland Gazette* of October 18, 1749. Assateague was probably already laid level by the storm of December 6, 1744; see *Maryland Gazette* January 17, 1745. This storm had tides of seven feet above normal. Five thousand head of cattle and horses drowned in lowlands as well as several negroes. Wharves carried away and vessels ashore, some forced over marshes six or seven miles making it impossible to get them off. In comparison, the 1749 storm surged 15 feet. At Lewes, Delaware just inside Cape Henlopen an inlet was opened from Whorekill Creek to the Delaware Bay which permitted small vessels to traverse. Breaches in Assateague Island were very likely.

1750. Spanish warship *La Galga* drove ashore on September 5, 1750 near Maryland-Virginia line.

1753. William Gore's inventory listed, cattle 48, 6 piggs and hoggs, 24 shoats, 33 sheep, 1 horse, 1 mare, and 3 young mares. There was no mention of horses on the beach. Note the very large decrease in horses from what he received in 1719 from his father Daniel. Wills, 1752-1757 p. 188, ACC.

1757. In Virginia, on Nov 9, 1757, George Douglas who owned land north of the Maryland line, listed 2 heifers and 2 steers on Assateague and a 2 year old oxen was sent to Wallop's Island. No horses mentioned on the island.

1765. In Virginia, John Smith willed to sons John and James land on the island. Also, 29 cattle, 4 cattle on beach, 1 brown horse, 1 sorrel horse, 1 brown mare two years old on beach, 1 black horse, 1 year old on beach. Deeds 1767-1772 #3, Wills p. 148, inventory pp. 333,336, May 30, 1765, ACC.

1770. Daniel Gore wills daughter Susanna choice of any two horses. Benjamin Aydelott got 100 acres at Maryland line. Wills & Deeds 1767-1772 #3 p. 479, ACC.

1773. In Virginia, John Smith's inventory separates cattle and horses on Assateague and mainland. No horses mentioned on the beach but cows, heifers, bulls, and sheep are described. Will November 6, 1773. Will Book 1772-1777, p. 333, ACC.

1782. Personal property records of Accomack County. Daniel Mifflin, 14 Horses, 250 cattle; James Smith, 1 horse, 4 cattle; Margaret Teackle, 4 horses, 22 cattle; Thomas Teackle, 11 Horses, 100 cattle. No breakdown of livestock on beach if any for these land owners of Assateague. The total horses registered in Accomack were 3,870 and 16,018 head of cattle. The number of horses decreased over time. Some writers such as the National Park Service (http://www.nps.gov/asis/naturescience/horses/htm) have put forth that horses and cattle were kept on Assateague to avoid taxes, These records disprove this. Tax records for 1839 mention Isaac Lewis, William Lewis, and Mesiah Lewis all with horses on the "island." See 1840 below. Accomack County Personal Property Lists. VSL reel 4 and at JRW.

1792. Thomas Gore sold *Ragged Point* to Daniel Miflin, Book 1815-17, p. 27, ACC.

1793. Benjamin Aydelott had received 100 acres from Daniel Gore in 1770 bordering the Maryland line. His inventory in 1793 listed 8 slaves, some cows and oxen, and 2/3 of a pettiauger. Also listed an old sorrel horse, a young sorrel horse and mare, a colt, and a black horse. Assateague was not mentioned. Aydelott owned land on the mainland just above the Maryland line. JW8 p. 262, MSA.

1797. Thomas Gore sold *Little Neck* to Jonathan Watson. Book 1793-97, p. 451, ACC.

1821. Storm described in *Scribner's Monthly*, April 1877. Also *Norfolk and Portsmouth Herald* September 3-11, 1821. Horses were lost. Tax records for Accomack County 1820 indicate a total of 2,481 horses in the county, 1821 2,556, and 1822 2,433. A net loss of 127 horses. If these were all on Assateague it would have been a huge loss. Personal Property Tax Lists Accomack County at VSL microfilm.

1825. Storm. *Aurora and Franklin Gazette*. Issues from June 6-10, 1825, describe a storm worse than the one in 1821. Described by all as the most dreadful ever experienced. Horses must have been lost.

1829. Inventory of Jonathan Watson who owned *Little Neck* opposite *Ragged Point*, described, besides numerous cows, sheep, and oxen, 1 black mare, 1 grey, 1 sorrel, 1 sorrel mare, 1 black horse. Will Book 1828-1830, p. 237, ACC.

1831. *Snow Hill Messenger* of February 1, 1831 describes a snowstorm and high tide. A house on the beach floated off and carried to the opposite shore. A number of horses and cattle drowned.

1835. Dr. Thompson Holmes wrote his story for the *Farmer's Register*, (Petersburg, Virginia), p. 417. Dr. Holmes stated that the horses were gradually diminishing in number by neglect and on one island they were nearly extinct. He stated that thirty years before they were in much larger numbers. As to their origin he said there is no specific difference between them than those on the mainland except for their smaller size and superior hardihood. He said that this was an accident due to poor diet in the winter and "promiscuous copulation." However he stated later that, "Their winter subsistence was supplied abundantly by nature, the tall, dense, and heavy grasses of the rich flat lands, affording them green food nearly all winter." Prices paid for the horses were $30-$40 and horses on Morris Island of a "more recent origin" fetched $60-$70. Holmes said "I am perfectly assured that a small capital might be most profitably employed by a man of enterprise in horses, black cattle, and sheep. The largest and finest work steers of the Eastern Shore are raised upon these islands, without any expenditure for winter support: a proof that horses of full size, might be reared there, with judicious attention to the breed. ...they require much less grain than common horses. Regarding Assateague "Some hundreds of horses, cattle, and sheep, might be raised here, and annually sold without a dollar of cost, except the expense of a herdsman." He was well aware of the devastating effect of storms on the safety of the herd. He said that the horses of Assateague belonged principally to a company who mostly resided on the peninsula (mainland).

1839. A hotel was constructed somewhere near present day Ocean City. The *Worcester Banner*, (Snow Hill) of July 23, 1839 describes the building of the Atlantic Hotel. The article described it as a "temporary experimental affair" built very low to withstand the "assaults of the wind" and which will afford fine views of the ocean and the bay. Its first floor was the dining room and bar with five bedrooms in the attic above facing the bay with five more rooms built on the other side of the hall on the ocean side. News of this spread and left one observer to comment:

> We are surprised that an establishment of this sort was not
> thought of before. What a delightful summer retreat it will be
> to the inhabitant of the city and the country too, that lives
> remote from the water. We would not exchange the invigorating
> breezes from the ocean and the wild music of its roar, for all of
> the fashionable watering placer in the union.

This would have been the first hotel for Ocean City. Published histories of Ocean City cite the beginnings of Ocean City as when Stephen Taber first acquired the land in 1868. The first hotel after that date was the Atlantic Hotel built in 1875. Further evidence of the 1839 structure may be the "Beach House" used as a benchmark and signal and depicted in the 1849 hydrographic survey of the area. NARA, College Park. This information about the earlier beginnings has never been published.

1840. A partnership is formed and 880 acres of Assateague from the Maryland-Virginia boundary south is repatented to William J. Aydelott and his ten partners, James Aydelott, Samuel Payne, Moses Payne, William Payton, James Payton, Azuriah Ardis, James Ardis, William Veasey, Christopher P. Ball, and Benjamin Blades. Surveyor's Book #6, p. 84, ACC.

1844ca. Henry A. Wise of Accomack, later Governor of Virginia, said: "There has since long before the American Revolution, on the islands along the sea-board of Maryland and Virginia, a race of very small, compact, hardy horses, usually called beach horses. They run wild throughout the year, and are never fed." In describing the size he said of one it was so small a tall man might straddle one with his toes touching the ground on each side. See "The Equine F.F.V's" in the *Virginia Historical Magazine*, Vol. 35, 1927. Henry Wise was born 1806 at Accomack Tavern, son of John Wise V and Sarah Corbin Cropper. He studied law, moved back to Accomack in 1830 and then elected to Congress. Served ten years. Governor 1856-59.

1877. Howard Pyle visits Chincoteague and pony penning. He describes the wild horses and records the local belief of the origin of he horses. "How these horses came upon the Island is not known except through a vague tradition, for when the first settlers came there, early in the eighteenth century, they found animals already roaming wild about its piney meadows. The tradition received from the Indians of the main-land was that a vessel loaded with horses, sailing to one of the Elizabethan settlements of Virginia, was wrecked upon the southern point of the island, where the horses escaped, while the whites were carried to the mainland, whence they found their way to some early settlements." *Scribner's Monthly* Vol. XIII, April, 1877, No. 6. Early historical notes and records make no mention of the horses being present when the first patents were issued. In 1641, when Henry Norwood was wrecked on Kickotank Island south of Chincoteague, he described wolves on the island there. They would have been on Assateague as well and would have threatened the existence of horses if they were present. At that time horses were quite valuable. The colonists would have gone to the island to capture horses if they had been present. "A Voyage to Virginia," *Force's Tracts*, vol. iii, No. 10.

1883. The *Peninsula Enterprise* of September 6, featured an ad for the sale of horses on Revel's Island, another barrier island in Northampton County. These horses were described as Hambletonian, Morgan, and Bell stock distinguishing them from the Assateague herd.

1908. Clarence "Grandpa" Beebe married Ida Whealton February 18, 1908 at the Maryland line beneath one of the "Marriage Trees." *Peninsula Enterprise*, February 22, 1908.

1913. *Harper's Monthly Magazine* of October, article by Maude Radford Warren, titled "The Island of Chincoteague," describes the horses as strong, shaggy, small creatures, somewhat larger than Shetland ponies. The ponies were said to have come "from some wrecked vessel in the eighteenth or perhaps seventeenth century."

1929. Ralph Poole of the *Baltimore Sun* visited Chincoteague and describes the pony penning, "The origin of the Chincoteague ponies is shadowed in the mists of the past. They have roamed the island for many, many years; as long, in fact, as the oldest residents can remember, and longer. There is a tradition that the first one swam ashore from a Spanish ship, wrecked off Chincoteague in Colonial days." "The Isle of Ponies," Baltimore *Sun*, August 11, 1929.

1941. Year uncertain. Article in Baltimore *Sun* by Katherine S. Edmonds writing about Chincoteague and the horses. Paragraph heading "Swam from a Spanish Ship", Mrs.[Victoria Watson] Pruitt's grandfather, the eighteenth century Robert Watson, is authority for the story that a Spanish ship filled with horses was wrecked off Assateague, nearby island, and some of the horses swam ashore. This is the generally accepted version of the ponies origin and some who support it hold that the animals were stunted by their environment and by their diet of marsh grass… The ponies used to be bay, sorrel or black, with occasional white hoofs or white spot on forehead. Now many of them are spotted all over, the result of crossing with other breeds imported by one of the present owner's." Article found in Vertical File, Maryland Room EPL. See also Jonathan Watson, 1797 above. He was Robert Watson's grandfather,

1947. *Misty of Chincoteague* is published by Marguerite Henry.

1948. Victoria Watson Pruitt commented in 1948 that the horses on Wallops Island were closest to the old strain than any on presently on Assateague and Chincoteague. Her notes, *The Pruitt Papers*, 975.51pr ESPL. She refers to loss of horses in the storms of 1821 and 1837.

1961. The movie, *Misty*, is released by Twentieth Century Fox.

1962. A great northeast storm called the Ash Wednesday Storm devastated Assateague Island. A storm surge of seven feet swept the island and killed at least 150 of the 300 horses on the island. That year the Assateague Island National Seashore Park is created covering the area from Ocean City Inlet to the Virginia line. At that time there were only about ten horses in the Maryland section and were privately owned. By 1982, there were 80. http://www.nps.gov/asis/adhi/adhi7.htm.

1972. In October, *Misty* dies at age 26.

1977. Donald F. Stewart publishes his hoax on the *San Lorenzo* as being the source of the Assateague ponies. Baltimore *Sun*. July 24, 1977.

Chapter One: The King's Ship

52 Gunner by the Marqués de la Victoria

This ship is very similiar to *La Galga* as she has the same number of broadside guns (48), and 2 bow and 2 stern chasers making a total of 52. The quarterdeck cannon (4) were not always counted since they were often not placed. Drawing from the album of the Marqués de la Victoria, MN. See below, *La Galga de Andalucía*.

Interior View of *La Galga*

Drawn by Chip Bane and based on the Jorge Juan plans for a 52 gun warship found at the Museo Naval in Madrid, Contratacíon 2476, AGI, Secretaría de Marina, 397-1: Fol. 342 *Estados de las fragatas Hermiona, San Esteban, Galga y Paloma que salieron de Cádiz a Buenos Aires en los meses de mayo y noviembre de 1736*, AGS, and information found at http://www.todoababor.es/vida_barcos/nav_74can.htm

Father Juan Garay de Concepción

Contratacíon 2476, AGI. Within this legajo is a letter which says he left Peru with a companion. Another said on his return to Spain he had "companions." Lima 521 documents three went with him to Peru in 1741. He left Lima for Havana with 4,000 pesos in doublons. He left Havana with 4,800. He also added jewelry valued at 119 castellanos de oro. The differences can be inferred as property of the unnamed companion that boarded with him in Havana. His companions in 1741: Francisco García, a priest of the order of San Juan de Dios and secretary to Garay, Tomas Moreno, a priest of the order of San Juan de Dios and associate of Garay, and Melchor de Val y Bustos, his servant. Contratación 5484, n.3, r.16 – 11, AGI.

Andrew Connell

CO 137/59 NAE. *Virginia Gazette*, September 5, 1751 repeats Connell's account from the *Royal Jamaica Gazette*. After he returned there he became captain of the sloop *Mary*, registered in Kingston June 24, 1751. CO 142/5, CO 137/59, Jamaica, NAE. Fink's deposition, *Virginia Gazette*, July 25, 1751. In *La Galga's* register Contratación 2476, AGI.

James Maloney

CO 137/59, f. 39. NAE. In *La Galga's* register Contratación 2476, AGI. He gave an account of the wreck to the *Pennsylvania Gazette*, September 6, 1750. Returned to Jamaica in sloop *Ann*, CO 142/5, NAE.

Edward Ford

Contratación 2476, AGI.

Thomas Velando

Contratación 2476, 2527, AGI, Secretaría de Marina, 440, AGS.

Father Juan Martin

AAB Cádiz, 8118-113.

El Fuerte and *Harrington*

The *Harrington* entered Hampton, VA, July 10, 1745 from Jamaica registered to Jonathan Hanbury and Co., London, 1744, 400 tons, 20 guns 90 men, Captain John Hunter. Built on the River Thames in 1734. CO 5/1446 microfilm M225. JRW. Later captured by Huony on the *Fuerte*. AGI Santo Domingo 1501, AGS Secretaría de Marina, 400 – 2. The *Harrington* was often referred to by the Spanish as the *Arenton* (AGI Arribadas, 30) including when she was in Norfolk 1750 and more commonly know by her religious name the *Nuestra Señora de los Godos*.. The *South*

Carolina Gazette of February 23, 1747 gave this account: "Captain Edward Lightwood came in from Havana in Flag of Truce, the brigantine *Foesby*, with 18 English prisoners. [Taken] the *Harrington*, William James, Master, from Jamaica to London, on December 9, 9 leagues to windward of Morro Castle by a Spanish Man of War of 60 guns commanded by Capt. Daniel O'Honie…" Soon after that, Huony as commander of the *Fuerte*, arrested the English brig, *Prince Charles*, sailing from Jamaica under William Bedlow off the coast of Havana at Cabo Corrientes. It had 869 barrels of flour and "contraband" aboard. Huony had been on duty patrolling the coastline. AGI, Santo Domingo 1572. Havana, March 18, 1747. CO 142/15, NAE, Shipping Returns Jamaica. The *Harrington*, 26 guns, 75 men, loaded with sugar, rum, cotton, mahogany, and pimiento bound for London, November 20, 1746. The *Prince Charles*, William Bedlow, 12 guns, 80 tons, 30 men, had cleared Jamaica Dec 4, 1745. Apparently she was captured on return to Jamaica

Preparations in Havana
AGI, Contratación 5157-59, 2527, 2626, 2525; Santo Domingo 390-2, 1194, 1205; México 862, 515; Indiferente General 1548A, 2525. AGS, Secretaría de Marina, 318.

La Galga de Andalucía
1731. Built at Cádiz by Juan Cassanova and in service as of October 29, 1731. AGS, Secretaría de Guerra, Suplementos 564. 56 cannons, keel 58 codos, length 64 codos, beam 17 codos, 11 pulgadas, depth 8 codos, 7 pulgadas, and rated at 632 1/10 toneladas. A codo is 0.5747 of a meter. A pulgada is .0232 of a meter.
1732. Careened at Cádiz (Carraca), Secretaría de Marina, 303, AAB Cádiz, 8176.
1733. Secretaría de Marina, 252, AGS, mentions repairs.
1734. Armed with 54 cannon in Mediterranean. 22 twelve-pounders, 24 eight-pounders, 8 four-pounders. AGS Secretaría de Marina, 660.
1736. Part of expedition to Buenos Aires under command of Nicolas Geráldino. Secretaría de Marina, 393 ff. 486-535. AGS Secretaría de Marina, 397-1 f. 342.
1739. Anchored in Cádiz awaiting gunpowder. AGS Secretaría de Marina, 661.
1740. *La Galga* was at El Ferrol, Spain and had been ordered to leave on a privateering mission with Daniel O'Leary against the English on the coast of Guinea, Africa. She had permission to carry 400 to 454 men. Conde de Vega Florida was named captain by the King. The project was called off in 1741 by the King for a more important mission. Conde de la Vega Florida would later sit on the tribunal at Captain Huony's court martial. Secretaría de Marina, 398-2, 438 – 1, AGS. On May 21, 1740 Admiral Pensadoes sailed from Ferrol for Cádiz with a large fleet of warships which included the *St. Philip* and *La Galga*. June 4, 1741, 14 ships from Ferrol came in last summer at Havana. AGS, Secretaría de Marina, 398, f. 561,726. *Diario formado en Cartagena de Indias desde 13 marzo hasta 21 mayo 1741*. *Boston News Letter*, September 24, 1741; *Boston News Letter*, October 29, 1741; *Pennsylvania Gazette*, May 7, and 14, 1741.
1741. Graña, Spain. *La Galga's* officers and crew total 448. AGS, Secretaría de Marina, 398-2, f. 460.
1744. At Toulon, France, *La Galga* is listed as having 50 cannon. AGS Secretaría de Marina 315.
1745. *La Galga* was part of a squadron of 17 ships under the Marqués de la Victoria and was in the port of Cartagena, Spain. Her captain was Don Augustín de Idiaquez.
1747. *La Galga* is anchored at Cartagena, Spain. AGS, Secretaría de Marina 315.
1748. *La Galga* readies for Veracruz. AGS, Secretaría de Marina 315.

N. S. Guadalupe and *N.S. Los Godos* to Veracruz from Cádiz.
Contratación 2902 A, AGI.

Francisco Cagigal de la Vega
Santo Domingo 1204. Correspondencia del Gobernador de la Habana, Cagigal de la Vega, 1743

–1749, AGI. On October 10, 1734, he was a witness at Juan Manuel Bonilla's wedding in Cádiz. Tomo 23: Fol.57, *Libros de Funerales, Matrimonios y Bautismos*, ACH.

Mahogany Planks and *Mercedes*
Indiferente General 1548A, AGI. January 15, 1749. La Coruña (Galicia) letter to the Marqués de Ensenada. The *zumaca* of the King, the *Nuestra Señora de Mercedes* under Don Joseph Antonio de Gastañeta set sail from Ferrol for Cartagena, Spain on December 22 with crown correspondence but was forced to return on January 8 because of bad weather and unfit to sail further. She is here now being repaired and hopes to sail as soon as the weather improves. Secretaría de Marina 401 A – f. 382, AGS.

El Salvador, N. S. de Soledad, San Pedro
Contratacíon 2527, 2626, 2902 A, Arribadas 30, AGI.

Father Garay and the register of *La Galga*
AGI, Contratación 2476

Velando accounting for crew and Pedro de León Gomez, ship's boy
AAB, Cádiz 8118-113

Chapter Two: Twelve Days

Description of storm
AGI, Contratación 5157, 2527, Indiferente General 1990, AGI.
HMS *Triton* at Norfolk, Virginia, ADM 51/1012, ADM 51/886 and 4335, NAE.
HMS *Scorpion* at Charleston, South Carolina, ADM 51/1012, ADM 52/734-735, NAE. AGS
Secretaría de Marina 15-1, Oficiales de Guerra, 1751-2 Expediente 184, f. 599-600.
Those officers from *La Galga* who testified were: Daniel Huony, Joseph de la Cuesta y Velasco, Vicente Marcenaro, Manuel de Echaniz, Diego Guiral y Concha, Juan Bernardo Mayonde, Francisco Izaguirre, and Gabriel Muñoz. Captain Pumarejo of *Los Godos* filed his report at México 2971, AGI.

Henry Dalton.
Daniel Huony´s name appears at the end of one of the 1749 books as Commander of *La Galga* with the names of his six servants: Henry Dalton and Daniel Clark, both from Dublin. Two others were Spanish; Pedro Serrano from Sevilla, Francisco Rodriguez from Cádiz, and two were Italian; Bartolome Burgarin and Pedro de Arenas from Genoa. All of them had been with Huony on the *Fuerte* when she arrived in Havana in November, 1749. AAB Cádiz 8118-113.

Huony 1733
Contratación 2923. AGI. Weller, Robert, *Galleon Alley, The 1733 Spanish Treasure Fleet*, Robert Weller/Crossed Anchors (November 2001). Contratación 2902, No.2, f. 133 AGI, Entered Cádiz September 25, 1733. Five warships and thirteen merchant ships, which were part of the Tierra Firme fleet carrying a huge treasure back to Spain, were driven ashore into the Florida Keys, from Matacumbe to Grassy Key. Daniel Huony's ship was the only one to escape.
Calendar of State Papers: Colonial Series: America and West Indies, 1733 pp. 189-91, preserved in the Public Record Office (NAE), London : H.M.S.O., 1994.

Huony and *LanFranco*
Contaduriá 784, 892A 1738-39, AGI.

Huony at Boca Chica
Francisco de Paula Pavia. Madrid, 1873. (See Museo Naval: HMN 63). In the second volume of three, there is an entry for Huony on pages 199 to 201, MN.

In Havana
Secretaría de Marina 401 –2 ,695-97. Secretaría de Marina 318 Montalvo is the top official in the Port of Havana, Santo Domingo 1219 AGI.

Spinola taking crew
Secretaría de Marina 401, AGS.

Crown boat
Secretaría de Marina 318. AGS.

Huony ordered guns over
Officers testimony, see Description of Storm above.

Los Godos and North Carolina Wrecks
México 2971, AGI, *The Colonial records of North Carolina*, published under the supervision of the Trustees of the Public Libraries by order of the General Assembly, collected and edited by William L. Saunders. Originally published, Raleigh, North Carolina, P.M. Hale, 1886-1914. Vol. 1752. *London Gazette*, December 1, 1750.

Huony's own words
Found in his testimony, see Description of Storm

Bonilla at anchor
Contratacíon 5157, AGI.

La Mariana, and *San Pedro*
Pumarejo, México 2971, AGI.

La Galga off Fenwick
Second Pilot, Gabriel Joseph Muñoz, see his testimony, Description of Storm.

1748 fleet inspections
Secretaría de Marina 441, 315, 400 – 2, ff. 89-94, AGS.

Astilla
Stems and fragments of tobacco. A total of 214,283 pounds of tobacco products were loaded on board *La Galga*. Contratación 2527. AGI.

Repairs in Havana 1750
Report Of The Carpentry And Caulking Repairs Carried Out In The Port Of Havana During The Careening Of H.M. Frigate Named La Galga. Havana, 4 August 1750. Secretaría de Marina 401-2. f.699, AGS.

Los Godos into the Cheapeake Bay
Pumarejo, México 2971, AGI.

Crew lists for *La Galga* at the Archivo Álvaro de Bazan,(AAB)
Legajo 8118 – 111: for the year 1732

Legajo 8118 – 112: for the years 1732, 1734, 1735, 1736, 1741
Legajo 8118 – 113: for the years 1741, 1747, 1748, 1749, 1750, 1751

The wreck
Officers testimony, see Description of Storm, AAB Reales Órdenes, 6518. *Maryland Gazette*, September 5, September 12, 1750. *Pennsylvania Gazette*, September 6, 1750. *Boston News Letter*, September 6, September 20, October 11, 1750. *New York Gazette*, October 1, 1750. *West Indian Monthly Packet of Intelligence*, December, 1750. *Virginia Gazette*, September 5, 1751. *South Carolina Gazette*, October 22, November 5, 1750. *The London Gazette*, December 1, 1750. *Colonial Records of North Carolina*, published under the supervision of the Trustees of the public libraries, by order of the General assembly; collected and edited by William L. Saunders, Secretary of State. Raleigh, P.M. Hale State Printer, 1886-90. The *Maryland Gazette* of September 5, erroneously reported that the Governor of Havana was on *Los Godos*. An English account said that the intendant of Chile was aboard. Thomas Lee to the Duke of Bedford, CO 5/1338, NAE. James Maloney wrote from Philadelphia that "that there were various passengers of distinction travelling on the ship with large amounts of monies. Another large ship hit at Cape Charles..." AHN Estado. 4263A. No other verification of this was made.

Pedro Garaicochea at Accomack. *Pennsylvania Gazette*, Dec 27, 1746. Volume 28, Proceedings of Council p.395, MSA. Much is recorded about this man in contemporary newspapers and Spanish documents. He was one of the greatest Spanish privateers during King George's War, 1739-48. He made several trips to the east coast from Havana capturing numerous prizes and taking them to Havana.

Edward Ford swimming ashore
Ford was not named other than being referred to as the "English captain" by Huony. James Maloney was already described as an Irishman, and Andrew Connell was listed in the register as a Scotsman.

William Edgar
Pennsylvania Gazette September 6, 1750. Legajo 8118 – 113 AAB. Listed as a gunner, not as a prisoner, but most likely he was.

Three Ship's boys drowning.
Carlos de Medina and Pedro de los Reyes, said to be "long standing crew of the frigate." The third, Antonia Martinez. The *Maryland Gazette* of September 12 said two men had money tied to their waists and drowned and two others drowned when the raft capsized. Spanish records do not mention the money bags, and only one man, a soldier named, Andrés Almoguera, drowned from the raft. Huony and others said only a total of five had drowned. William Edgar was the fifth. Legajo 8118 – 113 AAB.

Indians
The crew made their way to land in Indian canoes (canoas de Indios). Letter, December 2, 1750, from the Duque de Sotomayor in Lisbon to the Marqués de Ensenada. Based on sailors testimony. Secretaría de Marina 503, AGS. Francisco Caro testified in London on December 6, 1750 that "After three days of being in this deserted area and without food a small English boat appeared." Estado 6917 AGS. But some unnamed person brought canoes believed to be an Indian.

Father Juan Garay de la Concepción saved his gold doubloons
AGI Contratación 2527.

Chests of money
Huony was able to cover expenses for maintaining crew out of his own money. He filed for reimbursement after his return to Spain. Secretaría de Marina 61, AGS; Reales Órdenes, 6518, AAB.

Twelve miles
The distance from the wreck site and Snow Hill Landing known today as Public Landing is about twelve miles as reported by Captain Huony. AGS, Secretaría de Marina 15-1, Oficiales de Guerra, 1751-2. Expediente 184, f. 599-600.

Description of Snow Hill
"Observations In Several Voyages and Travels in America," reprint from *The London Magazine* in the *William and Mary Quarterly* Vol. XV, No 3, January 1907.

Sheriff John Scarborough
Maryland Archives Series, Volume 28, *Proceedings of the Council of Maryland April 15, 1732 - July 26, 1753*. pp. 485-2, 493-90, MSA. Sheriff Scarborough reported to Governor Ogle in Annapolis about salvage activity. "They got off near two hundred Small Arms with Belts and Slings, Swords, and Bayonets, very large Coppers of Several Sizes and Small ones in aboundance, All her Runing and Standing Rigging, Iron Bars Crows and all Sorts of Tooles, many thousand Pounds of Tobacco made in Strong Wrappers. They have hove the Tobacco out for the Sake of Linnen Wrappers and the Tobacco now on board in good Order, There is some thousands of pounds worth of Mahogany on board for to do the Inside work of the King of Spains Pallace Doors & Windows &c. There is many thousands of pounds worth if it could be got before the Ship bursts with the Sea and Sinks into the Land, not more to add but hope your Excellency will at all times make your demands of anything in My Power to Serve you in Am Your Excellencys Most Hble & Most Obed' Servant.
J. Scarborough

P. S. She has many large Pieces
of Cannon on board two fine Anchors
at her bowes abundance of all Sorts of
Rigging and Sails in her hold and amount Supra"
The "Coppers" referred to are most likely pots or bowls and not necessarily made of copper. However, on the 1748 outbound trip the gunners were issued "copper bowls and pans." Contratación 1381, AGI. In Folder 43, Colonial Records, VSL, it describes two swivel guns, one large block, iron hoops, a pair of brass scales, a pump hook, 4 strapped blocks and a basket of trivial items were recovered by the Sheriff of Accomack from a nearby island.

William Gore
Executive Journals of the Council of Colonial Virginia, Virginia State Library, D. Bottom, Supt. of public printing, Richmond, VA 1925-1966.

News of the loss
Pennsylvania Gazette, September 6, 1750. *Boston News Letter*, September 6, September 20, October 11, 1750. *New York Gazette*, October 1, 1750. *West Indian Monthly Packet of Intelligence*, December, 1750. *Virginia Gazette*, September 5, 1751. *South Carolina Gazette*, October 22, November 5, 1750. *The London Gazette*, December 1, 1750.

In Norfolk
Secretaría de Marina 15-1, Oficiales deGuerra, 1751-2, Expediente 184, ff. 599-600, AGS. Contratación 5157, AGI. *Executive Journals of the Council of Colonial Virginia*, Virginia State Library,

D. Bottom, Supt. of public printing, Richmond, VA 1925-1966. *Order Book and Related Papers of the Common Hall of Norfolk*, Virginia, Brent Tarter Editor, Virginia State Library, Richmond, VA 1979.

Loss of the Mercedes
Letter from Daniel Huony to the Marques de Ensenada October 13, 1750.
The location was stated as six leagues north of Cape Charles in President Lee's letter of September 28, 1750, CO 5/1338, NAE. Another account said she was lost on Machapungo Shoals. *Maryland Gazette,* September 5, 1750. Hog Island on the north side of Machapungo Inlet was formerly known as Machapungo Island. The *Maryland Gazette* of September 5 said there were a "good many chests of money aboard." Spanish records do not reflect this although they said she was loaded with goods from the Royal Treasury. Folder 43, Colonial Records, Microfilm at VSL contains a letter from Thomas Lee to Sheriff Burton of Northampton County dated August 30, 1750 (September 10 NS) about the loss and the cargo salvaged from the *Mercedes*. Also contained in this folder is an account with Peter Hog where he names the salvagers as Abel, George, and Joseph Powell, some Floyds, and a Michael Nottingham has having been involved in the salvage. The Floyds and Powells owned the islands on each side of Machapungo Inlet, Hog Island to the north and Prout's Island to the south. See Whitelaw, Ralph T., *Virginia's Eastern Shore; A History of Northampton and Accomack Counties*. George Carrington Mason, editor for the Virginia Historical Society, Richmond, Virginia, 1951, Vol. I. Peter Hog's letter was dated September 2, Northampton, County and was written in French. The addressee was not disclosed but it was addressed to the "commander of one [of the ships]" who were at Norfolk. This must have been Captain Pumarejo. Contratación 5157, AGI. Captain Barrosa was later listed with the crew of *La Galga* in Norfolk. Legajo 8118-113 AAB.

Correspondence to and from Governor Ogle
Maryland Archives Series, Volume 28, *Proceedings of the Council of Maryland April 15, 1732 - July 26, 1753*. pp. 485-2, 493-90, MSA.

Peter Hog
Contratacíon 5157, AGI. *Executive Journals of the Council of Colonial Virginia*. Several references can be found of him in the Northampton County Court Orders, Northampton County Courthouse and his accounting is in Folder 43, Colonial Papers, Microfilm, VSL. He became Huony's attorney in his absence. In 1746, he was listed as custom's officer for Accomack County. NAE Class A.O. 15/43. Audit Office Enrollment Books, 1743-1747. Also at JRW.

Chapter Three: Hooked

Huony's letter
Maryland Archives Series, Volume 28, *Proceedings of the Council of Maryland April 15, 1732 - July 26, 1753* pp. 497-94 The letter was undated but received on November 14, 1750, New Style.

Dave Horner
The Treasure Galleons; Clues to Millions in Sunken Gold and Silver, Dodd, Mead, New York. 1971.

The Atocha
Lyon, Dr. Eugene, *The Search For The Atocha*, New York : Harper & Row, c1979.

Dahlgren's Raid
Col. Ulrick Dahlgren's Union cavalry passed through this area late in the evening of March 1, 1864 before defeating the Richmond Armory Battalion at the Battle of Green's Farm, just

south on Three Chopt Road. Dahlgren led his command toward Richmond on the Westham Plank Road (now Cary Street Road) for about half a mile. At Hick's Farm, five miles from the Capitol Square, his 500 cavalrymen encountered the local defense troops of the Departmental Battalion and the remnants of the armory battalion. After a brief skirmish in the darkness during a rain, snow, and sleet storm, Dahlgren retreated to rejoin Brig. Gen. H. Judson Kilpatrick's force on Brook Road. Dahlgren was killed the next day. http://www.mdgorman.com/ Written%20Accounts/Mercury/charleston_mercury,_3_3_1864.htm Richmond *News Leader*. August 18, 1962, Richmond *Times Dispatch*, August 19, 1962.

USS *Minnesota*
http://cssvirginia.org/vacsn4/original/monlog.htm

Nuestra Señora de la Concepción
Earle, Peter *The Treasure of the Concepcíon =: The wreck of the Almiranta*, Viking Press, New York, 1980. Grissim, John, *The Lost Treasure of The Concepción*, William Morrow and Company. Inc, New York. 1980. Cousteau, Jacques-Yves and Phillippe Diole', *Diving For Sunken Treasure*, Doubly Day & Company, Garden City, New York 1971.

Northern bounds at latitude 38
Can be found in, Letter from Thomas Lee to the Board of Trade (Duke of Bedford) September 29, 1750. CO 5/1327, NAE.

Herman's Map
Library of Congress, Map Division.

Edmund Scarborough survey
Virginia Historical Magazine, Vol. 19, Richmond, Virginia, 1911.
MSA, Vol. 54, Preface.

Fry-Jefferson Map
Library of Congress Map Division. Fry's report, CO 5/1327 May 8, 1751. NAE. Also M-243, JRW.

English account of distance
Maryland Gazette, September 12, 1750. For the Spanish account of a gun shot see declaration of Francisco Caro, Estado 6917, AGS.

La Galga's Manifest
Contratacíon 2476, AGI.

Wall Street Journal
The Mart, April 25, 1980.

Chapter Four: Storm on the Horizon

The USS *Constellation*
The frigate had been named for the "new constellation of stars" on the American flag. The *Constellation* displaced 1,264 tons and carried thirty-eight guns. Capable of cruising at fourteen knots, she quickly earned the name "Yankee Racehorse." The primary source for the back ground and history of the preservation of the *Constellation* and Donald Stewart's early years came from *Fouled Anchors: The Constellation Question Answered*, Dana M. Wegner, David Taylor Research Center, Bethesda, MD, September 1991. Hereafter referred to as *Wegner*. His bibliography was helpful as well. A very valuable source. Report DTRC 91/CT06, David Taylor

Research Center, Bethesda, MD, 1991. Available free on-line at the Naval Surface Warfare Center, Curator of Navy Ship Models web site http://www.dt.navy.mil/cnsm/faq_13.html

For the construction and early years of the *Constellation* see, Williams, Glenn F., *USS Constellation A Short History of the Last All-Sail Warship Built by the U. S. Navy*, The Donning Company Publishers, Virginia Beach, 2000, and Wegner, Dana M., "The Frigate Strikes Her Colors," *The American Neptune*, 55, #3 (Summer 1995).

Donald Stewart
For Stewart's position with the B&O Railroad see Deposition of Donald Stewart filed in Civil Case #9981, WCC, John Amrhein vs. Donald Stewart. Also see *Baltimore News Post*, June 1, 1953. On March 2, 1983, Chessie Systems Railroads confirmed to SEA. Ltd. that Stewart was employed as a clerk typist from April 3, 1950 to May 18, 1956. For the tunnel episode see Wetzel, George, *Baltimore Subterranean*, 1954 from the files of the Baltimore Museum of Science. This paper leaves Stewart unnamed but was verified in an interview on March 25, 1980 between this author and Mort Wood of Marathon, FL and a former member of the Maryland Gun Collectors Club who was present when Stewart led them to the tunnels. Also see letter to Walter Graham from John Lyman, March 8, 1958. John R. Lyman Papers, San Francisco Maritime Museum, HDC 278, Folder 816.

Stewart on TV in uniform. *Wegner*, p. 17, and John Lyman Papers. Letter from R. Walter Graham, Jr. MD to John R. Lyman, September 24, 1975. Graham reported that he had heard that Stewart had been picked up by the FBI masquerading as a naval officer, probably in the late 1940s. Folder 815. John Lyman Papers, SFMM.

Bureau of Ships and FDR Letter
See *Wegner*, p. 21.

Admiral Eller
See *Wegner*, p. 22.

Leon Poland
See *Wegner*, p. 24.

The spike and Stewart
See *Wegner*, pp. 24-5.

Howard Chapelle
See *Wegner*, p. 28.

"The Yankee Racehorse. The U.S.S. Constellation" which was published in the Maryland Historical Society's magazine of March 1961, and was co-authored by Leon Polland, John Schneid, Charles Scarlett and Donald Stewart, MHS. See also U.S.F. *Constellation Papers*, MS 1939, MHS.

Constellation was designated a National Historic Landmark
See *Wegner*, pp. 30-1.

The second spike
See *Wegner*, p. 27.

Constellation was the oldest ship afloat

For Stewart's quote see *The United States Frigate Constellation*, by Donald Stewart, [1967] MHS. Baltimore *News Post*, June 1, 1953. Stewart was quoted as saying, "We definitely cannot see the point to destroying this Maryland ship...the Navy seems to have preserved her sister ship, the *Constitution*, very well. Why sink the oldest ship in the U.S. Navy?" As a side note the frigate *United States* was broken up in 1840 at Norfolk after the Navy had spent $100,000 refitting her. She was 40 years old. *New York Herald* December 21, 1839.

Childish forgeries
See *Wegner*, pp. 42, 44.

Stephen Brayden and Captain Meade
See *Wegner*, p. 37 and 48.

Lloyd A. Olsson
See *Wegner*, p 38.

David Stodder
See *Wegner*, pp. 26, 50, and n134.

For Agnew's remark about the Naval Militia
See *The News American*, Wednesday, June 20, 1973

Stewart as Rear Admiral
See also *Wegner*. Stewart made statements to the author that he was a Rear Admiral. See Report to Governor Mandel, from Major Edwin Warfield, III, Adjutant General, State of Maryland Military Department. May 14, 1973. Copies of this provided to author by Hugh Benet of the Star Spangled Banner House, Baltimore, Maryland in 1983. Included in this is Stewart's letter dated December 6, 1971 to Mr. Earl Koberg, Director, Naval Ships Command, Department of the Navy, Washington, D.C. from Donald Stewart, Brigade of Naval Militia, found in Naval Sea Systems Command, Office of Public and Congressional Affairs, Washington, D.C.

Stewart's resignation and letter to Captain Taylor
Provided to the author by Hugh Benet, Star Spangled Banner House. Copies in author's possession.

Print of *Constellation*
In the author's possession supplied by Hugh Benet of the Star Spangled Banner House, Baltimore, Maryland, in 1983. Comment on Montague Dawson was made by Benet.

Details of the background of Atlantic Ship Historical Society
Found in deposition filed in Civil Case #9981, WCC, John Amrhein vs. Donald Stewart. Also, minutes of the Atlantic Ship Historical Society filed in this case. Copies of the tax returns for Atlantic Ship Historical Society were also obtained.

Stewart starts at $75 a week
Baltimore *Sun* June 16, 1974. Magazine Section.

"amazing documentation that has begun to clutter public archives
Lyman's statement about the rebuilding of the Constellation in 1853 found in his letter to John H. Kemble, Pomona College, January 5, 1972. John R. Lyman Papers, SFMM HDC 278, Folder 815.

Statement about the band of confidence men
See *Wegner*, p.52.

National Archives Stamp
See Wegner, p. 54 and discussion below, Donald Stewart the forger.

The *Sea History* Article, "Greenwich Letter," and Robert Erlandson
Wegner, pp. 57-9 and n153,154, Baltimore *Sun*, September 21,1975, and John Lyman Papers, HDC 278, Folder 816, San Francisco Maritime Museum. Lyman to National Maritime Museum, Greenwich, England, September 30, 1975; National Maritime Museum to Lyman, October 8, 1975; Erlandson to Lyman, October 20, 1975; Lyman to Erlandson, October 29, 1975. Erlandson reported this in the Baltimore *Sun*, September 21, 1975. "Frigate's Past Debated." *Wegner* and John Lyman Papers.

Stewart's resignation
Came from deposition filed in Civil Case #9981, in Worcester County, Md., John Amrhein vs. Donald Stewart, p. 56. Stewart says he resigned in 1975, no date given.

Raymond Thompson, Baltimore Sun
See Baltimore *Evening Sun* January 4, 1949.

Ocean Bird
The information about the *Ocean Bird* is from the Baltimore *Evening Sun,* January 4, 1949. A review of *Lloyd's Register of Shipping* at the Mariner's Museum failed to show a vessel named *Ocean Bird* for the period 1795-1800. The name William Carhart of the *Hawk* was always erroneously associated with the *Ocean Bird*. Therefore the *Hawk* and the *Ocean Bird* are one and the same. *Gazette of the United States and Philadelphia Advertiser* dated January 21, 1799. For more on this connection see *A History of Ocean City, Maryland*, by Mary Ellen Mumford, printed by Mayor & Council of Berlin, Mayor & Council of Ocean City, and Calvin B. Taylor Banking Co., 1958. Copy WCL. On the mainland across from Ocean City, at present day Captain's Hill, there is a lone tombstone that bears the inscription, "In Memory of Captain William Carhart who was shipwrecked on this coast, January 5th, 1799, age 38."

Spanish coins passed as legal tender until 1857
http://www.newworldtreasures.com/milledpillar.htm
http://www.coins.nd.edu/ColCoin/ColCoinIntros/Sp-Silver.intro.html

Spanish fleet of 1715
Wagner, Kip http://www.1715fleet.com/1715_fleet_and_kip_wagner_story.htm

Stewart publishes the *San Lorenzo* story
Baltimore *Sun*, July 24, 1977, EPL. The *San Lorenzo* story was also published in the *Resorter* in the July 15-31, 1979 issue at Ocean City, Maryland. No copyright notice. Dick Lohmeyer founder and editor of the *Maryland Coastal Press* owned the *Resorter*.

Cocos Island Treasure
Baltimore *Sun*, January 19, February 23, March 23, April 25, 1949.
Stewart also read about Art McKee and his adventures with the 1733 Spanish wrecks near Marathon, Florida in the Baltimore *Sun* articles of September 24, 1949. He would later claim to have worked with Mckee. Baltimore *Sun*, June 16, 1974, EPL.

Grosvenor East Indiaman

Kirby, Percival R., "The True Story of the Grosvenor, East Indiaman," African Affairs, Vol. 60, No. 241 (Oct., 1961), pp. 555-556

Various correspondence to and from Stewart and the National Park Service
Obtained through Freedom of Information request. Copies in author's possession. The report on the so called *"Ocean Bird"* was included in this.

Thirteen pages in support of the *San Lorenzo*
Supplied to author by FOIA request from National Park Service.

San Lorenzo marker
Photo by the author in 1983. This marker was later replaced. Bearss, Edwin C., *General Background Study and Historical Base Map: Assateague Island National Seashore,* Division of History, Archaeology and Historic Preservation, Washington, DC, 1968.

Albert Alberi
Facts related to Albert Alberi provided to the author by Alberi. He provided the author with the Stewart letter of February 6, 1978. The "original documents" Stewart said he found in 1949 on the 1750 fleet were no doubt the January 4, 1949 Baltimore *Evening Sun* article.

Information about the "rare coin" found on Assateague
Provided by the National Park Service through a Freedom of Information Request.
See also *The Daily Times*, Salisbury Maryland, November 6, 1979.

Details of the origins of SEA, Ltd
From author's first hand knowledge and in Stewart's deposition filed in Civil Case #9981, WCC.

Donald Stewart the forger
As to all of the forgeries mentioned in this chapter it is this author's opinion that they were manufactured by Donald Stewart. This conclusion was easily reached based on other documents that this author found to be fraudulent and prepared by him. He was certainly capable of the fraud and his alleged acts from 1949 to 1980 were totally consistent with those which this author knew that he committed from 1977 to 1985. This author also reached the conclusion that the documents referred to with a National Archives stamp were prepared and stamped by Donald Stewart. And based on this first hand experience there is no doubt that the employee caught with a National Archives stamp by Leon Polland described, but unnamed, in *Wegner*, page 54, is Donald Stewart. The description of the behavior of this unnamed employee is identical to the observations made by this author and others who knew Stewart. In the civil action #9981, WCC, filed by this author and others, Stewart produced a fraudulent document with the National Archives stamp on it. See also chapter 9. Evidence of Stewart's use of his historical society to generate cash can be found in the court papers of Case# 2-4-84-CI-244 filed in District Court of Maryland for Worcester County. The Historical Society received $6,500 from the Quarterdeck Restaurant for twenty one different items. Included were a cannonball, deadeye, and rigging block from the USS *Constitution*. The binnacle of the USS *Constitution* is documented as being property of the Atlantic Ship Historical Society which Stewart then lent to the Quarterdeck Restaurant. Other items mentioned as personal property of Stewart is the decommissioning bell of the USS *Constellation*. The minutes of the Atlantic Ship Historical Society of August 14, 1985 state that they "donated" the binnacle to the *Constitution* rather than return it from where they got it.

Stewart conning National Park Service
Baltimore *Sun* December 17, 1978. In the opinion of Larry Points, Chief of Interpretation,

Assateague National Seashore, "There is no doubt that he is an excellent historian. From what 'I've seen, he really knows his shipwrecks." Points later saw the light.

Chapter Five: The Race for the Greyhound

Maryland Beachcomber article
"Shipwreck: 18th century Spanish shipwreck reported off Delmarva," published in Ocean City, Maryland, May 16, 1980. Stewart's depiction of the wreck illustrated four stages of the wreck's deterioration. Of note Stewart described *La Galga* as 1,544 tons, 182 feet long and carrying 60 guns. See Notes, Chapter One, *La Galga de Andalucía* for actual dimensions.

Stewart's *Juno*
"Treasure ship sinks while crew of 425 is cast adrift, amid sharks." *Maryland Beachcomber*, May 22, 1981, by Donald Stewart. This story is obviously made up.

Stewarts resume
In the Sea, Ltd., Prospectus in possession of the author.

SEA Investor Meeting
The Wilmington *News Journal* of August 30, 1980 mentions the belt buckle with the Spanish coat of arms as well as Stewart's representation that *La Galga* was armed with bronze cannon, and was carrying 327 bars of silver and 1300 carats in gems. Stewart also told the reporter he was a former Navy diver. This article also mentions his alleged discovery of the *Ocean Bird*. See also *Washington Star*, November 11, 1980.

Chapter Six: In the Enemy's Camp

HMS *De Braak*
Sunk off Cape Henlopen, Delaware on May 25, 1798. It was rumored for centuries she was carrying Spanish treasure from a prize recently captured. The treasure legend proved later to be false. See Shomette, Donald, *The Hunt for HMS De Braak*, Carolina Academic Press, Durham, North Carolina, 1993.

For the *Conquistador* article
Maryland Beachcomber, April 18, 1980, "Of Hurricanes and Spanish galleons", by Capt. Donald F. Stewart. This story is a fabrication.

Juno
See *Juno* above.

Assateague Island Handbook 106. National Seashore 1980 Division of Publications, National Park Service, U.S. Department of the Interior, Washington, DC

Robert Marx
Marx, Robert F., *The Treasure Fleets of the Spanish Main*, World Publishing Co., Cleveland, OH 1968

——————, *Shipwrecks of The Americas*, Bonanza Books, New York .1983, This is a reprint of his *Shipwrecks of the Western Hemisphere*, 1492-1825. New York : D. McKay Co., c1975.

The Hidden Galleon

Burt Webber
For the details on the *Concepcíon* and Burt Webber see Grissim, John, *The Lost Treasure of The Concepcíon*, William Morrow and Company. Inc, New York. 1980.

Naval Records of the American Revolution
Naval records of the American Revolution, 1775-1788. Prepared from the originals in the Library of Congress by Charles Henry Lincoln, of the Division of Manuscripts. Published/Created: Washington, 1906.

Index The Papers Of The Continental Congress 1774-1789, Volume IV. Compiled by John P. Butler, Govt. Print. Off., 1978.

SEA records
Sea. Ltd. letters and memorandum referred to in possession of the author. Some of these were filed in the federal cases in Baltimore, see Chapters Eight and Nine and also the suit in Worcester County Circuit Court, case #9981.

Santa Rosalea
Stewart's account of the *Santa Rosalea* was recounted from memory by the author in 1984 during the civil suit against Stewart. Amrhein v. Stewart, WCC, Case #9981. The details on the alleged *Santa Rosalea* are as follows: Robert Marx published *Shipwrecks of the Americas*, Bonanza Books, New York. This is a reprint of his *Shipwrecks of the Western Hemisphere*. On page 163, item 160. "Year 1788. Spanish Merchantman *Santa Rosalea*, Captain Pardenus, sailing from Baltimore to Havana wrecked near Cape Henlopen but some of her cargo saved." Marx's source was based on the account described in *Lloyd's List*, copies of which can be found at the Mariners Museum in Newport News, Virginia. The entry in this paper dated September 16, 1788 says "*Santa Rosalia*, Pardenus, From Baltimore to Havanah, is drove on shore at the capes of Delawar and dismasted part of cargo saved." (Note that it is at this juncture that Marx misspells "Rosalia", this trivial error would be repeated by Stewart and others later). The real facts are as follows: On June 3, 1788 the *Santa Rosalia*, Captain A. A. Pardenus entered the port of Baltimore from Cádiz, Spain (see the *Maryland Journal and Baltimore Advertiser*, June 6, 1788, p. 3, col. 3 at MHS). She was rated at 300 tons and carried a cargo of 4,587 gallons of white wine, 9,689 bushels of salt, raisins, Jesuit's bark, and silk handkerchiefs consigned to Carey and Tilghman, merchants. (see Imports, Port of Baltimore, Naval Office S-205 at MSA. Also U.S. Customs Bureau, Baltimore Customs House, Record of Fees Collected, RG 36 E 1168, p. 140, NARA). No official record survived of her outbound cargo, but she cleared customs at Baltimore, July 11, 1788 for Teneriffe. (see *Maryland Journal and Baltimore Advertiser*, July 15, 1788). When ships are cleared they are free to leave but often cannot until a favorable wind. *Santa Rosalia* would soon encounter a wind less than favorable. A great hurricane hit the Capes of Virginia on July 23 (see *Early American Hurricanes 1492-1870*, David M. Ludlam, American Meteorological Society, Boston, MA, 1963). *Santa Rosalia* met the storm just outside the Virginia Capes. It was a very severe hurricane and it was reported that only two ships in Hampton Roads survived. The hurricane tracked up the bay and up the Potomac passing Mount Vernon where George Washington noted it on Thursday the 24th. It became known as "Washington's Hurricane". The *Pennsylvania Gazette* of August 20, 1788 printed an account written from Norfolk dated July 31 which said that "a Spanish ship with 4 thousand barrels of flour on board, from Baltimore for the Mississippi or New Orleans was wrecked on Cape Charles and the crew consisting of 30 people all perished" This same account described "a great many wrecks" along the coast, and hoped that the Delaware "escaped its effects." This paper and others fail to mention any ship losses at the Capes of Delaware related to this hurricane. Further, there are no other Spanish ships leaving Baltimore during this time period. This was verified in the *Maryland Journal and Baltimore Advertiser* and the Baltimore Port Records. There is no doubt that the ship lost at Cape Charles and the *Santa Rosalia* are one and

the same. Port records for Baltimore do not record any other Spanish ship for this time period. It is also clear that regardless where the *Santa Rosalia* wrecked she would not be of any commercial value to salvage today.

For the Spanish frigate of 1785 which did not wreck see AGI, Contratacíon 2589A,B, Cuba 1392, 1399, Indiferent General 2162B, 2209A. A voyage for this ship was recorded in "A Voyage of the Spanish Frigate Santa Rosalia, in 1774," by B Glanvill Corney, *The Geographical Journal*, Vol. 47, No. 1. January, 1916.

In the spring of 1981 Stewart gave the author a hull drawing he claimed to be the *Royal George*. Pasted onto the photocopy was his typewritten note giving the details of the *Royal George*. "A Draught of the British Privateer 'Royal George' Length in deck – 13-'-6", Beam Extreme – 28'. Draft 12'-6" Depth of Hold – 11' Burden in tons 324. The vessel was built in Canada, Circa – 1784 for the R.N., sold in 1788 on the stocks to the three Halfpenny Brothers. She wrecked on the shoals of Assateague Island, Behind the Isle of Wight in the county of Worcester (Maryland – U.S.) during a violent Noreaster in 1789." There is a very famous shipwreck, the HMS *Royal George* which wrecked at Spithead, Isle of Wight, off the south coast of England on August 29, 1782. This ship weighed 3,745 tons and had 100 guns. Stewart's confusion with this ship was no accident. All he needed was the Isle of Wight connection. The Isle of Wight across from Ocean City got its name from White's Island. A third *Royal George* was built at St. John's Lake Champlain in 1777. 386 tons, 96'6", 18 guns. From *American Ships of the Colonial and Revolutionary Period*, John F. Millar. Presumably broken up at the end of the war.

SEA files claim in Federal Court
U.S. District Court for the District of Maryland, CA R-81-51, R-81-52, R-81-53.

Judge Ramsey
From his obituary, Baltimore *Sun,* June 16, 1993.

April 9, 1981 Attorney General files
Docket Entry #9 and #11.

Juno Article
See *Juno*, Notes Chapter Nine.

Mrs. Clements
Interviewed by the author by phone in the spring of 1981.

Quattro
Lloyd's Register of Shipping, 1887. MM. Berman, Bruce D., *Encyclopedia of American Shipwrecks*, The Mariner's Press, Inc, Boston, MA, 1972.. p77. "*Quattro*, bark, [wrecked] February 17, 1887, Ocean City, MD."

Boiler Wreck
Author believes this was in a fishing guide published by ADC Map Co. prior to 1980.

St. Rosalia
For her history see Chapter Nine.

China Wreck
Discovered by the NOAA vessels *Rude* and *Heck* in 1972 at the mouth of Delaware Bay. Her cargo was cases of ironstone china with British hallmarks dating to the latter 1800s. This popular

sport diver's wreck routinely yields souvenirs. According to discoversea.com the identity of this wreck is the *Principessa Margherita di Piemonte*, of Naples, Italy. She was sailing from Plymouth, England to Philadelphia and was lost on March 12, 1891. No verification of this was done by the author.

May 18, 1982 Stewart was boarding the *Captain Cramer*
Minutes, Atlantic Ship Historical Society, filed in John L. Amrhein, Jr., et al. vs. Donald F. Stewart, et al., case #9981, WCC.

Motion to Intervene
Docket #18, CA R-81-51 in the U.S. District Court for the District of Maryland, Baltimore, MD.

Chapter Seven: The Hidden Galleon

1943 plat of Assateague
Plat Book #6, pp.17-18, ACC.

William Gore
His boundary on Assateague, Patent Book #7, p563 1687, VSL.
Wills & Deeds 1676-1690, p. 507, ACC.

Pope's Island
Patent Book PL #3, p. 475, Liber 22, p. 391, MSA.

No-Man's Land
After the patents for Pope's Island in Maryland and Assateague in Virginia in 1687, Virginia, contradicting Maryland's patent, patented 183 acres on the south end of Pope's Island to Hill Drummond in 1700. (Patent Book 9, 244, VSL). The survey began at "the mouth of a small thorofare and a small bay thence running west 172 poles (2,838 feet) to the thorofare and from thence south being surrounded with salt water and land locked on the east, west, and south by Assateague Island." Although not described, the west line appears to be the understood line between Maryland and Virginia. In 1711, William Whittington patented and surveyed a tract of 1300 acres in Maryland called *Assateague Beach* which ended at "the Divisional lyne betweenVirginia and Maryland." (EE#6, p292, Land Office MSA). This document also gave the distance from Pope's Bay to the ocean as 134 poles or 2,211 feet. It ended at the "low water mark." There has been very little erosion at this location since then. However, the Pope's Island 1687 Maryland survey was reaffirmed in 1713. (PL #3, p. 475, MSA). Virginia appeared to comply with the claim of Maryland to Pope's Island as they issued no patents on Assateague for the area between the Jenifer patent and subsequent Gore ownership to the line prescribed by Whittington in 1711. Maryland maintained its claim to Lower Pope's Island until 1883. This line was later described as the "Traditionary Line" in 1868. See Chapter 10, Figure 34.

Boundary line resolved in 1883
Peninsula Enterprise, December 6, 1883.

1668 Boundary
See *Southern Boundary of Maryland*, Commissioner on Boundary with Virginia, Thomas Lee, 1860.

Truitt, Reginald V.
And Millard G. Les Callette, *Worcester County, Maryland's Arcadia*, Worcester County Historical Society, Snow Hill, MD, 1977.

1840 plat
Surveyor's Book #6, p. 84, ACC. Treasury Warrant 14384, Reel #339, VSL.
Little Neck, Thomas Teackle Gore to Jonathan Watson, 1796. Deed Book 1793-1797. p. 451, ACC.

Alberi's letter from Stewart
In the author's possession and filed in Case #9981, Amrhein v. Stewart, WCC.

Two Swivel Guns
Colonial Records, Folder 43 Microfilm, VSL.

The Steamboat Bertrand: History, Excavation, and Architecture.
Jerome E. Petsche. National Park Service, U.S. Department of Interior, Washington 1974.
The *Bertrand* was 161 feet long, 32 feet 9 inches wide and five feet 2 depth of hold and rated at 251 tons.

Alberi on other's looking for *La Galga*.
His letter to the author December 27, 1982.

Wilson's Treasure
Truitt, Reginald, Worcester County, *Maryland's Arcadia*, p. 73.

Cook and Stewart
Stewart wrote Edwin Bearss, National Park Service Historian, June 12, 1985 and among other things claimed ORO, Inc. and the author were still pursuing the SEA, Ltd. wrecks. For more on this letter see Chapter 9. Stewart claimed in a letter dated July 16, 1985 to the members of the Constellation Committee that Richard Cook, a "disgruntled member" of Ocean Recovery Operations told him in 1983 that "Amrhein needed money, equipment, and my [Stewart's] research to operate his corporation." The minutes of the Atlantic Ship Historical Society dated November 22, 1983 describe a visit by Richard Cook to the house of Donald Stewart on July 19, 1983. It states that Cook was a member of ORO, and reported that ORO was attempting night-time salvage of the "previously discovered wreck sites." Stewart claimed to have written to Thomas Deming, Assistant Attorney General with the State of Maryland to complain of this alleged activity. The author's motion to intervene in the *San Lorenzo* case was filed on May 4. From that point on there was much publicity about Stewart's fictitious wrecks. There was never any desire by the author or ORO to return to these "sites." By July 19 Cook had already been dismissed from ORO as he insisted *La Galga* was in Maryland waters.

1859 Coast Survey map
Map of Assateague Island , U.S. Coast Survey, Triangulation and Topography by Charles Ferguson, 1859, Record Group 23, NARA, College Park, MD.

Scarborough's Statement
Volume 28, *Proceedings of the Council of Maryland*, April 15, 1732 - July 26, 1753, pp. 485-3, MSA

Correspondence with General Service Administration and Fish and Wildlife
Can be obtained through FOIA request from U.S. Fish and Wildlife Service, Region 5.

News of discovery.
Baltimore *Sun*, December 12, 1983.
The *Morning News*, Wilmington, December 13, 1983. B1.
Wilmington *News Journal*, "History, Hunch, May Reveal Hulk," January 1, 1984, p. 1.
Eastern Shore Times, December 14, 1983, *Washington Post*, December 13, 1983.

The Virginian-Pilot, on Holloway, January 5, 1984, and Wilmington *News Journal* January 9, 1984. *Eastern Shore News*, December 19, 1983.

President Nixon's Executive Order No. 11593
http://www.cr.nps.gov/history/online_books/anps/anps_7b.htm
In part it says:

Sec. 2. Responsibilities of Federal agencies. Consonant with the provisions of the acts cited in the first paragraph of this order, the heads of Federal agencies shall: (a) no later than July 1, 1973, with the advice of the Secretary of the Interior, and in cooperation with the liaison officer for historic preservation for the State or territory involved, locate, inventory, and nominate to the Secretary of the Interior all sites, buildings, districts, and objects under their jurisdiction or control that appear to qualify for listing on the National Register of Historic Places.

Sec. 3. Responsibilities of the Secretary of the Interior. The Secretary of the Interior shall: (a) encourage State and local historic preservation officials to evaluate and survey federally owned historic properties and, where appropriate, to nominate such properties for listing on the National Register of Historic Places.

Letter from Broadwater, Smithsonian, Stieglitz
These letters are in the authors possession but can be obtained through FOIA from U.S. Fish and Wildlife Service.

Schooner *Hawk*
Gazette of the United States and Philadelphia Advertiser, January 21, 1799. See also Chapter 2.

1839 Baltimore *Clipper*
October 31, 1839.

1857 Dollars
http://collections.ic.gc.ca/bank/english/emay73.htm
http://www.collectsource.com/Americas.htm
http://www.coins.nd.edu/ColCoin/ColCoinIntros/Sp-silver.intro.html

Pitts, William
Copies of old certificates of return patents and field notes. Worcester Room, Worcester County Library, Snowhill, Maryland.

The *Samaritan, Boston Columbian Centinal* of December 15, 1830
See also the *Baltimore Patriot*, December 24, 1830. A total of nine bodies were found. Two hundred mahogany logs were recovered as well as a quantity of logwood. The *Salem Gazette* of December 17, 1830 repeated a letter written by John Powell, the Wreckmaster of Worcester County to the *National Gazette*, dated December 4, Berlin, Maryland. He said the brig had gone to pieces. At that time six bodies had been found, four white and two black. The *Salem Gazette* December 21, 1830 named John O. Abbot as master and mate, and Jeremiah Wheelwright, both of New York, were part of the lost crew. See also the *Samaritan*, from Newburyport, Massachusetts. Newbury Port Registers 1789-1870 at the Mariners Museum. This ship's master was Isaac Brown and gave its dimensions as a brig 177 tons, 78 feet 2 inch. long, 22' 10' wide, 11 5/4' depth, condemned as prize October 14, 1812 and registered March 1, 1823 to Nathaniel Jackson of Newbury, Isaac Brown Master. 1829 *Lloyd's Register* said owner M. Jackson, 13 feet draft, single deck). A similar wreck occurred on the North Carolina coast in 1827. The English brig *Monarch* loaded with mahogany and 12,000 in specie from the Bay of Honduras was lost near Cedar Inlet. *U.S. Gazette* September 25, 1827. The *Gazette* February 10, 1829 comments on

the premium received for Spanish and Patriot dollars because of the civil war in Mexico. Most of the coins found in the area between Fourteenth and Eighteenth Streets in Ocean City were two reals or quarters.

Chapter Eight: Cast Away in the Court of the Admiralty

Nuestra Señora de Atocha,
Lyon, Dr. Eugene, *The Search For The Atocha*, New York : Harper & Row, c1979.

SEA, Ltd. federal cases.
In Civil Action 9881 in Worcester County, Maryland, Raymond Cardillo, attorney for SEA, Ltd. admitted that the only evidence of discovery of these shipwrecks presented to the federal court was his sworn affidavit. When asked to admit that each of these vessels as described in the complaint were in fact present he stated that "he lacks information or knowledge of them". In his defense, he pointed to Judge Ramsey's Opinion that they were there. He denied it was his "recommendation" to file the admiralty complaints even though his memo to the SEA, Ltd. Board on December 5, 1980 states "...I would urgently request the Board to authorize m[e] to engage co-counsel immediately, and to institute and action *in rem* in the United States District Court without further delay". When asked to admit that the shipwrecks were found prior to December 5th he said they had. When asked to admit that the wrecks were found after November 7, 1980 he stated that he lacked information to admit or deny and referred the plaintiffs to Ramsey's Opinion.

The *Central America*
Kinder, Gary, *Ship of Gold in the Deep Blue Sea*, Vintage Books, New York, NY, 1999.

Letter from Judith Armold to Judge Norman Ramsey
April 13, 1983. This letter about the potential problems admitted by the Attorney General of Maryland was never introduced into the official record on this case by the State. However the author filed this letter with the Fourth Circuit Court of Appeals and is available for inspection. Case #84-1151 and 84-2170, Richmond, VA.

Whydah case
The *Whydah* was a pirate ship lost off of Cape Cod, Massachussets in 1717, and found by Barry Clifford.

Eleventh Amendment Defense.
States must consent to being sued in a federal court.

John Harvey Letter
Can be found at Appellant's Reply to State of Maryland's Response to Informal Brief, filed December 13, 1984, in case #84-2170, United States Court of Appeals for the Fourth Circuit, Richmond, VA.

Cardillo's statement
Was recorded in Stewart's Workman's Compensation Case Civil Action M83-1606, U.S. District Court of Maryland, Baltimore, Maryland.

The Constellation Question
Howard I. Chapelle, and Leon Polland, Smithsonian Institution Press, U.S. Government Printing Office, 1970.

Baltimore *Sun*, April 24, 1983
The article quoted Stewart's accounts of his fictitious treasure.
3,973 gold doubloons
173,700 silver pieces of eight
255 bars of gold
303 bars of silver
A statue of the Madonna and a baptistery of solid gold
Plus all of the unregistered cargo

Baltimore *Sun* May 1, 1983.
"Investors Seek Proof in Sunken Ship Search," and *Maryland Coast Press*, April 29 and   May 4, 1983.

The *Juno*.
See the notes for Chapter Ten.

The *San Lorenzo* case.
CA R81-53 United States District Court for the District of Maryland.

The *Hawk*.
Details of her loss are found in the *Gazette of the United States and Philadelphia Advertiser* dated January 21, 1799. The captain's wife Ann published a notice as administratrix in the *Pennsylvania Gazette* of March, 9, 1799. It said he was late of Southwark, Philadelphia. See also Chapter Four.

Dr. Richard Passwater's letter.
Not part of the official record. Copy in author's possession.

K. H. Houston Matney to the author
May 18, 1983. In the author's possession.

Judge Ramsey's Opinion in SEA, Ltd. cases.
United States District Court, District of Maryland. Baltimore. Subaqueous Exploration & Archaeology, Ltd., and Atlantic Ship Historical Society, Inc., Plaintiffs, v. The Unidentified, Wrecked And Abandoned Vessel, Etc., et al., Defendants. Civ. A. Nos. 81-51, 81-52, 81-53. 577 F SUPP, 597.

SEA, Ltd Investor suit
John L. Amrhein, Jr., et al. vs. Donald F. Stewart, et al., case #9981, Circuit Court for Worcester County, Snow Hill, Maryland, *Maryland Coast Press*, February 1, 1984, p. 3. Also Baltimore *Sun*, January 30, 1984. *Maryland Coast Press*, May 4, 1983. *Maryland Coast Dispatch*, July 5, 1984. Baltimore *Sun*, January 30, 1984, Section B1.

Correspondence with Judge Ramsey.
In the author's possession.

Appeal
Case #84-1151, United States Court of Appeals for The Fourth Circuit, Richmond, VA
In Re: John L. Amrhein, Jr. Subaqueous Exploration and Archaeology , Ltd., et al, v. The unidentified, etc, et al.

State acknowledges deficiency
SEA, Ltd., v Unidentified Vessels, CA R81-51, 52, 53, Second Supplemental Memorandum of

Defendant on Jurisdictional Issues. U.S. District Court for the District of Maryland, Baltimore, MD. SEA spent approximately $300,000 looking for make-believe ships and treasure. Had the State called for an evidentiary hearing in the beginning, the investors would have been spared a great deal of this.

The Society for Historical Archaeology newsletter dated March 1984:
http://www.sha.org/Publications/publications.htm

Affidavits of Little and Bastian
Docket Entry #11, SEA, Ltd., v Unidentified Vessels. See also Maryland Natural Resources Code § 2-301. At this writing it appears to have been repealed. http://www.dsd.state.md.us/comar/Annot_Code_Idx/NaturalResIndex.htm
Former language included, "A person who knows the location of any archaeological site in the state is encouraged to communicate the information to a reputable museum, an institution of higher education, a recognized scientific or historical institution or society or the Geological Survey. See also 16 USC §470 a (b) (3)(A) and (B). (B) which says "It shall be the responsibility of the State Historic Preservation Officer to: (1) Direct and conduct a comprehensive statewide survey of historic properties; this high priority responsibility entails locating historic and archaeological resources at a level of documentation such that the resources can be evaluated for potential nomination to the National Register of Historic Places."

Letter to Tyler Bastian
Copy of this letter can be found in case #84-2170, United States Court of Appeals for the Fourth Circuit, Richmond, VA. Appellant's Reply to State of Maryland's Response to Informal Brief, December, 11, 1984. Today the inventory of archaeological sites can only be viewed by "qualified individuals." "All material relating to Maryland's archeological sites is accessible only to qualified researchers with prior approval from the Office of Archeology." See http://www.marylandhistoricaltrust.net/library.html. In existence since the beginning of SEA, Ltd., the State of Maryland also seated the five-member Advisory Committee on Archaeology comprised of professional and avocational archaeologists and at least one person who was an expert in shipwreck research. An afternoon at the Library of Congress reviewing contemporary newspapers would be enough to convince a researcher that the shipwreck claims by Stewart were unfounded. See also The Maryland Historical Trust, *Annual Report 1983*, Department of Economic and Community Development.

Duty of an Attorney
4 *American Jurisprudence* 2d AMICUS CURIAE §5 1962.
Also stated here, "An attorney who deliberately fabricates evidence, or knowingly permits fabricated evidence to be entered into the record without informing the court of the fact, is guilty of perpetrating a fraud upon the court." The Fourteenth Ammendment prohibits State prosecutors or other State officials from allowing fraudulent testimony to be used when they have knowledge of such, even though they did not solicit such testimony. See e.g. Reickauer v Cunningham, 299 F 2d 170, 172 (CA 4th, 1962). One who accepts the fruits of fraud, knowing of the means by which they were obtained, is liable therefore even though he had not personally participated in the fraud. 37 *Corpus Juris Secundum* FRAUD §61 b(2).

Decision of Court of Appeals
Case #84-2170 Denial of Motion to Vacate, Unpublished Opinion.

Article II, Section 2 of the U. S. Constitution requires that there be a real case or controversy, not a hypothetical one and the parties may not by stipulation invoke the judicial power of the United States in litigation which does no present an actual case or controversy. See Memphis Light, Gas, and Water Division v. Craft 440 US 1, 56 LED 2d 30, 98 S. CT 1554 (1978).

Dr. Harvey's letter.
See above.

Federal Rules of Civil Procedure
Rule 8(d) Effect of Failure To Deny. Averments in a pleading to which a responsive pleading is required, other than those as to the amount of damage, are admitted when not denied in the responsive pleading. Averments in a pleading to which no responsive pleading is required or permitted shall be taken as denied or avoided. It is the author's position that since he challenged the existence of the defendant by verified motion and alleged fraud, that Stewart and his historical society should have answered the pleading and that the State of Maryland should have officially stepped forward with what it knew.

"We believe the truth is more important than the trouble it takes to get it."
Publicker v. Shallcross, 106 F 2d 949, 952 (CA 3rd 1939).

Owen, David,
"Some Legal Troubles with Treasure: Jurisdiction and Salvage", *Journal of Maritime Law and Commerce*, April 1985. 16 J.Mar. L. & Com. 139 http://www.jmlc.org

Entry of Judgement
See rules 58 and 79 FRCP as they relate to entries of judgement.

Letter of Edwin Bearss to Amrhein
In reviewing the court docket for the *San Lorenzo* case the author found that his motion to intervene had not even been entered on that docket, it was buried in the *Royal George* case which he had not bothered to intervene in. His letter of transmittal and Motion to Supplement Pleadings both refer to attached exhibits. The court docket says "June 11, 1985 No. 39 Motion of John L. Amrhein, Jr. to Supplement Pleadings, and Attachments." These attachments were not in the file when retrieved from storage September, 2002, but are clearly documented as having been part of the record.

Timely mailing of court orders.
Rule 77(d) FRCP Notice of Orders or Judgments. Immediately upon the entry of an order or judgment the clerk shall serve a notice of the entry in the manner provided for in Rule 5(b) upon each party who is not in default for failure to appear, and shall make a note in the docket of the service.

Judge Ramsey's letter August 5, 1985
In the author's possession.

Reliance on SEA Ltd, cases
Keller, Paul N., "Salvor-Sovereign Relations: How The State Of Illinois Destroyed The Lady Elgin" 30 J. Mar. L. & Com. 279. Zych v. Unidentified, Wrecked and Abandoned Vessel, Believed to be the SB "Lady Elgin," 746 F. Supp. 334, 1991 AMC 359 (N.D. Ill. 1990).

Chapter Nine: Rosalia's Revenge

Worcester County District Court, Snowhill, MD

Case # CL-112 March 21, 1984. Stewart admitted to the *Eastern Shore Times* of August 27, 1980 that he received the detector from Garrett. Garret was told by Stewart that he would get 1% of all treasure found in return for the detector. On January 17, 1984 he assigned by letter the detector to the author for $1.00. Correspondence from Garrett September 16, 1983, and January 17, 1984 in author's possession.

Shipwrecks in the news

Wilmington News Journal. June 13, 1985, August 17, 1986.
Delaware State News June 13, 1985.

"Santa Rosea Lea"

C.A. No. 85-312 C.M.W, United States District Court for the District of Delaware, and others: The *China* 85-315, the *Cornelia*, 85-314, the *Adeline* 85-313, the *Three Brothers*, 85-311, the *Faithful Stewart*, 85-310. The *China* wreck was later identified as the *Principessa Margherita di Piemonte,* according to the DiscoverSea Museum in Fenwick, DE.

Background on *De Braak*

Shomette, Donald, *The Hunt for HMS De Braak: Legend and Legacy*, Carolina Academic Press, Durham, North Carolina, 1993. Cites Stewart's letter to Zwaanendael Museum in Lewes, DE. *De Braak* file, July 12, 1956.

The *Santa Rosalia*

See Notes Chapter Six, *Santa Rosalia*

The *Cornelia* and other IRRC wrecks.

See the *Pennsylvania Gazette* of March 3 and 10, 1757. For the *Adeline* see Robert Marx, he says it wrecked in 1824 but the *National Gazette and Literary Messenger* (Philadelphia) of December 13, 1823 reported the loss of the *Adeline*. Since the vessel actually wrecked in 1823 it is again obvious that IRRC used Marx solely as support for their claim on this wreck. For the *Three Brothers*, see *Shipwrecks off the New Jersey Coast*, by Walter and Richard Krotee, 1965. Krotee gives identical coordinates for the *Faithful Steward* and the *Three Brothers*. The authors were unsure of the date so it is safe to assume that they had no contemporary historical references. There was a *Three Brothers* lost in January 1812 under Cape Henlopen, see *United States Gazette* January 12, 1827. For the *Faithful Steward* see the *Pennsylvania Gazette* of September 14, 1785. Except for the *China Wreck*, these five vessels are identical to the five Donald Stewart gave to the author in November, 1980 to research.

Howard Chapelle

See Shomette, p. 45. He refers to the *Smithsonian Journal of History* article "H.M.S. De Braak: The Stories of a 'Treasure Ship.' Spring 1967, pp. 57-66.

Stewart and *De Braak*

See Shomette, p. 168, 197. *Maryland Beachcomber*, August 15, 1980. Stewart describes a huge treasure on board the *De Braak* when she sank.

Stewart and missing documents.

At the Worcester County Library in Snow Hill, Maryland the author, in 1984, examined Volume 28, *Proceedings of the Council of Maryland April 15, 1732 - July 26, 1753*, of the Maryland Archives Series and found that the pages referring to the wreck of *La Galga*, had been cut from the volume. It is not known who did it or when, but whoever did had a motive.

Letter of Edwin Bearss
June 12, 1985. Copy of letter was sent to the author by Charles McKinney of the National Park
Service. Also found in Demand on Stewart to Produce Documents in Worcester County Court,
Civil Case #9981, in Worcester County, Md., John Amrhein vs. Donald Stewart and Atlantic Ship
Historical Society, Inc.

Stewart to Constellation Committee
Copy provided to author by Hugh Benet, Star Spangled Banner House, 1983.

Baltimore *Evening Sun* January 4, 1949
See also Chapter Four. This article provided the inspiration for Stewart's fictitious *San Lorenzo*
and his later quest for *La Galga*.

Spanish Coins were legal tender until 1857.
http://collections.ic.gc.ca/bank/english/emay73.htm
http://www.coins.nd.edu/ColCoin/ColCoinIntros/Sp-silver.intro.html

Stewart's Answer to Interrogatories and production of Documents.
Worcester County Court House Civil Case #9981, in Worcester County, Md., John Amrhein vs.
Donald Stewart and Atlantic Ship Historical Society, Inc.

Wall Street Journal Ad
April 25, 1980 in The Mart, See Chapter Three also.

Stewart's Deposition
Filed April 8, 1986, Worcester County Court House Civil Case #9981
On March 2, 1983, Chessie Systems Railroads confirmed to SEA. Ltd. that Stewart was employed
as a clerk typist from April 3, 1950 to May 18, 1956.

Horner, David
The Treasure Galleons; Clues to Millions in Sunken Gold and Silver, New York, Dodd, Meade 1971.

Potter, John S.
The Treasure Diver's Guide, Garden City, N.Y., Doubleday, 1960.

Letter from Victoria Stapells Johnson October 10, 1985
In the author's possession.

Notation "Page 424" Maryland Archives
Volume 28, *Proceedings of the Council 1732-1753*. p. 497. MSA.

National Archives Stamp
The document Stewart produced as a letter dated April 15, 1785 was obviously a fabrication. Yet
there was the stamp of the National Archives. This is the proof that Stewart had his own stamp
made which he used previously in his fabrications related to the *Constellation*. See Chapter Four.

"Santa Rosea Lea"
See discussion above. This spelling was obviously deliberately contrived and was no accident.

For stock sales by IRRC
Joe Sater's *Antiques and Auction News*, June 30, 1986, Delaware. By June of 1986, IRRC had sold
forty one units at twenty five hundred dollars each. The article said that the IRRC prospectus

said that the six wrecks they had arrested contained the potential for hundreds of millions in treasure recoveries.

IRRC cases decided.
Indian River Recovery Co., Plaintiff, v. *Adeline, Santa Rosea Lea, Faithful Steward, Three Brothers* and *Cornelia,* Her [their] Appurtenances, Furniture, Cargo, etc., Defendant,v State Of Delaware and Ocean Watch, Applicants for Intervention. Civ. A. Nos. 85-310 CMW to 85-314 CMW. 30 J. MAR. L. & COM. 253 June 11, 1986.

The *China Wreck* Civ. A. Nos. 85-611 CMW to 85-613 CMW and 85-646 CMW to 85-648 CMW. Indian River Recovery Co. v. *The China,* 645 F. Supp. 141, 1989 A.M.C. 50, D. Del., September 30, 1986.

Indian River Recovery Co. V. *The China* United States District Court, D. Delaware. Indian River Recovery Co., Plaintiff, v. *The China,* her appurtenances, furniture, cargo, etc., Defendant, v. Ocean Watch, Intervenor. Civ. A. No. 85-315 CMW. Sept. 30, 1986. Indian River Recovery Co. v. *The China,* 108 F.R.D. 383, 3 Fed.R.Serv.3d 1401, D. Del., December 03, 1985.

San Lorenzo material
From the National Park Service through FOIA request.

Obituary, Donald Stewart
Baltimore *Sun* March 20, 1996.

History of St. Rosalia
http://www.stthomasirondequoit.com/SaintsAlive/id262.htm
http://www.catholic.org/saints/saint.php?saint_id=157
http://www.newadvent.org/cathen/13184a.htm
Calascibette, Emmanuele, Villa-Diego, Bernardo de, imp
La Rosa de Palermo, antidoto de la peste y de todo mal contagioso, Santa Rosalia, virgen esclarecida ... que viuio Anacoreta, y solitaria en los desiertos / la escriue ... el R.P.D. Manuel Calasibeta Clerigo Regular, orden de N.P.S. Cayetano. Madrid, 1668. BN

Chapter Ten: Found, Refound, Found Again.

Ocean City Today, Spring/Summer 1990.
The *Santa Clara* was a fictitious ship concocted by Donald Stewart for his SEA, Ltd. adventure. See also Chapters Four and Seven. The schooner *Hawke* did in fact wreck in the vicinity of Twenty-Second Street, January 1799. Captain Carhart, the *Hawke's* captain, was buried immediately across the bay. The subdivision known as Captain's Hill derives its name from Carhart's grave and his wreck. As for the *Santa Clara,* Alpha Quest appears to be relying on SEA. Ltd. as the source since the statement "circa 1785" indicates they were not in possession of any archival information that would substantiate the wreck's existence. For the *Santa Rosalia,* it appears they relied on Marx even though he had misspelled it as "Rosalea" or perhaps Marx's source, *Lloyd's List.* This ship was lost near Cape Charles, Virginia. See Chapter 9. See also the *Baltimore Evening Sun,* August 31, 1989. Copy of this magazine in author's possession.

Maryland Coast Press, Berlin, Maryland March 28, 1986.
This author found no independent proof that the *San Lorenzo, Santa Maria, Santa Clara,* or *Royal George* wrecked in 1829 or any other time at Ocean City. Stewart had published the date for the his *San Lorenzo* as 1820, The dates 1789 for the *Royal George* and 1798 for the *Santa Clara* were

his unpublished representations but made to the author. Stewart later denied those dates. See Chapter 9. All of Stewart's "wrecks" are unsupportable historically.

Permit VRMC #89-0671-2.
There is some evidence that Cook's rediscovery of *La Galga* occurred in 1987. His archaeologist, Daniel Koski-Karell published an account in 1988 and filed in the Eastern Shore Public Library called *Shipwreck, Horses, and Treasure: a Tale of Old Assateague*. Discovery was said to have been in August 1987. Sea Hunt, Inc. v. Unidentified Shipwrecked Vessel or Vessels, etc., Answer Of Intervenors and Claimants Alpha Quest Corporation and Richard L. Cook, Case # 2:98cv281, U. S. Court for the Eastern District of Virginia.

The Maryland-Virginia Boundary line
Various references to the Maryland-Virginia line in this chapter will be found below.

1632. The Charter of Maryland. Maryland Archives Series, Volume 549.

1668. The boundary line on the mainland is surveyed by Edmund Scarborough. The line was supposed to be a due east line but was drawn north of east in error. *Virginia Historical Magazine*, Vol. 19, Richmond, Virginia, 1911. Maryland State Archives, Vol. 54, Preface. See also Augustine Herman's map, Chapter 1, Figure 3. In 1668, the Calvert-Scarborough line was not run over to Assateague. See 1686 below.

1683. Virginia issues patent for 200 acres on the south end of Assateague, bound south by the inlet and north by the boundary line. Patent Book #7, p. 269, VSL. This puts the line in the vicinity of latitude 37' 55."

1686. Somerset County surveyor, William Whittington, complained to the Maryland Council that "there is a certain Isthusmus or Peninsula of Marish & Piney Hummocks called and known by the name of Assateague Island lyeing and being on the Seaboard side within this Province containing at the least 15000 Acres the southward end of which is reputed to be within the bounds of Virg^a by which pretence some persons are about to take up or Pattent a considerable quantity thereof in the right of Virg^a under which notion (by reason the divisionall line between this Province & Virginia has not been yet run there) encroachm^t maybe made upon the right appertaining to the R^t Honble the Lord Proprietor which may be an ill consequence for the future. Wherefore it is humbly offered to your Hon^{re} mature considerations &c. Upon Consideration whereof this Board judges it necessary the Divisionall Line between Virg^a and this Province on the eastern shore be anew run out..," See *Proceedings of the Council of Maryland, 1667-1687/8*, Vol. 5, p. 536. MSA.

1687. April 16. Patent to Daniel Jenifer and William Stevens for 3,500 acres. Bound on south by inlet and north by boundary line running from bay to sea. The line did not cross Pope's Island as it was not mentioned. Patent Book #7, p.563, VSL. Maryland issues Certificate of Survey for an island of 400 acres called Long Island to John Pope and Samuel Hopkins. The survey describes the bounds as "near unto Assateague Island and the Divisional Line between our said province of Maryland and the Collony of Virginia." The Island was then known as Long Island. Patent Book PL #3, p471. MSA.

1689. Jenifer sells the Virginia portion of Assateague totaling 3500 acres to Maximilian Gore. The boundary is the same as 1687. Wills & Deeds 1676-1690, p. 507. ACC.

1696. Maximilian Gore's will divides Assateague up into necks between his son Daniel and stepsons, John, James, and Thomas Smith. The boundary is not mentioned. But see 1840 below. *Great Neck* was given the nominal size as 500 acres in 1686. In 1840 a detailed survey says 448 acres, ACC.

1700. Virginia patents 183 acres on south end of Pope's Island to Hill Drummond. This parcel is bound east, south, and west by Assateague Island and surrounded by a thoroughfare of salt water. The north bound is a line drawn west to east 2,838 feet. It was not described as the bounds of Maryland and appears to fall a little south of the line described in 1711 below. The land in this patent was already claimed by Maryland in the 1687 grant. Patent Book 9, 244, VSL.

1711. William Whittington receives patent for 1300 acres called *Assateague Beach* in Maryland. The southern limit is the boundary line. This line is about 630 yards south of the present line. Land Office Patents EE #6 p. 292, MSA.

1713. Pope's Island survey is recorded and patent issues. Same metes and bounds as 1687. This survey was clearly in contradiction to the 1700 patent to Hill Drummond above. Patent Book PL #3, p. 475, MSA See also Plat Book #6, pp.17-18, ACC.

1719. Daniel Gore's Will. Selby Gore gets *Great Neck* as far as the divisional line. The residue (unspecified acreage) of land on the beach between the line and James Smith to the south went jointly to William and Selby Gore. Language implies that not all of *Great Neck* is considered in Virginia. See 1840 below.

1731. The processioners of St. George's Parish, Accomack County stated, "the lines if any upon Pope's & Assateague Island which we could not procession for that we ourselves know no lines on either of said Islands." Accomack County Vestry Records Microfilm Reel 136, VSL.

1733. Daniel Welbourne's will conveyed his interest in "Hope's Island", believed to be Pope's Island. Wills p. 99, ACC. There appears to be double ownership between Maryland and Virginia. See 1743. Welbourne had inherited from Hill Drummond. Drummond's will, 1715-29, pt. 2, p. 222, ACC. No sale or conveyance by will was noted after this in the Virginia records.

1736. Whittington's *Assateague Beach* is subdivided and reference is made to the same boundary line as 1711.

1743. The processioners of St. George's Parish, Accomack County stated, "no lines to be found on Assateague and Pope's Island on Virginia part." Signed by William Gore. That same year George Pope sold to Adam Spence one moiety of 400 acres of Long (Pope's) Island. Book A, p. 48. WCC.

1750. September 29, 1750, President Thomas Lee of Virginia writes the Duke of Bedford in England and describes the line as an east line ending about latitude thirty eight degrees. This is about 1.5 miles south of the line described in 1711.

1750. The captain of *La Galga* is told that he is on Assateague Island, in Virginia and on the border of Maryland. A survey or experiment was done in October drawing an east line south of the preconceived notion of the boundary as related to him by the local people.

1751. Joshua Fry and Peter Jefferson survey Virginia and publish their map in 1752. Their map shows the boundary as an east line south of latitude thirty eight. From that point on and into the nineteenth century, maps depict the boundary as latitude thirty eight degrees. See Figure 4.

1755. The processioners of St. George's Parish, Accomack County stated that there was no line to be found on Assateague, but also they no longer mention Pope's Island as they had in 1731 and 1743. This was repeated again in 1760. Signed both times by Daniel Gore.

1770. Daniel Gore wills 100 acres of Assateague and Pope's Island to Benjamin Aydelott to be laid out from "sea to bay and parallel with the Virginia Line." Daniel's son John got the acreage from there to John Smith's land (Ragged Pt.) This boundary seems to coincide with the line depicted in 1840. On this plat the south point of Pope's island appears to be accreted land extending from the old part of Pope's Island into Virginia territory. This appears to be the basis for Daniel Gore's will citing a line that crossed a portion of Pope's Island. This point was not described in the metes and bounds of Pope's Island in 1687. Will Book 1767-1772, p. 479, ACC. This parcel appears to have been forfeited to the Commonwealth of Virginia along with the remainder of *Great Neck* and *Ragged Point* as it was repatented in 1840 to William Aydelott and others. It should be noted that the Gore family had not previously acquired any of Pope's Island by patent or deed. See 1840 below.

1840. William Aydelott and others (see Notes, Chapter Twelve) receive a patent for 447 and 997/1000 acres from Virginia. The Maryland line shown is a due east/west line and intersects with the line shown in 1876 on the mainland of Virginia which is about 2,000 feet south of the present boundary on the mainland, demonstrating the still uncertainty of the line, even on the mainland. This plat comes very close to the description of *Great Neck* in 1719. On the 1840 plat (see page 149) is a small point of land lying in Virginia but considered part of Pope's Island. On the 1949 plat and deed from Nellie Burwell, parcel 4h for 6.7 acres is on the extreme southern end of Lower Pope's Island and described as being within the 1713 patent to John Pope and a part of *Holland's Addition to Margaret's Good Luck* 8-15-1874. See 1943 plat, page 141.

1846. The map of Samuel Mitchell shows the line on the mainland as the tangential line of Scarborough but the line on Assateague is nearly two miles south of its projection to Assateague from the mainland over Chincoteague Bay. The boundary on Assateague was shown as latitude 38°. Mitchell's map can be found at the Maryland State Archives or online at http://www.davidrumsey.com.

1858. Maryland and Virginia form a Boundary Commission.

1859. Topographical map notes a "Boundary Tree" about 400 feet south of the 1840 survey line. Map of Assateague Island , U.S. Coast Survey, Triangulation and Topography by Charles Ferguson, 1859, Record Group 23, NARA, College Park, MD.

1864. Patent from State of Maryland to James Holland. Described as 4h in deed book 168, p. 380, ACC. The details are found in WL&WS #3 p. 518, MSA. Worcester Circuit Court December 8, 1870 decreed land of Margaret Gibbs to be sold by John Handy Trustee, see ITM No 2, p. 138. Peter Watson acquired from Handy, ITM #2, p. 442, WCC. This land later became part of Virginia. Peter Watson's inventory of April 3, 1884 mentions one beach mare on beach worth $50.

1860-68. Field work to recover the Calvert Scarborough Line. De La Camp, *Part of the line between the Chincoteague Bay and the Atlantic Ocean*, John de la Camp, MSA. At the north end of south Pope Island is indicated an "old stone monument." This apparently had not been recognized previously. See also Pope Island patent 1864 above. The stone could have delineated property boundaries. The Maryland patent of *Holland's Addition to Margaret's Good Luck* dated 1864 and totaling 67 acres, referred to a stone on east side of lower Pope's Island as its starting point. The Maryland-Virginia line was south of this. WL&WS #3, p. 518. MSA. See also WET #1, pp. 419-20, ITM #2, pp. 442-39. See also notes Chapter Seven, "no-man's land." It was always Maryland's contention that Lower Pope's Island was in their jurisdiction. The 1840 plat and other deeds in the Accomack County Court House bear this out. The Coast and Geodic Survey surveyed the tangential line of Scarborough. RG 23 T890b, National Archives, College Park, MD. In 1862, they also looked for a due east line across peninsula. See T890a.

De La Camp's report, *Report of the Commissioners appointed by legislatures of Maryland and Virginia to run and mark the division line between Maryland and Virginia, on the Eastern Shore of Chesapeake Bay*. W. Thompson printer. Annapolis Maryland, 1868.

See *Southern Boundary of Maryland*, Commissioner on Boundary with Virginia, Thomas Lee 1860. Lt. Michler in 1858 recovered 30 trees, one gate, and ruins of an old house in the Calvert-Scarborough line of 1668 with the help of locals. Except for two marks they were not more that 350 feet out of line. He measured the magnetic variation and concluded that Scarborough drew his line with the aid of a compass and proceeded on a due east magnetic line which created the error of 5° 15′ north of east as we see it today. He stated that Scarborough's error might have been intentional evidenced by the fact that he did not survey the west side of Pocomoke River. He merely sailed up the Pocomoke River. Michler concluded that it could be inaccurate as he had no plats of survey from either county. MSA. But this did not yet settle the boundary on Assateague or the mainland. See 1876 below.

1876. Maryland and Virginia. John and Kate Franklin sell land to the Worcester Railroad Company. The survey recorded shows the boundary line runs through the north part of Franklin City. This line extended east intersects the 1840 line on Assateague. Deed Book 1876-77, p. 475, ACC.

1883. The boundary is finally monumented and the line on Assateague is moved north to its present location. *Peninsula Enterprise*, December 6, 1883, ESPL. After the boundary change in 1883, D. J. Whealton sold Lower Popes's Island to oysterman James R. Pitt, Book 79, p. 581, ACC. Described as 170 acres for $185, bound on north by "new state line" and the ditch. Whealton had acquired by Special Commissioner, C. Floyd Nock, October 24, 1902, Book 1902-1903, p. 669, ACC. The property had formerly been Jesse Bowdoin's and foreclosed on as he was a creditor of Whealton's. Whealton was the highest bidder getting it for $100.

Koski-Karell's account
Koski-Karell, Daniel, *Shipwreck, Horses, and Treasure: a Tale of Old Assateague*. 1988, Box 9, No. 6, ESPL.

For 1990 account
Ocean City *Today*, Spring/Summer 1990 Author's copy.

Gary Gentile
Shipwrecks of Delaware and Maryland 1994. His LORAN numbers in the appendix pointed to the same location as his latitude and longitude.

Margolin 1994
Blanton, Dennis B., Sam Margolin, *An Assessment of Virginia's Underwater Cultural Resources*, Virginia Department of Historic Resources, College of William and Mary, 1994. and Margolin, "Contrary to all law and justice": the unauthorized salvage of stranded and sunken vessels in the greater Chesapeake, 1698-1750" from *North Carolina Historical Review*, Vol. 72, no. 1, January, 1995.The author in June of 2005, had a chance meeting with Charles Mazel, Ph.D at Jost Van Dyke, BVI. He said he was with Margolin in 1983 in his attempt to locate *La Galga*. See Riebe below.

The *Virginian-Pilot* , Norfolk, Virginia March 26, 1997
See also the *Washington Post*, July 7, 1998 for background on Benson.

Benson's Report
The King's Frigate "La Galga" and the 1750 Treasure Fleet, by Ben Benson. Box 13, No. 24, ESPL

Quicksilver International
Quicksilver International, Inc. v. The Unidentified, Wrecked and Abandoned Vessel Sailing
Vessel, Case # 88-618-N (E.D. Va.) Quicksilver and bronze bell, *The Virginian-Pilot,* September 21,
1997.

Cook's meeting Benson
From court testimony. It was here that Cook alleged that Benson borrowed his research.
Benson's belief that horses were on *La Galga* may have come from the author's 1983 report.

Juno Anchor and plate
The Virginian-Pilot, March 26, 1997.

James Alone.
The Washington Times, August 31, 2000. The 1850 census for Accomack, County lists a James
Lunn, 40 years old, head of household and a sailor. His birth was approximately 1810. This may
be the great-grandfather of James T. Lunn who drowned in 1913. If so, he was born well after
1802 the year the *Juno* was lost.

Shipwrecks in the *"Juno"* area
Sloop from Georgia struck on bar trying to get into Chincoteague. *Pennsylvania Gazette,*
September 19, 1771.

March 10, 1793, a small brig came onto Jengoteague Shoals opposite north end of Accomack,
wrecked and full of water, part of cargo saved by island people, masts lay along side. *Gazette of
United States,* April 6, 1793.

A brig from Baltimore, carrying salt from Turks Island, cast ashore on Chincoteague Bar in a gale
the Saturday before December 26, 1794. Probably the brig, *Trial,* Captain Hall. *The Philadelphia
Gazette and Universal Daily Advertiser.* There was another vessel seen on the beach between
Sinepuxent and Phoenix's Island.

Brig with yellow sides and plain black stern ashore 50 miles south of Cape Henlopen, people
unloading cargo of coffee and sugar. *Baltimore Federal Gazette,* July 23, 1800.

In the War of 1812, a sloop was chased on Chincoteague Shoals by armed brig *Revenge.* *Navy of
U.S.* Emmons, George Foster, Gideon & Co Washington, DC, 1853.

Sloop *Sally,* Captain Hand, Philadelphia to Norfolk, cast away December 31, 1804, on
Assateague Beach, vessel lost. *Federal Gazette,* January 27, 1805.

Sloop *Sarah Ann,* Captain Taylor, from Fredericksburg to Philadelphia, with wheat and tobacco,
cast away on Chincoteague Shoals, February 17, 1798. No survivors. *Norfolk Herald,* March 24,
1798.

U.S. Gazette of September 18, 1827 refers to a great gale. Schooner *Moses,* James Benson master,
from Saco, Maine to Richmond, Virginia, lost on Ship Shoal of Chincoteague. Crew saved, vessel
and cargo lost.

Topaz, Brig, Captain Dubois, from Cape Haytien for New York with coffee, cocoa, etc., lost on

Chincoteague Shoals, July 11, 1822. *Baltimore Republican*, July 20, 1822.

The *Borneo*, of Boston, was seen totally dismasted and bowsprit gone on April 19, 1801, in latitude 37' 40" longitude 69' full of water, cargo of flour and rice and three bags of gold four pistoles. *New York Spectator*, May 6, 1801.

Brig *Juno* to New York went to pieces on Chincoteague Monday or Tuesday before April 15, 1817. *Norfolk and Portsmouth Herald*.

Pennsylvania Gazette of November 16 and November 23, 1758, reported the *Kingston* lost on Chincoteague Shoals, also a snow, and a third vessel between Assateague and Chincoteague Shoals.

Schooner *Lisbon*, Captain Cox, from Petersburg to Philadelphia, was lost off Chincoteague Shoals in latitude 38, vessel lost, crew saved. *Baltimore Federal Gazette*, December 7, 1799.

The *Norfolk Herald* of December 19, 1796 reported the brig *Peace* ashore "at Chincoteague" with a cargo of mahogany and logwood, from Bay of Honduras.

Benson leaving Cook
Court testimony *Sea Hunt* 2:98cv281, U. S. Court EDV.

Benson permit and ASA
Permit VRMC #97-0163 and VRMC #97-0498 Details were found in Sea Hunt v Unidentified Shipwrecked Vessel or Vessels. Entry #25 p. 11. Abandoned Shipwreck Act Pub.L. 100-298; 43 U.S.C. 2101-2106 http://www.cr.nps.gov/archeology/submerged/intro/htm http://www.cr.nps.gov/local-law/FHPL_AbndShipwreck.pdf

$250,000 spent
The Virginian-Pilot, March 26, 1997.

Publicity and MAHS
The Virginian-Pilot, March 26, 1997. January 26, 1998, *Washington Post*, July 7, 1998.

Benson files in federal court March 11, 1998
Testimony recorded by Susan V. Ash. Transcription filed March 25, 1998, Entry #12. *Sea Hunt* 2:98cv281, U. S. Court EDV.

Cook intervenes
May 11, 1998, Entry #15. *Sea Hunt* 2:98cv281, U. S. Court EDV.

Benson contacting others.
Benson never contacted the author. If he wanted to all he had to do was ask Cook where he lived.

Author's GPS unit
GPS Unit Lowrance LMS 160. The article was actually in the *Washington Post* of December 13, not 14.

Virginia steps in on May 20
Filed May 22, 1998, Entry #23. *Sea Hunt* 2:98cv281, U. S. Court EDV.

Testimony September 15 hearing
Recorded by Susan V. Ash, official reporter, transcript filed October 21, 1998, Entry #74. *Sea Hunt* 2:98cv281, U. S. Court EDV.

History of the *Juno*
There are several accounts of the loss of the *Juno*. Primarily two. One was an account from the *Columbian Centinal* of Boston, Massachusetts dated November 3, 1802. The other was Francisco Duro in his *Nafragios de la Armada Espanola* written in 1857. The two accounts are mostly consistent except for the final moments of the wreck. The first account comes from the schooner *Favorite*, Captain Pourland, who was sailing from Madeira to Boston, he fell in with the *Juno* on October 24th and found her in great distress and taking on water. The *Juno* had left Porto Rico on October 1st headed for Cádiz, Spain and encountered severe weather where the ship was damaged. Two anchors and all of the artillery forward of the main mast were thrown overboard on October 23rd. The *Favorite* took on board three officers, one named Don Francisco Clemente, and four marines from the *Juno* to coordinate signals and a possible rescue. The position given by the *Favorite* was latitude 37° longitude 67°. This was over three hundred and fifty miles off the Capes of Virginia. (It should be noted that the determination of longitude in those days was often imprecise). The ships sailed together northward for three days propelled by a fresh southwesterly wind. The desperate Spaniards were continuously working the pumps and unable to stop the leak. Duro's version which seems to be based on Clemente's account, said that on the 27th the *Juno* lost her rudder and at noon their position was latitude 38° longitude 69.56°. It should be noted here that in both accounts there was no mention of soundings being taken. Soundings are taken to determine how close a vessel is to land. In deep water farther out to sea, calculations of longitude would have been made and relied upon absent the calculation of water depth. This last position translates to two hundred and fifty miles off Assateague Island. At ten in the evening the wind shifted to the northwest and there was a violent squall. The *Columbian Centinal* says it started early morning on the 28th. The gale continued and at nine a.m. the mainmast went over the side and the foremast was rendered useless. All four pumps were manned. The *Juno* made signals to the *Favorite* that they needed to abandon the ship but the *Favorite* could not maneuver close enough. The *Juno* was seen to roll as if nearly full of water. The *Centinal* reported that a heavy fog ensued and the *Favorite* lost sight of the *Juno* for about a half an hour and when the fog cleared she was no longer to be seen. Duro reported that at dawn of the 28th the *Favorite* had lost sight of the *Juno* from the night before. Duro's account was taken from Lt. Clemente's description of events and written over fifty years later. The question unanswered is what was the *Favorite's* position on the 28th when she lost sight of the *Juno*? It is obvious that the *Favorite* could still sail well and she remained with the lumbering *Juno* who was dangerously full of water. From noon the 28th until ten that night it appears from the accounts that the ships were still on a north to north west course. The difference in the two known reported positions which spanned seventy two hours was sixty miles to the north and about ninety miles to the west. No report ever mentioned being "in soundings," a depth of about 200 feet. Because of the difficulties of accurately determining longitude, sounding the bottom was the best method of finding an approaching shore. The distance traveled by report translates into a speed of more than two knots. That would put her position about latitude 38° 10' and longitude 70° at ten pm the 27th. Clemente had reported that when the wind changed she was forced under bare poles and drove for about ten miles by the northwest wind. This probably put her back to her noon position, which would have been still about two hundred and fifty miles off of Assateague Island, Virginia. The wind continued driving the ship to the south east as the wind was from the northwest, the *Juno* had no formal rudder, only a steering oar. By the time she disappeared on the morning of the 28th the *Juno* would not have been any closer to land. Benson's theory can now be deduced. The *Juno* would have to had traveled at a minimum two hundred miles to the west to reach the southern end of Assateague Island as he has claimed. The ship would have to have remained afloat for days and still be capable of

sailing, this of course after the officers had signaled that they needed to abandon ship on the 28th. In the admiralty case filed by Benson, Spain submitted some documents from the Don Alvaro de Bazan Museum Archives at Cuidad Real entitled File #31, of the Expeditions to the Indies. There was a translation of Clemente's account which was incomplete, and an account from the Charleston, South Carolina dated November 13, 1802 which stated that it was a from an article dated November 2, 1802 from Boston. The South Carolina article said the position of the *Juno* on October 24th was latitude 36° 44' longitude 76° 16'. This position today would be over dry land near the Virginia/ North Carolina border, an obvious error. The *Favorite* had reported their position as latitude 38° longitude 67°, 474 miles from Assateague. This same article stated the treasure on board at "700,000" pesos as the Boston account said "100,000." Spain submitted documents from Don Alvaro de Bazan Museum Archives at # 130 which included proof that the treasure was offloaded onto the warship *Asia* in Puerto Rico. There is a third account which deserves mentioning. This one was published in the Maryland *Beachcomber*, May 22, 1981, and written by Donald Stewart. The headlines read "Treasure ship sinks while crew of 425 is cast adrift, amid sharks." This version picks up after the *Juno* apparently has wrecked. Stewart describes the ship as having wrecked off Fenwick Island, Delaware. This author was with him when he led SEA, Ltd. on a futile search for the wreck on Fenwick Shoals, which lies five and one half miles east of the Maryland/Delaware line at latitude 38° 27' north. This colorful but unsupportable account was based on the "log" of the American brig *Columbia* which only Donald Stewart has "seen." The log describes the events of Thursday, October 29 the day after the *Juno* separated from the *Favorite*. The *Columbia* spotted flotsam scattered for over a mile and survivors struggling in the water amongst feeding sharks. Stewart's account said that the *Columbia* began firing grapeshot at them but "that it had no effect on them as they went about their fiendish task." The story went on to describe a Spaniard being rescued and taken aboard the *Columbia* and was carried all the way up the Chesapeake Bay to St. Michael's, Maryland. The Spaniard was not so lucky as he died in the harbor aboard ship. But Captain Lewis supposedly memorialized the Spaniard in his (Stewart's) log book;

> St. Michaels, Maryland Port to – Harrison's Dock the crew delivered the body of Antonia Lopazario to the cedar plank coffin. He was taken by cart to the old Church Burying Ground where I read over him from the Good Book. I could not summons the local parish as the rector was on the Island (Tilghman or Kent) and as there seems to be no interest of the town in a dead Spanish soldier we sent him to rest without further ceremony under a cedar shake carved with his name, age and death date. May God have mercy on his young soul.

If this account were true it is unlikely Stewart would have given it away for free in the local paper. If the account is true then neither Benson nor Quicksilver, International have found the *Juno*. Rest assured this story is untrue.

The Virginian-Pilot, July 22, 2000,
"Spain Owns Coastal Shipwrecks Court Bases Decision On 1902 Treaty"

NOAA Database of Wrecks.
http://historicals.ncd.noaa.gov/awois/awoisdbsearch.asp

1983 Report by author.
The report entitled *Report: Discovery of an historic Spanish Shipwreck on Chincoteague National Wildlife Refuge, Assateague Island Virginia,* John L. Amrhein, Jr. President, Ocean Recovery Operations, Inc. 1983. Copies were sent to various libraries and government officials which included the Worcester County Library. The report is no longer there.

Benson on boundary line.
His report, ESPL. See above.

Cook's Report.
Cook, Richard, and Daniel Koski-Karell, *An Account of the Spanish Wreck "La Galga" and the Loss of the Treasure Fleet of 1750*, self published, c1989, MM. It's not known what Mrs. Clements told Cook about the coins but she told this author in 1981 that the coins were found north of the boundary fence.

Dale Clifton and 1751 coin.
See Benson, ESPL. The author interviewed Dale Clifton of the DiscoverSea Museum, Fenwick Island, Delaware in 2005 and he confirmed finding the coin in the vicinity of the Riebe/Cook/Benson site, but when the author asked to see it he said it was in Florida and not on display in his museum.

Koski-Karell
His report, ESPL. See above. The name "Mahoney" was used by the English in several documents when they first heard Huony's name. Later, Maryland and Virginia archival documents used "Huony." Stewart always used "Mahoney" to appear to have knowledge superior to the author and others familiar with the archival documents. See Chapter Six, at the author's first meeting with Stewart.

Borrowed research and evaluation of Cook's research.
Benson's report ESPL. Benson later denied Cook's allegation on September 15, 1998. He did say that he had read Cook's book found in a library. Transcript of September 15, 1998 hearing *Sea Hunt v Unidentified* filed at #74. For Mathew Smith surveyor of Dorchester County, see Unpatented Certificate of Survey, Dorchester County #366, MSA. Stewart swore in his Admissions of Fact in Civil Case #9981, in Worcester County, Md., John Amrhein vs. Donald Stewart that Henry Lloyd was surveyor of Dorchester County. Later in his deposition he said that Henry Lloyd was a surveyor from Pennsylvania and had a summer home in Cambridge, Dorchester County, Maryland. The entire narrative put forth as coming from the journal of a Henry Lloyd is a fraud.

Iron items and fittings on *La Galga*. Cannonballs 1737
Iron fittings and ballast on *La Galga*. Secretaría de Marina 397-1, f. 342, Estados de las *Hermonia, San Esteban, Galga y Paloma* que salerion de Cádiz a Buenos Aires en los mesas de Mayo y Noviembre de 1736, AGS. Cannonballs, Secretaría de Marina 660. Carraca, 22 July *Estado de la artillería de los bajeles de la Armada*, AGS. The presence of the cannon ballast for the last voyage was uncertain as the ship had been documented as having been careened or repaired at least three times since 1734, in 1745 and 1747 at Cartagena, Spain, and at Havana in 1750 just before her last trip. For the last trip from Spain in 1748 the records describe the ship carrying "enjunque" or heavy ballast and cargo details list 1842 iron bars. In 1750, *La Galga* was not carrying an extremely heavy load and may have required more ballast than usual. In 1748, Ensenada does not consider it necessary to take the ballast out of these ships to make the additional storerooms, "...in order to make these, the ballast can be moved either more to the bow or to the stern of the ships and so leave the necessary space for the storerooms, this can be done on the three ships within 15 days". From past experience, Ensenada estimates it would take three days to take the ballast off a 70 cannon ship. "..In order to make sure an armed ship without ballast does not capsize, it is necessary to take care that the heavy iron ballast which will take the place of the space left by the other ballast is well placed..." *La Galga* may well have been carrying iron ballast when she wrecked.

La Galga covered with sand.
Letter from Joseph de la Cuesta y Velasco to the Marqués de Ensenada, October 13, 1750 "The frigate was covered in sand", and Daniel Huony that same day to Ensenada "The hull was abandoned as it was full of water between decks, to the steerage and in the stern, up to the windows of the saloon and buried in sand." Secretaría de Marina 15-1, AGS. Diego Guira testified that "it was decided to run the ship aground as it was completely forded. The Spanish word here was *desguazada*. In English, ford means "shallow place where a stream may be crossed by wading or driving through." This literal translation may be describing the inlet. Guiral also testified that "the frigate was amongst sandbanks (*bancos*) and stone reefs (*arrecifes de piedras*). These "stone reefs" may have been oyster shells which is further evidence of an inlet.

Benson's SW analysis.
The south west path suggested by Benson seems logical as the winds were northeasterly. But the path from Winter Quarter Shoal to its resting place is northwest. The south west winds of the previous days may have created a northbound current opposed by a north east wind on September 4th. Thus *La Galga's* path to her final resting place would have been northwesterly as opposed to southwest. Captain James Maloney had testified (*Pennsylvania Gazette*, September 6, 1750) that they had hit Chincoteague shoals. On December 9, 1750 in Lisbon, Lt. Marcenaro told Francisco Varal (Indiferente General 1990, AGI) that after they struck the shoal the ship was 3 or 4 leagues from shore. Today there are no shoals that would stop a ship of a 17.5 foot draft anywhere else that would correlate with a two hour drift time on September 4th from 2pm to 4pm. Winter Quarter Shoal lies two miles south of latitude 38° and three miles south of his suggested site.

Charles Ferguson
Charles Ferguson's notebook RG 23, Entry 124, Descriptions of Benchmarks, #24411, NARA, College Park, MD. Besides the three wrecks mentioned in December of 1839, (see *Baltimore Clipper*, January 9, 1840, via *Worcester Banner*, December 21, 1839) the *New York Herald* of September 4, 1839 reported a gale which wrecked over 100 ships at Norfolk. There may have been losses on Assateague. For the *Sunbeam*, see *New York Observer and Chronicle*, April 1, 1852. This gave the location as seven miles above Assateague Light. The *Georgia Telegraph*, April 27, 1852, gave details of the tragedy. Also note in Edwin Bearss, *Historical Background study of Assateague Island* that two wrecks are noted on the beach in this area.

Benson evaluates *La Galga* site as a pre-1820 shipwreck
His report, ESPL.

Lloyd's Register of Shipping
Mariner's Museum, Newport News, Virginia.

A list of wrecks in the area of *La Galga.*
United States Gazette, Philadelphia of June 14, 1825 reported a storm on June 4 wrecking numerous vessels from Delaware Capes to Winter Quarter.

The *Pennsylvania Gazette* of April 28, 1768 reported a snow storm on April 17, 1768 where 5 vessels were lost between Sinepuxent and Assateague. Most people drowned or died of cold.

Maryland Gazette of January 25, 1749 reported a sloop from Boston that was cast away near Sinepuxent.

Baltimore Clipper of January 9, 1840 repeats news from *Worcester Banner* of December 21, 1839 about three ships ashore.

October 14, 1755. Heavy winds between Cape Charles and Cape Henlopen. 8-10 vessels ashore, two seemed large and almost sunk 20 leagues south of Cape Henlopen, one large sloop on Sinepuxent and other small vessels. *Maryland Gazette*, November 7, 1755.

The *New York Herald* of May 31, 1839 reported the *Polly*, Ireland, capsized off of Sinepuxent Beach in a squall. Crew brought in by *Extra* from New York to Philadelphia.

Robert and James, sloop, from South Carolina, drove ashore 20 miles south of Sinepuxent July 29, 1723. *American Weekly Mercury*, August 22, 1723.

Sarah, a sloop from Providence, to Rhode Island cast away on Assateague December 1, 1718. *Boston News Letter*, February 9, 1719.

Sophia, schooner, Thomas Massey, from Philadelphia to Baltimore, seen in the breakers on Eastern Shore of Maryland and Virginia. *Norfolk and Portsmouth Herald*, December 23, 1821.

Ship *Kingston*, Captain Bendall, from Jamaica to Philadelphia, lost on Chincoteague Shoals, a snow was lost nearby. *Pennsylvania Gazette*, November 16, 1758.

The *Pennsylvania Gazette* of November 11, 1759 reported an unknown sloop, Edmund Morton, master, sank latitude 38 off Assateague in storm, carrying 500 barrels of flour.

The ship *Endeavor*, Captain York, of Philadelphia, from Barbados, was lost September 13, 1760 on Chincoteague Shoals. Cargo and vessel totally destroyed. About ten people drowned. *Pennsylvania Gazette* September 25, 1760.

The *Pennsylvania Gazette* of August 12, 1762, reported that Captain Baird had been taken by a Spanish privateer between Wilmington and Sinepuxent, they scuttled his vessel but she ran ashore on Assateague Beach.

The *Pennsylvania Gazette* of March 21, 1765 described six vessels laden with grain were cast away on Virginia's coast.

Captain Parker in an unknown sloop from Metomkin to Philadelphia, ran ashore between Sinepuxent and Chincoteague and was lost. *Pennsylvania Gazette*, October 23, 1766.

A small sloop from Amboy, John Hamton, master, was overset on October 17, 1767, off Chincoteague, the masts, sails, and rigging carried away, and one man drowned. The rest continued on the wreck a considerable time till she drove ashore in Accomack County, the master returned home. It was doubtful whether the vessel would be got off. *Pennsylvania Gazette*, December 10, 1767.

A sloop, from Hispaniola to Philadelphia, was cast away on Chincoteague the Sunday before June 8, 1774, the vessel and cargo lost, but people saved. *Pennsylvania Gazette*, June 8, 1771.

The *Norfolk and Portsmouth Herald* of February 25, 1822 reported a schooner named *Jarvis* or *Janus* from New York to New Bern ran ashore on Winter Quarter Beach.

A great storm of early June, 1825 was recorded in the *Aurora and Franklin Gazette* of Philadelphia from June 6-10. June 9 says 32 sail of large and small vessels on shore between Chincoteague and Cape Henlopen. The entire shore covered with goods. June 11 says schooner *Speculator*, Bishop, from New York to Currituck was seen bottom up off Chincoteague, masts gone deck ripped up.

Also the sloop *Dusty*, Miller, of Snow Hill seen bottom up, side stove in.

Schooner *Charming Mary* seen sunk, about 10 feet of her lower masts above water, 4 leagues north of Chincoteague. The vessel reporting was in 6 fathoms and saw the schooner inshore. Topmasts standing, fate of crew not known. Barrels of beer seen floating. September 29, 1806 per *Norfolk and Portsmouth Herald*, October 1. 1806.

Sloop *Comet*, Walpole, from Richmond or Norfolk laden with coal, went ashore inside Chincoteague Bar, Thursday before Dec 2, 1830, via *Norfolk and Portsmouth Herald*, December 3. The crew and materials were all saved except a small anchor. *The Daily Chronicle*, Philadelphia, December 7, 1830.

Depositions on the loss of schooner *Kitty*. Several unnamed ships were described as being lost on Assateague between 1755 and 1764. Exchecquer E 134/8 Geo3/Trin 3 and E134/8Geo/mich 4, NAE.

Huony's statement on wreck October 13, 1750.
Secretaría de Marina 15-1 AGS.

Huony's Letter to Ogle
Huony to Ogle Maryland State Archives, Volume 28, *Proceedings of the Council 1732-1753*. p. 497, MSA.

John Henry's notes
John Henry surveyor of Worcester County, Maryland, found at the Maryland Historical Society.

Weather from HMS *Triton's* logs, Norfolk, Virginia
ADM52/ 734-735, ADM 51/1012, NAE.

The use of a large sextant
Maryland State Archives Series Vol. 73, *Land-Holder's Assistant* p. 167. In 1682, William Penn met Lord Baltimore by appointment in Maryland, and produced a letter from King Charles II directing the settlement of their mutual claims, and requiring that the northern limits of Maryland should be determined by the admeasurement from its southern boundary with Virginia of *two degrees*, according to the *usual* computation of *sixty* miles each. Lord Baltimore objected to this that his patent mentioned no specified number of degrees, but went absolutely to the 40th degree of north latitude; that nothing, therefore remained to ascertain but, where his northern line intersected the Delaware, which he proposed to determine by an observation on land, by a *sextant of six feet radius* belonging to his opponent; and in reference to the King's opinion that he must necessarily begin at the *degree 38*, he alleged that his charter said no such thing, and that a royal mandate could not *take away* what had been granted under the great seal. Mr. Penn's argument in opposition to this was, that Watkins's Point was *presumed* to lie in the 38th degree, and that Virginia might otherwise be wronged if her claim should be to that degree. For further mention of sextant see Proceedings of the Council of Maryland 1667-1688, Vol. 5, pp. 381-82, Correspondence of Governor Sharpe. Volume 9, p. 473, Maryland State Archives. For more on the precision of land measurement during the period see Danson, Edwin, *Drawing the line: How Mason and Dixon Surveyed the Most Famous Border in America*, John Wiley, New York, c2001.

Ralph Justice as actor and witness
Ralph Justice was not named by Huony to Governor Ogle. However records show that he was in Norfolk in early October, and Huony did name him in his letter to President Lee in

Virginia. The letter was presented to the Council on October 17, 1750 (OS). See *Executive Journals, Council of Colonial Virginia*, p. 337. JRW, CO 5/1446, Port of Hampton Inwards from September 29 to December 2[5], 1750 and Outwards to December 26, 1750. Registered in on October 1, 1750 (October 12, New Style), the *Promising William*, Captain Ralph Justice from Philadelphia with cheese, butter and one ton of iron. Ralph Justice was also an Accomack County Justice of the Peace. He was absent from court during this time. The *Promising William* left for Philadelphia and arrived by October 18. Thomas Cropper was captain so it appears that Ralph Justice remained in Norfolk. The *Promising William* cleared Philadelphia by October 25, for Virginia, Thomas Sheal was captain. On December 26, he and the *Promising William* cleared for Philadelphia but the *Gazette* does not record his entrance. He must have returned to Accomack. The Virginia port records do not record the entrance, but the later clearance again for Philadelphia, see *Pennsylvania Gazette*, October 18 and 25, 1750. Ralph Justice's will and inventory Book 1757-61 pp. 324-329, ACC, included 2 carriage guns, an old mahogany stock, and two old brass gun barrels, 6 old guns and gun barrels, 38 pounds of old iron.

Warner Mifflin
Mifflin, Warner, *The Defence of Warner Mifflin Against Aspersions Cast On Him On Account of His Endeavors To Promote Righteousness, Mercy and Peace, Among Mankind*, SLW.

Journal of the Executive Council.
Executive Journals of the Council of Colonial Virginia, Virginia State Library, D. Bottom, supt. Office of Public Printing, Richmond, VA, 1925-1966.

16 defendants
Folder 43, Colonial Records of Virginia. Microfilm.

Mifflin's House
Whitelaw, Ralph Whitelaw, *Virginia's Eastern Shore; a History of Northampton and Accomack counties.*, George C. Mason, editor, Virginia Historical Society, 1951, 1968. Dr. Thompson Holmes married Elizabeth Ann Stockly a descendant of Daniel Mifflin. He inherited *Pharsalia*. See Introduction for more on Holmes.

Latitude 38° as boundary
For the line at latitude 38°, Thomas Lee to Board of Trade and note that in 1682, Watkins's Point was considered to be at latitude 38°. See Maryland State Archives Series Vol. 73 Land-Holder's Assistant, p. 167.

September 15, 1998 Testimony
Susan V. Ash official reporter *Sea Hunt* 2:98cv281, U. S. Court EDV.

Spain files claim December 23, 1998
Sea Hunt, Entry #80.

Coins 1857
http://collections.ic.gc.ca/bank/english/emay73.htm
http://www.collectsource.com/Americas.htm
http://www.coins.nd.edu/ColCoin/ColCoinIntros/Sp-Silver.intro.html

Benson claims ships are not warships
The Virginian-Pilot, July 10, 1998.
Benson values *Juno* at 83 million and carried 700,000 pieces of eight.
Washington Post, July 7, 1998, Benson quoted as saying "in our exhaustive research, we have

not found any manifest or document to support the idea that the *Juno* carried a huge treasure," Later, June 29, 1999, *The Virginian-Pilot*, "Judge: Spain gets all of ship's loot." Benson says appraiser says it's worth "83 million."

Spain submits docs on treasure
USA Today, May 7, 1998, Rafael Conde of the Spanish Embassy in Washington stated that there is no treasure on the *Juno* because it was transferred in Puerto Rico to the *Asia*.

April 1, 1999 Testimony
Zahn, Hall & Zahn official reporters, *Sea Hunt* 2:98cv281, U. S. Court EDV.

April 1, 1999, Alpha Quest dismissed
Sea Hunt, Entry 124.

La Galga belongs to Virginia
Sea Hunt, Entry 128.

Children's comments
The Virginian-Pilot, August 1, 1999.

Comments by Addis
The Virginian-Pilot, June 30, 1999.

Appeals Court
Case Nos. 99-2035 and 99-2036 Fourth Circuit Court of Appeals, Richmond, VA.

Central America
Kinder, Gary, *Ship of Gold in the Deep Blue Sea*, Vintage Books, New York, 1998.

Benson:" If I had it to do over again"
The Virginian-Pilot, May 1, 2000.

Benson: "My involvement has ended"
The Virginian-Pilot, October 19, 2000.

Artifact inventory
Annual Report on Target Verification Activities within Virginia Marine Resource Commission Permit Areas #97-00163 and #97-0498, James R. Reedy, Jr. R2 Underwater Consultants., Moorehead City, North Carolina. December 15, 1998. Contract Archaeologist for Sea, Hunt, Inc. Copy at Sea Hunt, Inc. v. Unidentified Shipwrecked Vessel or Vessels. Entry # 160, November 17, 2000. There is reference to seventeen additional artifacts not included in the inventory and displayed at Sea Hunt's counsels' office in Richmond. Filed by Spain at #130 Supplemental Brief of the Kingdom of Spain on the Issue of Salvage. See also March 2, 2001, transcript, Entry #185. It was suggested by Virginia that the additional artifacts came from disassembled conglomerates already listed.

Riebe's hunt for *La Galga*
Letter from K. A. Dierks, Environmental Engineer to Koski-Karell of Seabay Salvors Co. dated March 30, 1982. This letter was supplied to the author in 1983 by Albert Alberi. This letter documents Koski-Karell's relationship with Riebe and that they filed for an exploration permit on November 24, 1980 with the State of Virginia. By October 7, 1981 Riebe had withdrawn his application. It appears from the letter that *La Galga* had not been declared as historic by the Virginia Historic Landmarks Commission. The letter also states that Koski-Karell had consulted

with the Research Center for Archaeology at William and Mary College. This Center sponsored Sam Margolin's research in that same area. See Margolin above. In 1990, Riebe published. *Treasure Wrecks Around the Globe, 900 -1900 A.D.* He disclosed the location of his *La Galga* site as "600 – 800 yards" south of the current boundary. He said that he was the first to apply for a state permit in November of 1980 but had been frustrated by government bureaucrats. Riebe pointed out that *La Galga* had been sought by many treasure hunters and historians but no treasure had been discovered. In 2002, he published *Chronicles of Shipwrecks and Sunken Treasure, 900-1900 A.D.: A Guide for Undersea Explorers*, Seven Seas Publishing, Beaufort, NC. Here he deleted reference to his past involvement but added by footnote that the "wreck has been sought since November, 1980," and that the King of Spain has asserted title to "anything of value found at the wreck site."

March 2, 2001 Virginia testimony.
Gloria Smith reporting transcript at #185, May 2, 2001.

List of wrecks by Sea Hunt
Benson *The Spanish Treasure Ship "Juno" lost in 1802,* ESPL His company Sea Hunt, Inc. filed a list of shipwrecks documented to be in the area with the VMRC. (See brief of Kingdom of Spain, docket entry #163) There were only four from 1750 and 1802. In fact there were many more ships in this area. See above.

Spain highlights Maryland document.
For Spain's reliance on Benson's evidence November 20, 2000, see Kingdom of Spain's Reply in Support of Motion to Terminate Appointment of Substitute Custodian to Enforce Judgement and For Other Relief. And for *La Galga* Supplemental Reply Brief of The Kingdom of Spain on the Issue of Salvage. June 14. 1999.

Mifflin's statement on people
Exchecquer E 134/8 Geo3/Trin 3 and E134/8Geo/mich 4, NAE.

1750 Indians.
An unidentified sailor from *La Galga* testified in Lisbon to the Duque de Sotomayor that they made there way ashore in Indian canoes. Secretaría de Marina 503, AGS. Francisco Caro, caulker, testified in London that it was not until the third day that an English vessel had arrived, Estado 6917, AGS.

William Tyndle
William Tyndle or Tindall: Court Orders of September 25, 1750 p. 448, ACC. Accomack ordered William Gore and to take Tindall's inventory. Records showed that the court would order someone close to the deceased to take inventory. George Douglas, also a land owner of Assateague, was ordered as well. Tindle did not own land in Accomack County. The 1840 plat of Ragged Point, see Surveyor's Book #6, p. 84, describes the house there as "Tindall's House." It sits close the edge of Calfpen Bay. In 1796, there was a neighboring feature called "Will's Hole." Today it is called "The Will Hole." Records show that since at least 1696 a herdsman lived at this location. The Accomack record pointed to Tindyle in Kent County, Delaware. His death bed will was found at the Delaware State Archives dated August 31, 1750 . He died on August 28, 1750. A Govey Trippet met William Tyndle about six miles from Luke Manlove's house in Misspillion, Delaware. Next day he took sick and gave his non cupatative will to Trippet at his father's house leaving his personal possessions to his father. Kent Co. Wills K-1, Roll #3, p. 25. He had personal property in several places in Kent County. Inventory taken September 3, 1750, in Delaware. All dates old style. The date of his death new style is September, 7th. It is most unlikely he was on Assateague when *La Galga* came ashore. In 1850, in the Descriptions of Stations by the Coast

and Geoditic Survey, this house is described as "Lonesome House" and was occupied by a "Mr. Paine" See Charles Ferguson above.

Line through Chincoteague
Boundary line through Chincoteague. The first patent on Assateague was April 16, 1683 to Col. Jenifer and Col. Stevens which was for 200 acres on south end of Assateague, bound on the north by the Maryland line. Patent Book 7, p. 269, VSL. Book 6, p. 400, Daniel Jenifer got 1500 acres on Gingoteague Island bound NE on Maryland Line. See also Book #8, p. 168, 1500 acres on Jengoteague Island bound north by Maryland line to William Kendall and John Robins April 18, 1691. Cullen's statement line through Chincoteague, SLW Annex.. Report and Accompanying Documents of Boundary Commission, 1873. Deposition of John Cullen, p.167.

Virginia's 1994 Inventory
Blanton, Dennis B., Sam Margolin, *An Assessment of Virginia's Underwater Cultural Resources*.

Spaniard's contention *La Galga* still in Virginia.
Records found at the Archivo Alvaro de Bazan at Cuidad Real, Spain, documents what was said on the beach. The ship's accountant Don Joseph de la Cuesta y Velasco took roll call on the beach on September 9th and made this notation in the crew list: "...the troops and crew serving on the frigate *La Galga* on land at the island of Assateague, close to the mainland of Virginia (where the ship hit)..." Also *La Galga's* register Contratación 2476, AGI. In the covering note made by the Marques de La Victoria on March 10, 1751, he stated *La Galga* was lost "off an island close to Maryland in Virginia." Secretaría de Marina 15 –2, Ex. 184, f. 50 AGS. For Guiral, see Secretaría de Marina 15 –2, Ex. 208, ff. 732 – 737, AGS. More confusion about the wreck's location is derived from two English captains both of whom were traveling as prisoners. One was Andrew Connell, a Scotsman, (*Virginia Gazette*, September 5, 1751, CO 137/59) NAE and the other, James Maloney who the Spaniards described as an Irish Catholic. (see his testimony in the *Pennsylvania Gazette* of September 6, 1750. Both of these men gave an account of the wreck after having gained their freedom. Captain Maloney was given control of navigation of *La Galga* when they arrived off the coast of Virginia. This was done as he was acknowledged as being familiar with the coast. Although the records do not mention him by name they do refer to him as the Irish Catholic captain. Andrew Connell later described having floated to shore on pierces of the wreck with the other prisoners when he made his declaration in Jamaica on December 25th. They each gave somewhat conflicting statements as to location. Maloney described the wreck going ashore on Chincoteague Island when he arrived at Philadelphia. It was clear they were on Assateague and impossible to be on Chincoteague since that island is behind Assateague. But Maloney may be alluding to the latitude of Chincoteague instead. It may also suggest that he went first to Chincoteague after leaving the wreck site. Here he would have received food and water. Andrew Connell on the other hand said they "drove ashore on the coast of Maryland." He did not mention Assateague either. He most likely landed on the Maryland mainland as the rest the Spaniards and prisoners had after leaving the wreck. If the issue of location was not discussed on the beach in his presence then he might later deduce he wrecked in Maryland. This could also account for similar statements in the *Maryland Gazette*.

Broadwater's letter
John Broadwater, Senior Underwater Archaeologist, State of Virginia, to John Amrhein, January 31, 1984. Amrhein's response to him February 6, 1984. In that letter, the author informed him that his group was willing to donate their time and use of the portable magnetometer for the purpose of verification. Broadwater was encouraged to seek the necessary permit. The author informed Broadwater that he would have attempted this on his own but that State and Federal Governments tend to discourage such initiatives and that National Geographic and the Smithsonian were watching the developments. Copies of these letters were sent to the Refuge

Manager, the Director of Fish and Wildlife, the Consulting Archaeologist for the National Park Service, and the archaeologist for the State of Maryland. These letters can be obtained from the USFWS through the Freedom of Information Act, part of the Amrhein File.

Virginia Code on Historic property
http://www.dhr.virginia.gov/homepage_general/down_load_codeva.htm
See also National Historic Preservation Act of 1966, Section 1 *(16 U.S.C. 474)*

Virginia told Court Sea Hunt not obligated to surrender artifacts
Testimony March 2, 2001, Gloria Smith reporting, filed May 2, 2001, Entry #185.

Testimony March 16, 2001
Susanne V. Ash official reporter filed at #184, April 23, 2001.*Sea Hunt* 2:98cv281, U. S. Court EDV.

Virginia and Spain agree on artifacts
Entries #169 and #175

Court orders artifacts turned over
Entries #187 to #191.

Spain asks for sanctions
Entry #191.

Case closed
Entry #193, August 3, 2001

Chapter Eleven: The Trial of Captain Daniel Huony

Arrival in Spain
February 27, 1751. Bay of Cádiz, aboard the *Alerton*. Letter from Huony to the Marqués de Ensenada. AGS, Secretaría de Marina 401 –2. f.704. The *Virginia Gazette* of June 13, 1751 claimed that the Spaniard's "rose against" the crew of the *Allerton*.

Sloop *Industry*
Letter from the Marqués de Ensenada to Vara y Valdés, Madrid, December 15, 1751. Ensenada said Lt. Marcenaro arrived from Norfolk in *La Bella María*. AGI, Arribadas 31. Hampton/Norfolk port records do not list such a ship but show the sloop *Industry*, Captain Samuel Tennant, clearing for Madeira September 13, 1750 OS, 50 tons, no guns. The *Industry* returned from Lisbon in ballast July 24, 1751. CO 5/1446 M225, JRW. Marcenaro wrote on December 9 after his arrival in Cádiz to the Marqués de Ensenada that after they arrived at Norfolk on September 19, "there was an English sloop ready to set sail for the island of Madeira and port of Lisbon. I was given the commission by Don Daniel Huony to embark on the said sloop with the correspondence for His Majesty and Your Excellency. I was given instruction to put this in the hands of his Excellency the Ambassador upon reaching Lisbon. However because of the bad weather we have had, we were unable to come into the port of Lisbon and the captain of the sloop decided to put into Cádiz. I arrived at this port on December 9 and delivered the referred to correspondence to the Marqués de la Victoria so that it can be sent to you. I left on the sloop from Norfolk on the first of October and stopped at Hampton which is 6 leagues away for five days because of the bad weather. In this interval the sloop captain realized that some of the cargo was damaged which meant we had to return to Norfolk incurring a delay until October 16 when we set sail. We arrived in Madeira on November 19 and left on the 21st of the same month [for Cádiz]…" Secretaría de Marina 15 – 1. Expediente 184. f. 599 – 600. AGS.

Marqués de Ensenada to Marques de La Victoria
AGS, Secretaría de Marina for the years 1751-52, 15A, Expediente 184 fols. 596 – 613.

Daniel Huony
Huony born in Tullamore, Clarke County, Ireland. Archivo Histórico Provincial de Cádiz
Tomo 1.006 fols. 19-20. Irishmen in the employ of Spain became known as, "Wild Geese."
Stradling, R.A., "The Spanish monarchy and Irish Mercenaries: The Wild Geese of Spain 1618-
68." *Irish Academic*, Portland Oregon, 1994.

1714.   As of August 25, he was Piloto Principal.
1715.   January 8, 1715 Alférez de navío.
1717.   June 1, Teniente de fragata.
1720.   Returned to Cádiz with General Baltasar de Guevara with a treasure fleet in
        September.
1727.   January 8, Teniente navío. He sailed to the Indies with General Lopez Pintado
        returning to Cádiz in 1729.
1730.   Served on *La Potencia*. Sailed to the Indies with the Marqués de Mary.
1731.   February 10, Capitán de fragata *El Fuerte*.
1733.   Captain of the *San Joseph* alias *El Africa*. the ony ship to survive the hurricane that
        wrecked the fleet of Admiral Don Rodrigo de Torres y Morales at the Florda Keys.
1737.   Huony was commander of the warships *León* and *Lanfranco* which sailed to
        Veracruz with azogue and merchandise.
1739.   The *Almiranta de azoques* (mercury) *Nuestra Señora de Pilar* alias *Lanfranco*,
        Capitán de Fragata don Daniel de Huony sailed to Veracruz from Cádiz arriving
        in March, 1738. The *Capitana* was the *León*. It is most likely that Huony sailed
        aboard the *León*. On February 2, 1739, and after numerous delays, the following
        ships set sail from Veracruz on the return journey to Spain: 2 *navios de azoque*:
        the Capitana, *León*, and the Almiranta, *Lanfranco*, escorted by the squadron under
        Don Joseph Pizzaro; *Guipuzcoa, Castilla, Incendio, Esperanza*, and also by the
        San Juan of the Windward Fleet.
1740.   August 28, Capitán de navío of the *San Felipe*.
1741.   At the Battle of Cartagena, wounded April 3. Commanded the *San Felipe*. Later
        that year, Commander of the Galleons. Returned to Spain in the *San Felipe*.
1744-   Capitán of *El Fuerte* in the squadron of General Andrés de Reggio patrolling
1749.   the coasts of Cuba.
1749-1750.   Capitán of *La Galga*.
1752.   May 29, Huony took command of *Princesa* and *Galicia*, both of seventy-four
        guns. His first mission was to escort two merchant vessels en route to the Indies
        out beyond St. Vincent, Portugal.
1755.   May 30, Jefe de Escuadra.
1760.   July 13, Teniente General of the Spanish Navy.
1771.   June 14, Died and buried at Isla de León, Cádiz. Archivo Catedralicio Histórico
        de Cádiz.

Cuerpo General, 561 – 620 Archivo Álvaro De Bazan. Viso Del Marqués.
Galeria Biográfica de Los Generales de Marina, 1700 a 1868. Vicealmirante D. Francisco de Paula
Pavia. Madrid, 1873. Museo Naval: HMN 63. In the second volume of three, there is an entry for
Huony on pages 199 to 201. AGI, Santo Domingo 1572, 1207. AGS Secretaría de Marina, 398-2. f.
726, Secretaría de Marina, 442.

War of Jenkin's Ear
Gentleman's Magazine June, 1731, p. 265.

Also known as the War of Austrian Succession and King George's War.
http://www.usahistory.com/wars/jenkins.htm

Huony *Real Fenix*
From his testimony, Secretaría de Marina, 15 – 1. Expediente 184, AGS. Arribadas 31, AGI.

Cartagena, Spain
Secretaría de Marina, 315, 441, AGS.

Ensenada and Navy
Hargreaves-Mawdsley, W. N., *Eighteenth Century Spain, 1700-1788: A Political and Institutional History*, MacMillan, London, 1979.

The Royal Palace
Sancho, José Luis, *Guide to Palacio Real*, Estudios Gráficos Europeos, 2004.

Smell of mahogany
September 6, 1746. Report entitled " *Maderas de caoba existentes en el Puerto de Santa Maria (Cádiz)* " Legajo 479, caja 1381 – 18209. Expediente 6, APR.

Bonilla loses ship.
The *Nuestra Señora de los Remedios* was owned by two widows of Utrera, Doña Manuela de Cifuentes and Doña Angela de Prado. Their husbands were Don Luis and Don Agustin de Utrera. Doña Angela later remarried. AGI Contratación 1522, Arribadas 17, and 134 A, Contratación 2902A, 5155, Mexico 2980, Indiferente General 1989; *Maryland Gazette* June 16, 1747. *Pennsylvania Gazette*, April 30, 1747. ADM 1/2583 ADM 51/135, HCA32/134. NAE.

Don Juan de Eques and mercury fleet.
See end leaves MPD, 63,43 Secretaría de Marina, AGS.
For background on mining and mercury process see, Marx, Robert F., *The Treasure Fleets of the Spanish Main*, World Publishing Co., Cleveland, OH 1968.

La Galga lading
AGI Arribadas 29, 178-B. Indifferente General 2724, 1989. Contratacíon 1381, 2918. AAB, Reales Órdenes, 6518. MN, Tomo XXXIV, docs. 80 and 81. AGS, Secretaría de Marina 315, 400 - 2, 441, 600, *Estado de la artillería*. Documentation of the 1748 outbound voyage of *La Galga* demonstrates in great detail the items and their quantity put on board. Registered at Cádiz, November 30, 1747: All the officials were allowed barrels of wine and aguardiente depending on their position. The higher ranking men were "owed" up to 50 barrels, the midshipmen and the chaplain were permitted 25 for their use and the rest had only 2 to 10 barrels. (Note, a quintal is a little over 100 pounds and an arroba is one quarter of a quintal.)

Don Francisco Rodriguez, first surgeon: 12 arrobas oil, 3 barrels of almonds, 3 barrels of raisins, 8 jars of olives, 6 jars of capers, 18 hams, 6 dozen chorizo, 6 arrobas dried vegetables, 4 lbs. allspice, 1 flask of spirits.
Captain D. Francisco Bonechea: 6 hats, 4 dozen bottles of beer, 4 dozen serviettes, 4 tablecloths, 12 kegs of olives, 2 quintals each of raisins and almonds.

Antonio Palua and Jaime Ferrer quartermasters: 2 jars of vinegar, 8 jars of oil, 4 arrobas of raisins, 4 arrobas of almonds, 8 jars of olives, 8 hams, 1 lb. allspice, 4 arrobas of dried vegetables and 3 quintals of biscuit.

Each gunner: 1 copper bowl and pan, 2 pewter plates, 2 arrobas of oil, 5 arrobas of dried vegetables, 1 lb. allspice, 1 jar of olives, 4 hams, 1 arroba of aguardiente and 2 arrobas of biscuit.

The Commander Don Blas Barreda: 380 barrels of aguardiente, 320 barrels of wine, vinegar, 400 bottles good red wine, 350 jars of oil, 10 cases other spirits, 18 quintals of raisins, almonds, figs, 60 tablecloths with serviettes, 16 arrobas fine wax, 1 ream of paper, 100 lbs. fine spice, 16 arrobas of chocolate, 8 arrobas of sugar, 30 quintals of flour, 24 quintals of sweets, 24 quintals pickled fish, 10 quintals of rice, pulses, 4 boxes crystal glasses, 100 small boxes of plums from Marseilles, 12 arrobas of lard, 4 quintals salt pork, 50 hams, 10 calves, 50 mutton, 12 pigs, 50 turkeys, 800 hens, 500 salted tongues, 8 arrobas of salmon and tuna, 4 arrobas of prunes, 2 arrobas of coffee.

Some of the passenger's belongings were listed: Joseph de Araujo y Rio and his son Bartolome. They traveled on the ship with 8 chests of clothes, 2 bottle holders and a chair, various textiles, 63 yards of veiling for nuns, a dressing table, various pieces of silverware, religious stamps and prints, 6 jars with tobacco from Seville, ivory tipped cutlery, 10 pairs of scissors, and a weighing scale.

Manuel Joseph de Borda sailed with 2 bottle holders with wine and spirits, a chest of his clothing with 18 shirts, 2 hats, a mosquito net, 4 reams of paper, various books, a writing case and a sleeping bag.

The Captains of the Battalions were issued the following clothing for their troops:
400 blue shirts, 600 white shirts, 200 quality shirts for the sergeants, 200 cravats, 150 pairs of breeches, 120 pairs of buskins (half-boots), 250 pairs of stockings, 200 pairs of shoes, 600 ribbons for uniforms, 50 lbs. colored thread, 50,000 needles, 200 pairs of buckles, 400 combs, 6 reams of paper (for official correspondence), 150 hats, 150 simple waistcoats, 120 linen cassocks, material for sacks and tablecloths, 130 belts, 120 flasks, and 120 cutlasses.

In addition to the mercury cargo *La Galga* carried 1,842 bars of iron weighing 908 quintals, 30 pounds, 46 medias. Also, 4 fluting irons, 66 bars of fluting irons, 500 rakes weighing 45 quintals, 17 pounds; 81 sacks each weighing 62 lbs. containing nails, tacks and studs, totaling 50 quintals, 22 lbs.

Admiral Liaño
AGS, Secretaría de Marina 400 – 2.

Admiral Hawke
Admirals of The Caribbean, Francis Russell Hart, Houghton Miflin Co., Boston and New York, 1922. Hawke off Cádiz, *Maryland Gazette* May 25 and June 8, 1748. Hawke's fleet having blocked Cádiz for some time was blown off by a brisk gale which prevented his being joined by Cotes, thus saving the Spanish Squadron. Richmond, W.W., *The Navy in the War of 1739-48*, The University Press, Cambridge, 1920.

La Galga at Toulon
AGS. Secretaría de Marina, 440. *La Galga* is with three other frigates *Javier*, *Retiro* and *Paloma* in Toulon, France. She was part of the squadron under Don Juan Joseph Navarro and her captain was Don Francisco Maldonado. The name of the *maestre de jarcia* was Tomás Velando who later served as Master of Supplies on her last voyage. In March, all the artillery and munitions were removed from the 4 frigates and distributed amongst the rest of the squadron which sailed to Cartagena. *La Galga* and the three other frigates remained in Toulon for the following months. In February, when she arrived at Toulon from Spain, those that were sick were sent to the hospital San Mandrier. Of the 153 ill from the 16 ships, only three were from the *La Galga*. *Estado*

de los individuos que de los vajeles de la Escuadra del jefe Juan Joseph Navarro existen enfermos en este hospital. 27 febrero 1744. By June, there were many more. List of the officers and crew on *La Galga* in June - *Estado de los oficiales mayores, guardias marinas…que se hallan a bordo de las 4 fragatas que estan en este puerto. Toulon 8 junio 1744.* In mid August, it was reported that *La Galga* needed repairs before setting sail. She had not been careened for five years. Her exterior wood sheathing was completely inadequate and some of her boards had come loose. None of these repairs had been done during the eight months she had been in the port of Toulon. The opinion was that she would not be able to get through the rigors of another winter. By the end of August, 1744, it had been decided that the four frigates should sail back to Cartagena, Spain, and once more, form part of the squadron of Don Juan Joseph Navarro, the Marqués de la Victoria. The ships left Toulon on September 9 and arrived in Cartagena, Spain on September 17. "… *La Galga* having been repaired in the best way possible." *La Galga* was careened in Cartagena in 1745. AGS, Secretaría de Marina, 313.

Jenkin's Ear. *Gentleman's Magazine* June, 1731, p. 265. For the battle at Cartagena see *Gentleman's Magazine* May, June 1741, *Pennsylvania Gazette* May 7, 1741. AGS, Secretaría de Marina, 398-2, f. 726. Diario formado en Cartagena de Indias desde 13 marzo hasta 21 mayo, 1741. Secretaría de Marina, 441, AGS.

Cape Cantin Affair
Richmond, W.W., *The Navy in the War of 1739-48,* The University Press, Cambridge, 1920. *Maryland Gazette*, May 25, June 8, 1748. HMS *Eagle*, ADM 1/1604, NAE. Letter from Hawke, April 20, 1748, ADM 1/88, NAE.

La Galga continues after Cape Cantin
AGS, Secretaría de Marina 400 –2.

Stowaways
AGS, Secretaría de Marina 400 – 2. f. 108.

The fleet of Juan de Eques Arrives at Veracruz
AGS, Secretaría de Marina 401–2, f. 31. At Havana 401 –1. f. 32. Reales Órdenes, 6518, AAB.

Privateers and Don Pedro Garaicochea
Maryland Gazette: February 24, 1748, June 8, 1748, June 22, 1748, July 6, 1748, July 20, 1748, August 10, 1748. *Boston News Letter*: May 12, June 16, June 30, July 21, September 1, 1748. *South Carolina Gazette*: July 20, 1748. HMS *Otter,* ADM 51/662. HMS *Hector*, ADM 51/425, NAE. Garaicochea had sent a boat into Sinepuxent inlet, ten miles to the north, on November 12, 1746 with five Spanish Negroes armed only with a makeshift scythe, boarded a sloop in the bay, and split a man's head open killing him and wounding another. They then sailed south towards Chincoteague Inlet, captured and plundered a sloop bound to Philadelphia which they let go, and then entered Chincoteague Inlet. The locals were alerted and with an armed attack, subdued the Spaniards, shot one who drowned, and the other four were put in jail in Accomack. *Maryland Gazette*, December 2, 1746. Trial of four Spanish Negroes, November 11, 1747. AGI, Escibania de Camara 71A 1752. Pedro Garaicochea y Ursúa, Capitán de Corso de La Habana.

Admiral Knowles and Havana
AGS, Secretaría de Marina, 400 – 2, 401. Log of HMS *Lennox*, ADM 51/521, NAE. In October 1748, Garaicochea on the *Nuestra Señora del Carmen*, alias *La Galga*, captured one of the fleet convoyed by the warship *Lennox* which was part of the Knowles squadron. The Governor of Havana informed General Knowles that his frigate would be returned in exchange for the

Spanish *Conquistador*. *Maryland Gazette*, April 12, 1749. Governor of Havana retaliated by taking prizes for Knowles taking of the *Conquistadore*. Knowles said he would not release it until his master's pleasure was known. *Maryland Gazette*, August 31, November 16, December 14 or 19, 1748.

The war ends
HMS Glasgow. ADM8/26, NAE. *Boston News Letter*, July 28, 1748, *Maryland Gazette*, May 3, 1749. But the Spaniards still pillaged Brunswick, NC after the cessation was declared. *Maryland Gazette*, September 28, 1748.

Eques arrives in Havana
Treasure on *La Galga*, Secretaría de Marina 401 –1. f. 32, AGS.

La Galga and Don Daniel Huony in Havana
Huony ordered by Reggio to take *La Galga* to Veracruz. AGS, Secretaría de Marina, 316.

Pearls
AGI, Santo Domingo, 1813, Arribadas 31-32.

Reggio sails
Reggio sailing, 60 million aboard. Duro, Cesáeo Fernádez, *Armada Espanola Desde la Unió de Los Reinos de Castilla y de Leó*, Madrid, 1895-1903. AGI, Contratacíon 5155-56, 377-82, Santo Domingo, 387. Mark Forrester wanted to stand trial. *Boston News Letter*, June 16, 1749.

La Galga's treasure transferred
La Galga leaking, July 17, 1749. Aboard *La Galga* off the coast of Havana. Letter from Fernando de Varela to Huony on *Fuerte*. AGS Secretaría de Marina 401 –2. f 174. Letter from General Benito Spinola to the Marqués de Ensenada. Havana, July 20, 1749. *La Galga* and *Fuerte* arrived here from Vera Cruz on July 18. *La Galga* was leaking and the General of the New Spain fleet was Huony. Spinola, "..orders that the necessary officers check and clean the keel. If the ship is ready at the same time as my fleet, I will take her and if not, I will leave her behind so that the work can be executed..." AGS, Secretaría de Marina, 401 –2. f. 173. *La Galga's* cargo off-loaded, AGS Secretaría de Marina 401. In a letter from Francisco Cagigal de la Vega, the Governor of Havana, to the Marqués de la Ensenada on August 6, 1749, he backs up Spinola´s decision to sail without *La Galga*, "and that the need to repair these vessels impeded their ability to continue sailing with the haste which both the General and I would have liked." Santo Domingo, 1501, AGI.

Spinola leaves for Spain
On December 4, Spinola's fleet was hit by a fierce hurricane in latitude 30° 23 minutes and 183 leagues east of the Florida Straits. In a shattered state, they continued eastward, but by January 1750 they were forced into Martinique to take shelter and make repairs. Some of the merchant ships went on but the warships remained until April 16 waiting for favourable weather. Spinola arrived at Cádiz on June 8, 1750, with treasure consigned to the crown valued at nearly sixteen million pesos. Spinola, who had taken the pearl necklace destined for the Queen from Huony, proudly informed the Marqués de Ensenada that they had safely arrived and that he would deliver them immediately. Arribadas, 31, Contratación, 5157, AGI. *Armada Espanol*, Duro.

In Havana, Montalvo and mahogany
Secretaría de Marina, 318, AGS. Contratación, 5157, AGI.

Anchors required on *La Galga*
Secretaría de Marina, 397-1, f. 342, AGS. *Estados de las fragatas Hermiona, San Esteban, Galga y*

Paloma que salieron de Cádiz a Buenos Aires en los meses de mayo y noviembre de 1736. Both the *Paloma* and *La Galga* were fitted with five *anclas grandes* and three *anclotes* (kedge anchors) for their voyage to Buenos Aires. Anchors on *La Galga* August 18, 1750 was based on officers testimony at the trial. There were then three *anclas grandes* and two *anclotes*.

In Norfolk
Francisco Caro. Secretaría de Marina, 503, AGS. *Pennsylvania Gazette*, September 6, 1750. AHN Estado 4263, AGS Estado 6919, AAB. Pumarejo, Mexico 2971, Contratación, 5157, AGI.

The *Harrington* is the *Nuestra Señora de los Godos*.
See the *Harrington*, Chapter 1.

Petitions to Council
Executive Journals of the Council of Colonial Virginia, Virginia State Library, D. Bottom, Supt. of public printing, Richmond, VA 1925-1966. CO 5/1338, NAE.

Hunter of *The Virginia Gazette*
Virginia Magazine of History, V32, 1924.

Sheriff Burton of Northhampton County, Virginia
Colonial records Folder 43 Microfilm, VSL.

Ogle to Lee
Volume 28, *Proceedings of the Council of Maryland, April 15, 1732 - July 26, 1753*, pp. 492-89.

Juan Ramos and Francisco Miguel
Cádiz – Contaduría, 8118 – 113, AAB.

Inspections of *Los Godos* and *San Pedro*
CO 5/1338, NAE.

Felipe García
Letter from Felipe García to Bonilla. Norfolk, October 18, 1750. Consulados, 861, f.175, AGI.

President Lee to Duke of Bedford and Board of Trade
CO 5/1338, CO 5/1327, NAE.

Thomas Lee presented a letter from Captain Huony
Executive Journals of the Council of Colonial Virginia, pp. 336-7

Ralph Justice, Thomas Crippen, Thomas Bonnewell named in Huony's letter.
All three were neighbors south of Chincoteague Inlet and in the vicinity of Kickotanck Creek. Thomas Bonnewell, Deed Book 1692-1715 p. 143. He had 300 acres at the head of Kickotank Creek. On November 27, 1750, Bonnewell appeared in court for assaulting Thomas Sheal, captain of Ralph Justice's vessel, *Burwell*. Order Book, ACC. In 1754, Bonnewell was master of the *Burwell* belonging to Ralph Justice. M226 1754-1770, JRW. The *Promising William* left Norfolk and entered Philadelphia, *Pennsylvania Gazette*, October 18, 1750. William Crippen, Captain of *Promissing William*, December 12, 1751.

Ogle to Robert Jenkins Henry
Volume 28, *Proceedings of the Council of Maryland, April 15, 1732 - July 26, 1753*
pp. 493-90.

Velasco takes roll call in Norfolk
Cádiz – Contaduría, 8118 – 113, AAB.

November storm
Huony refers to the late storm in his letter to Governor Ogle. It was received by Ogle November 14, NS. The log of HMS *Triton* riding at Norfolk was used to ascertain the dates of this northeast storm.

Ralph Justice is the informer.
See notes Chapter Ten.

Peter Hog Attorney.
Executive Journals of the Council of Colonial Virginia, p. 361. Colonial records Folder 43 Microfilm, VSL. In 1746 he was Collector of Customs for Accomack County, Enrollment Books A.O. 15/43 1743-47 NAE and JRW.

President Thomas Lee to the Duke of Bedford November 17
CO 5/1338, NAE.

Los Godos passengers apply for help
Order Book and Related Papers of the Common Hall of Norfolk, Virginia, Brent Tarter Editor, Virginia State Library, Richmond, VA, 1979 pp. 79-80. *Executive Journals of the Council of Colonial Virginia* pp. 333-340. Contratación 5157, AGI.

Nov 1, Peter Hog accounting
Colonial records Folder 43 Microfilm, VSL. *Executive Journals of the Council of Colonial Virginia*, p. 361.

José Carvajal y Lancaster to Ambassador Richard Wall
Secretaría de Estado, E 6917 – 6-7, 6918 – 4, E 5847 – 5, AGS

John Hunter's warehouse
Letter from Pumarejo to Bonilla or in his absence, Pedo M. de Ortega. Norfolk, December 1, 1750 fols. 212-213, Consulados, 861, AGI.

The Spanish leave Norfolk on the *Dorothy* and *Allerton*
Allerton, Ship, 100 tons, 8 guns, 22 men, James Wallace, entered the Upper District of James River on July 4, 1750. Cleared customs at Hampton on December 22 OS for Cádiz. *Dorothy*, ship, 160 tons, 12 guns, 17 men, James Lucas, built in Maryland in 1748, owned by James Johnson & Co. Cleared for Cádiz, December 31, OS, AGI México, 2971, CO 5/1446 microfilm M225, JRW. *Gaceta de Madrid*, March 16, 1751, AMS.

Dates of departure from Norfolk and Hampton
Cádiz – Contaduría, 8118 – 113, AAB. The records for the Port of Hampton only give the date vessels are cleared to sail, not actual sailing dates.

Huony insisted that it made more sense to put into Cádiz
February 27, 1751, Bay of Cádiz – Aboard the *Alerton*. Letter from Huony to the Marqués de Ensenada, Secretaría de Marina 401 –2, f.704, AGS.

Arrive in Spain
See arrival above.

Father Garay
Contratación 2476, 2527, 5484, n.3, r.16, AGI.

Huony's Court Martial
Vida de D., Juan Josef Navarro, Primer Marqueˊs de la Victoria, pro Josef de Vargas y Ponce. Josef de Vargas y Ponce. Madrid, Impr. Real, 1808. In 1745, *La Galga* was part of a squadron of 17 ships under the Marqués de la Victoria and was in the port of Cartagena. Her captain was Don Augustín de Idiaquez who was now one of nine Capitanes de Navío who sat on the tribunal. Huony's testimony and others found at AGS, Secretaría de Marina, 15 – 1, Expediente 184.

La Galga's Register
Contratatacíon, 2476, AGI.

The Palace
See Palace above

Back in Virginia
Colonial Records, Folder 43, microfilm, VSL.

Huony restored to duty
AGS, Secretaría de Marina 15 –2, Expediente. 291, f. 917, 16 – 1, 442. See also Francisco Paula Pavia above.

Huony's funeral
Huony was buried at the Parroquia de San Francisco in San Fernando (Isla León). See Huony above. *Galeria Biográfica de Los Generales de Marina, 1700 a 1868.* Vice Almirante D. Francisco de Paula Pavia Madrid, 1873. MN: HMN 63, Volume 2, pp. 199-201.

Chapter Twelve: The Legend

Background on Chincoteague
Turman, Nora M., *The Eastern Shore of Virginia*, 1603-1964 Eastern Shore News, Onancock, VA, 1964.

Mariner, Kirk C., *Once Upon An Island : The History of Chincoteague*, Miona Publications, New Church, VA, 1996.

Wise, Jennings Cropper, *Ye Kingdome of Accawmacke; or, The Eastern Shore of Virginia in the Seventeenth Century.*, The Bell Book and Stationary Company. Richmond, VA, 1911.

Whitelaw, Ralph T., *Virginia's Eastern Shore; a History of Northampton and Accomack counties.*, George C. Mason, editor, Virginia Historical Society, 1951, 1968.

Harper's Monthly Magazine of October, article by Maude Radford Warren titled "The Island of Chincoteague," 1913.

Holmes, Dr. Thompson, "Some Accounts of the Wild Horses of the Sea Islands of Virginia and Maryland", *Farmer's Register*, Petersburg, Virginia. July 30, 1835, p. 417.

Scribner's Monthly, Scribner & Co. New York, New York Volume 13, Issue 6, 1877.

Henry, Marguerite, *Misty of Chincoteague*; illus. by Wesley Dennis. Rand McNally, Chicago, 1947. Aladdin Books, New York, 1991.

Spanish documents, Indians
AGS, Secretaría de Marina, 503, Estado, 6917. The last of the Assateague Indians and neighbouring tribes began to leave the area around this time, and most of the tribes consolidated with the Nanticokes at their reservation at Indian River, Delaware, forty miles to the north. Others travelled north into Pennsylvania. A few remained behind and intermarried with the whites. Seabrease, Wilsie G., *Nanticokes and Other Indians of Delmarva*, Easton Publishing Co., Easton, Maryland. 1969.

Henry A. Wise and Coventon Corbin.
George Corbin's land on Assateague mentioned in deed James Stewart to John Lewis, Deed Book 1793-97, p. 130 ACC. George may have inherited from his father. Coventon's will p. 161, Will Book 1777-80, ACC. It said George got "land on islands not yet given." Daniel Gore to George Stewart 1757-1770 pt. 1 p. 284. James Stewart to John Lewis, Deed Book 1792-1797, p. 130. William Silverthorn to Joshua Whealton 175 acres on Piney Island next to Chincoteague. Deed Book 1797-1800, p. 51, ACC. This island is directly opposite Assateague where Lewis lived. Joshua had two sons, Eba and William. His wife was Sally, believed to be Sally Lewis.

Jonathan Watson and early land owners of Assateague
See Notes, Introduction.

George Stewart and the Lewis Family
Deed Book 1839-41 p. 521, David Watson's land bound south by Isaac Lewis. Deed Book ACC 1793-97, p. 136. John Lewis bought 44 acres behind sand hills on Assateague from James Stewart, November 3, 1792. Isaac, April 21, 1821 purchased 46 acres for 46 dollars bound NE by his own land, p. 57. In 1783, Isaac owned 11 horses and 21 cattle. Personal Property Taxes, 1783-1792, Accomack County. VSL. William Lewis lived on Assateague in 1820 per map of Accomack County, Surveyed and Drawn Under the Direction of John Wood, VSL. The estate for a William Lewis was sold 2-6-1797 indicated four children including Sally and William. See Ronnie Beebe below. John Lewis mentioned in Dan Mifflin's will, p. 218 near sand hills and Arthur Cherrix.

1835 description of horses
Dr. Thompson Holmes wrote his story "Some Account of Wild Horses of the Sea Islands of Virginia and Maryland" for the *Farmer's Register*, Petersburg, Virginia. P. 417. Dr. Holmes said that the "The horses of the island belonged principally to a company, most of whom resided upon the peninsula. No other care of them was required, than to brand and castrate the colts, and dispose of them at marketable prices..." The total number of horses in Accomack for that year was 2,521. In 1782, the first year for taxation, the count was 3,870. Some have put forth that horses were put on the island to avoid taxes. In 1835 the tax per horse was 6 cents. Records show that taxes were paid by Zadock Watson (son of Jonathan Watson) for 5, Elby Whealton for 3, and William Whealton for 4 island horses. Records show that horses were concentrated in the hands of the Whealtons, Watsons, and Lewises. As for the company mentioned by Holmes, there was listed an Eba and William Whealton & Co. in 1840 who paid taxes on horses. See 1840 partnership below.

Santa Margarita
Lyon, Dr. Eugene, *The Search For The Atocha*, New York : Harper & Row, c1979. Interview with Dr. Eugene Lyon, January, 1983. Duncan Mathewson, 2005.

Ronnie Beebe

Ronald's father Harvey was Clarence "Grandpa" Beebe's brother. He described D. J. Whealton as an uncle, see D. J. Whealton below. He said that Sally Lewis married Joshua Whealton and that she was part Assateague Indian.

Truitt
Truitt, Reginald V. and Millard G. Les Callette, *Worcester County, Maryland's Arcadia*, Worcester County Historical Society, Snow Hill, MD, 1977.

Paul Watson
Reverend Paul Watson born September, 1890 .Federal Census Worcester County
Peter Watson, ITM #2, p438-9, ITM #9, p577, ITM #10, p606. Worcester County Land Records, Snowhill. The "ditch" is mentioned in Book 79, p581. ACC. D .J. Whealton to James R. Pitt. The land was known as Lower Pope's Island and was bound on north by the new state line and the ditch. The island was later named after James Pitts.

1842 Hurricane
American and Commercial Daily Advertiser, July 18, 1842 via *Norfolk Herald*. For an authoritative study on inlet formations see Leatherman, Stephen, *Barrier Island Handbook*, University of Maryland, College Park, Maryland, 1979.

Area East of 1840 Patent.
Patent April 9, 1897 by Treasury Warrant to John W. Fields for 749 acres. Another patent for 39.94 acres was patented by Fields on January 18, 1919. Land Office Records VSL. See Figure 20.

Will Hole
See the discussion on William Tyndle, Notes Chapter Ten.

D.J. Whealton
D. J. Whealton married Annie Scarborough Aydelott TDP #R 25-27, WCC. She was the daughter of William J. Aydelott who married Eleanor Marshall, March 14, 1839. Nora Turman, *Marriage records of Accomack Co. 1776-1854*, Heritage Books, 1994. D. J. Whealton became a member of the 1840 partnership. See below.

1840 Partnership
1840 plat, Surveyor's Book #6, p. 84. ACC. Treasury Warrant 14384, $17.60 plus $4.65 in fees. Survey dated August 18, 1840. Land Office, Reel 339, VSL. 1850 Worcester County, MD census gave occupations and ages of partners. While Moses Payne and Christopher Ball sold out early there is evidence that Samual Payne and Azuriah Ardis saw future profit in their Assateague venture. On December 3, 1842 Moses Payne sold two pieces of property called *Peterson* and *Wakefield* in the vicinity of the Maryland line to Samuel Payne and Azuriah Ardis, GMH 6, p. 109. They paid $1,000 for the land but sold it later to William J. Aydelott for $400 on July 6, 1843, GHH 6 p.462. Payne and Ardis did not sell out their partnership interest. Ardis held on until he died in 1869. Moses Payne sold his partnership interest Jan 16, 1843 to Samuel Payne, Azuriah Ardis and William J. Aydelott for $100, Book 43 p. 499, ACC. On September 23, 1853 Christopher Ball sold his share to the other partners but Moses Payne was back in the partnership, Book 44, p. 353. On December 18, 1843 James Aydelott sold out to the other partners for $100, Book 44, p. 525, ACC. On April 15, 1844 James Ardis sold out to the partners for $100, Book 44, p. 697, ACC. Transaction does not mention boat or bull. On July 17, 1847 Benjamin Blades sold out to the partners for $150, being one-eighth part of partnership. Cow boat conveys but no mention of livestock, Book 57, p. 478, ACC. November 15, 1856, Book 60, p 54, Ardis, Payne, Aydelott to James Payne, Moses Payne's interest for $100. June 20, 1868, John W. Payne to W. J. Aydelott for $200 his share, Book 69, p. 416, ACC. 1873 Samuel Payne willed to Ira Payne of Accomack all

interest in Ragged Point and all interest in partnership horses and sheep owned by himself and James Payne and all interest in cow boat, GTB #3, pp.6-7, WCC. December 30, 1886, Brittingham, Ira Payne, and John Payne each sold to E.P. Timmons for $100 one seventh share in joint stock of Ragged Pt. on Assateague part of the original 880 acres from 1840. Book 58, 1885-87, p. 662, ACC. January 20, 1887, Benjamin Payne sold to E.P. Timmons for $185 1/7 part of 880 acres, Book 59, p 1, ACC. January 11, 1887, D. J. Whealton bought in, Book 59, pp.699-700, and on September 9, 1899, D.J. Whealton sold out to E.P. Timmons of Philadelphia for $125 a 1/7 part. Book 78, p. 484, ACC. For the partners livestock ownership: Benjamin Aydelott, not a partner, inventory 4-5-1853, D356, 480 Wills WCC, on Assateague three ox, one heifer, sixteen sheep, owned for bay horses but not mentioned on island; Partner Benjamin Blades 12-9-1856 pp. 566,656 mentioned 1 white mare, 1 ox, 1 cow, sheep and hogs, not described as being on the island; John Payton inventory February 17, 1857, besides cows, steers, hogs, etc., he had one grey mare and it was not described as on the island; William Payton January 25, 1861,TPP p. 608, WCC, leaves sons John and William interest in Assateague and cow boat and one "beach pony" 2nd choice, and a 1st choice cow and pair of oxen, daughter Sarah one 1st choice beach pony, daughter Harriet Ann Boston, one beach pony 4th choice; William Veasey on March 26, 1867 leaves wife Sally farm and lands on Piney Island and tract called Ragged Pt. (Assateague) with four "beach mares" and their colts, and five "beach mares and colts" on Piney Island. All mares and colts to be 1st choice and selected by Kendal Jester or his son Isaac, his adopted son William to get one beach horse, nephew Mitchell Pilchard one beach horse, in his inventory EH#5 WCC he described a "horse net" and gave values for the horses, 1 white horse $60, 1 bay horse $48, 2 beach horses @ $125 each, an old beach mare $45, a sorrel beach horse with a white spot on face $65, the list includes others not on beach, legacy to his wife one grey beach mare, 1 white mare, 1 large sorrel mare, 1 young sorrel mare, one horse with short main, son William got one black horse; Azuriah Ardis, March 16, 1869, p. 513, wife Sally got in lieu of dower interest in Assateague, a small carriage, and my "best beach mare", grandson William Chapman his interest in 880 acres on Assateague and cowboat, daughter Mary got one beach mare 1st choice and one cow, daughter Susan Aydelott, one beach mare 2nd choice and one cow, daughter Missouries Anna, one beach horse 3rd choice and one cow, inventory TT #8, WCC, one grey mare $175, 1 young horse $80, 6 island ponies @$40 each, 1 beach horse $40, 1st choice beach horse $50, 2nd $45, 3rd $45; GTB #3 p. 6-7, WCC. William J. Aydelott, TDP #12, p. 25-27, WCC, daughter Annie Scarborough wife of D.J. Whealton.

Conversation with Cook.
Cook told the author in 1983 that he obtained this information by interviewing local fisherman. The oyster plat book 1895-1897 at ACC says a Jonathan T. Archie, Daniel Emory, and George H. Bowdoin had 9.9 acres of Pope's Bay oyster grounds near this spot. Others are also recorded.

Surgeon's instruments
1 *chifo* or *trocar* (pointed tool with three cutting edges), 1 *herrín* or hook, 1 claw hammer, 1 instrument for extracting teeth, 2 curved needles. AGS, Secretaría de Marina, 401 – 2. f. 698.

Holloway, Wilmington *News Journal*
The Virginian-Pilot, January 5, 1984, and Wilmington *News Journal* January 9, 1984.

Chapter Thirteen: Uncovered

"The story of each shipwreck is woven into the intricate tapestry of regional history."
http://ww.cr.nps.gov/nr/travel/flshipwrecks/text.htm

Also see Chincoteague National Wildlife Refuge
http://www.fws.gov/northeast/chino/history.htm. As of April 30, 2007

Remnants of Assateague Island's history can still be found on the refuge. For example, the famous "Chincoteague Ponies" are a present-day reminder of Assateague Island's past. Although no one is certain when or how the ponies first arrived on the island, a popular legend tells of ponies that escaped a shipwrecked Spanish galleon and swam ashore. However, most historians believe that settlers used the island for grazing livestock (including ponies and other farm animals) in the 17th Century to avoid fencing regulations and taxation

Perhaps the most famous shipwreck was the *Dispatch*, President Benjamin Harrison's official yacht. On October 10th, 1891 the ship ran aground 2.5 miles east by north of what is now the Woodland Trail, and 75 yards from the shore. The 730 ton schooner-rigged steamship was bound for Washington D.C. from New York City when she ran ashore just after 3 a.m. No deaths occurred, but what had once been the official yacht of Presidents Hayes, Garfield, Arthur, Cleveland, and Harrison was a total loss.

For reasons unknown, this site makes no mention of *La Galga*.

Author's GPS
GPS Unit. Lowrance LMS 160.

NOAA web site
http://historicals.ncd.noaa.gov/awois/awoisdbsearch.asp

Tyler Bastian 1986
Maryland Coast Press, Berlin, Maryland, March 28, 1986.

Susan Langley Report
Archaeological Overview and Assessment of Maritime Resources in Assateague Island National Seashore Worcester County, Maryland & Accomack County, Virginia, by Susan Langley, Phd., Maryland Historical Trust, for the Assateague Island National Seashore, National Park Service, Department of the Interior. Copy can be found at the Virginia Department of Historic Resources, Richmond. #AC-38.

H. Richard Moale
Notebook on Shipwrecks, Maryland-Delaware Coast, Family Line Publications, Westminster, Maryland, c1990.

Baltimore *Sun, San Lorenzo* Story
Sunday, July 24, 1977, magazine section.

HMS *Marlborough*
Pennsylvania Gazette March 24, 1763. The *Marlborough* was en route from Havana to England. See also Log Book HMS *Antelope*, ADM 51/50. HMS *Culloden*, 51/219. NAE.

Lloyd's Register and *Lloyd's list*
At the Mariner's Museum, Newport News, Virginia. The Register does not list wrecks, only construction and ownership details. *Lloyd's List* is a newspaper recording ship news including wrecks.

Lancashire County Record Office
Mr. Tim Hughes, www.timhughes.com, performed the searches for the author related to this archive.

Joan Charles
Mid-Atlantic Shipwreck Accounts to 1899. Self published 1997.

Charles Wilson treasure
See Notes Chapter 5.

Maryland Archives documents
Maryland State Archives Volume 28, *Proceedings of the Council 1732-1753.* p. 497, MSA.

Report to Broadwater
Broadwater's acknowledgement of author's report is found in his letter to the author dated January 31, 1984. Copy of letter in possession of U.S. Fish and Wildlife Service.

Underwater Archaeological Joint Ventures
In 2005, at Jost Van Dyke, British Virgin Islands, the author met Charles Mazel who worked with them searching for *La Galga* in 1983. He said they were unsuccessful in locating the wreck.

Juno site form
DHR ID# 44AC0402.

Virginia Code
http://leg1.state.va.us/cgi-bin/legp504.exe?000+cod+10.1-2301

National Historic Preservation Act of 1966
http://www.cr.nps.gov/local-law/nhpa1966.htm

"If they were ever found"
See Chapter Ten, Notes, court transcript.

Benson's Report
The King's Frigate "La Galga" and the 1750 Treasure Fleet, by Ben Benson. ESPL, Box 13 No. 24.

Judge Clarke, September 15
See Chapter Ten, Notes, court transcript.

Huony gives up ship
Maryland State Archives, Volume 28 *Proceedings of the Council 1732-1753.* p. 486, MSA. "The owner of the land owns the ship." Huony's testimony in Spain, Secretaría de Marina, 15-1, AGS. "And although it is true that an official wanted to set light to what was left of the frigate above water, he later voted to the contrary with the rest upon reflection that burning a wrecked ship is only done at a time of war so that the enemy cannot take advantage of anything left. As there was no such motive because our King is at peace with the country in which we found ourselves, doing this would not be of any benefit to our Master. Rather it was hoped that we would be assisted by the commander of the colony and as well, we feared resentment from the local population through whose territory we were to travel if we set fire to the ship. Due to ignorance and greed they might have thought, as often happens, that the remains of a shipwreck could be claimed by them. This can all be certified by the purser of the same frigate who was present."

Research in England: National Archives SP 94/138-144, CO 5 326/31-32 Board of Trade, CO 5 306-307, CO 5 385-386, NAE. Secretary of State. British Library: Duke of Newcastle, mss #33,030. Papers relating to the affairs of the American and West Indian Colonies. There was a great deal of correspondence between Ricardo Wall, Spain's Ambassador to England, the Duke of Newcastle and the Marqués de Ensenada.

IRRC Cases in Delaware
See Notes, Chapter Nine.

Advisory Opinion
"It is elementary that a federal court has no power to render such an opinion." Owen, David, "Some Legal Troubles with Treasure: Jurisdiction and Salvage", *Journal of Maritime Law and Commerce*, April 1985. 16 J. Mar. L & Com 139 http://www.jmlc.org Alabama Federation of Labor v. McDory, 325 U.S. 454, 465 (1945). And for the *Juno*, Spain was given party status to the case without any proof by anyone that the alleged wreck was Spanish. Can Spain be made party to the suit and then be awarded a wreck based on an unsupportable allegation?

Boundary line discussion
See Notes, Chapter Ten, The Maryland-Virginia Boundary Line.

Abandoned Shipwreck Act
http://www.cr.nps.gov/archeology/submerged/intro.htm
http://www.cr.nps.gov/local-law/FHPL_AbndShipwreck.pdf

Wildlife Service "no plans to investigate"
Letter from Charles Benner, Sales Division, General Services Division, September [20], 1984, to the author. Copy with U.S. Fish and Wildlife Service.

National Register of Historic Places
Guidelines for nomination
http://www.cr.nps.gov/nr/publications/bulletins/nrb20/vsintro.htm

CFR Historic preservation
http://www.access.gpo.gov/nara/cfr/waisidx_02/36cfrv1_02.html

Steamboat *Bertrand*
http://www.fws.gov/historicPreservation/publications/pdfs/SteamboatBertrand.pdf
http://www.fws.gov/midwest/desoto/
Petsche, Jerome E., *The Steamboat Bertrand: History, Excavation, and Architecture*. National Park Service, U.S. Department of Interior, Washington 1974. The remains of this wooden stern-wheel steamboat lie in 15 feet of water at De Soto Bend in the Missouri River, in the De Soto Wildlife Refuge. She was built in 1864 and sunk in 1865. Owned by the U.S. Government, Fish and Wildlife Service. Listed in the National Register as nationally significant.

Daniel Lenihan and Larry Murphy
Lenihan, Daniel, *Submerged: Adventures of America's Most Elite Underwater Archaeology Team*, Newmarket Press, New York, 2002. Larry Murphy's testimony at Docket # 74, Civil Action 2: 98cv281, Norfolk, Virginia, September 15, 1998, Susanne V. Ash, reporter.
Edward Dethlefsen
Trupp, Philip Z., *Tracking Treasure*, Acropolis Books Ltd., Washington, DC, 1986.

HMS *Fowey*

http://www.imacdigest.com/hms.html
http://www.cr.nps.gov/archeology/submerged/NRShips.htm
Legare Anchorage Shipwreck. This wooden British merchant vessel, named HMS *Fowey*, wrecked in 1748. Her scattered remains are buried in Biscayne National Park. Owned by the U.S. Government, National Park Service. Listed in the National Register as part of an archeological district. This wreck is nationally significant.

Yorktown wrecks
Yorktown (Shipwreck 44Y088) lying in 20 feet of water about 500 feet offshore. This ship had been fairly well preserved in silt and clay. In 1982, a cofferdam was built to isolate the hull from the river. The wreck was later identified as the *Betsy*, merchantman. This wreck and others nearby are considered nationally significant. Of the eleven wrecks listed on the National Register for Virginia, all but two are at Yorktown. The other two are Confederate Civil War vessels.
http://www.nist.gov/lispix/MLxDoc/demo/MASJ/d_bkg_sub.html
http://www.cr.nps.gov/archeology/submerged/NRShips.htm
http://www.historyisfun.org/news/yvcoverview.cfm

Huony to Ensenada
Letter October 13, 1750 from Norfolk, Virginia. Secretaría de Marina 15-1, AGS.

Executive Order 13287
http://www.gsa.gove/Portal/gsa/ep/contentView.do?P=PLA&contentID=16910&contentType=GSA_BASIC

Kirk Mariner
Once upon an Island: The History of Chincoteague, Miona Publications, New Church, Virginia, 2003.

Rich Pomerantz
Wild Horses of the Dunes, Courage Books, Philadelphia, Pennsylvania, 2004.

Evidence submitted to federal court on June 10, 1985.
The evidence consisted of a detailed analysis of Stewart's documentation which disproved Stewart's *San Lorenzo* story and the letter from Edwin Bearss, National Park Service Historian who acknowledged to the author the illegitimacy of the story. The motion was misfiled as docket #39 in the *Santa Rosalea* case #R-81-51, U.S. District Court, Baltimore, MD. The evidence attached was removed sometime after it was filed.

Prospect for excavation of *La Galga* site
The *Baltimore Sun*, January 30, 1984 Dennis Holland said money appropriated to the refuge system is strictly for the preservation of wildlife and that "it would be foolish" to spend money meant for wildlife on archaeological excavation. But he said that the refuge would consider a permit for private excavation.

Epilogue

Bonilla's Funeral
Archivo Histórico Provincial de Cádiz. Sección de Protocolos Tomo 5754 Fols. 1132 – 1137.
Archivo Catedralicio Histórico de Cádiz. Libros de Funerales, Matrimonios y Bautismos, Tomo 16: f. 56.
History of the Royal Palace
Sancho, José Luis, *Guide to Palacio Real*, Estudios Gráficos Europeos, 2004.

Church doors from mahogany
Sancho, José Luis *"La Planta principal del Palacio Real de Madrid"*

History of the Archivo General de Indias
http://cvc.cervantes.es/obref/arnac/indias/
http://www.mcu.es/jsp/plantillaAncho_wai.jsp?id=61&area=archivos

James Gould
Court filings U.S. District Court Middle District of Florida (Tampa) 8:07-cv-00614-SCB-MAP
Odyssey Marine Exploration, Inc. v. The Unidentified Shipwrecked Vessel Transcript of
Proceedings Sea Hunt, Inc. v The Unidentified, Shipwrecked Vessel or Vessels, etc. U.S. District
Court for the Eastern District of Virginia, March 2, 2001, Gloria Smith reporter, March 16, 2001,
Susan Ash reporter.

1835 Pony Penning
Holmes, Dr. Thompson, "Some Accounts of the Wild Horses of the Sea Islands of Virginia and
Maryland", *Farmer's Register*, Petersburg, Virginia. July 30, 1835, p. 417.

Sovereign Exploration Associates International, Inc
Their efforts to recover artifacts from the alleged *La Galga* and *Juno* sites was obtained from a
press release found at www.otcfn.com dated February, 2006 and their web site www.sea-int.com.

Odyssey Marine
http://www.shipwreck.net/
http://www.gibfocus.gi

Spain loans artifacts to the NPS
http://www.cr.nps.gov/archeology/sites/npSites/assateague.htm
It is not known for sure whether the anchor discovered is Spanish. But what is known is that
ships often lost or abandoned their anchors. Because of this, any vessel trading at a Spanish
port in Mexico, South America, Cuba, Puerto Rico, or Spain might well purchase a replacement
anchor that would have Spanish characteristics.

Index